# HISTORY OF CEYLON

# HISTORY OF CEYLON

AN ABRIDGED TRANSLATION OF

PROFESSOR PETER COURTENARY'S WORK

TRANSLATED BY

M. G. FRANCIS

GYAN

*Published by*

Gyan Publishing House
5, Ansari Road
Daryaganj, New Delhi-110002
Phone: 011-47034999, 9811692060
E-mail: books@gyanbooks.com

*Distribution Network*
gyanbooks.com
India, USA, Canada, UK, Australia, France



ISBN : 978-81-212-3507-5 (PB)
First Published, Mangalore, 1913

2nd Impression 2020

*Printed at:* Gyan Press, Delhi.



**History of Ceylon**
Translated by: M. G. Francis

# HISTORY OF CEYLON

AN ABRIDGED TRANSLATION OF

PROFESSOR PETER COURTENAY'S WORK

BY

M. G. FRANCIS

---

MANGALORE

PRINTED AT THE CODIALBAIL PRESS

1913

# INTRODUCTION

According to the Decree of Pope Urban VIII we declare that in using in this history the terms *Saint*, *Confessor*, *Martyr* and in speaking of *Miracles* etc. we only follow the ordinary manner of speech among people, and that we do not intend in any way whatsoever to prejudge the decision of the Church, which alone has the right to bestow these titles and qualifications in their true and complete sense.

# INTRODUCTION

The history of Ceylon begins with the landing of the Portuguese in the first weeks of November 1505. We have no historical documents older than this date.

The Mahawansa, the Rajavaliya, the Rajaratnacara and other chronicles of this kind, compilations made in the latter part of the eighteenth century, have their interesting side, but no serious writer will ever consider them as historical documents.

Davy goes perhaps too far, when he calls these books: — „A tedious and unprofitable historical romance." — Tedious they certainly are, nevertheless it is not improbable that they contain some scraps of local tradition and some real historical facts, but they are utterly worthless for the historian and of no use to him.

The Portuguese, did not care to gather together the historical facts of the period preceding their arrival, as the Spaniards did in Mexico. The reason is, that during the 56 years after they had established themselves in India, they cared less about Ceylon. They could certainly have done it, as on their first landing at Galle and Colombo, they found already the Ceylonese in a rather advanced state of civilisation, so far as civilisation goes with heathenism.

An interesting question would be to know, if there were Chrisfians in Ceylon before the Portuguese period?

It is said that the Gospel of our Lord has been preached in Ceylon by St. Thomas the Apostle. This does not seem impossible; nay, it seems even probable that St. Thomas, who lived in Malabar and afterwards suffered martyrdom on the Coromandel Coast, at Kalaminur or Mailepuram, might have visited Ceylon. There is however no authentic tradition of the fact, such as we have of the Apostle's visit to Sindh, to Malabar and to Mailepuram.

There also exist a very old tradition that one of the wise men of the East who came to Bethlehem to adore the Infant Jesus was a native of Ceylon. His name was Peria Perumal and he was King of Jaffna. Later on, baptised by St. Thomas, he took the name of Casper.

These are but vague traditions of facts which might be true, and are certainly possible, for at that time India and Ceylon were in communication with the Roman Empire, and better known in Europe, than they were a thousand years later.

It is a historical fact that just at the time when St. Peter was Pope and resided in Rome, and the Apostles were still living, the Roman Emperor Claudius received an embassy from a King of Ceylon. And according to the tradition, the Apostle St. Thomas, on his voyage to India, travelled together with an embassy of a Rajah of Northern India. At the time of Emperor Constantine the Great a large portion of the inhabitants of Sind were Catholics, and St. John Damascene mentions there many Bishops, anchoretes and monks.

Three ancient writers speak of the Christians of Ceylon: Cosmas Indicopleustes who wrote in the year 563. Abu-abd-Allah Mohamed Edrissi, an Arabian writer, speaks of them in 1154, and finally Sir John Maundeville, an English Catholic Knight who visited Ceylon in 1330.

Cosmas is a serious writer and can be trusted, but it seems that the Christians mentioned by him in Ceylon were not natives, but a colony of Merchants from the Malabar Coast who were trading in Ceylon.

Edrissi cannot be trusted. He never travelled himself but wrote what he had heard from others, without satisfying himself of the truth of what they related.

As regards Sir John Maundeville, it is enough to read his extravagant adventures to judge the value of his book.

Marco-Polo who visited the Island in 1284, does not mention Christians, and the great Missionary, the Blessed Oderic of Udine who came to Ceylon in 1318, and John Marignolli whom Pope Benedict XII had sent as Delegate to China, and who on his return voyage in 1348 remained four months in Ceylon, would certainly have mentioned the Christians, if there were any.

The Portuguese who landed in the Island in 1505 found no Christians and no tradition of Christianity.

The rise of Mahomet and his faith and the subsequent wars and conquests of the Arabs, rose a barrier between Europe and Southern and Eastern Asia, and for eight centuries India and Ceylon remained separated from civilisation, isolated and with no contact with the western world. Europe had even forgotten the existence of these distant countries.

The Popes alone did not forget them. They knew that, in these unknown lands, there lived millions of men, redeemed by the blood of our Lord Jesus Christ, who were buried in the most abject idolatry and worshipped the devil.

In 1252 Pope Innocent IV started the first missionary society for the conversion of the East. It was composed of Franciscan and Dominican Friars, and was called: SOCIETAS PEREGRINANTIUM PRO CHRISTO.

We have already mentioned one of the most famous members of this Society, the Blessed Oderic of Udine, who, at the beginning of the fourteenth century, visited Persia, India, Ceylon, Indo-China, Sumatra, Java, the Philippines, China and Tibet and, during this long, and at that time most difficult voyage, had baptised more than 30,000 heathens.

Nor were the Popes satisfied by merely sending missionaries to these distant countries, they had relations with their Sovereigns, at that time, when the other European rulers did not know even of their existence.

We have already mentioned John Marignolli the Papal Delegate to China. Benedict XII, Clement VI and their successors maintained friendly relations with the Emperors of China, and before the Portuguese had set foot for the first time on the shores of that vast empire, there had already been eight Archbishops at Pekin.

India too did not escape the solicitude of the Sovereign Pontiffs, who had already established missions there two centuries before the Portuguese. Franciscan and Dominican Friars preached the Gospel in India. The centre of their missions was Thana, now a small town near Bombay. On the 8th April 1330, Pope John XXII erected an Episcopal See at Quilon.

One century later Pope Eugene IV sent to India the first Delegate, the Blessed Albert of Sarteano (1439). His two secretaries were Lawrence of Levanto who became later on General of the Franciscan Order and the Blessed Thomas of Florence, whose feast we celebrate on the 30th October. The two immediate successors of Albert of Sarteano, as Papal Delegates in India, were Gandolphus of Sicily (1443) and Louis of Bologna (1454—1457).

We mention these facts in order to show that, whilst the whole world had forgotten the lands of the far East, and the names of China, India and Ceylon were hardly even known in civilised Europe, the Popes alone never abandoned them and never ceased in their endeavours to bring these distant peoples to the Catholic Faith.

Towards the end of the fifteenth century, two great

European nations, the Spaniards and the Portuguese were endeavouring to acquire the empire of the seas.

Their bold and enterprising sailors were exploring the ocean in order to discover new and long forgotten countries. Their conquests became of such extent, that Pope Alexander VI, fearing a conflict between these two great powers, and using of his supreme right as Vicar of Christ, traced on a chart of the world, a line from the North to the South Pole and, by a decree dated 1493, ordered that the Spaniards were to pursue their discoveries to the West, the Portuguese to the East of that line.

This historical chart, with the line traced over it by the hand of Pope Alexander VI has been carefully preserved, and may be seen in the library of the Sacred Congregation of Propaganda in Rome.

A few years later, on the 22nd May 1498, Vasco de Gama landed at Calicut, and India, after eight centuries of isolation, became again connected with the civilised world.

The affairs in Ceylon were at that time in a most critical situation. All the trade of the Island was in the hands of the Moors. The wealth which this trade brought them rendered them powerful and gave them a great ascendency over the native Rulers of the country. They took profit of their quarrels and, sustained by the Zamorin King of Calicut whose subjects they were, their aim at this epoch was to become the absolute masters of Ceylon. The arrival of the Portuguese saved the Singhalese from the slavery of the Moors.

The Singhalese owe to the Portuguese their national existence. Had not the Portuguese landed then in Ceylon, there would be no Singhalese to-day, they would have all become Moormen.

# PART I

# THE PORTUGUESE ALLIANCE

## 1505 — 1554

# CHAPTER 1

## LAWRENCE D'ALMEIDA

Seven years had elapsed since the Portuguese were established in India. The Viceroy Dom Francis d'Almeida had
1505 despatched his son Dom Lawrence to pursue some Moorish pirates who from the Maldive Islands infested the Southern Coast of India.

The squadron commanded by Dom Lawrence had left Cochin in the month of November 1505. When already approaching the Maldives, they were met by a heavy storm which gradually grew fiercer and fiercer. Aware of the danger which threatened the squadron, d'Almeida summoned his captains and Fr. Vincent, the chaplain of the fleet, to a council, in order to decide in face of the imminent danger if it were not more prudent to sail back to Cochin.

Opinions were divided, some of the captains urged to go on, others advised to return to Cochin. Fr. Vincent, asked for his opinion, answered that they should wait till next morning and in the meantime pray God to make them know His will. And such was the esteem in which the venerable Franciscan Friar was held by the captains that all agreed to follow his advice.

Fr. Vincent passed the whole night in prayer and in the

morning after having celebrated the Holy Mass to which Almeida and all his officers assisted:

— „Brethren, he said, it is the will of God that we should deviate from our course, and He will soon manifest to us the reason. He neither wishes us to proceed to the Maldives nor to return to Cochin. God wishes us to drift before the wind, and He will guide us to a land to whose people He wants us to carry the Faith of Jesus Christ." —

The officers listened in silence to these prophetic words, no one attempted to controvert them. The squadron sailed before the wind, the storm continuing. The sailors murmured, thinking themselves in the vicinity of the Maldives and expecting every moment to be wrecked on the reefs. But soon they sighted land. It was the Coast of Ceylon. They anchored in the harbour of Galle where they stopped for some days to take fresh water and gather some informations about the country. Learning that further up there was another anchorage, nearer to the residence of the King, they followed up the Western Coast and arrived at Colombo on the 15th November 1505.

The narration of the Rajawali about the arrival to Colombo of a very white and beautiful kind of men who wear shoes and hats of iron, eat a sort of white stone and drink blood, is childish and absurd.

Ceylon was already well known to the Portuguese, although they had not yet visited the Island. The Portuguese were now since seven years settled at Cochin, a town with which Ceylon was in continual commercial intercourse, and the Singhalese knew perfectly well who were these white men who had landed at Galle and at Colombo.

Lawrence d'Almeida, struck by the beauty of the country and by the good and pre-possessing manners of the people, endeavoured to enter into friendly relations with the inhabitants of Colombo. With this object in view, he ordered those under him to pay liberally for all articles the natives would bring for sale, and to treat all who ventured on board his ships with courtesy and kindness.

Meanwhile the news of the arrival of the Portuguese reached Kotta. The King Dharma Prakrama Bahu was a man of superior intelligence. His kingdom was threatened by the Moors whose power increased every year. He was not strong enough to oppose them and he knew that, sooner or later they would make themselves masters of his kingdom, depriving him of his crown and reducing his people into slavery.

He therefore asked himself if he could not use the Portuguese against the invading Moors. This idea having taken possession of his mind, he became very desirous of forming an alliance with these strangers. Tales of the daring enterprises of these white faced warriors which he had heard, and their powerful weapons unknown in Ceylon inflamed his mind, and he felt sure that the same would inspire terror to the Moors, and stop their endeavours to become masters of the south of Ceylon.

The King therefore assembled his council and they decided that an embassy should be sent to Colombo, headed by a chief called Chakra Raja, to convey to Almeida the greetings of the King and enter into friendly relations with him.

Almeida received Chakra Raja with great honors, and in return sent a brilliant embassy to Kotta. He selected as his envoy Payo de Sousa, a knight of noble birth, who surrounded himself with all the pomp possible, so that the embassy should be worthy of the King of Kotta. Chakra Raja procured a number of elephants and accompanied de Sousa. But instead of conducting him directly to Kotta which is only a few miles distant from Colombo, they made such a detour, that it was not till after three days of a painful and fatiguing march that they reached Kotta.

Payo de Sousa understood at once that they were promenading him across the country, crossing and re-crossing again the same river, but, as he wanted to explore the neighbourhood of Colombo and acquaint himself with its strategical possibilities, he raised no objection.

What was the reason of this silly stratagem ? Was it to give the King time to prepare a proper reception, or to conceal from the Portuguese the fact that the residence of the King was so near from the place where their squadron was anchored ?

The King gave audience to Payo de Sousa in a large half darkened hall laid with beautiful persian carpets. He was seated on a throne raised six steps above the floor of the hall and draped with cloth of gold. He wore a white dress and had on his head a kind of turban adorned with large pearls and with precious stones. He had valuable rings with emeralds and diamonds, and his slippers were adorned with rubies.

The hall was lighted with great wax tapers in silver candlesticks of exquisite workmanship. Courtiers in rich dresses lined the walls on both sides of the throne.

Payo de Sousa, clad in green velvet, advanced towards the throne and saluted the King according to the custom of the courts of Europe. Dharma Prakrama Bahu was pleased, but his courtiers were scandalized, as they were in the habit of prostrating on the ground before their sovereign, and took it therefore as a sign of disrespect.

The King invited de Sousa to sit on a grand chair on the right of the throne and put him a number of questions about Europe, Portugal and King Dom Emmanuel.

After this preliminary audience, political affairs were discussed and a treaty concluded, by which Prakrama Bahu recognized the King of Portugal as his paramount Lord, promised to pay a yearly tribute of six elephants and a certain quantity of cinnamon, on condition that the Portuguese protect him against his enemies and help him in his wars.

The treaty was read in public and engraved on large gold medals in Singhalese and in Portuguese.

Some superficial authors have put forward the tale that Payo de Sousa was received at Kotta by a court official who personated the King, and that he never saw Prakrama Bahu. The Portuguese had too much experience of Oriental ways to allow such a trick to be played upon them, and would certainly not allow such an insult to remain unpunished.

The same authors pretend that the treaty was an invention of Lawrence d'Almeida as, during the twelve following years, no tribute has been paid to the Portuguese.

The treaty was undoubtfully real but it is not known if it had been ratified by the Viceroy, who had too much on his hands in India to desire to interfere with the affairs of Ceylon. During these twelve years the Portuguese never came to Ceylon, they could not therefore exact the tribute, which was not properly a tribute, but rather an indemnity for the help which Almeida promised to the King in his wars against his enemies. As the Portuguese did not fulfil their obligations, they could not claim that the King fulfil his. The treaty remained in abeyance. The fact is that, as soon as the Portuguese returned to Ceylon, they renewed the same treaty with some modifications.

Lawrence d'Almeida remained yet a short time at Colombo to take in a cargo of cinnamon. On a rock near the place where his squadron was anchored he built a chapel dedicated to St. Lawrence, his patron, in which Fr. Vincent used to say Mass every day.

When the squadron had to leave the Island, Fr. Vincent asked to be left behind, and devote himself to the conversion of the Singhalese, but Almeida would not consent to leave him alone without any protection, and he had to return with him to Cochin.

When a Portuguese fleet was starting with the intention to visit or to discover some new or unknown country, they used to carry with them *padrãos* or stone pillars on which were engraved the royal coat of arms of Portugal, which they erected as a monument in the place where they landed.

As Almeida when leaving Cochin had no intention to visit a new country, he did not take with him a *padrão*. He had therefore the arms of Portugal engraved on a rock close to St. Lawrence chapel.

This rock, whose very existence had almost been forgotten, was discovered on the 5th of November 1898 when demolishing an old house close to the ancient Battemburgh battery. Although damaged by the scratching on it of a clumsy cross and of a later date referring to the death of a man who has been buried at its foot, the place having served as a burial ground, its authenticity cannot be disputed.

This engraved rock is the most ancient Christian monument of Ceylon. It marks the place where Holy Mass had been first publicly celebrated. Hence Catholics ought to take great interest in seeing that such a valuable historical monument be carefully preserved.

## CHAPTER 2

# LOPO SOAREZ D'ALBERGARIA

Notwithstanding the enthusiastic reports made by Lawrence d'Almeida on the beauty of Ceylon and the sympathetic
1509 nature of the Singhalese, neither his father nor his successor, the great Alphonsus d'Albuquerque, thought of adding the Island to the sphere of Portuguese influence.

Albuquerque, having added to the Portuguese colonial empire Ormuz on the Persian Gulf and Malacca which commanded the route to China, thought only of organizing his new conquests.

Nevertheless, since the conquest of Malacca which was soon to become the second metropolis of the East, the importance of Ceylon as a strategical station between Cochin and Malacca became so obvious, that, when Lopo Soarez d'Albergaria was leaving Lisbon to succeed Albuquerque as Viceroy of India, the King of Portugal Dom Emmanuel ordered him to erect a fortress in Colombo.

Soarez landed in Cochin on the 8th September 1515 and, two years later, on 10th September 1517, set out for Ceylon with a fleet of seventeen vessels.

During the twelve years that had elapsed since the departure of Lawrence d'Almeida, the Moormen had laboured to strengthen their power in the south of the Island. They had gained over several influential Singhalese chiefs and reduced King Dharma Prakrama Bahu to the position of a nominal sovereign.

Hence, when Lopo Soarez d'Albergaria reached Colombo, the Moormen did their best to force the King to openly
1517 declare himself against the Portuguese and oblige them to leave the Island.

But the Viceroy had already sent to Kotta a noble knight called John Flores, to whom the King granted an audience, and so far was he from wishing to drive the Portuguese away, that he decided on the contrary, to secure their support to liberate his country from the overwhelming tyranny of the Moormen.

On the very next day after the departure of Flores from Kotta, Prakrama Bahu went to Colombo to meet in person the Viceroy. The Moormen thought it more prudent to conceal their resentment and made him a grand reception whilst the Portuguese greeted his arrival with salves of artillery.

In the afternoon the Viceroy landed in a magnificent gilt boat. The King received him at the entrance of the palace. He was surrounded by the chiefs, but was easily distinguished by his long white beard and his noble and venerable aspect. He saluted the Viceroy and, notwithstanding his protestations, forced him to take precedence.

Two armchairs were placed on the throne and, when they were seated, the King was the first to speak. He excused himself that owing to his old age he could not have been the first to visit the Viceroy on board his vessel, but he had come to meet him at Colombo, a thing he had never done before for any one.

After exchanging the usual compliments, Soarez asked for permission to erect a small fort and establish a commercial factory at Colombo. The King asked for a delay of two days to discuss the question with his councillors for, he said, although in his country the King could do what he liked, yet it is customary to ask in all important matters the opinion of the chiefs.

The evening was then spent in friendly conversation between the two old men and, on taking leave of the King, Soarez was enchanted with his wisdom, his dignity and with his polished manners.

Hardly had Prakrama Bahu returned to Kotta, when the Moors exasperated at the result of the interview, collected their forces and those that their supporters could place at their disposal and, being determined at all cost to prevent the Portuguese from erecting the fort, attacked them suddenly, but far from being able to contend against the discipline of European troops and of their artillery, they were repelled after having heavily lost in the battle.

King Prakrama Bahu irritated by the treachery of the Moors sent an embassy to the Viceroy and, after some days, concluded with him a treaty based on that which he had signed with Lawrence d'Almeida. The text of this document was as follows:

— The lawful sovereign of the universe, direct descendant of the Kings of Anuradhapoora, greater than the whole earth. Born of the race of the gods of Ceylon, lawful sovereign of the kingdom of Kotta and of the kingdoms of Jaffna and of Kandy, and by inheritance of that of Dambadeniya, owner of Adam's Peak, protector of the Law of Buddha. Descendant from the son of the sun, carrying a star on his forehead; master of all sciences and lawful successor of Vijaya Bahu. We, King Dharma Prakrama Bahu, in the heart of our kingdom, called during forty years by the name of Sagara — We are content and it pleases us much to give unto the King of Portugal, annually four hundred measures of cinnamon, twenty rings set with Ceylon rubies and ten elephants with tusks — on condition that the present Viceroy, and the Viceroys that shall succeed in India Lopo Soarez d'Albergaria shall be obliged to favour and aid us against our enemies, as is their duty towards a vassal, that we are, of the King of Portugal. —

Soarez having obtained the permission of the King erected a small fort at Colombo on the same hill at the foot of which Almeida had built St. Lawrence's chapel. The works being completed in January 1518, he left a garrison of one hundred men under the command of John de Silveira and returned to Cochin, after a stay of four months in Ceylon.

A Priest named John Monteiro de Setuel remained with the garrison as military chaplain. It is not known whether he was a Franciscan or a Secular Priest. He erected a church on the site of Almeida's chapel and laboured for eighteen years for the conversion of the Singhalese of whom he baptised a large number. He is considered as the first Missionary of Ceylon and died at Colombo in 1536.

A few weeks after the departure of the Viceroy King Dharma Prakrama Bahu was poisoned by his son Vijaya, who was led to commit this horrid crime by the Moors, who could not pardon the old King for having frustrated, by his alliance with the Portuguese, their plan of making themselves masters of the southern and western part of Ceylon, and that just at the moment when they had nearly attained their end.

# CHAPTER 3

# VIJAYA BAHU

Hardly had the parricide Vijaya Bahu mounted on the throne of Kotta, when he sent a secret embassy to the Zamorin,
1518 the Moorish Raja of Calicut to ask his help against the Portuguese.

The Zamorin sent him eight vessels and a good contingent of soldiers who, on landing at Colombo were joined by the Moormen of the place and some Singhalese who had been gained to their party, and they besieged the Portuguese fort.

John de Silveira who could not defend it with his hundred soldiers, determined on a bold stroke. On the night of 20th June he made a sortie, attacked the Moorish camp on three different sides and inflicted them a heavy defeat, so that the Moormen fled in haste to their vessels.

Vijaya Bahu frightened by this unexpected issue hastened to send to Colombo some of his grandies, to congratulate Silveira on his victory and to excuse himself for not having hastened to his aid, as was his duty as a vassal of the King of Portugal, but, he said he had no time to concentrate his troops.

Silveira knew very well that it was the King himself who had appealed to the Zamorin, but in order not to break up his apparently friendly relation with him, he dissimulated his anger and sent a courteous reply.

This affair persuaded the Portuguese that, if they wanted to remain at Colombo, they would have to build a more substantial fort, and garrison it better.

When therefore Lope de Britto was appointed to succeed to Silveira he brought with him reinforcements as well as materials and workmen to re-build the fort on a better plan.

He was however continually disturbed by the inhabitants of Colombo whom the Moors had gained to their side.

Finally losing patience, Britto attacked the town, on the
1519 evening of 15th June 1519, seized the leaders, executed some of them and retained as prisoners the others. This however did not intimidate the Singhalese, who were a brave and hardy race, and, being constantly urged by the Moors, they did not cease to molest Britto and to oppose to his building the fort.

This state of things continued till May 1520, when King Vijaya
1520 Bahu, seeing that the forces of the Portuguese were greatly reduced, for they had lost many men in these constant skirmishes with the Moors and with their partisans, openly declared himself against the Portuguese. He repudiated the treaty passed between his father and Lopo Soarez d'Albergaria on the plea that, having been made without the consent of the people it had no value, and marched against Britto at the head of 27,000 men.

To this force Britto could only oppose 80 Portuguese soldiers and 200 sepoys. He was therefore obliged to shut himself up in his fort, which was nearly completed, but not yet sufficiently provisioned, and wanting in water supply so much, that the besieged had to cut their way arms in hand to the neighbouring wells.

Vijaya Bahu and the Moors commenced the siege of the fort on 7th May 1520. Britto could not have resisted long to such an overwhelming force, if it were not for his artillery, which gave him a great superiority over his badly armed foe.

The siege had already lasted five months, and the soldiers that survived were nearly reduced to the state of walking skeletons, when a sail appeared on the horizon: Anthony de Lemos was bringing to the besieged provision and a reinforcement of 50 men sent by the Viceroy.

Britto did not loose a moment in communicating his plan to Lemos and, whilst Lemos cannonaded the King's camp, Britto attacked it with only hundred men. The camp was taken.

Nevertheless, the King and his allies the Moors, who had taken to flight rallied their scattered troops and the same evening advanced in order of battle against the handful of their conquerors.

The Singhalese at that time had no artillery, but they possessed a formidable engine of war in the shape of trained elephants, which, with long and sharp swords fixed to their tusks, made a terrible havoc in the ranks of the enemy.

Twenty-five such great beasts marched at the head of the King's army. Their sight disconcerted the Portuguese soldier, but

Britto and Lemos directed their artillery against the terrible looking animals. At the first discharge of the guns, the elephants, most of them severely wounded took flight, and stampeded in disorder through the King's army throwing the men on the ground and killing a great number with their swords and under their feet. The defeat was complete and the Portuguese remained masters of the field and of Colombo.

Britto inflicted a severe punishment to the treacherous inhabitants of the town, who, since his arrival had made common cause with the Moors and had thus been responsible for so much bloodshed. He burned a part of the town to the ground, and in order to inspire more terror, many of the known partisans of the Moormen were tied to the doors of their houses and set fire to the roofs. But Britto took good care to leave the women free, and ordered his soldiers to fire the roofs so that the flames should not reach the prisoners before their wives could cut their bonds. The terror was therefore great, but none perished in the flames.

The King, having thus twice experienced the superiority of the Portuguese forces over those of the Moors, saw clearly that he could not count on the numerical weakness of the garrison of the fort, as it could easily be reinforced from Cochin. Humbled by his defeat, having lost a good deal of prestige in the eyes of his subjects, he sent an embassy to Britto suing for peace.

Britto himself had great need of this peace to establish himself more firmly in Colombo and finish the construction of the fort. He therefore received the King's envoys with honor, and insisted only on the renewal of the treaty of 1517 which was signed again by the King and himself.

This was an act of political prudence. There is no doubt that, after his brilliant victory and at this moment when the King had lost the support of the Moors, and the confidence of his people, Britto could have shown himself more exacting. But the object of the Portuguese at this period was not the conquest of the Island, of which they had no thought. All they wanted was to have commercial relations with Ceylon, be allowed to export the products of the Island and possess a military station to protect their trade. With such an end in view, it was wise to treat the King with regard and to be friendly with the people. It was necessary to show them that, whilst they were strong enough to defend their right acquired by treaties, they were also desirous to maintain friendly relations and peace.

The renewal of the treaty exasperated the Moormen. They saw that they were not strong enough to re-gain their influence by force of arms, nor to return to their former method of exciting the people against the Portuguese; for the Singhalese, by nature peaceful, were already tired of all this bloodshed which brought them no profit.

The Moormen therefore carried their intrigue to the court of Kotta, no longer in the hope to gain the King to their ends; for, rendered wise by the recent events, he would no longer listen to their solicitations. What they now undertook was to provoke a revolution in the palace and get rid of Vijaya Bahu, who would no longer allow himself to be an instrument in their hands.

5

They began to sow discord between the King and his sons, and succeeded so far that, it is said, the King seriously thought to disinherit the three princes and to transfer the rights of succession to a more distant relative!

Did he really intend to do so, or was it a clever invention of the Moors, the fact is that the princes rebelled against their father. They were popular in the country, the King was not liked by the people, so that the ranks of the rebels daily increased. With the aid of the King of Kandy they marched on Kotta, took the town and dictated their terms to the King.

For the time being the rebel princes did not dare to go further through fear of the intervention of Britto who, though willing to go to the King's help, as indeed he was bound to do by the treaty, but he had only a few soldiers exhausted by the late war, and was therefore powerless.

A few weeks later, King Vijaya Bahu was murdered by a Moorman named Soleiman who was paid to do the deed by the King's sons. Thus the parricide Vijaya Bahu perished by the hands of his own children.

Meanwhile the three princes divided among themselves their father's treasures and kingdom.

The eldest, Bhuwaneka Bahu, became King of Kotta. The second, Rayagam Banda, received in the division the province of Rayagam, and the youngest, Mayadunnè, who was to acquire in the history of Ceylon a sad notoriety, became Raja of Sitawacca.

## CHAPTER 4

## MAYADUNNÈ

During the next three years peace does not seem to have been disturbed. King Bhuwaneka Bahu fearing more and
1521 more the ever increasing ambition of his brother Mayadunnè, drew nearer to the Portuguese. For the time being the power of the Moors was broken. The people of Colombo and the surrounding country were beginning to appreciate the advantages of the neighbourhood of the Portuguese traders. Many had been converted to the Catholic Faith. The prosperity of the city was increasing and the development of trade enriched the natives.

King Dom Emmanuel of Portugal died in 1521, and was succeeded by John III, one of the greatest monarchs mentioned in history.

Wise, prudent, a born administrator, John III became alarmed at the rapid extension of the Portuguese colonial empire. The up-keep of the forts they had constructed everywhere for the protection of their trade necessitated considerable expenses and a large number of soldiers. The cost of the fleets that had to be maintained to keep up the communications with the distant establishments which extended from Brazil to Japan, and protect the commerce of half the world, pressed hard on the financial resources of Portugal. These colonies could not be organized on a solid basis, scattered as they were along the coasts of South America, Africa and Asia. They certainly brought great riches, but the strain on the mother country was unbearable.

John III therefore deemed it more prudent to put a stop to further colonial expansion. With this object in view he ordered that Ceylon should be abandoned, and the Viceroy sent Ferdinand de Lemos, the brother of Anthony, to Colombo to demolish the fort and to bring back the garrison to Goa.

But opposition arose from the least expected quarter. King Bhuwaneka Bahu protested energetically on the ground of the treaty of 1517. This treaty enacted that in return for an annual tribute paid by the King of Kotta, the Portuguese were bound to aid him in his wars with his enemies. How can this condition, said the King, be fulfilled without a permanent garrison in Colombo?

In face of such a protestation on the part of Bhuwaneka Bahu Ferdinand de Lemos and Lope de Britto found themselves in an embarassing position, for there could be no doubt that the treaty obligations were binding.

Subject therefore to the sanction of the Viceroy, and with the consent of Bhuwaneka Bahu, Lemos and Britto decided that the fort at Colombo should not be demolished, and as the King was not wanting in troops, for, at any moment he could raise an army of 25,000 men, and what was needed for such a force to become really powerful, was only to have them organized and trained according to European tactics and commanded by European officers, a body of twenty Portuguese would be left in Colombo, under the command of Nuno Freire d'Andrade.

The Portuguese then, evacuated Colombo and, during the
1523 thirty-one years that followed (1523 to 1554) Ceylon was not reckoned as one of their colonies. If at times they sent troops to the Island, it was only in fulfilment of the obligation imposed on them by the treaty of 1517, to aid the King in his wars against his enemies and, as we shall see later on, scarcely was the war ended when the troops were withdrawn to Goa.

Andrade and his twenty men considered themselves rather in the service of Bhuwaneka Bahu than in that of the King of Portugal, and betook themselves to Kotta to organize the King's army.

Also from time to time, some Portuguese merchants would, on their own initiative, come to Colombo for trade; Missionaries too established themselves on the Island, but the Portuguese Government gave up all intention of acquiring Ceylon and, if King John III still remained the nominal Suzerain of Kotta, it was only because the King of Kotta was unwilling to give up the advantages of his vassalage, which obliged the Viceroy of Goa to defend him against his enemies.

Hardly had the Portuguese left Ceylon, when the Moors began again to hope to conquer for themselves the kingdom of Kotta.

The Zamorin, Raja of Calicut, sent them four vessels with five hundred soldiers under the command of one of his generals called Galeacem, who anchored in Colombo harbour and sent an embassy to Kotta to announce to the King the news that the Portuguese had abandoned India as they had abandoned Ceylon.

The King, very much alarmed by these news, hastened to summon Nuno Freire d'Andrade, who assured him that the news were false, a mere stratagem of the Moors, and that, if he gave him a sufficient number of soldiers, he could easily defeat the troops of the Zamorin.

Meanwhile Galeacem made preparations to land his small army. But the inhabitants of Colombo rose in a body to oppose his landing. They had learned in these years to appreciate the advantages of the alliance with the Portuguese. From being formerly robbed by the Moormen they now saw their trade protected. From a mere sea coast village Colombo was becoming an important town; its prosperity increased year by year. The people selling to the Portuguese such products of the country which formerly had no value whatever were growing richer, trade was flourishing, and they did not care to return to the ancient tyranny of the Moormen.

Nevertheless, Galeacem effected his landing, but meanwhile Andrade had arrived from Kotta at the head of six hundred Singhalese soldiers. The twenty Portuguese from the fort joined him and helped him to place the native soldiers in battle array according to European tactics. These Singhalese soldiers were brave and, when well commanded, were not to be despised.

On the morning of the 15th February 1524, the Moors were

1524 attacked. The struggle was a bloody one, but they were defeated and took to flight. Some with their chiefs succeeded in reaching two of their vessels and, at once, put out to sea. Others took refuge in the territory of Mayadunnè. Andrade seized two ships and returned victorious to Kotta.

Though conquered, Galeacem was not discouraged. He returned to Calicut to prepare another expedition, and on the 3rd May landed again at Colombo. But Andrade at the head of the King's troops inflicted him another defeat, and he fled leaving four vessels in the hands of the victors.

After this brilliant victory, King Bhuwaṇeka Bahu wishing to break the faction of the Moormen, ordered all those who lived in Colombo to leave his kingdom within three days. They all sought refuge at Sitawacca where Mayadunnè received them with honors and great hospitality.

After their recent defeats, the Moormen saw clearly that, without some powerful ally, even with the help of the Zamcrin they would not be able to re-gain their old ascendency in the south of Ceylon, nor monopolise the trade of the Island which, before the arrival of the Portuguese, was entirely in their hands.

They cast their eyes on Mayadunnè, an ambitious, unscrupulous and enterprising prince, who for long time was desirous of getting rid of his elder brother and possessing himself of the throne of Kotta.

They began to flatter him and to fan his ambition, and, in a short time the little court of Sitawacca became the centre of intrigues round which gathered the Moorish faction. Urged by them, Mayadunnè entered in communication with the Zamorin.

Bhuwaneka Bahu being informed of these intrigues and
having been told that the Zamorin was making great
1526 preparations to invade his kingdom, sent in the first half of 1526 an embassy to Goa to ask help from the new Viceroy Lope Vaz de Sampayo, who promised to succour him.

The occasion soon presented itself. Mayadunnè thinking himself now strong enough to openly declare his rebellion, assembled an army of 30,000 men. The Zamorin sent him a well armed force of 2,000 Moors under the command of a renowned leader named Ali Ibrahim Marikar. The united forces marched against the King and laid siege to Kotta, while Bhuwaneka Bahu and Nuno Freire d'Andrade gallantly defended the town.

The Viceroy, faithful to his promise, hastened to send reinforcements under the command of Alphonsus de Mello Zuzarte. As soon as the departure of the Portuguese fleet from Goa was known at Ceylon, Mayadunnè and Ali Ibrahim Marikar hastened to raise the siege, the former flying to Sitawacca and the latter joining his ships and sailing to Calicut, so that when de Mello arrived to Colombo, there was nothing for him to do but to pay his respects to the King of Kotta and to return to Cochin.

Mayadunnè, loosing courage and now seeing clearly that, though the Portuguese had abandoned Ceylon, they yet remained faithful to the treaty with the King of Kotta, and considered
themselves bound to come to his aid when the necessity
1528 arose, humbly sought his brother's pardon for his

rebellion, sued for peace and offered to pay him a yearly tribute; and, during the eight years that followed (1528 to 1536) lived in peace with his brother. Nor could he count on the Zamorin, who, discouraged by his recent defeats, did not wish any more to interfere with the affairs of Ceylon.

As mentioned before, Andrade leaving to one of his subordinates the command of the small garrison of the fort of Colombo, had established himself at Kotta where he organized the King's army and fortified the town after the European system.

He was an old man of great piety and zeal for religion and employed a good deal of his time in instructing and converting heathens. He helped Fr. Paul of St. Bonaventure, a Franciscan, to build a church at Kotta where they formed a small Catholic community.

As already stated, humbled and discouraged, Mayadunnè remained quiet for nearly eight years. But the Moormen, who had been for so many years masters of the country, did not resign themselves to the loss of their power. They began again their intrigues with the Zamorin and with Mayadunnè. To the Zamorin, their Sovereign, they pointed out the commercial value of the Island, and never ceased to excite the ambition of Mayadunnè showing him in glorious colours the possibility of exchanging his small principality of Sitawacca for the throne of Kotta, which, in the eyes of the Singhalese, ignorant of the world outside of their Island, seemed to be the height of power.

At first, Mayadunnè resisted to their solicitations, and even once, when a Moorish force landed on the shores of Ceylon, he paid them a large sum of money to induce them to quit the country. He was prudent and he feared consequences. He knew well that a Portuguese fleet could reach in a few days Colombo from Cochin, and thus he might lose his principality of Sitawacca without which, as a base of action, he could never hope to put into execution his ambitious projects on the throne of Kotta.

The Moormen however won him gradually over, and finally induced him to write to the Zamorin a letter proposing
1536
an alliance against his brother King Bhuwaneka Bahu, and promising to the Zamorin that, when he becomes King of Kotta, he will recognize him as his paramount Lord and pay him a yearly tribute.

The Zamorin sent him an army of 4,000 soldiers under the command of Paichi Marikar, his brother Cuniale and the old Ali Ibrahim Marikar. They landed at Colombo in October 1536, and Mayadunnè having joined them, they laid siege to Kotta.

King Bhuwaneka Bahu asked help from the Viceroy Nuno da Cunha, who ordered the Governor of Cochin, Martin Alphonsus de Sousa, to proceed to Ceylon with the forces he had at
1537
his disposal. The same as has happened to de Mello Zuzarte happened now again: When de Sousa landed at Colombo in January 1537 he learned that the Zamorin's troops had left for Calicut nine days before, and that Mayadunnè had been reconciled with his brother.

Martin Alphonso de Sousa was a man of great merit, and a few years later he made for himself a great name as Portuguese

Ambassador to the Pope, Viceroy of India and friend of St. Francis Xavier.

Seeing the object of his expedition frustrated, he nevertheless thought it his duty to go to Kotta to pay his respects to the King who received him with great honors, and then returned to Cochin.

Notwithstanding the peace concluded with his brother, Mayadunnè did not cease his intrigues with the Zamorin, and Paichi Marikar was preparing a new expedition.

Hardly had a year elapsed, when he embarked again for Ceylon at the head of 8,000 men. The Governor of Cochin,
1538 Martin Alphonsus de Sousa, was watching his progress. Seeing that the Moors had already escaped twice before the Portuguese could reach Ceylon, he resolved to attack them on sea. He pursued Paichi Marikar's squadron, overtook him in the bay of Beadala near Rameseram and on the 20th February 1538 defeated him completely.

Before Mayadunnè could hear of the defeat of his ally, King Bhuwaneka Bahu marched against him, gained a decisive victory and conquered his capital Sitawacca. Mayadunnè fled from the battle field and sought refuge with his brother Rayagam Banda.

Such was the state of affairs when M. A. de Sousa landed at Colombo, proceeded at once to Kotta and placed himself at the King's disposal. His intention was to finish once for ever with Mayadunnè, now that he was deprived of the aid of the Moors and thus assure the peace in Ceylon. But the cunning Mayadunnè having foreseen this, had written to the King a humble letter begging his pardon and suing for peace. Bhuwaneka Bahu showed the letter to Sousa who answered him that he had already twice pardoned the rebel, who had each time broken his promises and should therefore no longer rely on his word. Seeing however that the King was rather inclined to reconciliation he added that, he had come to Ceylon with no other object than to bring him help. The King was therefore free to do what he thought best, if he thought that the peace would be more advantageous for his kingdom. Sousa remained yet a few days at Kotta and then returned to Cochin.

Mayadunnè remained quiet for a whole year. Then, on the death of his brother Rayagam Banda, he seized his
1539 principality, which according to the laws of the country ought to have reverted to the King. Bhuwaneka Bahu, who desired at any cost to avoid a new conflict, had the weakness to ratify his brother's usurpation.

The annexation of the province of Rayagam to the small State of Sitawacca increased Mayadunnè's power and, as the Portuguese had at this time their hands full, engaged as they were in a war with several Indian Rajas, he considered the moment propitious to rebel again against the King. The Zamorin sent him new reinforcements commanded by Paichi Marikar and his brother Cuniale who anchored at Putlam, left there their troops, and proceeded alone to Sitawacca.

The Viceroy, Don Garcia de Noronha, faithful to the treaty,

and in spite of the war in which he was engaged in India, sent to the King's aid a small army commanded by Miguel Ferreira.

Ferreira went straight to Putlam, defeated the forces of the Zamorin, landed then at Colombo and proceeded to Kotta.

The Portuguese commander wanted to march straight on Sitawacca and put once for all an end to those revolts of Mayadunnè. But the King opposed his plan, saying that it was repugnant to him to destroy his own brother.

Ferreira replied that he had come to Ceylon to establish peace, and that it was useless to think of peace, as long as they did not deprive Mayadunnè of the means of causing trouble. It was easy to drive the Moors from Ceylon, but of what advantage was it when, the moment the Portuguese left the Island, the rebel prince called them back again? The Portuguese had already come three times to Ceylon, and each time, the King, by his excessive weakness towards his younger brother, had prevented them to put an end, once for all, to these disgusting wars. He finally declared, that the Portuguese had serious work in India and could not amuse themselves with such useless expedition, and therefore, if this time again the King would prove an obstacle to their action, they would disassociate themselves from the affairs of Kotta, and abandon the King to his own resources.

This last argument made an impression on Bhuwaneka Bahu, and he consented to march on Sitawacca.

Ferreira led the vanguard of 300 Portuguese. The King followed at the head of 7,000 soldiers, the flower of his Singhalese army, and his son-in-law Weedeya Raja brought up the rear with 11,000 men.

They encountered no resistance till they reached the walls of Sitawacca, wherein Mayadunnè had shut himself with all that was left of the Zamorin's army.

Ferreira wished to take the town at once, but the King would not lend him his troops on the plea that he could not participate in the ruin and perhaps even in the death of his brother.

Meanwhile Mayadunnè sent a letter to the King, humbly begging for peace and swearing on the head of his father (whom he had helped to assassinate) that henceforth he would be always faithful and obedient.

The King assembled his council and they decided that peace and pardon would be granted to Mayadunnè on condition that he would dismiss the Moors of the Zamorin, to whom a safe conduct would be granted through the territory of Kotta, to Colombo, where they could embark for Calicut.

This dècision of the King rose the anger of Ferreira. Old warrior that he was, he knew that Sitawacca could not resist a single assault, and that with the taking of the town and the death or capture of Mayadunnè, the war would end and peace restored in Ceylon for many years. But, without the co-operation of the King's army, he could do nothing with his handful of men.

Nevertheless, he surrounded the town so that none could escape unobserved and sent word to Mayadunnè that if he would not deliver into his hands Paichi Marikar and Cuniale, he would attack and capture the city, take him prisoner and send him in chains to Goa.

Two days later, they brought to Ferreira the heads of the two Moorish chiefs whom Mayadunnè had cowardly murdered.

The death of Paichi Marikar and of Cuniale broke the power of the Moors. Henceforth they had to cease their endeavours to become masters of Ceylon, and became a factor no longer to be reckoned with. The Zamorin, discouraged by so many reverses and fearing more and more the rising of the Portuguese power on the western coast of India, renounced for ever to his ambition of conquering Ceylon, and gave no more support to Mayadunnè. The power of the Moors in Ceylon was crushed for ever.

Thus it happened that the Portuguese with their arms and with their blood, shed on the field of battle, saved from destruction the national existence of the Singhalese. Had not the Kings Dharma Prakrama Bahu and Bhuwaneka Bahu allied themselves with the Portuguese, the Singhalese reduced to slavery by the Moors, would have lost their nationality, and even their name would have remained unknown to history.

Let us pause now for a moment to consider the strange and apparently inexplicable conduct of King Bhuwaneka Bahu in the events narrated above.

It is difficult to suppose that this King, who had procured the death of his father, was moved only by brotherly love.

He was certainly strong enough to reduce to obedience

Mayadunnè alone. But he would not have overcome Mayadunnè allied with the Zamorin and the Moors, and therefore he wanted the Portuguese alliance.

He feared nevertheless, that the Portuguese may some day think of conquering Ceylon, he wished therefore to keep for them an enemy in reserve in the person of Mayadunnè.

To maintain his power with the aid of the Portuguese, and to check at the same time the velleity of the Portuguese to become themselves masters of his kingdom, he spared them an enemy. That was the secret of the policy of Bhuwaneka Bahu.

On the other hand, these wars were no more now so easy for the Portuguese as they used to be years ago when the Singhalese had no other arms than swords, spears and arrows.

Frightened as they were at first with the fire arms they never had seen before, the Singhalese, industrious and clever, had hardly picked up on the battle field some Portuguese muskets, when they began to make them, and in a short time they had reached such a perfection, that their weapons were superior to those which the Portuguese imported from Europe. And, towards the end of the Portuguese domination in Ceylon, the King of Kandy, not only possessed 20,000 muskets, but he had in addition a cannon foundry.

## CHAPTER 5

# THE EMBASSY TO LISBON

King Bhuwaneka Bahu had no son. His only daughter was
1540 married to Weedeya Raja a prince of royal blood.

His younger brother Rayagam Banda was dead, thus Mayadunnè was the presumptive heir to the throne of Kotta.

The events however of the last fifteen years showed the King clearly, what would be the consequences if his rebellious brother should succeed him.

Though well nigh for sixteen years the Portuguese had given up their military station at Colombo, they had maintained their trade with Ceylon. A number of Portuguese merchants had settled at Colombo round the church of St. Lawrence, of which, at this time Fr. Henry, a Franciscan Friar, was in charge.

Mayadunnè had identified himself too much with the Moors, and owed them too much, being in fact a mere creature in their hands, to be able to change his policy. He hated the Portuguese, who, up to the present had prevented him from usurping his brother's throne. On the other hand the Portuguese distrusted him too much to accept his alliance, even if he offered it.

It thus became clear to the King that if his brother were to succeed him as King of Kotta, the Moors of Calicut, sure of his protection, would do all possible to re-gain their past power. The

Portuguese from their side, out of necessity to protect their growing commercial interests, would be naturally obliged to a military occupation of the coasts of the Island. There would thus issue a deadly conflict between the Portuguese and the Moors, and whichever be the victors, the independence of the kingdom of Kotta would be lost for ever.

Now the Moors wanted to conquer the Island, to become absolute masters of it. On the other hand, the Portuguese at this period, did not think even of adding Ceylon to their already too extensive colonial possessions. They were contented of having assured by treaty free trade with the kingdom of Kotta, they had a civilizing influence on the people, they respected their national independence, and whilst their trade brought them certainly great profits, they enriched at the same time the natives, by buying the products of the land and opening a new market for Singhalese export.

King Bhuwaneka Bahu having to choose between two alternatives preferred naturally to be the vassal of the King of Portugal than to see his people enslaved by the Moors. The only hope of his kingdom remaining independent was in the alliance with the Portuguese. Mayadunnè was the chief obstacle, and he was his heir presumptive.

The people hated Mayadunnè, who ruled his States of Sitawacca and Rayagam with tyrannical cruelty, and trembled at the thought of his becoming one day their King.

Bhuwaneka Bahu resolved, since it was not against the laws

and custom of the country, to transfer the succession to his grandson Dharmapala, the son of his daughter and of Weedeya Rajà.

The boy was carefully educated by a tutor whom the Portuguese writers call Tamita Ramale, which is evidently a corruption of his Singhalese name. He was one of the first Ceylonese converted to the Catholic Faith. He trained the royal child with great care, inspired unto him the principles of virtue and secretly instructed him in the Catholic Religion. And the boy, intelligent and precocious, listened with great interest when his teacher spoke to him of God and of His Law.

In order to make certain young Dharmapala's succession to the throne, the King, having acknowledged himself vassal to the King of Portugal, knew that, according to the feudal law, the consent of the Suzerain was required.

Bhuwaneka Bahu cared little for the feudal laws of Europe. But he wanted to profit by these laws to secure to his grandson the support of the Portuguese, for he well knew, that once the King of Portugal had recognized young Dharmapala as lawful heir to the throne of Kotta, the Viceroys would be bound to secure him his rights and protect him against the aggressions of his grand-uncle Mayadunnè.

Bhuwaneka Bahu determined therefore to send an embassy to Lisbon, but he had great difficulty to find amongst his nobles one who would consent to undertake this voyage, which in those days took nearly a year.

He finally chose two officials, one named Salappu Aratchi, the other Proybila Rale. They were not high functionaries of the court, but they were the only ones who could be persuaded to undertake the voyage.

The two ambassadors embarked at Colombo, and were received with honors at Goa by the Viceroy Steven de Gama who sent them on to Lisbon under the care of a Portuguese nobleman Francis de Sousa Tavarez, who spoke fluently Singhalese and could act as interpreter. They took with them a statue representing the boy Dharmapala and a rich golden crown studded with precious stones.

The voyage was prosperous; they arrived at Lisbon in 1540, where they had a grand reception. All the court dignitaries met them at the landing.

Seated in gilt carriages and accompanied by the Marquises of Ferreira and of Villa-Real, they drove to the royal palace, and were received by King John III seated on a magnificent throne.

The Singhalese ambassadors deposited at the feet of the King the presents sent by Bhuwaneka Bahu and handed him the King's letter written on a palm leaf. The letter ran as follows:

— Sun of the world, Planet that is never eclipsed, Whale of the ocean and Lion of the earth. Light of battles, King of Kings, merciful, wise, just, holy, admirable, victorious! We Bhuwaneka Bahu, an ant that crawls at Your feet, relying on the promptings of Our heart and not on the little merit We may seem to have in Your esteem, We beg of You to confirm Our grandson Dharmapala, as heir to Our kingdom, so that, after Our death, he may revive Our spirit, and, with Your powerful aid, triumph over those who would dispute his rights to the throne. In return for the benefit You would thus confer on Our poor merits, We promise to pay punctually the tribute as established by treaty, and to leave You in possession of those places which We have already given to You, which are Yours, and will be Yours, on condition that You succour me in my reverses of fortune. —

Some days later, amidst a brilliant assembly, the ambassadors placed before the King the statue of the boy Dharmapala, and John III rising on his throne placed on it the royal crown, amidst sounding of trumpets, and roaring of guns.

Then followed great festivities and the Singhalese ambassadors were much impressed with the greatness and glory of the King of Portugal.

They remained at Lisbon till the annual departure of the Portuguese fleet for India. King John III gave them a letter to Bhuwaneka Bahu, in which he put but one condition to the protection that he granted, and that was, that Bhuwaneka Bahu should allow the Franciscan Fathers to establish a Mission in his kingdom, and would leave them free to preach to his people the Gospel of Christ.

The Ambassadors left Lisbon on a vessel called the Santiago
1541 and had for companions of their long voyage, the new Viceroy, Martin Alfonsus de Sousa who, when Governor of Cochin, had already been twice in Ceylon, St. Francis Xavier who was going to India as Papal Delegate, and seven Franciscan

Fathers whom the King of Portugal was sending to establish a Mission in Ceylon. These were the Fathers: John de Villa Conde the Superior. Anthony de Pedrão, Francis of the East, born in India and educated at Lisbon, Edward Chanoça and three others whose names are not known.

Leaving Lisbon on the 7th April 1541, they wintered at Mozambique and reached Goa on the 6th May 1542.
1542 St. Francis Xavier and Fr. John de Villa Conde formed on the voyage a holy friendship which they retained till death.

At Goa, the Viceroy equipped two vessels and sent the ambassadors and the Franciscan Missionaries to Ceylon. He sent with them two knights, Edward de Menezes and Francis Carneiro, bearers of a letter to the King of Kotta, in which he informed his old friend King Bhuwaneka Bahu of his promotion as Viceroy, promised to bring him help whenever required and recommended to him the Franciscan Fathers who were going to Ceylon to establish a Mission.

The King was well satisfied with the result of the embassy in all respects except one, the arrival of the Missionaries. Superstitious Buddhist that he was, he had regarded with no favourable eye the conversions to the Catholic Faith that were taking place among his subjects.

At first he would not allow Fr. John de Villa Conde and his companions to exercise their Apostleship in his kingdom, but, fearing the anger of the King of Portugal, whose protection he needed, he yielded to the inevitable and finally confided the education of prince Dharmapala, his grandson and heir, to Fr. John.

Fr. John de Villa Conde must be considered as the founder of the Missions in Ceylon. It is true that before him there had already been three priests in the Island: Father John Monteiro de Setuelo and Fr. Henry a Franciscan both in charge of the church of St. Lawrence at Colombo, and another Franciscan, Fr. Bonaventure, who built a church at Kotta. They had converted a number of heathens and established Catholic communities in both towns, but there were no organized Missions in the Island, till the arrival of Fr. John and his six Franciscan companions.

Fr. John de Villa Conde resided at Kotta where, as tutor to the young prince Dharmapala he had his quarters in the royal palace. Hence he had many occasions to approach the King and to speak with him of Religion. But Bhuwaneka Bahu was obdurate in his heathenism, never ceased placing obstacles to the apostolate of the Franciscan Fathers, so that, the fruit of their labours, as mostly in the beginning of Missions, was the conversion of a small number of villagers.

About this time Fr. John de Villa Conde, wrote a long report to St. Francis Xavier on the prospects of the Ceylon Mission, of which he drew a rather gloomy picture owing to the bad will of the King.

Yet, the first Christians of Ceylon, gave a martyr to the
**1543** Church of Christ.

A year had already passed since St. Francis Xavier was labouring in India. He was then on the Fishery Coast near to

Tuticorin, and the news of his wonderful apostolate had reached Ceylon.

At that time there were still in the Island some Bikshun or Bonzes who had some instruction or, at least, passed for being instructed. They held a meeting at Dinavacca to discuss the doctrine which St. Francis Xavier was preaching in India.

One of them, more learned than the others, openly declared his opinion that the doctrine of transmigration was an absurdity and that St. Francis Xavier was right to teach, that the soul after death would go to heaven, purgatory or hell according to its merits. These words of the Bikshu gave rise to a great uproar, and the speaker was accused of perverting the doctrine of Buddha, and, as he persisted in his opinion, he was condemned to be deported to a peninsula at Arrakan to be tried there for heresy.

Whilst waiting in prison at Trincomalee for the departure of the ship that was to carry him to Burma, he was visited by some Catholics. He questioned them eagerly on the doctrine of the end of man, not that he had any idea of becoming a Christian, but in the sole view of learning how better to answer to his Judges.

Finally, touched by the words of a Portuguese called John de Silva, who often came to speak with him of Religion, he asked for Baptism. Silva called over Fr. Francis Antunes a young deacon, native of Goa, who was labouring on the opposite coast of India with St. Francis Xavier, who instructed and baptised the Bikshu.

On being carried to Arrakan the brave confessor of the Faith answered to his Judges that, being now a Catholic, he would not discuss with them the teachings of Buddha, but would teach them the doctrine of Christ. He was condemned to death and was the first among the Ceylonese to gain the crown of martyrdom on the 5th December 1543.

In concluding this period of the history of the kingdom of Kotta, we cannot omit to mention the calumnies with which the Portuguese have been overwhelmed by superficial writers of the past century who, not caring to go to the authentic sources of history, and disregarding the first rules of critic, contented themselves with copying one another.

It is amazing the amount of thrash which even more serious writers give to swallow to their readers under the name of history.

In the text-book of Ceylon history prescribed for the English schools in the Island, and which every school boy has to learn, (page 102), speaking about the epoch, the author says:

— „ The Portuguese gradually extended their possessions in „ Ceylon, and, in doing so, they did not spare neither the lives „ nor the property of the Singhalese. In their anxiety to secure „ wealth and power, they were utterly careless of the rights of the „ natives of the Island and committed many acts of cruelty and „ injustice. The Singhalese maddened by the oppression to which „ they were subjected, made a vigorous attempt to get back their „ independence." —

Let us analyze this statement in the light of history.

In the first place the text-book imposed for the use of the schools is wrong in giving the dates of 1527 to 1542 for the reign of Vijaya Bahu. This King reigned from 1518 to 1521. But let it pass.

— „The Portuguese gradually extended their possessions in Ceylon." — Which possessions? All they had at this time was a small fortlet manned by 20 soldiers at Colombo, a few commercial stores in the same town and a church at Kotta, all built on land given them by the King, and the land at this epoch was of no great value.

— „And in doing so they did not spare either the life or the „property of the Singhalese." — It is rather a bad compliment to the Singhalese to presume that they were unable to defend their life and their property against twenty soldiers and a dozen of merchants.

— „In their anxiety to secure wealth and power." — Wealth yes, certainly. Even in our times merchants come to Ceylon, not to get bankrupt but to acquire wealth. But they develop at the same time the trade, they open new markets and, in securing wealth for themselves, at the same time they enrich the country. As to secure power, the Portuguese had long ago evacuated Ceylon which remained for all these years outside their colonial policy and it was only on the demand of the King of Kotta that they did not dismantle their fortlet at Colombo and left there twenty men. If they had wanted power, with an army of one thousand men sent from Goa or from Cochin, they would had crushed Mayadunnè and his Moorish allies and conquered in no time the kingdom of Kotta. All what they wanted, at this epoch, was free and unmolested trade.

— „They were utterly careless of the rights of the natives of

„the Island." — The natives of the Island were well able to care themselves for their rights, and the author should point out what were these rights which were violated.

— „And committed many acts of cruelty and injustice." —

The only act of cruelty mentioned was the fact of Britto tying the rebels to the doors of their houses and firing the roofs. But we have seen how the thing had been done, and the reason why he did it. As to injustice, we will admit that the Portuguese merchants cheated sometimes the Singhalese by overvaluing the goods they were selling, but this was nothing in comparison to the amount to which the Singhalese merchants cheat now the European and American tourists. Many traders unhappily are not always honest.

— „The Singhalese maddened by the oppression to which „they were subjected, made a vigorous attempt to get back their „independence." — It would be rather interesting to know, when and where this vigorous attempt has been made. History does not mention any. We have seen wars, and war brings always a certain amount of bloodshed and oppression. But in these wars, the Portuguese, a mere handful of brave, determined men, acted only as auxiliaries in the army of the King of Kotta. They helped King Bhuwaneka Bahu to defend his throne, the freedom of his people and the independence of his ancient kingdom, against the rebel Mayadunnè, who for his own interest, for the ambition of becoming a shadow of a King, had sold his native country to the Moors, and helped them in their endeavours to reduce the low-country Singhalese into slavery.

King Bhuwaneka Bahu, by allying himself with the Portuguese against the Moors and Mayadunnè their puppet, who, without this alliance, would certainly have conquered the kingdom of Kotta, saved the Singhalese from destruction, from utter annihilation. If the Singhalese nationality still exists, if they have not been forcibly transformed into Moormen, they owe it to the Portuguese.

We have allowed ourselves this disgression in order to dispose, once for all, of the thrash accumulated by some authors of the last century, who wrote about the Portuguese period of the history of Ceylon. They can all be refuted with the same arguments, so that we will have no need to return to this subject.

## CHAPTER 6

# THE MARTYRS OF MANAAR

The north of Ceylon and the Vanni formed another independent kingdom, that of Jaffna, populated with Tamils,
1544 and was ruled at that time by King Sagara Raja a cruel tyrant, who had usurped the crown by depriving of his throne the legitimate King, who was his elder brother.

The Portuguese had little intercourse with Jaffna. Some merchants from Cochin visited it from time to time, a few had settled in the town and Fr. John de Villa Conde had sent to Jaffna a Franciscan Missionary, Fr. Peter, to provide for their spiritual wants.

The Jaffna Tamils, who were in constant intercourse with the Parawers of the Fishery Coast, were the first in Ceylon to hear about St. Francis Xavier and the numerous conversions which he made in the south of India; his influence over the Portuguese, his wonderful miracles and his great kindness to the poor and the humble, and they desired greatly to approach and know him.

The inhabitants of the Island of Manaar were the first to send to him a deputation, begging the Saint to come over to them and to instruct them in the Catholic Faith.

St. Francis Xavier was at that time busy in Travancore, where he was making many conversions. He could not leave these new

Christians. He sent therefore to Manaar a young Goanese priest who had been his constant companion since the first days of his arrival to Goa. St. Francis Xavier struck by his virtues had a great affection for the young man, who was then a deacon, and he, out of love for his master, on the day he was raised to the holy priesthood took his name, and was hence known as Fr. Francis Xavier.

In sending to Manaar his favourite disciple, St. Francis Xavier predicted that his Mission would be very successful, and in fact, in a very short time he baptised more than six hundred pagans and established at Manaar a fervent Christian community.

The wrath of the King of Jaffna had no bounds when he heard of the conversion of the Manaarese. He sent to the Island a body of armed men who seized in one night all the Christians and brought them to the village of Passim.

Wonderful was the heroism of these new converts. Interrogated each separately if they were Christians, when by a denial they could have saved their lives, all, without exception, acknowledged that they were, the parents answering for their little children, and all, six to seven hundred, were cruelly put to death.

The young priest Francis Xavier was of the first to shed his blood for Christ. He was the first native priest to suffer martyrdom.

---

King Sagara Raja thought that this massacre of the Manaarese had eradicated Christianity from his kingdom, when a few days later he learned that his own eldest son was a Catholic. The young prince had formed a friendship with a Portuguese merchant named Andrew de Sousa who instructed him in the Catholic Faith, and he had been secretly baptised by Fr. Peter.

The King, in his anger, tried all possible means for inducing his son to give up his Faith. Seeing at last that nothing could shake the courage of the youth, he condemned him to death. He was executed and his body thrown into the field to be devoured by the wild beasts. But in the night Fr. Peter and Andrew de Sousa went in search of the body and gave a Christian burial to the martyr prince.

Great wonders happened on his grave. A Cross of fire appeared over it so resplendent, that the people, attracted by this extraordinary spectacle, could not bear its sight. Many fled in terror, others moved by the grace of God asked for Baptism and professed openly their Faith. The King ordered many of them to be put to death.

All this happened in November 1544, and these facts have been authenticated by historical documents: A letter of St. Francis Xavier, another of the brother of the martyred prince to King John III of Portugal and a third of Andrew de Sousa, an eye witness, to Cardinal Henry, the brother of John III, which is still preserved in the State Archives of Lisbon.

King Sagara Raja had a sister, a lady of a superior intelligence and of indomitable courage. She too, unknown to her brother the King, was a Catholic. She had brought up as Catholics two boys, the younger son of the King, a brother to the martyr prince, and her own son, who according to the laws of succession was the rightful heir to the throne.

The event above related made her see what would be the fate of the young princes, if the King happened to know that they were preparing for Baptism. She determined therefore to remove them from his wrath. As to the danger for herself the courageous woman did not care; she was ready to die for her Faith. All her affections were centered in the boys whom she had gained to the Faith, and all her anxiety was now to save them.

She sent for Andrew de Sousa, who chartering a small vessel embarked with the young princes and brought them to St. Francis Xavier who was then in Travancore. St. Francis pressed the boys to his heart and shed over them tears of sorrow and joy: of sorrow at the news of the sad events of Manaar and of Jaffna, and of joy, that God had chosen these two innocent souls in the very family of the tyrant who had murdered his Christians.

As the royal boys were rather backward in their studies, St. Francis Xavier sent them to Goa to St. Paul's College. The King of Portugal took personal interest in their welfare. Writing on the 17th March 1546 to the Viceroy John de Castro, he approved St. Francis Xavier's action in placing them in the College, but directed that they should be lodged in the city and that the colonial treasury provide generously for their support, so that they could live in a manner and state befitting princes of royal blood.

The princes were baptised at Goa; the King's son took the name of John. We do not know the name which was given to his cousin. He died very young. Prince John too followed him soon in the grave. He was no more alive in 1560.

King Sagara Raja, hearing of the flight of the princes could not restrain his anger. It was not alone hatred of Christianity that urged him, but fear lest the Portuguese should mix themselves up with the affairs of Jaffna, since he was but an usurper, and his brother the lawful King, whom he had treacherously deprived of the crown, and who since led a miserable life hiding in the Vanny, had also fled to Goa, where, after having received Holy Baptism, old and broken down, he no more thought of re-gaining his kingdom, but to the end of his life, kept to piety and good works.

A short time afterwards, ten members of the principal families of Jaffna embraced the Catholic Faith. They fled to Nagapatam whence they crossed to Goa where they found a honorable refuge.

King Sagara Raja was disheartened. Fearing the vengeance of the Portuguese, he did not dare to persecute the Christians, whose number was increasing in Jaffna and in the neighbourhood of the town.

The events related above gave much anxiety to St. Francis Xavier. He clearly saw that, if the massacres of

1545 Manaar and Jaffna were left unpunished, the progress of Religion in the north of Ceylon would become impossible and the life of the Christians would always be in danger.

He sailed therefore to Cambay where the Viceroy was at that time (January 1545) to treat with him of these events and represent him the consequences of such crimes remaining unpunished.

The Viceroy, Martin Alphonsus de Sousa, was seized with

horror at the recital of the Saint, and at once ordered a fleet to be made ready at Nagapatam, to capture Jaffna, take Sagara Raja a prisoner and put him to death.

The fatherly heart of St. Francis Xavier shrank at the great indignation to which the affairs of Jaffna gave rise in the Viceroy's mind. He feared the punishment to be too severe and endeavoured to allay his anger against Sagara Raja. The Viceroy, admiring the saint's charity, ordered that if the King was taken prisoner, his fate should be decided by St. Francis Xavier.

Having thus settled the matter with the Viceroy, St. Francis Xavier returned to Cochin, whence he proceeded to Nagapatam to hasten the preparation for the expedition. But unforeseen circumstances caused the expedition to be put off, and the saint, broken hearted at the dangers to which the Catholics of Jaffna would remain exposed, left Nagapatam for Mailepur on the 5th April 1545.

Martin Alphonsus de Sousa having completed his term of office was succeeded by John de Castro. Among the instructions given to the new Viceroy by King John III in March 1546, we read the following:

— „ The cruel outrages of the tyrant of Ceylon, against those of his subjects who had embraced the Catholic Faith, oblige Us to command you to inflict on him, though late, a sure and severe punishment, so as to show to the world, that We are determined, to grant every possible protection to the poor people who renounce the errors of heathenism, and its diabolical superstitions." —

However, neither John de Castro, nor his successor could

carry out the orders of the King. Their hands were full with Indian affairs, and it was not till fourteen years later, that war against Sagara Raja could be undertaken.

## CHAPTER 7

# THE KING OF KANDY

The central part of Ceylon, occupied by the kingdom of Kandy, was by far the largest of the three States into
1546 which the Island was divided. It extended from one sea to the other, and included at that epoch, the hilly centre of Ceylon, with the plain a little beyond Anuradhapura and Kalpe, the seven Kortes with Chilaw, Putlam and Kalpentyn, the whole province of Uva, and the district of Battecaloa.

The King of Kandy Jayaweera, who had been always opposed to Christianity and had refused the entrance in his dominions to the Franciscan Missionaries, had a quarrel with Mayadunnè, who now, since several years at peace with his brother, had employed his leisures in strengthening and exercising his army, and he was much afraid that Mayadunnè should declare him war.

Having seen how the Portuguese alliance had been advantageous to his cousin Bhuwaneka Bahu, he wrote to Fr. John de Villa Conde that he desired to become a Christian and invited the Franciscan Missionaries to come into his kingdom.

There was no doubt, that, at this time, King Jayaweera was not sincere, his real motives were only the fear of Mayadunnè, and the hope of being helped by the Portuguese.

Nevertheless, Fr. John de Villa Conde hastened to send to

Kandy two Missionaries, the Fathers Pascal and Gonzalo. King Jayaweera received them with great honors, gave them permission to preach the Gospel in his dominions and gave them a beautiful site in the town for building a church.

Whatever might have been the personal motives of the King, his kindness towards the Missionaries impressed the people and helped much the Fathers in their apostolic work, and the conversions which they made in a short time were so many, that the Superior was obliged to send two more Franciscans to Kandy, the Fathers John of Calvo and Peter Maddalena. This was in 1545.

King Jayaweera received willingly the Missionaries at his palace and often spoke with them of Religion, but he seemed to put off more and more his intention of becoming a Christian. At last he cooled down so far, that the Kandians fearing his displeasure, did not dare to declare themselves Catholics, and the number of conversions diminished so much, that there was no more work in Kandy for four Missionaries, so that Fr. John de Villa Conde re-called two to Kotta, and Fathers Pascal and Gonzalo remained alone at Kandy.

Fr. Pascal nevertheless went often to visit the King. He describes him of being of such inconstant character that one day he would desire Baptism, and the next seemed more hardened than ever in his heathenism. Nevertheless his conversations with Fr. Pascal made a greater and greater impression on his mind.

At length the decisive moment arrived: Mayadunnè declared war against Kandy. The King of Kotta, Bhuwaneka Bahu, who for the last six years had lived in peace with his brother remained neutral, but King Jayaweera had no confidence in this neutrality, and feared that one day or another he would join his brother and march with him on Kandy.

He wrote therefore to the Viceroy John de Castro begging for help. The Viceroy sent him forty Portuguese soldiers who were joined by three Franciscan Fathers one of whom was Fr. Simon of Coïmbra. It was the first time that the Portuguese interfered with the affairs of Kandy.

One must not wonder at the small number of soldiers the Portuguese Viceroys were sending to the help of the Kings of Ceylon. The King of Kotta and the King of Kandy had sufficient armies of their own. All that was needed to assure them the victory over their enemy, was to place these troops under the command of European officers, and for this a small number was sufficient.

For the rest ancient writers, speaking of these wars, only mention the number of European troops, and generally do not mention the number of Sepoys, of whom the Portuguese at that time had a strong contingent in India.

The small party of Portuguese arrived in Colombo, but King Bhuwaneka Bahu, under the plea of his neutrality,
1546 refused them the permission to pass through his territory. They sailed therefore to Trincomalee whence they marched to Kandy.

When on their half way the commander of the troop received

a letter from King Jayaweera, in which he wrote that, having concluded an honorable peace with Mayadunnè, there was no longer any reason to delay his conversion to the Catholic Faith, and therefore he had been baptised by Fr. Pascal and taken the name of Emmanuel. He further stated, that he had so far kept the matter secret, for fear of a rising of his Buddhist subjects and that, he only awaited the arrival of the Portuguese to openly declare himself a Catholic, and urged them to hasten their arrival.

They reached Kandy on Thursday of the holy week of the year 1546. The King sent some dignitaries of his court to meet them and the Franciscan Fathers were driven to a house prepared for them, and informed that, the church built by Fr. Pascal being small, the King had ordered one of the principal heathen temples of the town to be cleansed and transformed into a church.

Next day they removed from the temple all the remaining emblems of paganism, erected an altar, and, on Easter Sunday, Fr. Simon of Coïmbra celebrated a solemn high Mass in the presence of the King and of his court. Next there was a grand procession and Fr. Pascal preached in Singhalese.

The sermon finished, King Emmanuel Jayaweera stood on his throne and announced to his people his conversion to the Catholic Faith.

Then Fr. Simon of Coïmbra baptised five Kandyan chiefs and other catechumens. This was the first time that Kandy witnessed such a ceremony.

During the stay of several weeks that he made at King

Emmanuel's court, Fr. Simon also gained over the Raja of Battecaloa, a member of the Kandyan royal family, who, shortly after his Baptism, wrote a letter to King John III, which is preserved in the Archives of Lisbon. He said:

— „ Fr. Simon of Coïmbra has instructed me in the truth and in the holy Catholic Religion. This I much desired, before all for the salvation of my own soul, and next to become a brother in arms and a brother in the Faith to Your Most Faithful Majesty." —

Whatever the first motives of King Emmanuel Jayaweera had been, at the beginning his frequent intercourse with Fr. Pascal, and the inspired words of that great Missionary had made on him a great impression, and there can be no doubt that now he was sincere, and we will see later on that he paid with his life his attachment to the Catholic Faith.

After the departure of Fr. Simon of Coïmbra for Goa, Fr. Pascal remained at the head of the Mission of Kandy. King Emmanuel Jayaweera built a beautiful church which he dedicated to the Immaculate Conception. Many heathens attracted by the majesty of the Catholic worship and the amiability of Fr. Pascal asked for Baptism. Fr. Pascal is rightly considered as the founder of the Mission in Kandy.

All these details are confirmed in a letter which Fr. Simon of Coïmbra wrote to the King of Portugal on the 25th December 1546.

He relates the kind reception that was given to him at Kandy, and adds that King Emmanuel Jayaweera desired much to have his Queen baptised together with his two children, a girl and a boy, but it had been deemed prudent to defer their Baptism until the agitation caused by his conversion among his Buddhist subjects had died out, the more so, as a number of Bikshun or Bonzes employed by Mayadunnè, were going through the villages and exciting the people to rise against their King.

He praises much the son of the King, as a talented, intelligent lad who ardently desires to receive Baptism and to see the whole kingdom converted to Christianity.

We know nothing more about the young prince. He probably found his death, together with his father at the siege of Kandy in 1548.

The girl was baptised later on, and became Queen of Kotta, as the wife of King Don Juan Dharmapala.

## CHAPTER 8

# ST. FRANCIS XAVIER

As we have seen in the preceding chapters, the Catholic Faith had began to extend itself over the Island of Ceylon,
1548 and St. Francis Xavier who was at that time Delegate of the Pope in the East determined to visit the Island. A report from Fr. John de Villa Conde which reached him at Manapad in January 1548, in which the Superior of the Ceylon Missions complained bitterly of the old King Bhuwaneka Bahu, who was putting all possible obstacles to the progress of Religion, decided St. Francis Xavier to delay no more his visit to Ceylon.

In the beginning of February 1548 he chartered a small vessel from Manapad to Jaffna. He first landed at Manaar: He went to Passim, where he prostrated himself on the ground and kissed the earth watered by the blood of the martyrs.

The plague was raging in the Island and decimating the inhabitants, who were dying at a rate of more than a hundred a day. No sooner did they learned that the Great Father was at Passim, they ran to him to the number of three thousand weeping and begging him to deliver them from the plague. They were nearly all heathens. St. Francis Xavier told them to wait three days. He retired to a solitary place and passed these days in prayer offering to God the blood of the martyrs of Passim, and after the three days had passed, the plague disappeared and the sick recovered.

Many asked for Baptism, and St. Francis Xavier had the consolation of baptising them with his own hand. Not being able to remain with them he got a Franciscan priest from Jaffna and put him in charge of his neophytes.

Was it real plague from which St. Francis Xavier saved the Island of Manaar? The old writers give often the generic name of plague to small-pox, and other highly infectious diseases. In any case, it was a severe scourge, if on a small and, at that time, thinly populated Island, more than a hundred a day were dying.

Fearing for his new Christians of Manaar the fate of the former, St. Francis Xavier resolved to go to Jaffna to see the King Sagara Raja.

On his way he put in at a small Island, which the Portuguese called the Island of the Cows, and the natives Ninundiva. It is said that St. Francis Xavier brought there back to life the child of a Moorman. We have unfortunately no details of this miracle.

The Island in question formed obviously part of the Jaffna Archipelago, and was probably one of the islets which the Dutch later on called Middleburgh and Delft, and which officially still bear that name.

King Sagara Raja had lost much of his former haughtiness. He knew that the King of Portugal had given the Viceroy John de

Castro a peremptory order to dethrone him and to inflict on him an exemplary punishment for the massacre of the first Christians of Manaar, and that John de Castro was only waiting for the end of the war which he was at that moment making against the Moorish pirates who were infesting the coast near Bombay, to undertake the conquest of his kingdom. He was afraid.

He received kindly St. Francis Xavier and promised him all he asked. But the saint had not much faith in the words of the tyrant, for, on leaving the harbour of Jaffna and looking on the receding coast he uttered these prophetic words: — „Unhappy Island, how many dead bodies will cover your shores, and with how much blood will you be inundated.“ —

At Jaffna St. Francis Xavier met a ship which was sailing to Galle.

When the news spread in Galle that St. Francis Xavier was on board the ship which had cast anchor in the harbour, a Portuguese named Michel Fernandez, who lived in that town and was dangerously ill, sent word to beg him to come and see him, as his house was on the way from the harbour to the Franciscan Convent, where he had to take up his abode. St. Francis Xavier entered the house of Fernandez, consoled him, heard his confession, and told him that he was going to say Mass for his intention. Whilst he was celebrating Mass, Michel Fernandez rose from his bed completely cured.

St. Francis Xavier did not stay at Galle, he left for Colombo probably on the same day.

At Colombo St. Francis Xavier had the consolation of meeting again his friend and companion of his voyage from Lisbon to Goa Fr. John de Villa Conde. They conversed together on the progress and wants of the Missions; Fr. John having decided to go to Lisbon, they arranged how he should represent these wants to King John III and the Superiors of the Jesuit and the Franciscan Orders.

From Colombo St. Francis Xavier went to Kotta, to pay his respects to the old King Bhuwaneka Bahu. Crafty, full of experience, the King understood from the very first that he had to deal with a man who could not be easily deceived and he spoke openly with St. Francis Xavier.

He told him that he clearly saw that the Catholic Religion was the only true one, and the only one which gave certitude, that Buddhism was absurd and its precepts a heap of incredible ignorance. Nevertheless his father and his grandfather died in that religion, and if he were to renounce it, his heathen subjects would rebel against him. For the same reason he could not allow the Franciscan Fathers to make numerous conversions, for then, the Buddhists would side with Mayadunnè, and he would lose his crown. He would permit the Franciscan Fathers to preach the Gospel in his whole kingdom, if the Viceroy would give him a hundred European soldiers to protect his capital and his person.

St. Francis Xavier perceived at once the duplicity of the King and his deep hatred for the Catholic Religion. He understood that all he said was only a subterfuge to obtain from the Viceroy reinforcements, which would have given him a decisive advantage over his rebel brother. He told the King that he would submit the question to the Viceroy, and hoped himself to return to Ceylon with the desired reinforcements.

But he had fathomed to his lowest depths the perverse soul of Bhuwaneka Bahu, and he wrote later to the King of Portugal: — „Your Majesty need not doubt that the King who reigns in Ceylon is a declared and implacable enemy of Christ." —

At Colombo St. Francis Xavier received a lettter from Fr. Pascal the Missionary at Kandy, inviting him in the name of King Emmanuel Jayaweera to visit him. It appears that, from the time of his conversion King Emmanuel had trouble with his Buddhist subjects who were incited by Mayadunnè.

St. Francis Xavier set out for Kandy, a distance of 70 miles from Colombo, partly across mountains and forests on paths only passable on horseback or on foot.

King Emmanuel Jayaweera received him with great honors. They had long interviews in which the King explained to St. Francis Xavier the state of the country, the ferment of the Buddhist party who, irritated at his conversion to the Catholic Faith were intriguing to overthrow him and to place on the throne a pagan prince, his younger brother Cumara Banda. And they decided to ask the Viceroy to place at Kandy a Portuguese garrison, to protect the person of the King and the life and property of the Christians.

On his return to Colombo, St. Francis Xavier was joined by

the ambassador whom Bhuwaneka Bahu was sending to the Viceroy.

On their arrival at Goa on the 20th March 1548 they learned that the Viceroy had left for Bassein. The ambassador, the same Proybila Rale who had gone to Lisbon seven years ago, remained at Goa to await his return. St. Francis Xavier proceeded to Bassein, where on hearing his report John de Castro decided to send over to Ceylon the garrison asked for by the Kings of Kandy and of Kotta.

Meanwhile Proybila Rale was befriended by the Jesuit Fathers of St. Paul's College at Goa. Already at Lisbon he had been much impressed by the majesty of Catholic worship. He now occupied his leisure in Goa in studying the Christian doctrine which was explained to him by the Jesuit Fathers, and he and some of his followers were solemnly baptised by St. Francis Xavier in the presence of the Viceroy.

Two other notable conversions which happened at this period rejoiced the heart of the great saint. These were that

1549

of the Sultan of the Maldives and of the young Raja of Trincomalee.

In February 1549 St. Francis Xavier visited Cochin. He met there the young Sultan of the Maldives who, having been driven out of his islets by his rebellious subjects, had taken refuge in Cochin. The Viceroy refused to mix himself up with the Maldivian affairs, the Sultan having lost all hope to re-gain the possession of his throne, established himself in the town, where he was converted to the Catholic Faith and baptised by St. Francis Xavier. He lived to a very old age residing sometimes at Goa and sometimes at Cochin entirely given to works of charity, respected by all on account of his virtue and of his piety. He was one of those who had the happiness of assisting at that Mass of St. Francis Xavier, when the saint was miraculously raised in the air.

Trincomalee was one of the small States of Ceylon usually given as appanage to younger sons of royal houses. It depended on the King of Jaffna.

Vaniana Raja, the Ruler of this small State died, leaving his son aged only eight years under the guardianship of his uncle. But Sagara Raja the King of Jaffna taking profit of the boy-Raja's youth invaded his State and annexed it to the kingdom of Jaffna.

The child and his uncle with a following of forty retainers fled and sought refuge on the Fishery Coast residing at Tuticorin and sometimes at Manapad where they were befriended by Fr. Henry Enriquez one of the companions of St. Francis Xavier, who often visited them, consoled them in their exile, and by and by baptised them all. The young Raja taking the name of Alphonsus.

His uncle tried to re-conquer his nephew's dominions and landed at Trincomalee at the head of a company of Catholic Parawers. But they were defeated by Sagara Raja and had again to take refuge in India.

St. Francis Xavier took care of the young Raja Alphonsus of Trincomalee. He placed him at St. Paul's College at Goa where the Jesuit Fathers gave him a solid education. We next hear of him at the siege of Jaffna in 1560. Later on he accompanied Don Anthony de Noronha in an expedition against Mangalore. One night, when least expected the Portuguese were surprised by a large body of Moormen. In the battle that followed young prince Alphonsus met his death after performing prodigies of valour. He was scarcely twenty years of age. Thus died a Catholic prince of great promise.

His companions in exile returned later on to Ceylon, where one of them, whose name unhappily had not been preserved by history, by his good example and his great influence, converted a large number of pagans.

## CHAPTER 9

# FATHER JOHN DE VILLA CONDE

We have seen in the preceding chapter how in his conversation with St, Francis Xavier the old King Bhuwaneka Bahu

1546 had declared that he would cease to put obstacles to the apostolate of the Franciscan Fathers if he could obtain from the Viceroy, that a garrison of one hundred Portuguese be sent to Kotta. In order to understand the reason of this demand of the King it will be necessary to remember the events of the last few years.

Mayadunne the King's rebel brother, deprived of the help of the Moors and having come to understand that even with their help, he would never be able to overcome the King allied with the Portuguese, the more so, as the Zamorin had lately concluded a treaty with the Viceroy, and would moreover never pardon him the treacherous murder of Paichi Marikar; fearing the loss of his own States of Sitawacca and of Rayagam, thought it more prudent to put aside for the time being his ambitious views on the throne of Kotta, as the King of Portugal having confirmed the young prince Dharmapala as heir to Bhuwaneka Bahu, it was evident that the Viceroy would give him strong support against any usurper.

And therefore since the conclusion of peace with his brother in 1540 Mayadunnè had kept quiet, organizing in the meantime his army and strengthening the frontiers of his State.

The hostilities were renewed in 1546. The provocation this time was given by Weedeya Raja the son-in-law of the King, who, having had a quarrel with Mayadunnè, without the knowledge of Bhuwaneka Bahu who was weakened by age and infirmity, with the troops under his command, marched suddenly on Sitawacca, took the town and reduced it to ashes.

His triumph however was of short duration, for being drawn into an ambush by Mayadunnè, he was defeated and taken prisoner.

The old King who, as we have seen, desired peace with his brother, wrote to him assuring that it was without his knowledge that his son-in-law had commenced hostilities and asking to let free Weedeya Raja for a reasonable ransom, so that he might punish him severely.

Mayadunnè, inflated with his success, sent an insolent reply, saying that the only ransom he would accept for Weedeya Raja was the crown of Kotta.

Weedeya Raja, however, succeeded in a few days in escaping from prison but, fearing the anger of the King, remained in hiding, till his son Dharmapala could obtain his pardon, which was easily granted by the King, the more so because being a skilled warrior, and his brother having refused the peace he offered him, the King needed his son-in-law to command his army.

Weedeya Raja returned to Kotta, fell on his face at the feet of the King and promised him to raise an army of 20,000 for the defence of his throne.

The whole of the next year 1547 passed in desultory

1547 skirmishes. Both sides seemed rather anxious to avoid an encounter, ravaging each other's country, burning villages and murdering the poor villagers.

It was owing to this renewal of the war with his brother that old King Bhuwaneka Bahu, during his interview with St. Francis Xavier, had insisted so much that the Portuguese should re-establish their military station at Colombo, re-build the fort and garrison it with one hundred men.

During the seven years' peace which the Island had enjoyed, before the new outbreak of hostilities between the King and Mayadunnè, the Franciscan Missionaries had worked with activity at the conversion of the heathens, hindered by Bhuwaneka Bahu, who once went even as far as to expel them from his kingdom, but as a rule kept with them on friendly terms, fearing to lose the good-will of the Viceroy, putting nevertheless every possible obstacle to their work.

The best known Missionaries at this period were the Fathers John de Villa Conde, Superior and Vicar General under the Bishop of Goa to whose diocese the Island then belonged. Anthony Pedrão, Louis of St. Diego, Thomas of the Nativity, Anthony of St. Mary, Edward Chanoza, Francis of the East, Emmanuel of all Saints and Fr. Michel.

During the last seven years they had established native Catholic Communities at Colombo, Kotta, Malwana, Panadure, Galle, Welligama, Barberyn, Jaffna, Mantotte, Kandy and on the Islands of Manaar and Minundiva.

Now however, the renewal of the war with Mayadunnè, was for them a great blow. The villagers fled to the forests, the poor Christians were scattered, and so the Missions of the South which were giving the greatest hopes became disorganized.

They had to suffer much from Bhuwaneka Bahu. The older he grew, the more attached he became to Buddhist practices and superstitions. He had surrounded himself with Bikshun, astrologers and sorcerers.

The most influent among them was an Indian Brahmin who had for many years led a vagabond life. Seeing that the profession of a fakir which he carried in his own country did not pay, he passed over to Burma where, pretending to be a Buddhist he became a Bikshu. He next came to Ceylon, and settled in Kotta, where he passed himself for a great sorcerer. It was he who had persuaded old King Bhuwaneka Bahu to turn out the Franciscans from his territories.

Fr. John de Villa Conde, having charge of the education of the young prince Dharmapala, was staying at the royal palace, and had much to suffer from him, and each time that the Brahmin met him in the presence of the King, he provoked him to a discussion.

One day, moved by the Spirit of God, after having exposed in vain the trickeries of the Brahmin to the King, he told him that he would give him a sign of the truth of the Catholic Faith. He caused a large pile of wood to be fired in the courtyard of the palace. When it was all in flames he walked into the pyre and standing in the midst of the flames invited the Brahmin to follow him. The Brahmin hesitated, but the King had him seized and thrown into the fire, from which he emerged frightfully burnt, whilst the flames had not even touched the dress of the holy Franciscan.

After this, the King treated Fr. John de Villa Conde with great veneration, but yet he would not allow the Franciscans greater freedom in the exercise of their apostleship.

## CHAPTER 10

# BHUWANEKA BAHU

Hardly had the Viceroy John de Castro returned to Goa, in
April 1548 when he set about to realise the promise
1548
given by St. Francis Xavier to the Kings of Kandy and
of Kotta.

He organized an expedition comprising 150 Portuguese selected among his best troops under the command of Anthony Moniz Barreto, a young officer, but one who had already given proofs of great courage and unequalled energy, and who 28 years later became one of the ablest Viceroys of India.

Barreto landed at Kalutara, whence he proceeded to Kotta to pay his respects to the King, from whom he learned the changes that had taken place at Kandy.

After the departure of St. Francis Xavier, the Buddhist Kandian chiefs excited by Mayadunnè had rallied around Cumara Banda a pagan prince, a younger brother of King Emmanuel Jayaweera. They marched on Kandy, captured the town and reduced it to ashes. King Emmanuel was slain, his Queen Donna Maria had to seek her safety in flight, and Cumara Banda was proclaimed King of Kandy.

Bhuwaneka Bahu persuaded Barreto to punish the usurper and ɔ re-place on the throne of Kandy King Emmanuel's legitimate heir. Barreto was molested on the way by the troops of Mayadunnè. He lost many sepoys in these skirmishes, others deserted, so that when he approached Kandy he had but a few men left.

He had almost reached the gates of the city, when the Franciscans who were still in the town informed him, that King Cumara Banda, with a rather large army, prepared an ambuscade in a place where he would certainly annihilate the small Portuguese body.

Barreto, who was never wanting in determination in a moment of danger, burned his baggages, distributed to the soldiers provisions for a few days and as much ammunitions as they could carry and commenced a retreat towards the dominions of the King of Kotta.

Meanwhile Cumara Banda finding out that it was the Franciscans who had caused Barreto to retreat, had them put in prison and sent 8,000 men to pursue the Portuguese.

Barreto made a masterly retreat, which was considered among the best feats of arms at that period. With the handful of men he commanded, he fought continually for three days with the Kandyan forces pressing around him, and finally gained the frontiers of Kotta, where he met a convoy of provisions which Bhuwaneka Bahu had sent to his succour.

Notwithstanding this fact, Barreto unjustly suspected the King of having betrayed him, and their relations from that time were strained.

Meanwhile, the King of Kandy repenting of his treatment of the Portuguese, and fearing the vengeance of the Viceroy, sent an embassy to Colombo, with a letter for Barreto, in which he excused himself that the Kandyans, without his knowledge, had attacked the small Portuguese force, protesting of his friendship and proposing an alliance. But Barreto answered that he had no authority to make with him a treaty.

Barreto remained a short time at Colombo, where his unjust suspicions that the King had betrayed him were yet stronger confirmed by some local merchants. Bhuwaneka Bahu invited him to come over to Kotta. Anthony Moniz Barreto answered, that he would do so when the King will have fulfilled the promise he made to St. Francis Xavier of becoming a Christian.

The old King answered, that he thought seriously of doing so, but that he must make before a pilgrimage to a Hindu temple where he was going, they say, to offer to the gods a human sacrifice.

Bhuwaneka Bahu came over to Colombo and had an interview with Barreto. The young Portuguese officer had a violent nature, they quarrelled and separated in wrath.

Nevertheless, Barreto had to fulfil the promise given by the Viceroy to the King, he repaired the half dismantled fort at Colombo and garrisoned it with more than half the European troops he had brought with him to protect Bhuwaneka Bahu against Mayadunnè, and then left for Goa.

On his return to Goa, Anthony Moniz Barreto used all his

influence with the Viceroy George Cabral to persuade him to send an expedition against the King of Kandy and punish him for the affront he had given to the Portuguese.

The occasion did not take long to present itself. The King of Kandy had a son, the presumptive heir to the throne,

1549 named Caralea Banda. He was an intelligent young man of a mild and amiable character. It was he who had obtained from his father that the imprisoned Franciscans be set free. The lad was a great friend of Fr. Pascal and begged him earnestly to be baptised. The Father deemed it more prudent to delay the baptism because the prince was not yet sufficiently instructed, and also for fear of the King's anger.

Cumara Banda was however informed of the state of affairs and in his wrath disinherited the young prince in favour of an illegitimate son who was called after him Cumara Banda and he declared him heir to the throne of Kandy.

In the meantime, Caralea Banda knowing that his father had ordered him to be put to death fled with Fr. Pascal and the other Franciscans and took refuge in the forests. As he was much beloved by the people, he was soon joined by a large number of Kandyans so that he was in a position to resist to his father with his armed followers.

Fr. Pascal informed the Viceroy of the state of affairs and George Cabral hastened to send to Ceylon George de Castro at the head of 600 men. Castro sailed from Goa in January 1550.

Hardly had he arrived at Colombo when he hastened to Kotta

1550 where King Bhuwaneka Bahu, hardly pressed by the forces of the rebel Mayadunnè expected his arrival. They marched together against the rebel, gained several victories over him and became masters of Sitawacca.

Mayadunnè reduced to extremity, having lost the best of his two States, sued for peace and Bhuwaneka Bahu pitying the misery of his brother, pardoned him again, in spite of his having broken so often his promises. He even received him at Kotta with all the honors due to a prince of the royal blood. Mayadunnè swore solemnly that he would never again make war against the King, restored some districts that he had conquered and paid a war contribution of 100,000 gold pagodas. In return the King reinstalled him at Sitawacca.

The King of Kandy, Cumara Banda, seeing how easily Mayadunnè had been conquered, and fearing seriously for his own crown, wrote to George de Castro a rather humble letter in which he asked to be pardoned for the Barreto affair, putting all the blame on Mayadunnè, who, he said, had prompted him to act against his will, and promised him to get reconciled with his son Caralea Banda.

George de Castro sent him a favourable reply, intimating at the same time that he would himself visit the King at Kandy. He desired to go there with all his forces, thinking that such a military display would inspire the King with a salutary fear of the power of the Portuguese.

King Bhuwaneka Bahu did his best to dissuade de Castro from

this undertaking. He told him not to trust his cousin of Kandy who was of an unreliable character and always scheming treason. But de Castro answered the King, that he had been ordered by the Viceroy to go to Kandy, and he must obey to his orders.

As a matter of fact, Kumara Banda had made these advances with the object of drawing the Portuguese into the narrow mountain passes through which the road leads to Kandy, and where, not being able to use their artillery they would be easily overpowered by the 40,000 men which he had summoned to arms.

Castro left Kotta in the beginning of April, and was already entangled in the mountains when he became aware of Cumara Banda's treason.

He held a council of war, and it was decided to retreat before the overwhelming forces of the King. Castro was not so determined in his actions as Moniz Barreto had been, he did not burn his baggages, and encumbered by his transports his retreat was necessarily slow.

Hardly had they extracted themselves from the mountain passes when they found themselves surrounded by the Kandyans.

In front of such overpowering forces, the Portuguese comparatively a handful of men could not hope to escape, so with their usual courage, they ranged themselves around their chief, determined to sell dearly their lives.

Meanwhile the Kandyans sent against them a huge elephant, trained for war, having long swords fixed to its tusks. The furious beast was causing terrible carnage, when a Franciscan, Fr. John de Calvo, facing the elephant with a Crucifix in his hand, exclaimed:

— „Fierce beast, in the Name of God, thy Creator, stop!" — The elephant stopped and, suddenly turning round, rushed on the Kandyans, making a terrible havoc in their ranks.

Castro took profit of the confusion to extricate himself and continued his retreat, day and night harassed by the Kandyans. He was marching towards Sitawacca, hoping to find there a refuge, but Mayadunnè barred him the passage, and thus, placed between two enemies, the Portuguese would have been annihilated if Bhuwaneka Bahu had not sent to their rescue all his available troops.

Castro led back to Kotta the remains of his brilliant escort. It was a disastrous retreat. In the battle he had lost 457 men, and about 300 more in the retreat, one half of whom were Europeans, so that of the 600 men who had embarked with him from Goa only 220 remained.

Thus, the war with Mayadunnè had re-commenced again and whilst the rebel prince was devastating from one side the provinces of the kingdom of Kotta, the King of Kandy ravaged them from the other.

Old King Bhuwaneka Bahu commenced at last to bitterly repent of the policy he had followed towards his rebellious brother. Every time that, with the help of the Portuguese, he had vanquished him, he granted him his pardon, preventing thus his allies from finishing once for ever with Mayadunnè, and with these wars which were bringing so much suffering on the unfortunate people of the south of Ceylon.

The object of the King was to reserve an enemy to the

Portuguese, in case they should ever wish to conquer Ceylon or to render themselves masters of his kingdom. It had always been the policy of the petty Rulers of Ceylon to raise up quarrels between their allies and their enemies, and keep them constantly occupied, so as to make their alliance valuable to both sides and thus secure for themselves the position of an arbitrator.

Bhuwaneka Bahu had always been faithful to the Portuguese his allies, to whom in reality he owed his crown and the independence of his kingdom, but he thought it good policy to keep alive an enemy who would keep them busy, and prevent them to become perhaps too powerful. And that was the reason why he had always spared his brother Mayadunnè, and prevented the Portuguese to ever give him the final blow.

But now, grown old, after a reign of thirty years during which he had been continually in touch with the Portuguese he clearly saw that they had no thought whatever of conquering Ceylon. They had their hands full in India, and contented themselves with being free to trade in Ceylon, and exporting the products of the Island. And this trade even they considered only as a private enterprise of some merchants, which the government of the Viceroy had not even need of protecting, sufficiently protected as it was by their ally, King Bhuwaneka Bahu.

On the other side, Mayadunnè aspired openly to the crown of Kotta. He had made it the ambition of his life, and endeavoured to wrest it by force from his brother.

Each time the King was in danger, he called the Portuguese, who, faithful to the treaty of 1517, renewed in 1521, sent him help and after each victory Bhuwaneka Bahu had prevented them to finish once for ever with Mayadunnè.

After so many useless expeditions, the Portuguese were disgusted, they understood the meaning of Bhuwaneka's tricks, and there was a growing party at Goa, that advised the Viceroy to abandon the old King to the consequences of his disloyal policy, and to wash their hands once for all of the affairs of Kotta. In the present circumstances, they said, when the Moors had been crushed, and the Zamorin had become a vassal to the Portuguese crown, whoever sat on the throne of Kotta, even Mayadunnè himself, the Portuguese trade in Ceylon was safe, as it was evident, that he could never have maintained his power without an alliance with the Viceroy.

Mayadunnè, in his cunning, took advantage of this revulsion of feelings at Goa, and began to make advances to the Portuguese. He sent an embassy to Goa, but failed to gain there sympathy. He succeeded however to further discredit the old King in the Portuguese capital of the East.

Doubtless, as long as he lived, Bhuwaneka Bahu was strong enough to keep in check Mayadunnè, but he was old, and his heir, the young prince Dharmapala was a minor. His father Weedeya Raja would be Regent during his minority, and the King did not trust his son-in-law, who was certainly an able warrior but at the same time a consummate intriguer, and although united with him by interest, yet he was always inclined to the party that was opposed to civilisation, which was fast developing in Ceylon owing to the contact with the Portuguese and the influence of the Catholic

Religion, and desired the return to old barbarity. And the head of this party was Mayadunnè.

The old King grew despondent; often looking with tears in his eyes on his young grandson Dharmapala, whom he tenderly loved, he would exclaim: — „Oh! my child, this kingdom will not be thine!" — When the astonished youth asked him the reason of his sorrow he would answer, that a great astrologer had so predicted at his birth. This did not affect much the lad who, having been brought up from his infancy in the Catholic Faith cared little for astrologers and for their horoscopes.

Such was the state of affairs in Ceylon when, the new Viceroy Alphonsus de Noronha, had re-placed George Cabral. On his way from Lisbon to Goa he landed at Colombo towards the end of August 1550.

Whilst yet in Portugal he had been warned against Bhuwaneka, on account of his tricky disloyal policy, and at Colombo, the commander of the small garrison of the fort, Francis de Miranda, bribed, it is believed by Mayadunnè, further prejudiced him against the old King.

As soon as Bhuwaneka Bahu was apprised of the arrival of the Viceroy, he sent two of the principal dignitaries of his court to pay him homage and to invite him to Kotta. Noronha received them badly, and wrote an insolent letter to the King, telling him, that it was his duty to come first, and pay personally homage to the representative of his paramount Lord.

The King felt greatly offended, nevertheless unwilling to provoke a rupture with the Portuguese, he decided to go to Colombo, but was forestalled by Mayadunnè, who, accompanied by a brilliant suite, first visited the Viceroy, and at once gained his goodwill.

When Bhuwaneka Bahu arrived at Colombo, the Viceroy did not show him the respect due to his rank and to his venerable age. He received him badly and treated him as an inferior.

In vain did the King endeavour to clear himself of the accusations made against him, the Viceroy would not hear his excuses. They quarrelled, the King broke up the interview, left the Viceroy in anger, and returned to Kotta whence he sent the Viceroy a peremptory order, to quit immediately his kingdom. Noronha of course made nothing of this order; he remained at Colombo till the end of October, and then left for Cochin:

Portuguese writers unanimously condemn Noronha's conduct saying that it was unworthy of a Portuguese nobleman and of a brother of the Marquis of Villa-Real.

Bhuwaneka Bahu survived only a few months to his quarrel with the Viceroy. He was already 83 years old, felt himself getting every day weaker and was afraid of death. Seeing that medicines did him no longer any good, he surrounded himself with astrologers.

Weedeya Raja took profit of the influence which these astrologers had gained over the King and, paid by him they persuaded the old man that, in order to prolong indefinitely his life, he should give over the government of the kingdom to his son-in-law and retire to his country seat at Kelanya.

The King afraid of death, did so. He had been only a few weeks at Kelanya when, on the evening of the 29th December 1550, whilst seated as was his custom at one of the windows of his palace, he was struck in the head by a bullet fired from a musket, whence no one could say. The servants panic stricken crowded around him, and not one of them thought of pursuing the assassin.

In spite of all help rendered the King expired after an agony of three hours.

There is no doubt that Bhuwaneka Bahu was far superior in intelligence to the greater number of the ruling princes of India and Ceylon at that period. The constant intercourse with the Portuguese had civilised him, and developed his mind.

His whole conduct was regulated by a policy, which he deemed prudent, but in the circumstances in which he was placed was only partially so. His predominant idea was to secure the independence of his kingdom, or rather to keep the throne for himself. As the Moors endeavoured to conquer the country, he allied himself with the Portuguese. But in order that the latter should not become too powerful in Ceylon, and should always need his support for the security of their trading, he kept at hand an enemy for them in the person of Mayadunnè, hence his leniency for his rebellious brother. Such policy could succeed if the Portuguese were less strongly established in India, as it was, he forced them to assume, after his death a more efficient protectorate over Ceylon and left a heavy inheritance to his successor. He did not measure the strength of the Portuguese, and thought he would succeed at playing with them. In any case, what he did, he did for the good of the country, to assure its independence.

Bhuwaneka Bahu did not believe in Buddhism, but he remained attached to all its superstitions. He hindered the propagation of the Catholic Faith, among his subjects, for he feared that religion would create a bond between them and the Portuguese, whom he did not wish to become too powerful in his kingdom. On the other hand he permitted his presumptive heir to be brought up in the Catholic Faith because he saw that his successor would need more than himself the help of the Portuguese against his uncle Mayadunnè.

Personally Bhuwaneka Bahu was amiable and gentle, even merry and jovial to the point of sometimes wanting in dignity. He hated war and did his best to keep peace even with Mayadunnè. It was repugnant to him to condemn a criminal to death.

He was careful of the well-being of his people, and appreciated the civilisation which the intercourse with the Portuguese introduced in the country. His people loved him and, in his old age surrounded him with great veneration. Nevertheless, egotism and dynastic interest was at the bottom of all his actions. He was jealous of the independence of his country, but it was in order to keep himself on the throne. He loved his subjects and interested himself in their well-being, yet, at the same time, for his own interest he kept Mayadunnè, who was shedding floods of blood and devastating whole provinces.

Some superficial writers of the past century who wrote about Ceylon, without having taken the care to study authentic historical documents of the epoch, represent Bhuwaneka Bahu as a traitor, who sold his country to the Portuguese, and Mayadunnè, as a national hero who fought for its liberty.

In fact, the contrary is nearer to the truth.

At the time of the arrival of the Portuguese, the Moors were masters of the coasts, and their end was to conquer, if not the whole of Ceylon, at least the kingdom of Kotta. Mayadunnè sold himself to the Moors, helped to deliver into their slavery the low country Singhalese, in order to obtain from them in payment the empty title of King of Kotta.

On the other hand, the Portuguese, with whom Bhuwaneka Bahu had made an alliance, had at that time no idea of conquering Ceylon. They respected the national independence of the Singhalese, and helped them to keep it up. All they wanted was free and unmolested trade with the Island.

It was only nearly a century later, when the Dutch began to dispute to the Portuguese the monopoly of the trade of the East, and the native potentates of Ceylon began to seek Dutch alliance, that it became an imperious necessity to the Portuguese, in self defence, to extend their domination over the Island of Ceylon, to become masters of the kingdoms of Kotta and of Jaffna and of all the coasts, in order to prevent an alliance of their enemy the Dutch, with the King of Kandy.

But, at the time of Bhuwaneka Bahu, the Portuguese had no thought of conquering Ceylon. On the contrary, they fought for the Singhalese and at the side of the Singhalese in defence of their liberty and to save from destruction their national existence.

If Lawrence d'Almeida and Lopo Soarez d'Albergaria had not landed at Colombo, there would be now no Singhalese at Ceylon. They would have all become Moormen, or slaves to the Moormen.

If the Singhalese still exist as a nation, they owe it to the Portuguese, and to King Bhuwaneka Bahu, who, at a moment of national peril, when the Singhalese stood in danger of annihilation, had the good policy of allying himself with the Portuguese.

## CHAPTER 11

# ALPHONSUS DE NORONHA

The news of King Bhuwaneka's death resounded from one end to the other of his little kingdom, for the people had a
1551 sincere affection of their old King. The mystery which surrouuded his death gave rise to a thousand suppositions.

The Portuguese suspected that the assassin had been paid by Weedeya Raja, who was impatient to exercise an unlimited power during his son's minority, and even to take profit of his youth to usurp the crown.

On the other hand, Weedeya Raja and Mayadunnè did their best to persuade the people, that their King has been murdered by the Portuguese, which was absurd, as the Portuguese had nothing to gain, and on the contrary every thing to lose by the death of Bhuwaneka Bahu, who had always been their faithful ally and had favoured their commercial interests in Ceylon.

However Mayadunnè and Weedeya Raja had succeeded to excite the people to the point that, had not the Portuguese sought all refuge at Colombo, many of them would certainly have been killed.

Such was the state of affairs when the young King Dharmapala ascended the throne, under the guardianship of his lather Weedeya Raja, whom all the chiefs had recognised as Regent.

The position of the Portuguese residing in Ceylon had become unbearable. The people had been excited against them, and Weedeya Raja who had up to then been obliged to conceal his hostility, raised now the mask exercising his troops and fortifying Kotta.

On the other hand, Mayadunnè had proclaimed himself King of Kotta and made grand preparation to invade the kingdom and with arms in hand to dispute the throne to the young King Dharmapala.

News of these events having reached Goa, the Viceroy Alphonsus de Noronha, who was bound to protect the rights of Dharmapala, embarked with an army of 3,000 men and landed in Colombo on the 12th March 1551.

The doings of Noronha in Ceylon are not clear; there are different versions among the old historians. We will therefore narrate the facts, as we have gathered them from the most reliable documents.

After landing in Colombo, the Viceroy sent his son Don Fernando with a strong body of men to surround the town of Kotta so that none could escape, and to take possession of the royal palace. Weedeya Raja fled, leaving behind the young King who fell into the hands of Don Fernando.

The Viceroy, at Colombo, disgusted both the Singhalese and the Portuguese by his bad conduct, and his arrogance towards the native chiefs who came to pay him homage, even towards those who were most devoted to the Portuguese.

He marched on Kotta at the head of his army, seized the royal treasury, and allowed his soldiers to sack the town.

This exasperated the Singhalese to such a point, that 600 nobles of the kingdom of Kotta joined Mayadunnè. Noronha grew seriously uneasy. He summoned the young King, whom he had not as yet taken the trouble to see. The youth was brought to him nearly fainting with fright thinking that they would put him to death.

Instead the Viceroy received him with paternal kindness: — „My child, he said to him, you are the King, and not your father, who has been the cause of all these troubles. You are young, the King of Portugal has promised you his protection, and I trust that, with the help of God, your reign will be better than that of your predecessors." — He told him then, that brought up in the Catholic Faith, he should not delay any longer his baptism, and at the end excused himself for having seized the royal treasury, saying that he had done so with the object of using it to conquer all Ceylon and making him King of the Island.

After that, young Dharmapala was solemnly enthroned and all the chiefs came to pay him homage. A prince of the royal house called Senerat Banda was appointed Regent with the title of chief counsellor to the King. He was a good and clever man and very popular in the country. All that pacified the mind of the people and gave them great satisfaction as they were tired of the tyranny of Weedeya Raja.

After the solemn enthronisation, the Viceroy Noronha began to treat with the young King and with Senerat Banda, of an expedition against Mayadunnè, to finish once for all with the old rebel prince. He demanded the sum of 200.000 pardaõs as the costs of the expedition, of which half was to be paid in advance, and half after the expedition.

The King could not pay so large a sum to Noronha, who had seized the royal treasury; after long discussion he saw himself obliged to sell his personal jewels valued at 80.000 pardaõs. Noronha took the money and promised to the King to divide with him by half all the booty made during the expedition.

They marched against Mayadunnè. The Viceroy at the head of his 3,000 men, the King and Senerat Banda with 4,000 Singhalese troops. After several victorious encounters they took Sitawacca, and Noronha delivered the town to pillage.

He did not find the treasures he expected, as Mayadunnè had had time to bring them away in his flight to the mountains. Considerable riches however were found in the temples, which Noronha took for himself refusing to share them by half with the King as he had promised.

Mayadunne's position was now desperate, and with one blow, his power could be broken for ever. But for this last stroke some European troops were required, and the Viceroy did not seem disposed to continue the campaign and bring it to an end.

Senerat Banda seeing that the Viceroy seemed to like the young King, used him as a medium to ask him to lend them 500 Portuguese soldiers. Noronha replied that he would give the men when he received the balance of 20.000 pardaõs yet due. And when the young King replied that he was at the end of his resources, that the Viceroy had already taken all he possessed, and that it would be impossible for him to raise this sum, Noronha answered, that the season was too advanced and that affairs of state obliged him to return to Goa.

He then prepared to leave Ceylon, but not before having exacted by threats the payment of the balance of 20.000 pardaõs, and Senerat Banda had to sell his family jewels to raise this sum.

Finally Noronha left for Goa taking with him the treasures so shamefully acquired, leaving at Kotta a strong body of men under the command of John Enriquez to whom he ordered to re-build the fort of Colombo which at that time was in ruin.

The Viceroy's conduct and his incredible greed rose the indignation of all the Portuguese who sent an energetic complaint to the King, and John III, full of indignation wrote to Noronha the following letter dated from Lisbon 20th March 1552.

— „ We had clearly recommended to you to treat the native Rulers with all the respect due to their rank; and now We had complaints, which have been confirmed with a letter written to Us by the King of Ceylon, that you have disobeyed Our orders, and We wonder how will you reply to these accusations.

We command you, to act henceforth in such a manner as not to incur again Our displeasure, and if you continue in your ways, We will consider Ourselves as badly served by you; so take good care that no more complaints against you reach Us.

We command you in a particular way that the natives of Ceylon be well treated, for in doing so you will help their conversion to the Catholic Faith, a thing which Our late father King Don Emmanuel had so much at heart.

We warn you that if you fulfil Our commands, We will keep your interest in mind, but if you fail to do so, We will proceed against you with great severity." —

Later on, when the details of Noronha's dealings in Ceylon reached Lisbon, King John III in his indignation deposed him from his office of Viceroy, and ordered that everything he had taken from the young King of Kotta be restored to him. But these treasures did no more exist. The vessel on which Noronha was bringing to Lisbon his ill-gotten wealth, foundered near the Cape of Good Hope. Then, John III ordered that their value at least be restored to King Dharmapala, and it must have been a large sum, because it was paid up by the treasury at Lisbon in several instalments.

After the Viceroy had left Ceylon everything fell into confusion. Weedeya Raja came out of hiding and again assumed the Regency. His tyranny had no bounds. He exercised his vengeance specially on the Christians, destroyed several churches, and forbade the subjects of his son to become Catholics. The Franciscan Missionaries were obliged to hide in the forests, whence they visited the Christians at the risk of their lives.

But the fact that caused the Missionaries the greatest uneasiness was, that the young King Dharmapala, under his father's influence, or perhaps afraid of him, seemed to waver in his Faith.

Such was the state of affairs when the Viceroy Alphonsus de Noronha received the above mentioned letter of King
1552 John III. Frightened by the King's threats he began to make advances to Weedeya Raja.

He sent to Ceylon Michael de Cunha who concluded with this prince a treaty by which the Viceroy recognised him as Regent of Kotta and Weedeya Raja subscribed to the treaty of 1521 with the addition that he would leave the Catholics in peace.

This treaty established in Ceylon an ephemeral peace, and the Franciscan Fathers returned to their Missions and re-built their ruined churches.

## Part II

# THE PORTUGUESE PROTECTORATE

1554 — 1597

# CHAPTER 1

## WEEDEYA RAJA

Peter de Mascarenhas, appointed Viceroy in the place of
1554 Alphonsus Noronha, landed at Goa and took possession of his exalted office on the 23rd September 1554.

He brought instructions from King John III to build a large fort at Colombo and to place there a strong garrison.

This permanent military station established in Ceylon changed the position of the Portuguese in the Island. The simple alliance with the King of Kotta, which had lasted now nearly for forty years, became now a protectorate. The Portuguese did not intend to rule over Ceylon, to make the conquest of the Island, but they wanted more security for their trade.

This trade, in the last years had increased immensely, and they could not afford to have it now exposed to the oscillation of native politics. So long as Bhuwaneka Bahu ruled over the kingdom of Kotta, they could trust his wisdom and his fidelity to the treaty, as his interest was strongly bound with it. But now, with Weedeya Raja on one side and Mayadunnè on the other, they could not leave their trade unprotected.

A strong military station had become a necessity, and thus, still respecting the independence of the Singhalese States and the sovereignty of their Rulers, the Portuguese found themselves obliged to establish their protectorate over the whole kingdom of Kotta, which later on they extended all over Ceylon.

In November 1554, the new Viceroy appointed Edward d'Fça, commander of Colombo, who landed there with a number of masons and other workmen, and part of the materials required for the fort and 500 soldiers to garrison it.

This new departure in Portuguese politics displeased Weedeya Raja who was still Regent, King Dharmapala being yet
1555 a minor. His ambition was now to depose his young son and to proclaim himself King of Kotta. The establishment of a strong Portuguese garrison at Colombo had upset all his plans. He was most insolent towards d'Eça, and sought by all means to put obstacles to the building of the fort. D'Eça bore up all this with patience, for he well knew that he could not efficiently resist the aggressions of the turbulent Regent so long as the fort was not completed and placed in a state of defence.

How was it that Weedeya Raja, who certainly had had experience of the power of the Portuguese, dared now to stand against them, and that just at the moment when Mayadunnè having proclaimed himself King of Kotta was ready to dispute the throne to his son? The reason was one that an European mind could not even have tried to understand: He was the possessor of the tooth of Buddha, and, by the power of this fetish he hoped to overcome the Portuguese and Mayadunnè.

It is probable that in olden times they possessed at Ceylon a real tooth of Buddha. Even during his lifetime Buddha was venerated by his followers, he was the founder of their religion, and there is no reason to doubt that they carefully preserved his relics.

There is no doubt however that, at the time when Marco Polo visited Ceylon, that is in the year 1284, Buddha's tooth was already a fraud, for he describes it as being big and bulky.

At our period of the history of Ceylon, the tooth was in the possession of the Kings of Kotta, who considered it as their most precious heirloom.

It was a piece of ivory, other say of deer horn cut to the shape of the point of an elephant tusk about one and a half inch long and half an inch in diameter.

The tooth, at this epoch, was worshipped by all the sections of the inhabitants of Ceylon: by the Buddhists as the tooth of Buddha, by the Tamils who professed Hinduism as the tooth of their monkey-god Hannumant, the White Monkey, as they called him, and by the Moormen as a tooth of Adam.

That which gave to the object a special value was the general superstition, that he who possessed it was the lawful sovereign of the whole Island, hence, the Kings of Kotta took the title of Emperors of Ceylon and though not recognized, pretended to be Lords-paramount of the kingdoms of Kandy and of Jaffna.

After the death of Bhuwaneka Bahu, Weedeya Raja possessed himself of the tooth of Buddha. He always carried it about him, in a small box of gold hidden in his girdle. Young King Dharmapala, brought up, as he had been, from his infancy in the Catholic Faith, cared little for the fetish, and willingly gave it up to his father.

The superstitious Weedeya Raja really believed, it seems, in the magic of this strange talisman and hoped, by its virtue, to overcome the Portuguese.

In the meantime, King John III of Portugal having been informed of the persecution which Weedeya Raja had raised against the Christians, sent orders to the Viceroy Peter de Mascarenhas to make him a prisoner.

The Viceroy assembled his council, and they decided that, to capture the Regent of Kotta it would be necessary to declare war against him, which could not be done at that moment, their hands being full of petty wars with different Indian Rajas. Therefore it was deemed more prudent to postpone the execution of John III's orders and to try in the meantime to conciliate Weedeya Raja in an amicable way.

When however Edward d'Eça reported to the Viceroy the Regent's behaviour towards himself, the obstacles he was putting to the erection of the fort and the insults to which he was submitting the Portuguese residing in Ceylon, Mascarenhas resolved to carry out without delay the instructions of the King and sent orders to d'Eça to arrest Weedeya Raja, to send him over to Goa and to give over the government of the kingdom to Dharmapala, who was nearing the end of his minority.

It was easy to the Viceroy to give such an order, but not so easy to carry it out. To arrest the Regent of a kingdom, even of a small one, in his capital and in his own palace, the more so when one has at his disposal only a handful of soldiers, is rather a difficult task.

D'Eça was dining with a young Portuguese officer of noble family, Diogo de Mello Cutinho, when they brought him the Viceroy's despatch.

Seeing that he seemed much disturbed, young de Mello said laughing:

— „What is the matter, I bet that the Viceroy wants you to take a wife." — D'Eça was a confirmed bachelor, and his friends were always joking with him on the subject.

— „Yes, answered d'Eça, only the bride is not very tractable." — And he passed the despatch to de Mello. He read it and then said:

— „Well, captain, I undertake to bring you the bride." —

It was evident that the thing could not be done except by some act of daring. With the permission of his chief, de Mello took another officer into his confidence, they took twelve of their bravest soldiers and proceeded to Kotta at nightfall. ·The palace of the Regent being at the entrance of the town, the soldiers remained in hiding, a little distance from it, and the two officers went to pay a visit to Weedeya Raja.

The Regent received them with much courtesy. After a moment's conversation, seeing that they were alone de Mello said:

— „Do you know, Raja, that we did not come here for an exchange of compliments, but to arrest you and take you a prisoner to Colombo. If you make the least resistance, you are a dead man.“ —

So saying he seized him by the arm and held to his breast a dagger which he held in his hand. The other officer too was armed.

Weedeya was a brave man, but he was so stunned by surprise, that he did not resist. The guards that were at the gate of the palace were surprised to see their master going out at that hour with two Portuguese officers, but de Mello pressed to his breast the point of his dagger, and Weedeya said to the soldiers: — „It is all right, I will soon be back.“ — The unhappy prince did not think perhaps at that moment that he would never more pass the threshold of his home.

After this daring deed it was easy to de Mello, once out of the city, to re-join his escort and to bring his prisoner to Colombo.

D'Eça received him with courtesy, excusing himself that what has happened did not depend on his will, that he had to carry out the orders of the Viceroy. Then he reproached him his evil deeds and told him, that he would be sent to Goa to be judged there for his misdoing, but that he could trust the generosity of the Portuguese who would treat him with consideration. Weedeya Raja listened to all this with a dignity that struck all present.

After this he was loaded with chains and shut up in a damp tower where not even a bed was given to him, and he was obliged to sleep on a mat on the bare ground, which certainly caused great

these disturbances a favorable occasion to expel the Portuguese from Ceylon. He proposed an alliance to Weedeya Raja, and in order to cement their friendship he arranged a marriage between Weedeya and one of his daughters. This marriage however was the cause of their quarrel. It seems that a few weeks after the marriage Weedeya Raja sent back his wife to her father. Mayadunnè in his anger turned to the Portuguese and proposed to Lacerda an alliance against Weedeya Raja.

The moment was critical, so, notwithstanding the repugnance of all his officers, Pereira de Lacerda accepted his advances and a treaty was signed at Colombo, by which Mayadunnè declared himself a vassal to the King of Portugal and promised to pay the same annual tribute as that paid by the King of Kotta.

At the request of his new friend Pereira de Lacerda deposed from the Regency the faithful Senerat Banda and sent him in exile to Goa. It was in the middle of August. For this act of injustice he was severely reprimanded by the Viceroy Francis Barreto who in a letter dated 10th September 1555 wrote: — „The want of wisdom and experience in those who are in command is a defect which hinders them from attaining the end desired." — The Viceroy added that Senerat Banda would soon return to Ceylon where he must be received with all honors due to his rank and merits.

Senerat Banda remained a few months at Goa. Already strongly impressed by his conversations with Fr. John de Villa Conde, he had long since a strong inclination towards the Catholic Faith. He was further instructed by the Franciscan Fathers at

Goa and solemnly baptised in the Cathedral. He took the name of the Viceroy, his godfather.

The return to Ceylon of Don Francis Barreto Senerat Banda evoked great demonstration of joy. He was beloved by the Singhalese and highly appreciated by the Portuguese for his uprightness and enlightened mind.

He did not resume his functions as Regent, the young King having attained his majority, but was appointed Adigar, that is, prime minister.

The campaign against Weedeya Raja opened in 1556. Mayadunnè had mobilized an army of 30,000 men under the

1556 command of his illegitimate son Tikiri Banda, who was to acquire later on a sad notoriety in the history of Ceylon under the name of Raja Singha.

Although it was only after his father's death that Tikiri Banda assumed the name of Raja Singha, in order to avoid confusion we will from now call him by that name. He was only about 20 years of age, but already showed remarkable military talent as leader of irregular forces.

Alphonsus Pereira de Lacerda reinforced Mayadunnè's army with a contingent of 300 Portuguese and some companies of well trained native soldiers. When young Raja Singha who till now had only seen his father's irregular troops saw the Portuguese manœuvring, he was seized with admiration, and exclaimed: — „How can the sheep of Weedeya Raja resist such lions." —

Weedeya had only 14,000 men, a rabble of badly armed

villagers; but he had faith in the magic of the tooth of Buddha. He exposed the fetish to the view of his soldiers and promised them victory. He sustained a crushing defeat near the village of Palande and fled with a remnant of 6,000 men, taking refuge at Putlam with his cousin the Raja of the seven Korles.

Even there he would not remain quiet. He was rich and had brought with him great treasures. These he used to gain partisans and organized a rebellion. The Raja of the seven Korles was killed and Weedeya Raja seized the power.

But the people swore that they would never submit to the usurper. They implored aid from the King of Kotta. The new commander of the fort of Colombo Edward Rodriguez de Bulhão offered the King a company of European troops, to whom young Raja Singha joined himself at the head of a strong contingent, and marched on Putlam.

Weedeya Raja, as they approached, fled to Kandy, but Mayadunnè having threatened the King of Kandy to send against him his son Raja Singha, Weedeya Raja retired to Jaffna carrying with him all his treasures, which, though partly exhausted by his intrigues at Putlam, were yet very considerable.

King Sagara Raja of Jaffna received him cordially. Knowing that the vengeance of the Portuguese for the massacre of his Christians of Manaar was only postponed and hung still over his head, he gladly approved Weedeya Raja's plan of a league of the Kings of Jaffna and of Kandy with several petty Rajas of Ceylon, against the King of Kotta and the Portuguese with the object of expelling the latter from Ceylon. They were to demand help from the King of Madura and enlist an army of Badagas a tribe of marauders who lived in the mountains between Travancore and Tinnevelli. Weedeya Raja, whom the natives considered as a great warrior, was to direct the military operations, and Sagara Raja was to undertake to treat with the other princes.

Everything was ready to arrange the preliminaries. Several of the neighbouring Rajas had already been summoned to Jaffna, when an unforeseen event upset all their plans.

The King of Jaffna, Weedeya, and several Rajas proceeded to a temple at a short distance from the town to offer a sacrifice to the devil, in order to render him propitious to the league about to be concluded against the Christians.

According to the custom, the people of the place made a great reception to the King and to his guests. There was a display of fireworks. A badly directed racket set fire to a small powder magazine which exploded. A tumult ensued.

Not knowing the reason of the explosion, Weedeya Raja thought that the King of Jaffna, whose treacherous character was well known to him, had laid a trap to murder him. He drew his sword and threw himself on Sagara Raja. His followers did the same. The Jaffnese ranged themselves around their King. A bloody combat followed. Weedeya Raja was slain, his followers overpowered and massacred to the last.

Thus ended Weedeya Raja. He was a man of high stature, and of an imposing exterior. But under these physical gifts was hidden a cruel, proud and inconstant nature. He was a true barbarian. He had inherited from his father immense wealth; and to enjoy it sooner he had killed his father with an arrow which he had thrown to him from an ambush. His marriage with the King's daughter gave him a high position at the court of Kotta, but, a few years later, moved by jealousy he drowned treacherously the princess in the Kelany Ganga. He was a barbarian, and his death was certainly not a loss to Ceylon.

The King of Jaffna, Sagara Raja, seized Weedeya's treasures; but what caused him the greatest joy, he got the tooth of Buddha which had been found on the dead prince's body. As we know, the fetish was worshipped equally by the Tamils as a tooth of the White Monkey, their cunning-god Hannumant.

Sagara Raja had it mounted in a setting of gold enriched with sapphires and rubies, and deposited it in one of the principal Hindu temples of Jaffna.

Thus the tooth of Buddha or tooth of the White Monkey, which had been for long years a heirloom of the royal family of Kotta, came into the possession of the King of Jaffna.

## CHAPTER 2

# DON JUAN DHARMAPALA

Thus freed from the tyranny of his father, young King Dharmapala who had now come to age, assumed the

1556 government of the kingdom. From the very beginning, aided by his prime minister and faithful councillor, the Adigar Don Francis Barreto Senerat Banda, he gained the affection of his people.

Educated since his childhood in the Catholic Faith, sincerely attached to Religion, and affectionate to the Franciscan Fathers, who had been his teachers and the best friends of his not too happy youth, he naturally gave them entire liberty to propagate throughout the kingdom the Faith of Jesus Christ, and the conversions had become very numerous. New stations were started, and the Catholic communities of Colombo, Kotta, Galle, Welligama, Malwane and Barberyn greatly increased in number. The Adigar Don Francis Senerat who was a fervent Catholic helped the Missionaries with all his influence.

The great event however of the year was the conversion of the Karawoe caste, who inhabited the coast between Colombo and Negombo. All, with their chief were baptised to the number of 70,000.

The conversion of the Karawoe was considered even in Europe

as an event of great importance, as appears from a letter which John III King of Portugal wrote in March 1557 to Fr. Francis de Chaves, one of the Superiors of the Ceylon Mission:

After having praised Alphonsus Pereira de Lacerda as one who conscientiously served his God and his Sovereign, the King added: — „We felt great pleasure at the news of how God has designed through the instrumentality of the Fathers of your Order, to bring the nation of the Karawoe to Our holy Faith, and that 70,000 of them, with their chief had been baptised. May the Lord be praised for it. We strongly recommend them to your care, for it seems to Us, that their conversion is sincere." —

And certainly it was sincere, and they gloriously proved it during the century of cruel persecution at the hands of the Dutch Protestants, and remained up to now faithful and fervent Catholics.

It was however in Ceylon that the conversion of the Karawoe produced the greatest results:

Young King Dharmapala had been brought up in the Catholic Religion, but his grandfather Bhuwaneka Bahu, and then his father Weedeya Raja, had always opposed his being baptised. After that came the troubles which we have narrated in the preceding chapter, the young King was not yet firmly established on his throne, then the uncertainty of the peace with Mayadunnè, who, as was well known, would not fail to take advantage of such an occasion to excite the Buddhists against him; all that had induced Fr. John de Villa Conde, to persuade the young King, for the sake of prudence, to delay yet his baptism.

But now that the conversion of the Karawoe, a strong and energetic race, had increased by so many the number of Catholics, the Adigar, Don Francis Senerat Banda was of opinion that there was no reason for delaying any longer the baptism of the King.

Nevertheless, it was thought more prudent not to give much prominence to the ceremony, not to excite the heathens. Moreover it was not necessary to make it a public affair, as already all the people looked on the King as a Catholic.

King Dharmapala was quietly baptised at Kotta by Fr. John de Villa Conde, and took the name of John, Don Juan.

King Don Juan Dharmapala notified officially his baptism to the Pope Paul IV and to John III King of Portugal. Unhappily we could not trace the answer of the Pope. When Don Juan's letter reached Lisbon, King John III was dead, and had been succeeded by his grandson Dom Sebastian, a minor, under the Regency of his grandmother Queen Donna Catherina.

The Queen's answer to King Don Juan is preserved in the archives of Lisbon. She wrote:

— „ Interested as We are in your well being, We have been glad to hear that God has granted you this grace through the good and zealous Franciscan Fathers. Nothing more could be hoped for from their apostolic labour, and nothing less from your devoted youth. The Catholic Faith has rendered you greater and given you the means of saving your soul and enlighten you in the midst of darkness. As regards Mayadunnè, who has already done so much harm to his country, and now, induced by Satan does not cease to create disturbances, show him your strong resolution to follow always the commandments of God. You are a King, act therefore as a King, show courage in adversity and act with the prudence with which you are endowed. In this way you will always enjoy the favour of Our Viceroys and Our Governors, to whom We will give positive orders, that they protect your interests as if they were Ours, because We consider your interests as Ours, not only by reason of the treaty between your grandfather King Bhuwaneka Bahu with Our grandfather King John III, whom God keep in His glory, but also because the bonds of fraternity which unite Us, and which have now been confirmed by your zeal, fraternity which We disown and deny to the Kings who have sworn it, and did not fulfil their engagements." —

We see this letter was written in the name of the young King Dom Sebastian. In another letter addressed to Fr. Melchior of Lisbon, Superior of the Franciscans in Ceylon and dated 7th March 1558, the Queen Regent expresses her satisfactions, that King Don Juan Dharmapala's baptism had taken place under her Regency, and then she adds:

— „As regards the help that the King asks against Mayadunnè, let him be assured that, as the Viceroy knows well, it is Our will that those who follow the ways of truth be protected. The demand of the King will therefore be granted, and We will always keep in Our mind everything that he wants.

The Ceylonese prince whom the Viceroy has sent to Lisbon receives a careful education and We hope that one day he will be able to render some service to God." —

The young prince about whom the Queen speaks in her letter was an illegitimate son of Bhuwaneka Bahu. His education finished, he did not return to Ceylon but settled at Goa, where he remained till his death and was buried in the church of the Franciscan Fathers.

The baptism of the young King, as the Adigar Don Francis Senerat Banda had foreseen, did not create disturbance
1557 among the people. The Catholics naturally rallied round him, and most of the Buddhists remained faithful to him. They were attached to the old dynasty and loved their young King, who was of a sweet and amiable disposition, equally accessible to the rich and the poor, and took a great interest in the welfare of the people.

The Bikshun and a few Buddhist petty chiefs endeavoured to create some trouble at Kotta and in the neighbourhood of Galle, but King Don Juan Dharmapala brought them to order with energy, more than one would not expect at his age. The severe justice with which he prosecuted those who had rebelled against their legitimate sovereign made them understand that he knew how to curb the disturbers of peace, and made the people rally more and more around their young King.

Sincerely devoted to the Catholic Religion, full of zeal for the conversion of his subjects, ardently attached to Fr. John de Villa Conde, who had been the friend and support of his youth in the midst of a pagan and depraved court, where the poor lad, with his pure heart and natural tendency to piety and virtue, found himself out of place, King Don Juan Dharmapala used all his influence to help the apostolate.

He encouraged his subjects to become Catholics and by his gracious and charitable demeanour showed to the heathens the advantages of being governed by a Catholic King.

He started schools and orphanages and in the years which followed his baptism he built twelve churches in the neighbourhood of Colombo and Kotta.

One of the first cares of King Don Juan Dharmapala was the question of education. Under his predecessors, there were no schools worth of this name in Ceylon. The rich kept in their houses pundits to teach and educate their children. The middle classes were sending their boys to pansalas, where they were abandoned to themselves and where they took at least three years to learn to read in Singhalese, and some of them to write. The villagers and poorer classes were left in a state of utter ignorance.

Don Juan Dharmapala, with the help of the Franciscan Fathers, started a College at Colombo, an institute for higher studies, such as would be called a high school, and primary schools were opened in the villages. It was decided that Colleges or high schools would be started in all other towns, but this plan had to be postponed for want of able and qualified teachers.

These schools had to be endowed. The large number of conversions to the Catholic Faith resulted in many Buddhist temples, principally along the coast, being now deserted. These temples had large properties. Now according to the Singhalese law of this epoch, the King alone was the owner of the properties of the temples and of the pansalas who had only the usufruct, and in case of the temples getting ruined or suppressed, these properties reversed to the crown and the King could dispose of them according to his wish.

By a charter dated June 1557, King Don Juan Dharmapala gave up the revenues of the deserted temples to educational purposes for the endowment of schools and orphanages. The charter ran as follows:

— „ We, Don Juan I, by the grace of God King of Ceylon make known to all concerned, who will read the present charter, that acknowledging the benefits We have reaped from the knowledge of Our Holy Faith, in which We have been educated by the Religious of the Order of St. Francis, who now labour with Us for the conversion of Our people, and on the demand of Fr. John de Villa Conde, guardian of Our royal city of Kotta, and metropolis of all the kingdoms of Ceylon, to whom We owe the happiness of being a Christian. We give and grant to the abovesaid Franciscan Fathers, all the revenues of the Kelanya temple, with its properties situated on the other side of the river. Also the properties of the temple of Deladasde which has been converted into a church of Our Holy Saviour, as well as all the fields, gardens, revenues, rights and royalties of all the other temples which, in time, would be suppressed. And as We know that the Franciscan Order, because of the severity of their Rule can have no possessions, its end being exclusively the salvation of souls, Our royal will is, that, as Our predecessors have assigned these properties for the maintenance of

Bikshun and sorcerers, that they be now employed for the endowment of the Colleges and the schools which the said Franciscan Fathers have erected and will erect in future in Our kingdom." —

This chart given in 1557 was re-confirmed in 1562 and on the 19th January 1594.

The baptism of the King was soon followed by the conversion of many persons of high rank.

The Rajavali, a Buddhist chronicle written in the eighteenth century, insinuates that it was only women of lower castes, who, attracted by Portuguese gold, became Catholics, and some Protestant writers repeat this assertion.

On the list of the converts in the years 1556 and 1557 we see: Don Emmanuel Raja of the Seven Kortes, a scion of the royal house of Kandy, his wife Donna Beatrice and his children D. Juan and D. Antonia. The princes D. Philip and D. Juan cousins of Mayadunnè with their mother D. Catharina, and the wife of D. Juan. Another D. Juan a near relation to Mayadunnè. D. Philip, Mayadunnè's Adigar or prime minister who renounced his high position to embrace the Catholic Faith, his wife D. Maria, his son D. Philip and his daughter-in-law D. Anna. D. Catharina widow of the Dessawe of Velacem with her daughters D. Antonia and D. Francisca.

There is no doubt that the baptisms in the lower classes were more numerous, but the Catholic Missionaries worked among all alike, the great and the humble, the rich and the poor. And then, we must admit that, in Ceylon as elsewhere, there were at that epoch more villagers than princes.

Mayadunnè saw in Don Juan's baptism a favourable occasion to endeavour anew to possess himself of the throne of Kotta. He thought that his proclaiming openly his Catholic Faith would alienate from the King his Buddhist subjects.

For thirty-one years Mayadunnè had aspired to the crown of Kotta, and notwithstanding all his reverses, he still directed all his powers towards this end with all the tenacity of a barbarian.

He began now again by sending Bikshun and other agents to all the districts of the kingdom of Kotta to preach rebellion against the Catholic King.

On the 22nd June 1557 the Bikshun succeeded to raise a tumult in the very city of Kotta, but the revolt was suppressed at the first moment by the energetic action of the King. Edward Rodriguez de Bulhão, the commander of the Colombo fort, also came to his aid.

The King then ordered his granduncle's agents, who overran the kingdom preaching disaffection, to be seized. Among those arrested there were thirty Bikshun. All those whose guilt was proved were punished.

On the last days of November of the same year, Mayadunnè sent a large army commanded by his bastard son Raja Singha to besiege Kotta. The King was unprepared, as no one supposed that Mayadunnè would break so soon the treaty which he had concluded with Pereira de Lacerda only two years ago. He sent for help to Goa.

The siege had already lasted eight months, and the garrison of Kotta was reduced to the last extremity by famine when

1558 help arrived in the early part of August 1558, led by Rodriguez de Lacerda who brought 100 Portuguese soldiers and 3,000 Indian sepoys. He attacked the besiegers and forced them to raise the siege, but they re-trenched themselves in a strong position not far from the city. On the 20th August new reinforcements arrived led by the commander of Manaar, where the Portuguese had established a small fort, and on the same day Raja Singha defeated in a battle, had to beat a hastily retreat and the victorious troops entered Kotta.

The first thought of the King was to thank God for the victory, and he was joined in it by the inhabitants of the liberated town.

An imposing thanksgiving procession passed the streets of the city. Headed by the clergy of Kotta and of Colombo they carried banners of St. Francis of Assisi, of St. James and of St. Bernard on whose feast day the victory was won, of St. Lawrence the patron of Ceylon, of St. Thomas the Apostle and of St. Francis Xavier, though his beatification did not take place till sixty years later. The Portuguese officers in gala uniform, all the Catholic soldiers and the Christians of the town followed the clergy. It was for the first time that Catholic worship was celebrated with so much pomp in the southern capital of Ceylon.

George de Menezes who succeeded Rodriguez de Bulhão as

1559 commander of Colombo with King Don Juan Dharmapala continued throughout the following year the war with Mayadunnè, but it was a desultory affair and there were no events worthy to be chronicled.

## CHAPTER 3

# THE SIEGE OF JAFFNA

Francis Barreto having completed his term of office, the
new Viceroy Don Constantine de Braganza landed at
1548 Goa on the 3rd September 1548. Brother to the Duke of that name, and related to the King, he was a great Christian and one of the ablest Portuguese Viceroys who ever governed their settlements in India. He protected the Missions, and during the three years he was in office the Jesuit Fathers alone converted, on the western coast of India 20,737 heathens, and many more were baptised by the Dominican and Franciscan Fathers.

Old King Sagara Raja still reigned at Jaffna. Though since 1545 he always feared war with the Portuguese, yet seeing that years were passing and that the Viceroys occupied with more important affairs seemed to have forgotten him, he re-commenced molesting his Catholic subjects who, thanks to the zeal of Fr. Melchior of Lisbon and the Franciscan Fathers, notwithstanding constant persecution, were yearly increasing in number.

Their position in the kingdom had at last become very precarious until the arrival at Goa of the new Viceroy, to whom, Sagara knew, the Queen Regent D. Catherina had given precise instructions not to delay any more the punitive expedition against Jaffna.

These news disturbed the old King, and he ceased molesting the Christians. Fr. Melchior of Lisbon and his companions took profit of this truce, and in the space of two years, from 1558 to 1560, they baptised 2,000 heathens, built 25 chapels on the territory of Jaffna and 35 others in the adjacent Islands and around Ramaseram.

In the meantime Don Constantine de Braganza was preparing his expedition to Jaffna. According to the orders of the Queen Regent of Portugal, Sagara Raja had to be dethroned and the crown given to some prince of the royal house. Now Sagara's brother, the rightful King was dead, and also the two young princes educated at Goa. The choice of the Viceroy fell therefore on the young Raja of Trincomalee, a scion of the same house. He was now nineteen years of age, educated since his childhood in the Catholic Faith and had just completed his studies at St. Paul's College at Goa.

It was about that time that the plan has been proposed to establish a Colony of Catholic Parawers in the Island of
1559 Manaar and on the northern coast of Ceylon. A large number had already settled at Manaar with Fr. Henry Enriquez one of the faithful companions of St. Francis Xavier. They were expecting the result of the Viceroy's expedition to pass over to the coast of Ceylon, which thinly populated and covered with jungle would be rendered flourishing with the immigration of such intelligent, energetic and enterprising race as the Parawers.

Don Constantine de Braganza sailed from Goa on the 28th of
1560 October 1560 at the head of 2,500 men.

With 4,000 men, writes Fr. de Queiroz, the conquest of the kingdom of Jaffna was certain, but 2,500 were an insufficient force. In all their wars in Ceylon the Portuguese committed the error of bringing into the field an insufficient force and so, they gained victories, but could not afterwards take profit of them.

Together with the Viceroy were the young Raja Don Alphonsus of Trincomalee, Dom George Themudo Bishop of Cochin to whose diocese belonged Ceylon, and Fr. Anthony de Quadros, Provincial of the Jesuits in India.

After having landed in a convenient place Don Constantine de Braganza marched on Jaffna. But King Sagara Raja had prepared himself for the war. He met the Viceroy at the head of a great army. But his undisciplined forces could not withstand the tactics of the Portuguese, he was defeated, the Jaffnians fled, leaving their camp in the hands of the enemy and took refuge behind the walls of Jaffna.

The Viceroy besieged the town. The walls looked very formidable bristled with guns taken from vessels which had been wrecked on the coast. But they were there only for show, the Jaffnians not knowing how to manage them and having no ammunitions.

A general assault was decided. The Portuguese were preparing themselves for the battle like Christians. On the eve, they all went to confession. Next morning the Bishop of Cochin Dom George Themudo celebrated holy Mass on an Altar erected in the middle of the camp. The Viceroy and the officers received holy Communion from the hands of the Bishop and the men from the Priests. The signal for battle was given, and the small army advanced proceeded by a large Crucifix carried by a Dominican, Fr. Peter de Sousa.

The Jaffnese placed their greatest reliance in an enormous gun which they had placed behind one of the gates of the city. They had charged it with nails, bullets and copper coins. When the Portuguese advanced to the assault, they let them approach the gate, and opening it suddenly they unmasked the great gun and fired. But it was pointed too high and all this singular grapeshot passed over the heads of the Portuguese of whom twelve only were wounded.

Seeing the failure of their stratagem the Jaffnese fled in disorder leaving the gate open, and the Portuguese pulling aside the gun entered the town and after some fighting in the streets became masters of it, but not of the fort which was manned by the best men of Sagara's army, well provisioned and was better able to resist than the town.

Meanwhile King Sagara Raja did not trust his people, whose fidelity he doubted and fled to the Vanny, where he remained in hiding.

The Viceroy had committed a mistake for which he was to pay dearly. He failed to inform himself of the sentiments of the people. If he had only known of the hatred they had for their cruel and barbarous King; if instead of treating them as enemies, he had acted as a liberator, posing as an avenger of their long sufferings and proclaimed King without delay young Raja Alphonsus of Trincomalee, they would have delivered to him the tyrant, and the war would have been ended at once.

The Portuguese did not find in the town the booty they expected. The Jaffnese knew beforehand that the Portuguese were approaching and they had time to hide all that was precious.

Nevertheless, in the tumult which followed the assault, no one had thought about hiding the tooth of Buddha, and some Portuguese officers found it in the great temple of Nellore and brought it to the Viceroy.

The Bishop George Themudo wished to have it destroyed on the spot as an object of pagan worship, but some officers prevailed saying that it could be sold for a very high price to the King of Siam or to some other Buddhist potentate of the East, and bring much money to the treasury.

At last it was decided that the tooth will be carried to Goa as a trophy.

Fr. Melchior of Lisbon heard this decision with great indignation. He said that it was an offence to God, that in carrying away the thing as a trophy, instead of destroying it, they gave it only more importance in the eyes of the heathens, and he prophetized that for having preferred sordid lucre to the glory of God, the penalty will be that they would not attain the end they desired, and that their expedition will fail miserably.

Among the prisoners the Portuguese had taken there were some ladies of high rank. The Viceroy put them under the protection of two knights Antony de Noronha and Louis de Mello de Sylva who treated them with all the respect due to their rank.

One of these ladies was the wife of one of the King's son. She was a sweet and intelligent lady, and liked to speak with Bishop Themudo and with Fr. Melchior. At last she asked for baptism. When her husband learned she had become a Catholic, he had her poisoned.

As soon as order was re-established in the conquered city, a solemn thanksgiving service was held. Fr. Melchior of Lisbon celebrated the holy Mass. It was one of his last, as he was soon to win the martyrs' palm. The Bishop of Cochin then mounted the pulpit: Take everything for yourself, he said to the victors, glory, riches, power, everything that the world appreciates, leave only the souls to me. He then exhorted the authorities and all the Catholics to help him in the apostolate he was about to undertake, for it was in the hope of saving the souls of these unhappy heathens and to bring them to God, that had induced him to undertake this voyage and face the fatigues and perils of war.

Meanwhile the inhabitants of Jaffna who had fled from the town either before the siege, or in the days which followed the assault of the Portuguese, began to return to their home. The Viceroy did all in his power to gain their confidence. He loved the natives, and liked to converse familiarly with them and, notwithstanding that the fortress was still in the hands of the troop of Sagara Raja the city began to resume its usual aspect.

But the fortress, well provisioned and manned by a brave determined garrison made a stubborn resistance. Don Constantine understood, that to reduce the citadel would be a long and difficult affair. With the small body of men he had at his disposal he could not even think of taking it by assault, and he was not provided with the necessaries for a regular siege. He could not get them from Goa, for the treasury of the colony was empty. He was therefore reduced to a simple blockade, hoping to force the citadel to surrender by famine.

In the meantime, the Bishop of Cochin, with Fr. Melchior of Lisbon and some other Franciscans laboured actively to convert the heathens.

One day, Fr. Melchior in company with Fr. John went to administer the last Sacraments to a dying Catholic in the interior of the country. They were seized by Sagara Raja's soldiers, and brought before him. The King was overjoyed that Fr. Melchior had fallen into his hands, for he knew that it was he who had insisted on the destruction of the tooth of Buddha, or, as he called it, the tooth of the White Monkey and he wished to have his revenge.

The King had an idol of Ganesha brought and ordered the two Missionaries to adore it, and, as they refused to do it, they were beaten with rods, until they were covered with blood and then cast into prison, where they were kept four days without food.

Brought again before the King, and ordered to adore the idol they constantly refused. Sagara Raja seeing that Fr. Melchior had tears in his eyes, asked him why he was weeping. Fr. Melchior answered: — It is not the fear of death that has brought forth my tears. Man is weak and I was afraid of torture, but I have prayed God, and He has given me a soul of iron, and I will bear now with delight all torments for His Faith and for His greater glory. I weep considering your misery, who being a King chose to remain a slave to the devil.

They endeavoured yet once to induce the two Missionaries to worship Ganesha, and, on their refusal, the King ordered them both to be beheaded.

On his way to death Fr. Melchior of Lisbon made a touching prayer recommending his soul to God, offering his life for the conversion of the heathens of Ceylon and begging God to pardon his executioners.

The martyrdom of Fathers Melchior and John, was the beginning of a persecution of all the Catholics in the territory of the kingdom of Jaffna which was not occupied by the Portuguese.

Many refused to deny their Faith and were cruelly put to death. We could not ascertain the number of martyrs, but the historians say that their number was great.

Meanwhile the Viceroy besieged the citadel of Jaffna and the resistance of tne garrison became daily more serious, and threatened to bring to naught the end of the expeditions.

Dissensions and disorder broke out in the Portuguese camp.

Food and ammunitions were becoming scarce, and armed bands of Sagara Raja, infesting the neighbourhood of the town, murdered the soldiers that ventured themselves beyond its walls.

Such was the state of affairs when the King of Jaffna sent his son to the Viceroy to sue for peace. The prince was bearer of the proposal of Sagara Raja which were: that he would deliver up the Island of Manaar, which would thus become an immediate possession of the Crown of Portugal. He would declare himself a vassal to Dom Sebastian the King of Portugal and pay a yearly tribute. He engaged himself no longer to molest the navigation on the northern coast of Ceylon. Finally the Viceroy will restore to him the tooth of Buddha or as it was called by the Tamils the tooth of the White Monkey.

Don Constantine de Braganza received the prince with his accustomed courtesy, but he was not satisfied with the King's proposals. He refused positively to restore to the King the tooth, and added the following to Sagara Raja's other proposals. The King was to guarantee, that he would no more persecute the Christians. That no Jaffnese who would become a Catholic would be molested either by himself or by his officials; that the Missionaries will be free to preach the Gospel all over the kingdom of Jaffna, and a convent for the Franciscans, and a residence for the Jesuit Fathers had to be erected in the city. Moreover Sagara Raja was to deliver to the Viceroy all his treasures as well in jewels as in cash, and hand over the treasures of Weedeya Raja, to be restored to his son the King of Kotta Don Juan Dharmapala.

Sagara Raja consented to all the conditions imposed by the

Viceroy even to the delivery of his treasures. He only insisted upon the restitution of the tooth of Buddha, but met with a refusal of the Viceroy.

He then asked for the liberty of one of his sons who had been taken prisoner by the Portuguese, which the Viceroy equally refused. The reason was that the prince himself did not care to return to his father. He wished to be a Catholic and feared the fate of his brother who had suffered martyrdom sixteen years ago In fact the prince was baptised by the Bishop of Cochin, then settled in Goa, and remained there loved and honoured by all till his death in 1571.

Thus Sagara Raja, the greatest enemy of Christianity saw nearly all members of his family become Catholics: three sons, his brother, his sister, two nephews, a daughter-in-law, and his cousin the young Raja of Trincomalee.

Sagara Raja tried then to raise the people against the Portuguese, but he failed. Then fearing the loss of his
1561 crown, for he knew that though this expedition had been unsuccessful, and because it had been unsuccessful, the Viceroy, on his return to Goa would certainly prepare another and would again invade his kingdom with a more powerful army, he submitted to the conditions of Don Constantine de Braganza and a treaty of peace was concluded in January 1561.

Thus the chief object of the expedition to dethrone the tyrant Sagara Raja and to give the crown of Jaffna to the Catholic Raja Dom Alphonsus of Trincomalee failed. The treaty recognized even as lawful Sovereign of Jaffna the King whom for sixteen years the Viceroys of India had considered as an usurper. Nevertheless the treaty was advantageous to the Portuguese. It gave them over the kingdom of Jaffna the same rights which the Portuguese crown had acquired since 1517 over the kingdom of Kotta. It recognized their protectorate over the northern part of Ceylon without the onerous condition of having to help the King against his enemies.

Weedeya Raja's treasures were restored to his son King Don Juan Dharmapala, and Sagara Raja's jewels which he had to deliver to the Portuguese, proved to be of no much value, they scarcely paid the cost of the war. Of course there could be no control if the King of Jaffna surrendered all he had.

From Jaffna Don Constantine de Braganza went to Manaar to organize the new colony, which now depended directly on the government of Goa. He constructed a fort in which he placed a garrison of 150 European soldiers under the command of George de Mello de Castro, at whose disposal he left six armed vessels. He built a convent for the Franciscan Fathers, and eager as he was to promote the education of the people he fixed a site for a Jesuit College which however was erected only four years later in 1565.

The final result of the expedition naturally deranged the plan of colonising the northern coast of Ceylon with Parawers from India. They could do it only in Manaar where a large number of emigrants had already come and new parties were still arriving.

Once, when a fresh party was landing, the Viceroy with his

suite went to meet them. He welcomed cordially their chiefs and, lifting up in his arms a small Parawer boy (he loved the native children) he placed him before him on his saddle and led the new arrivals to the church where they were blessed by the Bishop of Cochin.

Among the Jesuit Fathers who took care of the Parawer immigrants at Manaar, Fr. Jerome Vaz deserves a special mention. He was a man of extraordinary zeal. He completely reformed the habits of the Portuguese soldiers, whom he transformed into fervent and exemplary Christians, and he alone baptised over one thousand heathens.

The Jesuit Fathers did their best to establish comfortably the Parawers at Manaar, but the whole plan of colonisation was deemed to be a failure. Home sickness seemed to have broken all their energy. In the year 1563, they were decimated by the plague. More than four thousands died in one year. Those who survived decided to leave these inhospitable shores, they re-crossed the gulf of Manaar and returned to their old homes.

## CHAPTER 4

# BUDDHA'S TOOTH

The news of Buddha's tooth having fallen into the hands of the Portuguese and carried away to Goa spread a gloom

1561 over the heathen population of Ceylon and reached even the opposite coast of Indo-China.

As said above it had been worshipped by all the sections of the inhabitants of the Island: the Buddhist Singhalese called it the tooth of Buddha; the Hindu Tamils worshipped it as the tooth of the White Ape, their monkey god Hannumant, and the Moormen considered it as a tooth of Adam. It was for all a kind of national fetish, and now it was gone from Ceylon.

Towards the end of February of the same year 1561, a vessel belonging to a Portuguese merchant called Martin Alphonsus de Mello who was trading between Goa and the coast of Burma, anchored in the harbour of Pegu.

When the news of the arrival of the well-known trader reached the King of Pegu he sent for de Mello, and desired him to sail immediately to Goa and ask the Viceroy to sell him the tooth of Buddha for whatever price he demanded.

De Mello, wishing to rid himself of this singular commercial transaction which certainly was not in his line, advised the King of

Pegu to send rather an embassy to Goa to deal directly with the Viceroy, and the King arranged the things so well, that the ambassadors, two high dignitaries of his court and two Bikshun or Punghees, as they are called in Burma, embarked on de Mello's ship bearers of a letter to the Viceroy.

Hardly had he cast anchor at Goa, in April 1561, when de Mello called on the Viceroy and related to him his singular adventure.

Don Constantine de Braganza received in solemn audience the envoys of the King of Pegu, who came immediately to the point: They offered, in the name of their King, in exchange for Buddha's tooth, a lump sum of 400,000 cruzados (825,000 Rupees) a perpetual alliance with Portugal and the obligation of revictualling the fortress of Malacca each time that its commander demanded. And they exhibited the credential which empowered them to sign the treaty in the name of the King.

The Viceroy surprised at such a proposal laid the question before the council. The treasury was empty, there was great need of funds for organizing the new conquests and maintaining the garrisons of numerous fortresses and the fleets that kept them in communication. Nearly all the councillors were of opinion that the offer should be accepted. The Archbishop of Goa, Dom Leo Pereira, vigorously protested, against restoring to the heathens this object of their worship, which would be favouring heathenism and an offence to God, and, not satisfied of his remonstrance at the sitting of the council, he preached on the same subject in the Cathedral.

The Viceroy then suspended the negotiations with the Burmese envoys and appointed a committee presided by the Archbishop and composed of the ministers of State, the Fathers Emmanuel de Serra Provincial of Dominicans, Anthony de Quadros Provincial of the Jesuits, the Guardian of the Franciscans, two Jesuit Fathers, the principal military and civil officials and a few Portuguese noblemen residing at Goa. Of twenty members of the committee, six only were ecclesiastics, all the others were laymen.

The Viceroy exposed the situation, the penury of the treasury and then retired to leave them free to deliberate. At first, the opinions were divided, as the government officials, who considered before all the needs of the State, were in majority. Then an old captain, the hero of many battles got up and said: — „Whoever of you can doubt that if our armies had always been victorious, it was because they were led by God. And this Great General had made more for Portugal's glory than all our Viceroys and all our Captains. If we restore to the heathens this object of their worship, the devil will use it to bite many souls, which certainly would be a great offence to God for which we alone would be responsible. Now, I ask you, would it be prudent to offend thus the Great General who had led us from one victory to another and covered our name with glory?" —

All the military men applauded the speech of the old warrior, the others were deeply impressed, and when they came to voting, it was decided nearly at unanimity that Buddha's tooth should not be sold.

The resolution was put in writing and presented to the Viceroy.

It said: — „That Buddha's tooth ought not be sold, since by selling it to the King of Pegu they would be inciting and favouring idolatry, and thus offending the Majesty of God, a sin, which cannot be permitted not only as in the present case to extricate the State from financial embarassments, but not even to save the whole world from imminent danger." —

Such was the verdict of the commission. Some civil officials grumbled. What is the use, they said, of destroying the tooth, when the Buddhist will make another and worship it again. The Viceroy seeing that there was logic in what they said, decided to give the greatest publicity to the destruction of Buddha's tooth

A rich pandal was erected on the shore of the Mandovi river not far from the Viceroy's palace. A large crowd assembled to witness the spectacle. The recent arrival of the envoys of Pegu and the extravagant offers they had made had excited the interest of the inhabitants of Goa. The crowd was immense: both shores of the river were lined with curious people, and the roofs of the neighbouring houses, says an eye-witness, were so loaded with people that it was seriously feared that they would break.

The Viceroy, the Archbishop and the principal ecclesiastics, civil and military dignitaries took place on the platform. Then Don Constantine de Braganza ordered the treasurer to bring the Tooth. He exhibited it to the people, having it identified by the officers who had found it in the temple at Jaffna, took it from the rich setting and handed it to the Archbishop.

The Archbishop threw it into a mortar, and, with his own hands reduced it into powder, then threw the parcels on burning coals. The embers and the ashes were next carried to the middle of the river, and thrown into the current.

Such was the end of Buddha's tooth, and one can easily imagine the despair of the Burmese envoys who assisted to its destruction.

## CHAPTER 5

# THE SIEGE OF KOTTA

Now returning to the affairs of Kotta, we have seen in another chapter how Mayadunnè having re-commenced war

1562 with King Don Juan, had placed at the head of his army his bastard son Raja Singha. We have interrupted then our narration at the events which occurred in the month of August 1559.

In the three years which followed that date, nothing worthy to be mentioned occurred. It was a small war consisting for the most part of pillage, in which Raja Singha distinguished himself by his cruelty and his courage.

But he had a formidable enemy in George de Menezes the commander of the auxiliary troops which the Viceroy had sent to Don Juan. Menezes was a warrior of indomitable courage and of a jovial sunny disposition. Once when at sea, he heard a soldier asking the cook for an onion: — „Glutton, he said, a soldier ought to be fond only of swallowing bullets." — On another occasion during a fight with Raja Singha, ammunition fell short. His soldiers got into panic and were shouting that they had no more powder: — „Fools, exclaimed Menezes, if you have no more powder, put sand into your guns or, if you prefer it, draw your swords and charge the enemy." — And they won the day.

Towards the end of 1563, Raja Singha, having received from 1563 his father, old Mayadunnè, reinforcements of well trained and armed troops, had the audacity to attempt to besiege Colombo, but repelled by the Portuguese he marched on Kotta.

Balthazar Guedes de Sousa commander of the fort of Colombo and his brother Gonzalo hastened to King Don Juan's help but, hardly had they entered the city with a small body of Portuguese troops, when Raja Singha besieged it. The siege lasted four months.

There were at that time at Kotta six Franciscan Missionaries: Fr. Luke, of whom we will have to speak later on, Fathers Simon of Nazareth, Martin of Guarda, Peter of Belem and two others.

The historian Diogo de Conto writes: — „ During this siege, King Don Juan, Balthazar Guedes de Sousa and some other knight, performed prodigies of valour, but the Franciscans did more than the others, for, with their incessant prayers, they fought more efficaciously the enemy. They exhorted the troops to fight gallantly, to ask God's pardon for their sins, and were always to be seen where the danger was greatest, administering to the wounded and bringing them out of peril.

On the 20th of December, the besieged made a vigorous sortie. They thought they would be able to surprise Raja Singha's camp, but the latter was on his guard. He surrounded the small body of Singhalese and Portuguese troops and cut off their retreat.

They fought bravely their way through the enemy's ranks and

reached at last the gates of the city, loosing heavily. They entered the city and the gates were closed.

Fathers Martin of Guarda, Louis of Amaral and Peter of Belem who had remained in the rear to minister to the wounded, were made prisoners, and Raja Singha after having endeavoured in vain to induce them to deny their Faith, ordered them to be hung on a tree.

At the beginning of the next year, Mayadunnè sent fresh troops to his son and Raja Singha fearing that, if the siege
1564 lasted longer the Viceroy should sent reinforcements to King Don Juan, determined to put an end to it by taking the town by assault.

The fight was terrible. While King Don Juan with his Singhalese troops defended the walls of the city, the Portuguese led by Peter d'Athaide who had succeeded in command to Balthazar Guedes de Sousa, dangerously wounded, made a sortie. In the midst of the fight, the brave Franciscan Fathers were seen everywhere unarmed, with the Crucifix in their hand, inflaming the ardour of the soldiers.

King Don Juan and Fr. Luke were always to be met where the assault was the fiercest. A Franciscan Father, whose name remains unknown, fell struck by a bullet when administering to a dying soldier. The enemy was on the point of becoming masters of the city. Peter d'Athaide pressed by numbers was rallying his soldiers around him for the last fight.

Fr. Simon of Nazareth fell then on his knees, and invoked the help of God. Whilst he was praying, he saw the Blessed Virgin Mary and St. Joseph, covering with their mantles the small Christian army. The assault was repulsed and Raja Singha suffered severe losses. The siege however continued, and the city was reduced to the last extremity. The provisions were exhausted and ammunitions began to fail. Surrender was inevitable.

Then Fr. Simon of Nazareth sought the King and offered to go to Colombo for help. At night, with a faithful native guide, he passed the enemy's lines and taking a winding turn through the forests he reached Colombo and embarked there for Manaar where Diogo de Mello Cutinho, the same who had so daringly arrested the Regent Weedeya Raja, was then in command Just at that time, Anthony de Costa Travasso had arrived from Goa to Manaar with six ships and a fresh contingent of soldiers. Without losing a moment de Mello and de Costa joined their troops and, with Fr. Simon they sailed to Colombo whence they marched on Kotta.

Raja Singha did not dare to meet them. His army was exhausted, he had lost 2,700 men. He therefore rose the siege and retired to his father's dominions.

Fr. Simon of Nazareth was received with joy and gratitude by the garrison and people of Kotta.[*]

In the meanwhile, several Viceroys had succeeded each other at Goa. Don Constantine de Braganza had governed till 7th September 1561. His successor was Francis Cutinho Count of Redondo who died on 19th February 1564. John de Mendoza governed the Colony till the arrival of the new Viceroy Anthony de Noronha who landed at Goa on the 3rd September 1564.

**1565** Anthony de Noronha took in hand the affairs of Ceylon.

There was no hope of making an end to the wars with Mayadunnè, since the old adventurer had clearly shown that no treaty of peace was sacred to him, as he broke them at his whim. There was therefore no other perspective than war and a war to the end. Now the strategical position of King Don Juan Dharmapala and of his Portuguese allies was defective. They had two important centres to defend: Kotta, the capital of the kingdom, and Colombo the emporium of the trade of Cevlon which has grown to an important city and in fact was already at that time the largest town in Ceylon. The King with his own resources could not resist his powerful grand-uncle, and the Portuguese contingent, which the Viceroys could not afford to be very large, was unefficient when divided between Colombo and Kotta.

It was therefore decided in the Viceregal Council that Kotta must be abandoned and the King induced to make Colombo the capital of his kingdom.

This decision caused a great sorrow to Don Juan Dharmapala: All the traditions of his race, and the history of his country were concentrated around Kotta, but he too saw plainly that with the change of circumstances and the great progress his kingdom has made in the last fifty years, Kotta could no more remain the capital, which must be transferred to Colombo, where the seat of Government, would be more sheltered, more secure and less exposed to the uncertainties of war.

Diogo de Mello Cutinho, the King's friend, having been appointed commander of the fort of Colombo in July 1565, King Don Juan transferred his residence to that city. Kotta was dismantled, all the fortifications demolished to the ground, all its guns, ammunition and war implements were brought to Colombo, and by degrees Kotta was reduced to the state of a humble village, whilst the rival city, became one of the most important Metropolis of the East.

Some English writers of the last century say that King Don Juan Dharmapala lived in Colombo in a state boarding on misery and entirely dependent on the Portuguese commander. Such assertion is historically false. Don Juan was the King, he ruled the kingdom and perceived its revenues. We see him at the head of his army in which the Portuguese served as auxiliaries.

There was, no doubt, a time, when the fortunes of war having turned against him he found himself, for a short time, in penury and distress, but then the Portuguese shared with him this distress.

This was the case in 1573 when Mayadunnè, having conquered nearly the whole kingdom of Kotta, Don Juan found himself reduced to the possession of the city of Colombo alone. The loss of the tributes he perceived from the provinces, and other revenues of the crown had reduced him to extreme penury. Disheartened and discouraged, he made better reproaches to the Portuguese commander, wanting him to re-conquer his kingdom and asking him large sums of money for the maintenance of his Court. He wrote petitions to the Pope and to the King of Portugal. But the commander had hardly soldiers enough to prevent Mayadunnè to render himself master of Colombo and was so short of money that he could scarcely support his small garrison.

These were however extraordinary circumstances, brought about by the fortunes of war and which did not last longer than the moment, help could be sent him from Goa. During his reign of more than forty years such thing happened twice only.

In ordinary times King Don Juan lived in great state at Colombo and enjoyed considerable revenues from tributes from the provinces and duties on the export of cinnamon and elephants. Reliable and almost contemporary writers like John Ribeiro and Fr. Ferdinand de Queiros say that he was rich, and even very rich. Then the Portuguese commander made the King pay the costs of all the military expeditions undertaken in his favour, which proves that the King had means of paying.

Further, it must not be forgotten that, at that time, the Portuguese were not masters of the country. They only had a number of commercial houses, factories as they were called and a fort in Colombo with a garrison barely sufficient to protect their trade and the King against Mayadunnè till reinforcements could be sent from Goa.

Don Juan was the King and it was he who ruled the kingdom. The King of Portugal was only recognized the Lord paramount, and, in order to maintain this suzerainty and their nominal protectorate, it was in the interest of the Portuguese to sustain the rights of Don Juan, to keep up his power and to raise his prestige in the eyes of his subjects.

There is among the Protestant writers a general tendency to lower as much as possible the Catholic King Don Juan, and to raise on a pedestal the adventurous pretender Mayadunnè whom they endeavour to represent as chief of the national party and defender of the independence of his native country against the Portuguese invaders. They insinuate, that the people of the whole country was devoted to Mayadunnè, and that King Don Juan maintained himself on the throne by the help of the Portuguese, whereas, in reality, the pretender was so abhorred for his barbarity that he could scarcely rely on the fidelity of the inhabitants of his own States of Sitawacca and of Rayagam, who fleeing from the tyranny of their Raja emigrated in mass into the territory of Kotta. Mayadunnè's dominions thus depopulated presented a miserable spectacle, whole villages disappeared, and the site of former fields and gardens was overrun with jungle.

On the contrary, the kingdom of Kotta though it had much to suffer from the pillaging bands of Mayadunnè was on the way of progress: Agriculture was improving, trade progressing, and the people whose prosperity was increasing began to appreciate the benefit of education.

Colombo had become an important city and ships from Portugal, Persia, Arabia, India, Indo-China and China were casting anchor in the harbour to take the products of Ceylon and Europe in exchange for those of their country.

In the year 1566 Dom George Themudo, the Bishop of Cochin, came to Ceylon on a pastoral visit. He had with him
1566 Fr. Melchior Nunez Barreto, the well-known Jesuit, one of the most zealous and ablest helpers of St. Francis Xavier.

They came first to Manaar to settle the question of the Jesuit College. George de Mello commander of the place handed them over the plot of ground selected for that purpose by Constantine de Braganza, the Bishop advanced the necessary money and laid the foundation stone of the building.

From Manaar, sailing around the northern point of Ceylon they proceeded to Nagapatam and to Mailepour whence they came to Colombo, where, taking their abode in the Franciscan Convent, they remained till January 1567.

Fr. Nunez, preached in the churches and, at the request of the Guardian gave lectures on scholastic theology to the Franciscan students.

## CHAPTER 6

# THE RE-APPEARANCE OF BUDDHA'S TOOTH

About the beginning of 1567, the King of Pegu, the same who had offered such large sum of money to the Viceroy

1567

Constantine de Braganza for Buddha's tooth, wishing to take a wife, consulted a famous astrologer, to find out in which of the royal houses of the East he should chose his Queen in order that his reign be propitious.

The astrologer drew the King's horoscope, and after days of study and meditation declared, that in order to bring happiness on his people, he should marry the daughter of the King of Kotta.

It was rather a delicate matter which presented some slight difficulty, for the King of Kotta, Don Juan Dharmapala had no daughter, and although at this time he was about 30 years of age, he was not even married, so that the King of Pegu, would have had to wait rather a long time for his proposed marriage.

On the other hand the ill-informed astrologer did not keep his secret, and every one now knew at Pegu that their King must marry the daughter of the King of Kotta, and that, if by some means or other he did not manage to marry a daughter of the King of Kotta all possible calamities would befall the kingdom of Pegu.

Placed in this difficulty the King of Pegu resolved to give the widest interpretation to the verdict of the astrologer. It is true, he said that the King of Kotta had no daughter, but, as he was the head of the royal house, every girl of that house could be considered as his daughter.

Now, Don Francis Barreto Senerat Banda, the nearest relative of the King, the same who was for a time Regent during his minority, had a daughter of marriageable age, and it suited to the King of Pegu to ally himself with King Don Juan the friend of the Portuguese. Although educated at the court of a Catholic King and daughter of a fervent Catholic, the young princess born before her father's conversion was a Buddhist like her mother, which shows that no one was forced to become a Catholic, as some writer pretend.

The King of Pegu sent an embassy to Colombo to ask King Don Juan for the hand of his cousin. The ambassadors were the same dignitaries of his court whom he had sent six years ago to Goa to buy Buddha's tooth. Don Juan received them in great state and the question of the marriage was settled.

Don Francis Senerat Banda not satisfied with his daughter mounting the throne of Pegu, and aware of the offers which the King had made Don Constantine de Braganza, imagined to take profit of the superstition of his future son-in-law and to play him a dirty trick.

In concert with King Don Juan, but with the greatest secrecy from the Portuguese commander and from the Franciscan Fathers, who would have certainly not allowed the fraud, he had a perfect imitation made of the tooth destroyed at Goa. He next tried to gain the confidence of the ambassadors and of the Burmese Bikshun or Punghees who accompanied them, a matter not difficult, for they considered themselves highly honoured, to be treated with so much regard by the father of their future Queen.

One day when they were about to start for a pilgrimage to the top of Adam's Peak to worship there the Sri-Pada, Don Francis Senerat Banda became confidential. He told them that he had become a Catholic to please his cousin King Don Juan, but at the bottom of his heart he had remained a faithful Buddhist. Once the confidences began, he went on, and related them how, when assisting at the siege of Jaffna (he had never been there), he had the supreme fortune to save from the hands of the Portuguese the tooth of Buddha, substituting a counterfeit which was destroyed at Goa. He further added to the amazed Burmese that, the King his cousin being a Catholic might probably oblige him to surrender it to the Portuguese, he had carefully hidden it in his house, where he kept it with reverence, as the most precious thing that existed on earth.

The Burmese ambassadors and the Bikshun astonished, at what they heard, begged of Don Francis to allow them to see the sacred tooth, and to render it due worship.

Don Francis flatly refused to do so, pretending that if King Don Juan came to hear of the matter he would cause the tooth to be destroyed, but finally yielding to their entreaties, after having made them swear the greatest secrecy, told them to come to his house, at night and disguised, taking great care not to be recognized.

The Burmese came at the fixed hour. Don Francis Senerat, feigning all kind of precautions, took them into a small room, the walls of which were hung with rich silk stuffs. In the middle of the room on a table surrounded with lighted tapers, perfumes and incense burning all around stood a richly gilded dagoba, covered with necklaces of rubies and sapphires. Don Francis rose the dagoba, and exhibited to the Burmese his counterfeit of the tooth. They prostrated themselves on the ground.

Overjoyed with their discovery the Burmese envoys begged Don Francis to give the tooth as dowry to his daughter, showing him, how she would be received at Pegu by the King and by the people if she were bearer of the precious relic.

But Don Francis Senerat answered them that for nothing in the world would he renounce to the felicity of possessing the sacred tooth. Such holy thing, he said, could be sold for a large sum of money but given never! They said, that the King of Pegu would willingly pay him the same price he had offered to Don Constantine de Braganza but, as they had not the money, the cunning Adigar, seeing how his fraud had succeeded, would not be satisfied with a verbal promise, refused to deliver to them the tooth saying he could not be induced to part with it.

Thus the young princess had to leave Colombo without it. King Don Juan did the things grandly: he gave her magnificent jewels and sent her off with a numerous court at the head of which was one of the principal headmen of his kingdom the Mudeliyar Andrew Bayam, a Catholic, and she was received at Pegu with all the pomp customary in the East.

Meanwhile, the King of Pegu, informed of the wonderful escape of the tooth of Buddha, was overwhelmed with the desire of possessing it. He despatched secretly to Colombo the ambassadors and the Punghees, bearers of the sum of 400,000 cruzados; they met Don Francis Senerat who, after much bargaining sold them the bogus tooth. They carried it at night to their ship, and immediately sailed for Burma.

The reception given to the tooth at Pegu surpassed by its pomp all imagination. We have the account written by an eye-witness, Anthony Toscano, a Portuguese trader, who at that time was a prisoner in the city:

When the news spread that the vessel was approaching the coast, all the Punghees or Bonzes of the neighbourhood, all in new yellow dresses and an immense crowd of people went to meet it at the landing, anxious to be the first to worship the tooth. A great number of boats richly adorned with flags put out to sea to meet the vessel, and when the dagoba with the tooth was landed it literally rested on gold, silver and precious silks.

The King ordered all his noblemen to go to meet the tooth, he himself remaining at Pegu to supervise the arrangements for its reception.

The tooth was carried up the river on a raft, under a canopy of rich and precious silks surrounded with burning tapers and followed by a long procession of gayly adorned boats.

The King in his state-barge went to meet the procession. When he saw it approaching, he retired to his cabin, took a bath, had all his body anointed with perfumed oils, and put on his richest robes. Then, getting on the raft and prostrated himself before Don Francis' Tooth and taking it with both hands, he placed it on his head, all the time muttering Pali invocations which he had learned by heart. Then re-placing it into the dagoba, they proceeded to Pegu. The air was filled with the odour of the perfumes burned on all the boats.

When they arrived at Pegu, the highest dignitaries of the court entered the water up to their knees, and lifting on their shoulders the litter with the tooth, carried it to the King's palace, and other noblemen all along the way, taking off their rich robes, laid them on the ground.

The tooth was deposited in the central courtyard of the palace, in a temporary structure ornamented with wonderful carvings, such as the Burmese alone know how to carve. The King prostrated himself on the ground, and remained so all the time the Punghees were reciting the pedigree of his royal house.

The tooth remained in this temporary abode for three months, until the temple erected purposely to keep it was finished.

Anthony Toscano adds, that the pomp was so great, and the expenditure so lavish, that, if the Emperor and all the Kings of Europe had put their riches together, they could not have afforded it. And the result was, that the people overtaxed and burdened with exactions rebelled against the King, who soon afterwards was dethroned.

Meanwhile King Don Juan and his Adigar Don Francis divided

1568 among themselves the four lakhs of cruzados, and enjoyed the fruit of their fraud laughing at the shabby trick they had played on the pagans. Although they had arranged the things secretly they could not resist the temptation relating it to some friends and soon the affair noised abroad so that a year had not elapsed when all Ceylon knew about it.

Wikrama Bahu, King of Kandy, who had succeeded his uncle Cumara Banda (he was a son of King Don Emmanuel Jayaweera), jealous of the successful commercial transaction of his cousin King Don Juan and his Adigar Don Francis Senerat Banda, determined now to try, if he too could not succeed in cheating the credulous King of Pegu. He sent to him an embassy with a letter denouncing Don Juan's and Senerat's fraud, stating at the same time that he alone was the possessor of Buddha's genuine tooth, and he would sell it cheaper if terms could be arranged, his envoy having full powers to arrange the transaction. And while awaiting the reply, he had a more or less exact imitation made, of the tooth destroyed at Goa and documents fabricated on ollas demonstrating its authenticity.

But before the arrival of his embassy the bubble had already burst. It seems that Mudeliyar Andrew Bayam had committed some indiscretion, news had come from Ceylon, and the King of Pegu was only too anxious to suppress all this affair which covered him with ridicule, the more so that all his people was indignant that he had made them worship Senerat Banda's fabrication instead of Buddha's tooth.

The King of Pegu therefore received with honor the embassy of the King of Kandy, but in the answer to his letter, made no mention whatever of the purchase of the new tooth. Wishing however to remain on good terms with the Kings of Ceylon he sent rich presents to Don Juan and to Wikrama Bahu and returned to the commander of the fort of Colombo all the Portuguese prisoners whom he had been detaining, among others Anthony Toscano.

Now King Wikrama Bahu was embarassed what to do with his tooth. The news that he had denied the authenticity of the tooth burned at Goa, and of the one sold to the King of Pegu, and declared himself sole possessor of the genuine article had spread throughout his kingdom, and many of his Buddhist subjects were indignant that he too had proposed to sell it.

Placed in this dilemma King Wikrama Bahu erected a shrine in a courtyard of his palace at Kandy. Deposed there his tooth with great solemnity, and prostrated himself before it, his subjects did the same. And such is the origin of the tooth of Buddha, which they now worship at the Dalada Maligawa at Kandy.

The fact of the destruction of the first tooth at Goa, was so well known at Ceylon, that neither the Tamils recognized Wikrama Bahu's fraud as the tooth of the White Monkey, nor the Moormen recognized it as the tooth of Adam. The Buddhists alone kept it as Buddha's tooth and worshipped it, at the beginning out of fear of their King, and afterwards out of sheer habit.

There are few events in the history of such unimportant

countries as was Ceylon at that epoch, that had been so well authenticated as the destruction of Buddha's tooth at Goa, and the subsequent frauds of Francis Senerat and King Wikrama Bahu.

Emmerson Tennent a former Lieutenant Governor of Ceylon, in his well known book on that Island Vol. II p. 199 says:

— „The fate of this renowned relic is so remarkable, and its „destruction related with so much particularity by the Portuguese „analysts and their European contemporaries, that no historical „doubt can be entertained, even were internal evidence wanting, „that the tooth now established at Kandy, is a spurious and „modern substitute for the original destroyed in 1560." —

And internal evidence is certainly not wanting: The tooth which at present is worshipped at Kandy is one and a half inches long and half an inch in diameter. They did not even give it the shape of a tooth.

Of course the educated Buddhists do not consider it as a genuine tooth of Buddha. It is certainly not a tooth. And if it is not a human tooth it cannot be Buddha's tooth. It is simply a fetish which they call Buddha's tooth.

## CHAPTER 7

# RAJA SINGHA

In the next year 1569 King Don Juan was married to the daughter of the late King of Kandy Don Emmanuel
1569 Jayaweera and sister to the present King Wikrama Bahu. Don Juan was then 30 years of age and the princess 24.

The commander of Colombo offered to the King two ships, commanded by Anthony Diaz de Lomba and Francis Gomez de Leitão, to bring his Queen from Trincomalee, and she was received in grand state at Colombo.

Since the siege of Kotta in 1565 Mayadunnè seems to have remained quiet and no mention is made of him until 1573 when he re-commenced the war with King Don Juan.

From the very beginning of the campaign, he shewed himself to be an enemy much more formidable than he had been before. During the nine years of peace he had organized his army. His son Raja Singha had drilled them as well as he could in European fashion. Big guns had been cast at a foundry established at Sitawacca and a large number of muskets made and kept in store.

Whilst his son Raja Singha supervised the armaments, old Mayadunnè versed as he was in all the intricacies of Oriental intrigues, endeavoured to gain to his sides the Buddhist chiefs in the kingdom of Kotta. He roused them against their Catholic King.

Having thus prepared himself for war, Mayadunnè invaded
1573 in 1573 King Don Juan's dominions.

This invasion was followed by the rising of Don Juan's Buddhist subjects.

All the partisans of old barbarity rallied round Mayadunnè. His name became the standard of the reaction against civilisation which, with the spread of Catholic Religion, the influence on the natives of their contact with the Portuguese, and King Don Juan's wise and enlightened government, was spreading rapidly in the south of Ceylon.

Don Juan's army was larger than that of Mayadunnè, but mostly composed of villagers of the coast who did not lack in courage but had not the fighting spirit of the mountaineers of the centre of the Island, less polished but more energetic. But he had the advantage of having at his disposal the Portuguese contingent, a mere handful of men, but to whom discipline and European tactics gave the upper hand over the native troops.

At the moment however when Mayadunnè had invaded the kingdom, the Portuguese commander had no troops to offer to the King. The treasury of Goa was empty and there was no hope of getting reinforcements from the metropolis.

The position was critical. Raja Singha was devastating the country. Mayadunnè was driving to rebellion the more powerful Buddhist chiefs, so that in a short time the whole territory of Kotta was conquered by the enemy and King Don Juan was reduced to the possession of Colombo alone.

Discouraged, reduced to great distress and such financial straits as he had never experienced in his life, the King appealed to the Pope and to the King of Portugal and complained bitterly of the commander of the fort of Colombo who himself was not better of and could not persuade the King that the fortunes of war are uncertain and changeable.

Mayadunnè at last triumphed; after forty-eight years, that he had been carrying on these wars, fortune seemed to smile on him for the first time.

But Don Juan's distress was of short duration. Diogo de Mello Cutinho, having been appointed for the second time commander of Colombo, brought reinforcements from Goa. He helped the King to re-conquer several of his provinces, whose inhabitants remained faithful to him but which had been delivered to Mayadunnè by their Buddhist chiefs. His forces however being insufficient, de Mello had to carry on a defensive war whose details are of no interest.

The hero of these wars, was Fr. Simon of Nazareth, whom we have already seen at the siege of Kotta. He was always with the Catholic soldiers. A man of indomitable courage, calm in the midst of most imminent danger, unarmed, with a Crucifix in his hand he exorted the dying, attended to the wounded. His sight alone inspired the soldiers.

In the first weeks of 1578, Diogo de Mello Cutinho was

1578 re-placed by Mathew Pereira de Sampayo, who continued a defensive war. But he was far from possessing the military talents and the experience of his predecessor, hence the balance turned again in favour of Mayadunnè.

On the 27th April 1579 Raja Singha laid siege to Colombo. It could hardly be called a siege, as, having no ships, the
1579 harbour remained open, and even from the land side, the town could not be completely blockaded. He nevertheless pitched his camp under the very walls of the city.

This state of things with intervals of truce and skirmishes lasted two years when, on the 18th February 1581
1581 Mathew d'Albuquerque, who, six years later was to become Viceroy, arrived with reinforcements.

Joining with the garrison, Albuquerque, attacked Raja Singha, who was defeated and had to seek safety in a hasty flight.

The victory was celebrated by a solemn procession of thanksgiving through the streets of Colombo.

Raja Singha had fled to Sitawacca, and soon the news spread through Ceylon that old Mayadunnè was dead. He was then 85 years of age.

The parricide Mayadunnè died by the hands of his son. Raja Singha had poisoned his father.

Raja Singha was 50 years of age, and thirsted for power. He could not hope to succeed Mayadunnè, as he was the youngest of his four sons, and moreover a bastard. He had the command of the army, that was his strength. On his return therefore from the siege of Colombo, he poisoned his old father and seized the power proclaiming himself Raja of Sitawacca.

Mayadunne, whose name resounded in Ceylon for sixty years, and who for 55 years posed as a pretender to the throne of Kotta, will always take a gloomy place in the history of his country.

A supporter of ancient barbarity against civilisation and Christianity, in order to attain the end of his ambition he caused floods of blood to be shed, the blood of his brethren, and he impoverished his country. From time to time the fortune of arms gave him an ephemeral power but, at the end of his career, after fifty-five years of fratricidal wars, his dominions did not extend over what he had got at the time when, together with his brother, he divided the spoils of their father whom they had murdered.

Notwithstanding all his intrigues, the mass of the population of the kingdom of Kotta, although the majority was still Buddhist, remained faithful to King Don Juan. Under his just and enlightened reign, and under the influence of Christianity they became civilised and cultured, and this march towards civilisation would have been much more rapid if the bloody invasions of Mayadunnè had not hindered the progress.

To the day of his death, Mayadunnè acted as a pretender, detested by the people whose King he aspired to be. The Singhalesé, an intelligent and clever race, naturally capable of high culture, appreciated too well the government of their Catholic King, to desire to exchange it for the rule of a cruel prince, who oppressed without pity his subjects, and a great number of the inhabitants of Sitawacca and Rayagam Korle fled from under his oppression and emigrated to the kingdom of Kotta.

There is no doubt that Mayadunnè was a man of character, to have been able with his scanty resources to sustain a war of 55 years, but history will always regard him as the personification of the reaction of paganism against Christianity, of barbarism against civilisation.

The parricide Raja Singha had become, by the help of the army, Raja of Sitawacca and Rayagam. He had no right to
1582 the throne being a younger son and a bastard, and he did not feel himself in security on his throne lest the people of his two states would side with the legitimate heir.

His first care therefore was to put to death his two elder brothers, and to exile the widow of his father to a place in the midst of the forests where she lived in fear and misery.

His third brother managed to escape,. and remained hidden in the mountains. Raja Singha discovered his retreat, and sent a company of soldiers to capture him. The unfortunate prince, afraid to fall into the hands of his cruel brother, took poison and made his wife and children do the same. At this sight, the men sent by Raja Singha to capture him could not restrain their tears.

These horrid crimes and other cruelties committed by Raja
1583 Singha, alienated from him his subjects. King Don Juan and the Portuguese commander of Colombo

thought it a favourable moment for a decisive blow, and, uniting their forces, they marched on Sitawacca, but Raja Singha was too experienced a warrior to be taken unaware.

At first he affected to despise his adversaries and sent against them one of his captains. The latter having been defeated, Raja Singha who, in the meantime had called to arms the veterans of his father's army, took up himself the campaign at the head of 150,000 men.

Not daring to attack the enemy in front, and being an expert in partizan warfare, he drew Don Juan's small army into an ambush which he had carefully laid in a place called Mooleriawe, where he attacked it at the same time from the front and from the rear.

Caught between two fires, in a narrow place where they could not use their artillery, King Don Juan and the Portuguese, lost 1,700 men, and had to make a hasty retreat to Colombo. Raja Singha remained master of the battle field.

Seeing that they had to do with more formidable forces than they had expected, Don Juan and the Portuguese commander sent for reinforcements to Goa.

The reinforcements having arrived, Don Juan with the
1584 Portuguese opened again the campaign.

Their army advanced along the Kelany river towards Sitawacca their implements of war being brought in boats up the river.

Raja Singha marched to meet them. He erected a battery in a place that commanded the course of the river, and armed it with two big guns that he had captured at Mooleriawe. Don Juan's army was advancing on the opposite side of the river. When the boats which were ahead, came within range of the guns, Raja Singha with a well directed fire, sent them all to the bottom of the river.

The King and the Portuguese having thus lost their ammunitions and implements of war, and also a great number of soldiers, had, of course, to retire, which however was done in good order. But the retreat was disastrous, for a party of Raja Singha's army had occupied in the rear some very strong positions, so that King Don Juan had to cut his way through the enemy to reach Colombo.

Raja Singha, intoxicated with these successes, was preparing to lay siege to Colombo, when he learned that Jayaweera II, King of Kandy who had succeeded Wikrama Bahu was taking up arms against him.

## CHAPTER 8

# XAVIER BANDA

Prompt in his decision, Raja Singha, knowing that after his defeats King Don Juan would not be able for some time to undertake a new campaign and, on the other hand, if the King of Kandy should attack him in the rear it could mean disaster, renounced to besiege Colombo and marched on Kandy with all his available troops.

The King of Kandy marched against him at the head of 60,000 men, an undisciplined rabble of untrained
1586 villagers mostly armed with spears and arrows and commanded by his cousin Veera Sundera, Raja of Peradeniya. The two armies met in the defile of Balane and the route was so complete that Veera Sundera could not even rally a sufficient number of men to protect the capital and had to seek his safety in flight.

Raja Singha entered Kandy. King Jayaweera with his Queen and his children sought refuge in the forests of the north of his kingdom, whence he proceeded to Manaar.

On hearing the news, King Don Juan hastened to his aid. He embarked for Manaar with a strong body of Singhalese troops, with the hope of joining there some Portuguese auxiliary forces and marched from Putlam on Kandy. But he arrived too late. King

Jayaweera II of Kandy was dead, and the Queen had preceded him by some weeks to the grave.

Jayaweera II, moved by the kindness with which the Portuguese and above all the Franciscan Father had received him, asked, a few weeks before death, to be baptised. He took the name of Philip. The Queen too had received Baptism on her death-bed. She wished to be called Mary and made a pious and edifying death.

King Don Philip Jayaweera recommended his children and his kingdom to the protection of the Portuguese. He had a son aged about twenty years, and a daughter Donna Catharina aged nine who had been baptised together with her mother.

The young prince was sent to Goa where he too was baptised under the name of Philip.

Some writers think that young prince Philip of Kandy was not the King's son, but his nephew whom the King had adopted and declared heir to the throne.

Among Don Philip's followers who had received Baptism together with him was a young man, his cousin. His pagan name was Wije Sundera, but he was commonly called Kunappu Banda and was the son of the Raja of Peradeniya Weera Sundera, the same who had lost the battle of Balane. Kunappu Banda took at his Baptism the name of Don Juan. This young man of great intellect and of striking beauty was destined to act a gloomy part in the history of Ceylon. He did not remain at Goa but returned to Colombo where he joined the King.

Meanwhile Raja Singha reigned at Kandy as the cruel tyrant he was in reality.

All those who did not pay him homage as their lawful King were put to death. In order to prevent a rebellion he had the Kandyans disarmed, a thing which was considered by these proud mountaineers as a supreme insult. He expelled the Franciscan Fathers and caused the church to be demolished.

Several Kandyan chiefs rebelled against him and joined the Raja of Peradeniya Weera Sundera who still resisted with the remnants of his army in one of the distant provinces, where they had proclaimed him King. But it was a royalty of very short duration. Drawn into an ambush Weera Sundera was made prisoner. He was brought in chains to Kandy, where Raja Singha condemned him to a horrid death: He was buried in earth up to the shoulders, and stones thrown at his head until he expired.

His elder son Don Juan Kunappu was then already at Colombo whilst his younger son Senevirat sought refuge on Adam's Peak where he remained in hiding dressed as a Bikshun.

The Raja of Peradeniya's cruel death however did not break the insurrection. On the contrary, exasperated by Raja Singha's cruelty and his tyrannical ways, the ranks of the rebels or rather of the defenders of their independence, were joined by other chiefs. At their head stood a royal prince, a Catholic, called Don Francis Cejaya Mudeliyar, better known by the name of Xavier Banda.

Xavier Banda gave proofs of great military talents, and gave a new life to the resistance. Weera Sundera was satisfied with a passive resistance in the mountains and forests of the interior. Xavier Banda took the offensive. He threw himself in the province of Uva, where his father had exercised a great influence, and whose inhabitants had not yet been disarmed by Raja Singha. He rose the whole province, organised resistance and was proclaimed King by the chiefs.

He accepted the title of King but, fervent Christian as he was, he did not allow himself to be led by pride. Laying aside all royal pomp, he continued his camp life, labouring hard for the liberation of his country from the yoke of the usurper. He entered into correspondence with King Don Juan, who encouraged him in his endeavours, promised him help and wrote to him that, in order not to raise the susceptibility of the Kandyans, he will place at the head of the troops he would send to help them, young Don Juan Kūnappu a prince of their own royal house.

These news rose the energy of the Kandyans. In the depths of their impenetrable forests they set themselves to make bows, spears and swords, and soon Xavier Banda informed King Don Juan, that they were ready for a general rising.

Meanwhile Raja Singha intoxicated by the conquest of Kandy, thought that with the death of the Raja of Peradeniya he had given the death blow to the insurrection. Thinking that he had sufficiently terrorised the Kandyan and having had them disarmed, he made little of Xavier Banda.

Inflated with his pride he now prepared to strike a great blow on King Don Juan and on the Portuguese. He commenced to make great preparations for the siege of Colombo, he drilled his army, and gathered together all the engines of siege in use at this epoch.

Nor did the Portuguese commander John Correa de Britto remain idle. He fortified the town and organized a corp of native soldiers commanded by Singhalese officers.

Before opening the campaign Raja Singha consulted the oracles to find out what would make the gods propitious, and he was answered that if he wished to conquer Colombo he must give innocent blood to the devil, much blood to drink and bathe in it.

Raja Singha then ordered fifty children below the age of ten years to be seized. They took them to the temple where they slaughtered them so that their blood flew unto a bucket which was placed before the idol of the goddess Kali.

And in order to render the devil more propitious he ordered the parents of the poor little children to be present at their slaughter.

After this horrid sacrifice Raja Singha proclaimed to his army that the gods would pour water into the Portuguese guns, and promised them a certain victory.

When the news of this awful deed reached Colombo the commander John Correa de Britto together with the ecclesiastical authorities, had services of expiations solemnly held. Holy Mass was celebrated in all the churches and processions in the streets.

Raja Singha appeared under the walls of Colombo with a

formidable force: 60,000 soldiers, 120 elephants drilled for war and 150 pieces of artillery.

The first assault took place on the 1st August 1586 the vigil of the Feast of Our Lady of the Snow.

The details of these battles are very interesting when we compare it with what is to-day the siege of a town. They fought hand to hand. Raja Singha's officers tore from the walls the Portuguese Standards, while the elephants with their tusks and their trunks carried away the guns from the ramparts.

De Conto relates in detail the stirring events of this siege which lasted nine months. He praises the bravery and skilful tactics of John de Britto, mentions the names of all those who distinguished themselves by their gallantry, and speaks highly of four Missionaries: Fr. Edward Chanoça, Commissary of the Franciscans in Ceylon, two other Franciscans, Fr. Louis of the Conception, Guardian of Colombo, and Fr. Emmanuel of Jesus, and a secular priest, Fr. Peter Diaz. Fr. de Queiros mentions another secular priest, Fr. Diogo Nunez who performed, he says, prodigies of heroism.

The great disadvantage for Raja Singha was, that having no ships, he could not shut up the town from the sea-side, so that it could be easily revictualled.

Some interesting details of the siege are given by an eye-witness, the Englishman Ralph Fitch, who, on his way from Bengal to England landed then at Colombo:

— „ We remained, he says, five days at Colombo to take water. Ceylon is a very fertile and beautiful Island, but for reason of the continual wars with the King, foodstuff is dear and rare and the

Portuguese who keep there a fort get all their provisions from Bengal.

The King besieged Colombo with 100,000 men. All his soldiers are naked, but there are among them several who are very clever with the musket. The King is dressed in a fine cotton cloth, beautifully dyed which hangs from the middle and covers the legs. He wears a very fine cloth on his head. The rest of his body is naked.

The elephants are not so big as those of Pegu which are enormous. The houses are small and built of cadjan. " —

Whilst Raja Singha was besieging Colombo, Xavier Banda was strengthening himself more and more in the province of Uva, and had become effectually the ruler of this part of the kingdom of Kandy.

King Don Juan had sent him an auxiliary force and 200 Portuguese under the command of young Don Juan Kunappu, who evinced more than ordinary military talents. All the Kandyans rallied around the son of their former chief. Kandy was re-taken, and the garrisons which Raja Singha had established in other places expelled.

Not satisfied of having re-conquered the whole kingdom
1587 of Kandy, they invaded Raja Singha's own territory and threatened Sitawacca.

Then Raja Singha who was besieging Colombo already for nine months, raised the siege in May 1587 and hastened to defend his hereditary States. But Don Juan Kunappu showed himself a formidable antagonist and always defeated him.

Whilst Don Juan Kunappu wrested from Raja Singha one district after the other, the Portuguese made a diversion in the south. Thomas de Sousa d'Aronches, pushed on as far as Dondra the southerly point of Ceylon, and destroyed the temple which was built on the promontory dominating the sea. He caused the idols to be thrown in the sea and took away considerable treasures.

Don Juan Kunappu in the centre of the Island marched from success to success, so that before the end of the year 1587, King Don Juan of Kotta found himself master of the greater part of Ceylon; he had re-conquered the kingdom of Kandy with the exception of the Uva province and the district of Chilaw which were in the hands of his friend and ally, Xavier Banda, re-established in its former limits the kingdom of Kotta and gained some districts from Raja Singha.

Raja Singha saw himself reduced to a small territory. His power was broken for ever. His glory had lasted only six years.

## CHAPTER 9

# SAGARA II

### KING OF JAFFNA

Whilst these events were taking place in the southern part of
1587 Ceylon, no less important things were happening in the north.

Peria Raja, King of Jaffna was taking no heed of the treaty which his predecessor had concluded with Don Constantine de Braganza.

He did not acknowledge the Portuguese protectorate, persecuted the Christians, and his rule was more tyrannical if possible than that of Sagara Raja I. At last, he put into his head to recover Manaar and landed in that Island at the head of an army. He was repulsed by the garrison of the Portuguese fort and fled to Jaffna.

The Viceroy, fearing lest this barbarous prince should ally himself with Raja Singha then master of the kingdom of Kandy, which would certainly endanger the Portuguese interests in Ceylon, and to avenge Peria Raja's aggression on Manaar decided to send a punitive expedition to Jaffna.

He gave its command to Andrew Furtado de Mendoza with instructions to dethrone Peria Raja, and if he were taken prisoner to put him to death.

In order to have him trained in European military tactics the Viceroy persuaded young prince Don Philip, the rightful heir to the throne of Kandy, to join the expedition.

Andrew Furtado de Mendoza was a renowned warrior, but what was more admired in him by his contemporaries, was not so much his courage and experience in military matters, as the great sanctity of his life.

On leaving Cannanore where he had received the Viceroy's orders, he recommended himself to the prayers of the Franciscan Fathers, and distributed abundant alms to the poor.

After a short stay at Goa he hastened to Manaar, where he was to organize the expedition. He was received there with great pomp. The commander of the fort with the whole garrison, the Clergy both Jesuits and Franciscans, and a large crowd of people met him at the landing. They took him under a canopy of cloth of gold to the church, where he prostrated himself before the Altar invoking the blessing of God. All were edified by his piety and his humility.

The preparations ended, Furtado held a council of war to which he called the two Franciscan Fathers Edward Chanoça and Francis of the East. None better than these venerable men had the experience of the affairs of Ceylon where they now worked for 45 years.

The Portuguese force left Manaar on the 26th October 1587, and the next day landed on the coast of Jaffna.

On the 28th, the Feast of the Apostles St. Simon and Jude, all officers and soldiers, having confessed on the previous evening, received Holy Communion. Fr. Edward celebrated a solemn Mass and gave benediction, and then they marched on Jaffna, and the evening found them encamped under the walls of the city.

Next morning, they stormed the walls; the defeat of the Jaffnese was complete, the town was taken. The King had taken to flight, but was found hiding in a temple, brought before Andrew Furtado de Mendoza who, obeying to the Viceroy's orders, had him beheaded.

The Queen and all the royal family were among the prisoners.

After having celebrated his victory by a solemn Te Deum, Furtado de Mendoza hastened to reassure the people and to restore order in the city. He allowed his soldiers to pillage the King's palace, but forbade them to touch private property.

Then, having called a meeting of the chiefs and of the principal inhabitants of the town,. who at the bottom of their heart were not displeased of having been liberated from Peria Raja's tyranny, he reassured them again and made them swear fidelity to the King of Portugal, then he swore in their presence that he would guard faithfully all their right and privileges.

Master of the kingdom of Jaffna, Andrew Furtado de Mendoza took seriously to heart the organisation of his conquest. He re-established order and confidence among the people, took measures to hinder the chiefs from oppressing the villagers, promoted agriculture and trade. Nor did he forget the Missions.

In his zeal for the conversion of this poor heathen people, he did all in his power to establish the apostolate on a strong basis. Several churches were built. The largest was erected in Jaffna under the title of Our Lady of Victory, which name was later, on account of the number of graces obtained in that sanctuary, changed in that of Our Lady of Miracles.

The Franciscan Convent was enlarged and a College annexed to it, in which solid education was given to a large number of boys. A new Mission was also started in the Island of Tanadiwa.

The kingdom thus re-organised, the question arose, what form of government was to be established, the policy of the Portuguese at that time excluding the idea of annexing any part of Ceylon to their Indian possessions. All they wanted was free trade in the Island, and to protect this trade, the garrisons which they held at Colombo and at Manaar were sufficient.

After having heard his Council and the Superiors of the Mission, Furtado de Mendoza decided to chose, among

1588 the members of the royal family, to which the people seemed to be attached, a prince, whose character gave a guarantee that he would make a wise and just Ruler, and proclaim him King of Jaffna, on the conditions of the treaty of 1560, that is that he would accept the Portuguese protectorate and pay to the Viceroy a yearly tribute.

The choice fell on a prince named Henderamana Singha Cumara, who was much beloved by the people, and he was proclaimed King under the name of Sagara Raja II, with the condition however that he should only act as Regent till his elevation to the throne had been confirmed by the Viceroy.

After having placed on the throne of Jaffna King Sagara Raja II, Andrew Furtado de Mendoza returned to Manaar where he distributed alms to the poor and expended large sums of money as dowries to poor orphan girls to enable them to marry honestly.

On his return to Goa he begged to be admitted into the Franciscan Order as a lay Brother. But the Superior of the Convent earnestly dissuaded him from doing so, pointing out that in his high position he could do more for the glory of God and the propagation of the Holy Faith. Twice again Furtado repeated his entreaties, at last, obedient to the advice of his spiritual director, he re-entered the public career. In 1609 he was acting Viceroy and then returned to Lisbon.

Andrew Furtado de Mendoza was a model of a Christian knight. His piety and humility were great. He preserved his virginity to the day of his death. Once, when at prayer during the siege of Malacca by the Dutch, the Blessed Virgin Mary had appeared to him.

## CHAPTER 10

# PHILIP II

### King of Kandy

The Kandyans after having regained their independence with
1587 the aid of the King of Kotta, getting over their first enthusiasm, began to doubt if they had not only changed one master for another. King Don Juan's army occupied the country, a Portuguese garrison was stationed in the capital, and in the north Furtado de Mendoza governed the kingdom of Jaffna which he had conquered, and it was not yet known if it would not be annexed to the Portuguese possessions in India. These facts greatly perturbed the Kandyans who were jealous of their independence.

To calm their apprehensions, Andrew Furtado de Mendoza, sent to Kandy prince Philip, the son of the late King Philip I Jayaweera who, as said above had accompanied him on his expedition to Jaffna, to take possession of the throne of which he was the rightful heir.

Furtado had the power to take this step, his command extending over the whole Island, he therefore acted in Ceylon as the representative of the Viceroy.

Before leaving Jaffna, Don Philip paid homage to the King of Portugal and signed a treaty by which he recognized the Portuguese protectorate over the kingdom of Kandy. The treaty was signed by Don Philip and by Furtado and countersigned as witnesses by the Franciscan Fathers: Bartholomew of St. Sebastian Guardian of Jaffna, Peter of Drago and Rodrigo de Chagos.

Thus, by the treaties with the King of Kotta in 1517, with the King of Jaffna in 1560 and with the King of Kandy in 1587, the King of Portugal had acquired rights of suzerainty over the whole Island of Ceylon.

When sending Don Philip to Kandy, Andrew Furtado de Mendoza ignored that Xavier Banda had already been proclaimed King of the chiefs. Xavier was powerful, and had many followers so that there was danger of a conflict. But Xavier Banda acted as a true Christian. He wrote to Don Philip that, in order not to create dissensions and perhaps shedding the blood of his brethren in this rather critical moment, and thus preventing perhaps that the throne of Kandy were occupied by a Catholic King; seeing that Don Philip was the rightful heir, he renounced to the crown which had been given to him by the chiefs and which he had already worn for nearly a year, recognized him as King, swore him allegiance and offered him his support.

Young King Don Philip made his entry into Kandy with great pomp, the Portuguese garrison of the town having been put at his disposal, he was installed in the royal palace, where Xavier Banda came to pay him homage and offer him his services.

As said above; Raja Singha had expelled the Missionaries from Kandy, now with a Catholic King on the throne, Fathers Edward Chanoça and Francis of the East re-organized the Mission and re-built the Church of the Immaculate Conception.

Don Juan Kunappu was appointed commander-in-chief of the army. He was disheartened and disappointed, for he had hoped that, in return for the great services he had rendered, the Portuguese would have set aside the rightful heir and conferred on him the crown of Kandy.

Nevertheless, he dissembled his anger and with the other chiefs paid homage to King Philip II.

In the bitterness of his heart he went to consult an astrologer and asked him what should he do to become King of Kandy. The astrologer gave him a subtle poison.

Meanwhile the Portuguese fortified Kandy and embellished the city which had been partially destroyed by Raja Singha and being satisfied of having placed a Catholic King on the throne, they surrendered into his hands the government of the kingdom and retired to Colombo whence they could more easily watch Raja Singha's movements.

Don Juan Kunappu was waiting for this opportunity. His intimacy with King Philip, his cousin, facilitated his perfidious designs. Scarcely had the Portuguese left Kandy when he found his way to administer to the young King the poison given him by the astrologer. Impatient to attain his end, it seemed to him that the poison did not act quick enough, he repeated the dose, and the King died.

Don Juan Kunappu assembled then his adherents, and he had many, thanks to the glory he had acquired during his campaign against Raja Singha and the fact that in truth it was he who had delivered the country from the tyranny of the usurper. In vain did old Fr. Francis of the East, whom he held in great veneration, exhort him not to stain again with a bloody civil war his country, which had already suffered so much. Don Juan Kunappu led by his pride and his ambition would listen to no advice.

Working on the superstition of the pagans, Don Juan Kunappu took possession of the tooth of Buddha, or rather of its duplicate, which had been made by King Wikrama Bahu and which had been taken from the Dalada Maligawa temple and hidden by the Bikshun, to prevent it from falling into the hands of Raja Singha. As said above the original of this tooth was believed to give to its owner the sovereignty of the whole Island, and Don Juan Kunappu who, as a Christian, certainly did not believe in the magic of the fetish, and well knew that the present tooth was only a fraud, nevertheless he seized it in order to impress the superstitious minds of the Kandyans.

At the first news of the death of King Philip and of Don Juan Kunappu's rebellion, Xavier Banda hastened to Kandy. He placed the royal treasury in safety and proclaimed King Don Philip's infant son, Don Juan I. But soon perceiving that, in face of the strong faction of Don Juan Kunappu, which was getting the upper hand he would not be able to maintain the boy on the throne, he thought of saving the life of the royal child and sent him to Colombo under the protection of the King Don Juan Dharmapala.

The news of the treason of Don Juan Kunappu fell like a thunderbolt on the Portuguese, who had not even suspected that, in presence of a rightful heir to the throne, he would not be satisfied with his appointment as commander-in-chief of the army, a position which gave him the first rank after the King.

The Portuguese garrison had left Kandy but a few days ago and not yet reached Colombo. When the news reached them they remained encamped at Gonoor, and the officer in command sent a messenger to the captain of Manaar John de Mello asking for reinforcements.

Meanwhile they received the summons of Don Juan Kunappu to evacuate Gonoor within six days, and, to enforce this peremptory order he advanced against them at the head of his forces. Their position at Gonoor being untenable, the Portuguese fell back on Colombo. Next day John de Mello arrived with reinforcements, but he was too late. Don Juan Kunappu had occupied all the strategical positions which defended the approach of Kandy and, to dislodge him would require a larger force than de Mello had at his disposal.

Don Juan Kunappu was master of Kandy, he did not dare however to assume the title of King, as he feared to alienate the yet powerful party of the old dynasty which was represented by two children, the infant King Don Juan I and his aunt Donna Catharina aged eleven.

# CHAPTER 11

## DONNA CATHARINA

The fears of Don Juan Kunappu were not without cause, for the majority of the Kandyans, faithful to their royal
1587 house, not only did not recognize him as King, but resolved to avenge on him the murder of Philip II.

The powerful Xavier Banda placed himself at their head, he gathered round him many Kandyan chiefs and prepared to resist the usurper.

Xavier Banda asked the commander of Colombo for help, but Francis de Silva knew from experience that Don Juan Kunappu was not an adversary to be treated lightly, and he had not sufficient troops at his disposal.

He took profit therefore of the passage through Colombo, on his way from Malacca to Goa, of Peter Lopez de Sousa, one of the eminent men at this epoch in India and asked him to explain to the Viceroy the position of the affairs at Ceylon.

As soon as he arrived at Goa Peter Lopez de Sousa put the question before the Viceroy Eduard de Menezes Count of Tarouca and before his Council. He represented the great strategical importance of Ceylon and the danger to the Portuguese of losing the position they have gained in the Island, and if they lost that position which unavoidably would be the case, if they were to find themselves face to face with two such enemies as Don Juan Kunappu and Raja Singha, they would be obliged to recover their lost position, what would not be an easy matter once the Portuguese had lost their prestige.

Lopez de Sousa's opinion had always a great weight in the Council of the Viceroy and an expedition was decided upon.

The Viceroy offered the command to Lopez de Sousa, but he refused on the plea of his old age and pointing out that this honour was due by right to the commander of Colombo Francis de Silva, who was certainly an able man and knew better than himself the country and the manner of warfare of the Kandyans. But the Viceroy and the Council insisted and Lopez de Sousa seeing that his refusal might cause the failure of the expedition which he considered so necessary in the interest of the Portuguese in the East, finally accepted the command.

Francis de Silva felt greatly offended, and it is said that, when required, he did not give the expedition the support he should have given.

Lopez de Sousa nevertheless, would not accept the command but on two conditions:

The first was that the expedition should not have for object the conquest of the kingdom of Kandy, but only to drive out the usurper Don Juan Kunappu and place the lawful King on the throne. This he said was the only way to assure success, for the majority of the Kandyans would rally around him. Otherwise, deep as was their love of independence, they would rather support the usurper than accept foreign yoke.

This condition was unanimously accepted by the Council.

But it was objected that Don Juan Philip II's son was but an infant. A long regency would follow, and under the present unsettled circumstances it would be rather dangerous as more than one of the powerful chiefs would attempt to seize the power. In order to avoid civil wars it would be necessary to keep in Kandy a strong Portuguese garrison, which seeing the young age of the King would have the appearance of a permanent occupation, and would certainly hurt the susceptibilities of the Kandyans.

They therefore decided to pass over the rights of the infant Don Juan, and to proclaim Queen of Kandy Donna Catharina the daughter of Philip I Jayaweera and sister to Philip II. She too was yet a child, having scarcely passed the age of eleven, but, in two years she could be married, and they should see to give her a husband capable of governing the Kingdom.

This decision was not an act of injustice to the infant prince Don Juan. The throne of Kandy was to a certain degree elective: according to the custom, after the death of the King, his Ministers, the three Adigars had the right to choose as his successor any prince of the royal house, and their election confirmed by the people by acclamation. In the present unsettled state of affairs, when there were no rightful Adigars, the right of election devolved on the Representative of the Lord paramount, the Viceroy.

It is true that the boy Don Juan had been proclaimed King by Xavier Banda. But it was an irregular election, and, that Donna Catharina's appointment was in conformity with the laws of the country is demonstrated by the fact that the Kandyan chiefs had no difficulty to recognize her as their lawful Queen.

The second condition proposed by Lopez de Sousa caused the highest degree of astonishment in the Viceroy's Council, and it was generally supposed that he only laid it down to get rid of the command of the expedition to which he did not aspire and which was being forced on him. He asked that Donna Catharina be given in marriage to his son Peter who would thus become King of Kandy.

Though such demand seemed extravagant, the majority of the Councillors, who wanted at all cost that the command of the expedition be given to Lopez de Sousa whom they considered as the man to bring it to a successful issue, began to argue that, after all the young Queen would have to be married, and that her husband should be a Catholic. Now the only princes of royal blood who could aspire to be her husband were Don Juan Kunappu, a rebel, and his brother Senevirat a Bikshu and a sort of barbarian. Both therefore were excluded. Why then should the young Queen not marry a Portuguese. Peter de Sonsa was of high lineage. His fidelity could not be doubted, and once King of Kandy he could easily lead his subjects to the Catholic Faith, and this was what Philip I now King of Portugal (Philip II in Spain) had most at heart.

These reasons prevailed in the Council and Lopez de Sousa's demand was unanimously granted on the conditions that the thing should be kept secret until the Queen had attained the age of twelve, and that before the marriage Donna Catharina and Peter de Sousa should take the oath of fidelity to the King of Portugal as their Suzerain, after which they would be left absolute masters of the Kingdom of Kandy.

The Viceroy gave to Lopez de Sousa the title of Governor of Ceylon, not because he would have to rule over the
1588 Island, which was governed by native Kings, but for the reason that he was too high a dignitary of the State to be appointed simple commander or captain of Colombo as they were officially called which corresponded to the rank of a Colonel. The Viceroy gave him therefore the rank of a Governor.

Lopez de Sousa left Goa at the beginning of 1588. He landed at Colombo and opened immediately the campaign. At Negombo he received a message from Xavier Banda, who put himself at the disposal of Queen Donna Catharina with an army of 25,000 men. These were good news, as the help of this powerful chief would decide the campaign in favour of the Queen.

Meanwhile Don Juan Kunappu, with an army of 30 to 40,000 men hastened to meet the enemy. He hoped to surprise old Lopez de Sousa who had only 4,000 men of whom 1,474 were Europeans before his junction with Xavier Banda's forces. But he was late, the two armies had already united, and he was defeated in a decisive battle.

Then nearly all the chiefs whom he had drawn to his party deserted his cause, to rally round that of Donna Catharina whom they considered as their lawful Sovereign, and Don Juan Kunappu vanquished and pursued fled to the forests where, fearing to be recognized, he lived for several weeks on roots and wild fruits.

The road to Kandy lay open. Lopez de Sousa and Xavier Banda entered the city without opposition.

They proclaimed Queen Donna Catharina, who was acclaimed

by the chiefs and by the people in Kandy and in the provinces.

It now remained to bring the Queen to Kandy. Since the death of her parents, she lived at Manaar under the care of a Portuguese lady Catherine d'Abreu wife of Gabriel Colaço who had been a friend to her mother.

The idea of returning to Kandy frightened the young Queen, she was only eleven years of age. She remembered the war with Raja Singha, the misfortunes of her father, their flight through the wild forests, the recent murder of her brother King Philip, all these sad memories filled the poor girl with terror. She begged with tears to be allowed to remain in her peaceful retreat of Manaar. She seemed to have the presentiment of the misfortunes that were to fall upon her. Finally she had to submit, and preparations were made for her departure.

Lopez de Sousa had sent from Kandy a brilliant escort to accompany her, Catherine d'Abreu Colaço had also to come, and they were joined by four Missionaries, two Jesuits and two Franciscans who were going to Kandy to take care of the Christians, as Fr. Anthony Schipano S. J. who had come with the troops from Goa, was unable alone to make all the work.

As the young Queen entered the rich palanquin in which she had to be carried to Kandy, the pole broke, and Donna Catharina got out of the palanquin saying with tears that it was a bad omen, that she would not go to Kandy. Then the commander of Manaar, who had been as a father to the royal orphan, took her by the hand and said:—„My child, we are Christians and such superstitious thoughts are unworthy of the followers of Jesus. Place all your confidence in God."—

Then the journey commenced. Eight days later, the young Queen with her brilliant retinue approached Kandy amidst an enthusiastic crowd. Lopez de Souza and Xavier Banda met her at the gates of the city, and her entrance into the town was a most splendid sight. Handful of gold coins were thrown to the people, 19 barrels, says an old chronicler; they reached the royal palace and three days later Donna Catharina was solemnly enthroned.

The reign of the young Queen seemed to have opened under happy auspices. All the people rallied round her, and it seemed as if peace and the progress of religion and civilisation would inaugurate a new era.

The rebel Don Juan Kunappu was in hiding and a price had been set for his capture. Notwithstanding the fact, the daring adventurer visited Kandy more than once in disguise to sow disaffection among the people and encourage his followers.

Lopez de Sousa and Xavier Banda reassured by their easy success relaxed their vigilance. The Portuguese troops, living in idleness and inaction were demoralized and their discipline grew lax. The native troops, hordes of unruly men, gave themselves up to the most brutal abuses.

Don Juan Kunappu, with his inborn cleverness and activity, availed himself of these circumstances to create disaffection among the people.

In the meantime Queen Donna Catharina had completed her twelfth year, Xavier Banda who had been the chief
1589 instrument of her restoration on her paternal throne, conceived the desire of marrying the young Queen. Being a cousin to her father the late King Philip I Jayaweera, he thought that his high birth and the eminent services he had rendered, gave him the right to aspire to her hand.

He opened his mind to Lopez de Sousa, who bound to keep secret that the hand of the Queen has been promised to his son Peter, answered evasively. He said that the Queen could not be married without the consent of her Suzerain, and that consequently the sanction of the King of Portugal was required.

Xavier Banda insisted. He suspected that there was something hidden under the Governor's answer as he was well aware that there was no need to apply to Lisbon and await the reply one year and perhaps more when the Viceroy had all the necessary powers. At last, one day, excited with anger he told to Lopez de Sousa: — „ Is that the recompense for all my services? You will bitterly repent of your refusal!" —

It is difficult to trace clearly what happened afterwards: Some old writers say that, in the first transport of anger he betrayed his Sovereign and entered into correspondence with Don Juan Kunappu offering to help him to seize the throne of Kandy on condition that he would appoint him Raja of Uva.

This hardly seems probable. Xavier Banda knew well that his marriage with Donna Catharina would be very popular among the Kandyans. He knew further, that nearly all the Portuguese officers, who were ignorant of the arrangements made in Goa, were in his favour for, in their opinion, there was not a man in Ceylon more fit to be placed at the side of Donna Catharina on the throne of Kandy, and the best proof, that he still hoped to obtain his end is that a few days after the quarrel we see him reconciled with Lopez de Sousa.

On the other hand, what would he gain by helping Don Juan to seize the throne of Kandy? Certainly, the rebel prince would accept all his conditions, and would show him every consideration in order to obtain the end of his ambition. But once firmly established on the throne, he would not fail to take a terrible vengeance for the wrongs and the ignominy he had suffered at Xavier Banda's hands.

Why should Xavier Banda offer to his enemy the crown to which he himself aspired, when he was powerful enough, in spite of Lopez de Sousa, and in spite of the Portuguese to marry Donna Catharina, the more so that it was an open secret that the young Queen was in love with him.

We are therefore inclined to believe rather the other version of the chroniclers who say: that Don Juan Kunappu, who, in his hiding place was always well informed by his spies of all that passed in Kandy, knew that Xavier Banda aspired to the hand of the Queen and that after having fallen out with Lopez de Sousa he got reconciled with him.

These news disturbed him greatly for he well understood that the union of the Queen with the powerful chief, would destroy for ever his chances of becoming King of Kandy.

Crafty, and always ready to meet whatever emergency he had recourse to a ruse:

He wrote a letter to Xavier Banda worded in such a way, as to appear to be an answer to advances made to him by Xavier. He wrote that he approved Xavier Banda's plan to murder Lopez de Sousa, to slaughter all the Portuguese, and deliver the town to him, and proclaim him King, and assured him that in recompense for this service he would make him Raja of Uva. He added that, as every thing was now ready Xavier Banda should no more delay to put his plan into execution.

Don Juan, confided this treacherous letter to a faithful servant instructing him, to allow himself to be arrested by the Portuguese outposts when pretending to be attempting to penetrate into the town of Kandy.

The ruse was fully successful, the messenger was captured and the letter delivered into Lopez de Sousa's hands. The old warrior saw at a glance the gravity of the disaster which would follow a rupture with Xavier Banda. He resolved without a moment's hesitation to make the sacrifice of his son's interests.

He assembled his officers and after having given them the letter to read he explained them the gravity of the situation, and said that there was no other way of getting out of it but the immediate sanction of Xavier Banda's marriage with the Queen Donna Catharina.

Some of the officers expressed the same opinion, but others objected saying, that it would have been a solution if the marriage had been sanctioned earlier, but now, that they had such evident proof of his treason, to put into his hands the supreme power as husband of the Queen, would only increase the danger, and after a short discussion they decided to get rid of Xavier Banda.

A few days later Xavier Banda who, suspected nothing, was attending a reception at Lopez de Sousa's residence. He wore on his breast a cross of exquisite native workmanship richly studded with rubies. Lopez de Souza having admired the jewel asked Xavier to lend it to him for a few days as he desired to have made one like it. The moment that Xavier Banda bent his head to take off the gold chain to which the cross was attached a Portuguese officer who stood behind him plunged a dagger into his back.

Thus died the great Catholic chief, on whom rested such great expectations.

When they announced to Donna Catharina what had happened, the poor child exclaimed with horror: — „ What have you done, his death will be for me and for you the beginning of unspeakable misery." —

The murder of Xavier Banda was the turning point in the history of the Portuguese in Ceylon. With that dastardly deed they had sealed their doom.

The news of Xavier Banda's murder exasperated the Kandyans. Not only Xavier's army of 20,000 men, but all those who had rallied under de Sousa's standard after Donna Catharina's elevation to the throne, left the town with their chiefs. Many returned to their homes, others, and they were by far the greater number, passed over to Don Juan Kunappu who had left his hiding place and now called upon the Kandyans to avenge the death of Xavier.

Thus, in a day the proscribed fugitive found himself at the head of an army of 25,000 men while Lopez de Sousa who had entered Kandy in triumph was reduced to the handful of men he had brought from Goa.

Don Juan did not march on Kandy; that was too easy a prey. He knew the Portuguese must quit the city, and he had determined to cut off their retreat. He threw himself on the road which led from Kandy to Colombo, if one can call a road a narrow tract which ran across mountains and forests on which scarcely few men could advance abreast. He had large trees cut and thrown over the footpaths, and dispersed his men so that they could harass without ceasing the handful of Portuguese.

Meanwhile, Lopez de Sousa, great leader amidst reverse, as he was on the days of triumph, seeing that all was lost, only thought of saving the young Queen and the few hundreds Portuguese, the remains of his army. He sent a messenger to Colombo asking for urgent help and commence his retreat towards that city. On the evening of the 5th October they camped at Gonoor. On the 7th they reached the narrow valley of Balane. Hardly had they entered it, when they heard the rolling of drums. Don Juan Kunappu had cut their retreat. Lopez de Souza gave then orders to fall back on Gonoor, but Don Juan had already closed the entrance to the valley. They were surrounded. It was late in the evening.

Lopez de Souza after having ascertained how far his position was desperate told to his soldiers that there was no hope and that they must prepare for death.

They passed the night in prayer. Before dawn, Fr. Anthony Schipano S. J. celebrated the Holy Mass and gave the Holy Communion to the soldiers, then taking the Crucifix he told them to adore Jesus Christ their Saviour and blessed them.

They ranged themselves in battle order and awaited the enemy.

At 7 o'clock in the morning a cloud of arrows fell upon them from the jungle on the mountain side and they were slaughtered without even being able to see the enemy. It was the signal of the battle. The Kandyans rushed upon them. The Portuguese performed prodigies of valour. Two Franciscans Fr. Simon of Luz and Emmanuel Pereira were killed when attending the dying and the wounded. They fought for three hours and at 10 o'clock, when the battle ceased, there remained only a small number of Portuguese covered with bleeding wounds.

Among the few survivors was Lopez de Sousa. He was taken before Don Juan, who treated him with great consideration, got native doctors to attend to his wounds, but all the care with which he was surrounded was in vain. On the third day, feeling himself on the point of death he sent for Don Juan, and recommended to him his young son Diogo who was among the prisoners, and Don

Juan, respecting the dying warrior's last wish set the youth free and sent him to Colombo with an escort.

The fate of prisoners who fell into the hands of pagan chiefs was not so fortunate.

Sixty, others say one hundred and twenty Portuguese, fell into hands of a Buddhist chief. He had them brought before him and ordered their captains Philip Toscano and Ruy d'Eça to deny their Faith, thinking that their example would entice the soldiers. When they refused he had them tied to trees and threatened to have them put to death. Both replied they would be happy to die for Jesus Christ. He then ordered an arrow to be shot at Ruy d'Eça's heart. They did it, but the wound not being mortal, he caused red hot irons to be applied to the wounds which he had received during the battle. D'Eça died under this torture. In the meantime Philip Toscano recited in a loud voice the profession of Faith. The Kandyan chief ordered him to be killed with arrows.

A soldier, whose name unfortunately is not known, seeing his officers die, approached the chief and told him, that he too desired to die for his Faith. They brought an elephant, who after throwing him several times in the air, threw him face downwards, and, placing his footh on his back and, after having torn off his arms and his legs, crushed his head.

In vain did they exhort the soldiers to deny their Faith, they were all tied to trees and pierced with arrows. Their martyrdom took place on the 9th of October.

Several Missionaries had followed the army. We have mentioned two of them who died on the battlefield when administering to the dying. Fr. Peter of Christ had also fallen on the battlefield. They thought he was dead but, after the battle, when the Kandyans were despoiling the corpses, they found him still breathing. According to their barbarous custom they cut off his nostrils and took him prisoner. Fr. Andrew de Chagas, fell into the hands of a Pagan chief who had him strangled.

Fr. Luke, whom we had already mentioned in the siege of Kotta in 1563 was at that time Superior of the Mission.

He was made prisoner by a chief, an apostate, whom he had himself instructed and baptized. The wretch had become a Christian for wordly motives under the short reign of Philip II. Not content of having apostatized himself, he wished to force the Priest who had befriended him to renounce to his Faith. Weakened by the wounds which he had received the previous day in the battle, all covered with blood, Fr. Luke, with apostolic courage reproached the wretch for his crimes. He ordered the Father to be tied to the stake and pierced through the heart with a lance.

Fr. Luke was born at Cannanore. He was a little boy, when in January 1545 St. Francis Xavier passing through that town. One day that the boy had committed some mischief and it seems that it happened rather frequently, his father was complaining to St. Francis Xavier: — „Fr. Francis, he said, Gregory is a great rascal.“ — „Leave the child alone, answered the Saint, he will become a great servant of God.“ —

Among historians, Fr. de Queiros and Fr. M. da Civezza say, that Fr. Luke was put to death by Don Juan himself. This is not admissible. History distinctly states that the Martyr was put to death by a chief whom he had himself instructed and baptized. Now Fr. Luke was parish Priest at Kandy, whence expelled by Raja Singha he retired to Colombo. Don Juan was instructed at Manaar and baptized at Goa. He certainly was not a fervent Catholic, but he never apostatized formally, and, if later, to please his Buddhist subjects, he sometimes took part in their idolatrous ceremonies, at the time when these events took place, he was rather disposed to show himself a Christian. None of the other Authors, even those who call him an apostate reproach Don Juan with Fr. Luke's death.

On the contrary, he himself treated his prisoners with much consideration, but he could not hinder, after the bloody day of Balane, the acts of cruelty committed by the Pagan chiefs, who had joined him, but whose master he was not yet.

Fr. Schipano S. J. was severely wounded whilst administering the Sacraments to the dying, and he too fell in the hands of the Kandyans. They led him to the temple and wished him to sacrifice to the idols. The Father was awaiting the palm of martyrdom, when Don Juan, hearing what was happening had him brought to Kandy, and set him free together with two Franciscan Fathers Francis of Christ and Peter of Lisbon and gave them an escort as far as the frontier of the kingdom of Kotta, in order that they be not molested on their way. He retained prisoners two other Franciscans, Fr. Louis and Fr. Gonsalo da Rosa, but as they were free to go about in the town, they administered to the spiritual wants of the Catholics of Kandy.

Don Juan Kunappu intoxicated with success, committed an atrocious action. The young Queen Donna Catharina being his prisoner he dishonoured her openly in the presence of his whole army, then taking her to Kandy he forced her to become his wife. The girl resisted with an energy above her age, but finally had to yield. The marriage amidst the tears of the unhappy Queen was celebrated with extraordinary pomp.

The marriage of Don Juan with Donna Catharina made him in the eyes of the people the lawful Sovereign of Kandy. He took the title of King and, according to the old Kandyan custom changed his name into that of Wimala Dharma.

## CHAPTER 12

# THE END OF RAJA SINGHA

The Kandyan chiefs made no difficulty in acknowledging as their King Don Juan Kunappu, now called Wimala
1590 Dharma. Donna Catharina was their Queen, it belonged therefore by right to her husband to rule over the kingdom.

Don Juan Wimala Dharma himself was a prince of the royal house; he was the eldest of the younger line, so that, the child Don Juan son of the late King Philip II having been excluded from the succession, he would have, in any case succeeded by the right of his birth to Donna Catharina.

The two branches of the royal house of Kandy descended from the two brothers King Don Emmanuel Jayaweera I, and the usurper King Cumara Banda. Donna Catharina was the great-grand-daughter of King Emmanuel, and grand-daughter of King Wikrama Bahu, the same who made the tooth of Buddha now worshipped at Kandy. Don Juan Wimala Dharma (or Kunappu Banda) was the great-grand-son of Cumara Banda. He was therefore after Donna Catharina the next heir to the throne.

The chiefs therefore, on his marriage with Donna Catharina recognized him as King and paid him homage.

Don Juan Wimala Dharma did not loose his time. He knew

that the Portuguese only awaited an opportunity to avenge the defeat of Balane. He therefore prepared for the struggle and put forth all his activity to organize an army and train it as far as possible in the European way. At the same time he fortified the frontiers of the kingdom.

Nevertheless, the Portuguese were not the first enemies he had to encounter. Gerome d'Azevedo who had succeeded to Lopez de Sousa, with the title of Governor of Ceylon and no more, as formerly, with that of commander of the fort of Colombo, was too able a general to risk himself against such an enemy as Don Juan without having prepared himself seriously for the struggle. He preferred therefore to put off to a later period the revenge for the bloody defeat of Balane, rather than risk himself with insufficient forces.

The first enemy with whom Don Juan had to fight was old Raja Singha, whose pride could not bear to see the man who had humbled him raised to the throne of Kandy. Now Don Juan having broken with the Portuguese and made them his mortal enemies, Raja Singha thought the moment opportune for him.

About the beginning of 1592 he marched on Kandy at the
1592 head of his troops. Don Juan, who was not without fear as to the result of the struggle with the old warrior, the more so that it was not improbable that the Portuguese garrison of Colombo would join him, went to meet him as far as Kaduganawa where he entrenched himself.

When Raja Singha approached with his army, he wrote to him that he was coming to inflict on him, the same death he had inflicted six years ago to his father. Don Juan answered that the issue of battles is in the hand of God and that he hoped to avenge his father's cruel death.

The two armies met near the village of Kaduganawa. The victory was with Don Juan. Raja Singha's defeat was so complete, that he had to save his life by a hasty flight.

Having collected the remains of his army he was retreating to Avisavella. Whilst traversing a forest near Ruanwelle Raja Singha descended from his elephant and walking barefooted in the jungle got a thorn into his foot.

The wound becoming very painful he called a native doctor to dress it. Raja Singha was detested by his subjects, and it is said, the native doctor, gained over by some chiefs, introduced poison into the wound.

Feeling death approaching Raja Singha was seized with a mad terror. His disordered life, all the atrocious crimes he had committed stood now before his eyes and he feared death.

He had been brought up in the Buddhist religion, but he abandoned it to give himself up to the Hindu devil worship, which suited better to his restless and gloomy nature. Now on his death bed, he feared less sleepy Buddha than the devils he had worshipped.

He sent for the Bikshun of a neighbouring Wihare and asked them if there were any hope in future life for a man who like himself had committed so many crimes.

The Bikshun, smelling money, for they thought that the more they frighten him, the more will he pay them in order that by their incantations they obtain him a better lot, answered that there was no hope whatever, that he would go to the bottom of hell, where the devils he had worshipped will torment him for all eternity.

Raja Singha, hearing their verdict, had them seized and burned alive.

A few days later he called the Bikshun from another Wihare and put them the same question. Made prudent by the fate of their colleagues they were less exacting. They answered, that the other Bikshun were simply stupid fellows. That certainly hell was the place where, after death, those who had committed great crimes would go. Nevertheless, the Bikshun by their incantations could procure him an intermediate place between heaven and hell.

They thought that Raja Singha would pay them much more for obtaining for him a place in Buddha's paradise. But Nirwana was too quiet a place for a man of his restless nature, and he was satisfied with an intermediate place. All that he feared were the devils in hell, once he could escape them, the rest was of little importance. He dismissed the Bikshun with presents. They were generously paid, but they had expected much more for piloting him into Nirwana.

Raja Singha died a few days later aged sixty years, or as they counted at this epoch 120 harvests of rice.

Raja Singha, was the sworn enemy of the Portuguese, of the Catholic King of Kotta Don Juan Dharmapala, and of the Catholic Religion, and this seemed a sufficient reason for some superficial Protestant writers, to set him up as a great national hero.

Pridham, the most serious perhaps of these authors writes:

—„ Raja Singha was an isolated beacon erect amidst the „ falling fortunes of his country: his quick perception enabled him „ to grasp an accurate view of its position; he traced the cause of its „ inferiority and, that discovered, devoted his whole energy to its „ removal." — (Ceylon Vol. I page 96.)

This makes him a great man; but let us see what says the Mahawanse, a Singhalese Chronicle, to which these same Protestant writers endeavour to give a certain amount of importance:

— „ Now Mayadunnè had a son named Raja Singha, who was „ an exceedingly cruel man. And he was want to accompany his „ father in his wars in diverse places; and being puffed up with „ victory, this great fool, in the wickedness of his heart, slew his „ father with his own hand and took possession of the kingdom, „ and was known as Raja Singha of Sitawacca." — (Wijesinghe's translation, chapter 93 page 325.)

The historian therefore must choose between the isolated beacon of Pridham, and the great fool of the Mahawanse, which though it has not any historical value is, nevertheless, to a certain point the echo of the traditions preserved locally by the natives. And it is obvious that a man cannot be at the same time, the beacon shining over his native country, and a great fool.

Raja Singha was certainly not the great fool that the Mahawanse calls him, but he was also far from being an isolated beacon.

During the life of his father he distinguished himself as leader of bands of plunderers, and by his cruelty which struck with horror even the pagans.

A parricide, a fratricide and murderer of his own son, he had a certain prestige as a warrior as long as his father's organisation of the army lasted. The victories of Mooleriawe and of the Kelany Ganga, his temporary conquest of Kandy gave him a certain glory. But, six years after the horrid crimes that had placed him on the throne of the small state of Sitawacca, conquered by Don Juan Kunappu, his career was finished, and he ended his life in obscurity.

Mayadunnè was an adventurer, but he was a strong man. Raja Singha was a hardy chief of bands of pillagers. He knew how to slaughter harmless villagers, and how to draw his enemy into an ambuscade, but he did not know how to make war. His place in the history of Ceylon is a secondary one.

Raja Singha, who had caused his only son to be put to death died without leaving a direct heir. Thus the throne of
1593 Sitawacca descended to his grandson, the son of one of his daughters, a child called Nicapeti who was proclaimed Raja under his grandmother's Regency. This princess was at that time in love with a stranger, a native of Southern India, whom she then made commander of the army, but who in reality ruled over the state.

The Singhalese chiefs jealous and discontented were strongly opposed to him, and the small state was all in disorder and the troubles increased every day.

King Don Juan Dharmapala and the Governor Jerome d'Azevedo resolved to take profit of the situation to interfere in the affairs of Sitawacca. They sent a small army under the command of Peter Homem Pereira, who after having defeated the Rani Regent's troops near Gurubewelle, entered Sitawacca without resistance. The Regent with the young Raja Nicapeti had fled to Dinawacca carrying with them all their treasures.

Pereira sent after them 150 European soldiers and a body of native troops under the command of John Rodriguez Camello and of a Singhalese officer. They were surprised to see the splendour of the small city of Dinawacca which they captured with hardy fighting. Young Raja Nicapeti was made a prisoner and all the treasures left by Raja Singha which were considerable fell into the conqueror's hands.

The two principalities of Sitawacca and Rayagam submitted to King Don Juan Dharmapala and were annexed to the kingdom of Kotta. The chiefs were tired of the long tyranny of Mayadunnè and of Raja Singha, and the people rejoiced at the change of master and oppressed as they had been till now, they were glad to come under the rule of the good and just King of Kotta who was much beloved by his subjects. And the kingdom of Kotta was restored in its ancient limits, such as it was before the division between the sons of Vijaya Bahu in 1521.

Thus ended the long war between Kotta and Sitawacca after it had lasted for 67 years, a war which, as we have already explained before, was nothing less than the reaction of ancient barbarism against civilisation, of heathenism against Christianity.

The boy Raja Nicapeti was taken to Colombo, where he was baptized by the Franciscan Father Christopher of the Mother of God who gave him the name of Philip. He was placed under the care of old Fr. Francis of the East, who was already in charge of the little prince Don Juan of Kandy. This venerable old man who laboured already for 51 years in the Missions of Ceylon held the place of a father to the two royal orphans each of whom was born to occnpy a throne.

Next year Fr. Jerome of the Holy Ghost Commissary General of the Franciscans in India was passing through Ceylon, and King Don Juan Dharmapala put the two boys under his care to be placed at the College in Goa where they could get a higher education than in Colombo.

About the middle of 1609, King Philip II of Portugal (Philip III in Spain, both kingdoms being at that time united under the same Sovereign), called them to Lisbon. On their arrival there they were received by Francis de Gama Count of Vidigueira grandson of the great Vasco, who had befriended them at Goa, when he was Viceroy from 1597 to 1600; and presented by him to the King.

Don Philip Nicapeti, who was the younger, and rather backwards in his studies was sent to the University of Coïmbra, where he fell sick and died in 1618.

Young Don Juan of Kandy when still at Goa expressed more than once the desire of becoming a Priest. He was ordained at Lisbon. The King had bestowed on him the title of Duke of Telheires and provided him with a very large income. He settled then at Madrid where the King of Portugal and Spain then resided and died in 1642 at his castle of Telheires leaving a very large fortune.

## CHAPTER 13

# DON JUAN WIMALA DHARMA

After the defeat and death of Raja Singha, Don Juan Wimala
1594 Dharma, who enjoyed already the fame of a great warrior, received the submission of several petty Rajas of Ceylon and became the most powerful Ruler in the Island.

He was certainly not wanting in talent, and the intimate contact with the Portuguese and the influence of the Catholic Religion had raised him above the level of his countrymen. He was both generous and barbarous: he rewarded with munificence and punished with a refined cruelty.

Notwithstanding his wars with the Portuguese he esteemed them greatly and often spoke with admiration of their honor and loyalty, he felt the want of their society who was more congenial to his more refined taste, than that of the rough Kandyans who at that time were much inferior to the low country Singhalese many of whom had got a careful education in the Franciscan College at Colombo, and he sought the society of the Portuguese who were detained at Kandy as war prisoners.

Don Juan Wimala Dharma was a barbarian, but one who had tasted civilisation and had always a hankering for it.

He allied himself later on with the Dutch, because he feared the Portuguese; but if the Portuguese, forgetting the past, had accepted as an accomplished fact his marriage with Donna Catharina and his ascension to the throne of Kandy, would have made him some advances, he would have gladly returned to them and become their most faithful ally. But the Portuguese were too proud to forget their reverses, and their repellent politics towards him cost them the loss of Ceylon.

Much is said of the apostacy of Don Juan Wimala Dharma. But there is no historical record of his having ever abandoned the Catholic Faith. On the contrary in the beginning of his reign we see him build churches, which he neither finished nor endowed. To gain the loyalty of his Buddhist subjects he at times took part in their worship, but he always spoke as a Christian. Having become a Christian from interested motives, Religion did not lay deep rooted in his heart, but he had had too much contact with civilisation not to despise heathenism. And we think that Ribeiro is right when he says that Don Juan Wimala Dharma was neither a Catholic nor a Buddhist.

1595 The annexation of Raja Singha's dominions to the kingdom of Kotta had increased King Don Juan Dharmapala's power, but it caused him all the same some trouble. The Buddhist chiefs who had at first willingly paid him homage, seeing now that under his strong and enlightened rule they were no more permitted to oppress the people and enrich themselves at the cost of the villagers, began to rebel against the King. They ravaged the country, burned villages and destroyed many churches.

The Governor Jerome d'Azevedo helped the King to subdue

them, and it was often necessary to send large bodies of troops against them.

The Missionaries had much to suffer during this petty war which lasted for several years. They all remained at their posts to protect the Christians and save them from the hands of the heathen aggressors. Many paid with their lives their devotion to their flock. Fr. Francis of Lapas was killed at Negombo. Fathers Bernard of the Immaculate Conception and Francis of Cannanorem Caymal, a native of India, were slaughtered at Malwane. Fathers Andrew of St. Setuval and Anthony of the Mother of God were hanged near Sitawacca after having suffered the most cruel tortures. They all belonged to the Franciscan Order.

Two Singhalese chiefs distinguished themselves in these petty wars by their courage and military talents: Don Ferdinand Samarakon and Dominic Correa Wikramasingha.

Dominic Wikramasingha was born of Catholic parents who had been converted to the Faith by Fr. John of Villa Conde, and had been very carefully educated. Related by marriage with several noble Portuguese families he was very rich and enjoyed the favour of both King Don Juan Dharmapala and Governor Azevedo. A spoiled child of fortune at the age of 30 years he had already attained the highest dignities in the kingdom.

This turned his head and, laid away by his pride, he conceived the ambitious project of cutting a kingdom for himself in the provinces of Raja Singha's old dominions, which had rebelled against King Don Juan. On the 17th September 1595 he betrayed

29

his King and passed to the camp of the rebels, who acclaimed him as their chief and bestowed on him the title of Raja. But defeated by Azevedo and by Samarakon he fled to Kandy, where King Don Juan Wimala Dharma received him with great honors, treated him as if he were a Sovereign prince and married him with the daughter of Anthony, the Raja of the Seven Korles, who a few months previously had been baptised with his family.

The Governor Jerome d'Azevedo having helped the King of Kotta to crush the greater part of the rebels, thought

1596 now the moment propitious to take revenge on Don Juan Wimala Dharma for the bloody day of Balane.

Well aware of the courage and ability of his adversary Azevedo acted with caution and prudence. In marching to the Kandyan frontier he endeavoured to gain the native chiefs, occupied the country to secure communications with Colombo, and re-build the small forts that Don Juan Wimala Dharma had destroyed after the defeat of Lopez de Sousa. In penetrating into the mountains, he caused the jungle to be beaten to dislodge any body of Kandyans that might lay hidden in ambuscade. Thus he arrived safely to the valley of Balane that had been the theatre of de Sousa's defeat.

Don Juan Wimala Dharma, able warrior that he was, knew that if Azevedo gained the first battle, the road of Kandy lay open to him, and he was prepared for the eventuality of a defeat.

Queen Donna Catharina whom he had so brutally forced to marry him, was rather his prisoner than his wife. If she fell into the hands of the Portuguese it would be in her name that they would carry on the war. Now he knew well that if the Kandyans fought loyally for him and for Donna Catharina, they would certainly refuse to fight for him against Donna Catharina who was their lawful Sovereign. He therefore secured the unfortunate Queen by despatching her to Nuwara Elliya, at that time a mere village amidst mountains covered with inaccessible jungle.

The encounter took place on the same battlefield of Balane which, seven years ago, had witnessed the tragic end of Lopez de Sousa.

Don Juan knew that his fate depended on the issue of the battle, he therefore displayed all his ability. He was to be seen everywhere, encouraging personally his troops, and leading them to the battle.

The Portuguese on their side burning to avenge the death of the soldiers of Lopez de Sousa whose bones were laying unburied around them, performed prodigies of valour, but their movements were impeded in the narrow valley where they could not use their artillery; they were crushed by the number, and the victory was with Don Juan.

Fr. Casper of the Kings, a Franciscan, who acted in Azevedo's army as military chaplain, fell covered with wounds when giving the last Sacraments to the dying. As he could not walk, and not even could hold on his seat, they tied him up on the back of an elephant to bring him to a place of safety. The animal frightened by the noise of the battle and wounded with an arrow rushed furiously through the jungle, and the unfortunate Father, was torn by the branches of the trees so that only shreds of his body were found.

Jerome d'Azevedo had made a mistake that the Portuguese and after them the Dutch and English always did in their wars with the Kandyans. They invaded the country with insufficient forces. They well knew from experience, that a handful of soldiers, drilled in the European ways were sufficient to defeat the badly armed and undisciplined hordes of the Kings of Ceylon. This however was right in the plains, where the troops could be set in battle array and artillery displayed, but not in these mountains covered with dense jungle where artillery was of no use, and where the Kandyans, in their own element, could easily crush them by their number.

Azevedo being defeated, retreated to Colombo. Among the prisoners he brought with him, was Dominic Correa Wikramasingha who had betrayed his King as related above. Don Juan Dharmapala condemned him to death. When in prison he showed sincere repentance for the atrocities he had committed during his rebellion and made a Christian and edifying death. He was executed at Colombo on the 14th July 1596. He was only 31 years of age. A man of no common ability and genius, if not led away by his pride, he could have rendered great services to his country.

Don Juan Wimala Dharma exasperated by the news of Don Dominic's execution with whom he was bound by close friendship caused his Portuguese prisoners to be horribly mutilated, and sent them so to Colombo.

The Portuguese soldiers of the garrison of Colombo already excited against the Governor to whom they attributed the disaster of the late Kandy expedition, were seized with horror at the sight of their mutilated comrades. They took their arms and ran to Azevedo's residence shouting: — „ Let us kill him, let us kill this dog! " —

Jerome d'Azevedo gave himself for lost, when some Missionaries threw themselves in the midst of the tumult and checked the soldiers. With their courageous and energetic action they re-established order and discipline, and saved the Governor's life.

The following event increased yet more Azevedo's embarassments: A well known Kandyan chief, Emmanuel Diaz, an old officer of Lopez de Sousa and a Catholic, who enjoyed great influence in the kingdom, quarrelled with Don Juan Wimala Dharma and entered in communication with Governor Azevedo in order to deliver Don Juan to the Portuguese.

Azevedo sent secretly to Kandy three Singhalese officers Albert Primeiro, Casper Pereira and Christian Jacob to arrange everything with Don Emmanuel Diaz and co-operate with him.

It was arranged that a body of Portuguese troops would surprise and seize the fort of Balane. At the same time Diaz with his party would render themselves masters of Kandy, seize Don Juan Wimala Dharma and bring him a prisoner to Colombo.

Don Juan, informed of these facts by his spies, saw the gravity of the position. He therefore hastened to get reconciled with Don Emmanuel Diaz by offering him the post of Adigar or prime minister, the highest that the King could bestow.

Now Diaz knowing that the Portuguese were already absconded in the forest in the neighbourhood waiting only for a word from him to surprise the fort, wanted to capture the whole body by giving the pre-arranged signal and bringing them thus into a trap. But the officer in command, informed of what was going on in Kandy, burned his baggages and made a hasty retreat to Colombo. Azevedo's agents were taken and executed in Kandy.

All these events made the breach between the Portuguese and Don Juan Wimala Dharma greater and rendered the latter more and more powerful.

## CHAPTER 14

# THE DEATH OF KING DON JUAN DHARMAPALA

After the failure of the Kandy expeditions, King Don Juan Dharmapala and the Governor Jerome d'Azevedo gave
1597 all their attention to the re-organization of the kingdom of Kotta which had much suffered from the wars with Raja Singha, the late rebellions and the incursions of the Kandyans.

The limits of the kingdom had been greatly extended by the annexation of old Mayadunnè's dominions of Sitawacca and Rayagam, and by the acquisition of the four Korles and a few other districts.

King Don Juan Dharmapala took always great interest in the question of education. He had renewed in 1591 his chart of 1557 by which he had given the properties of the Kelanya temple and some other deserted and suppressed Buddhist temples for educational purposes. Many primary schools had been started. The College of Colombo founded by the Franciscan Fathers was no more sufficient for the ever increasing number of students, and the Provincial of the Jesuit Fathers in India was approached with the proposal to start at Colombo a second College with a higher standard of studies.

The Missions though very much disturbed by the wars, were nevertheless progressing thanks to the zeal of the Franciscan Fathers.

There were now in the kingdom of Kotta 47 churches besides a great number of chapels and about 100,000 Catholics, which was a large number, if we consider how thinly populated was Ceylon at that time. It seems that the whole population of the Island did not attain at this epoch to a million of souls. The Karawoe alone were 70,000.

Many conversions were made among all classes. During the year 1595, Don Anthony Raja of the seven Korles, his daughter who soon afterwards married Don Dominic Correa Wikramasingha, his cousin Don Philip and Donna Maria the widow of the Maha Mudeliyar, a princess of royal blood, had become Catholics.

King Don Juan Dharmapala took a great interest in the Missions. He was already 60 years of age, and had been on the throne for 45 years, during which long period he had always remained faithful to the alliance with the Portuguese. Brave in war when he was young, and carefully educated, he was not gifted with extraordinary talents but being endowed with a straight and clear intellect, he understood all the advantages which his subjects, whom he really loved, could gather from the contact of the Portuguese and from the beneficient influence of the Catholic Faith, which soon raised the low country Singhalese to a degree of civilization by far superior to that of the Kandyans and of the Tamils of the north.

A good and devout Christian, very pious, mild, affable,

accessible to all, King Don Juan Dharmapala was much beloved by his subjects, who gave him many proofs of their fidelity during the wars with Mayadunnè and with Raja Singha.

In the latter years of his reign he gave himself up to works of charity and to promoting education among low country Singhalese. Since Kotta had been abandoned in 1565 he always resided in Colombo, where he lived in great state and in close friendship with the Governor Don Jerome d'Azevedo.

King Don Juan Dharmapala died on the 17th May 1597. He made a most edifying and Christian death, equally regretted by the Singhalese and by the Portuguese. He was buried with great pomp in the Franciscan church of St. Antony at Colombo.

Sixty years later, the church was desecrated by the Protestants, but King Don Juan's tomb still existed in 1762 when the Dutch Governor Schroeder mentions it in the instructions which he gave to his successor Van Eyk, and mentions that it was engraved on the tombstone that Don Juan in his will had bequeathed his dominions to the King of Portugal.

King Don Juan left no children. He had a step-sistèr Donna Maria, daughter of Weedeya Raja by his second wife the daughter of Mayadunnè. This princess, at that time, was a nun in a convent in Goa. His other relations were distant cousins who had neither right nor even pretended to the succession to the throne. With Don Juan Dharmapala's death, the royal dynasty of Kotta was extinct.

Now according to the feudal law, at the extinction of the family of the vassal, his dominions reverted to the Suzerain. The Kings of Kotta were vassals to the Portuguese Crown, so that even without the old King's testament, which in the case seemed to be a rather unnecessary document, on the sole strength of the treaties of 1517 and 1520, Don Juan Dharmapala having no legal heirs, the King of Portugal became *ipso facto* the rightful Sovereign of the kingdom of Kotta.

Nevertheless, as the Singhalese and the native chiefs knew little about the feudal law, the King, in order to legalize in their eyes such transfer of Sovereignty, made this will, bequeathing his kingdom to the King of Portugal, who even without this testament was *de facto* his legal successor.

Father de Queiros who, in the latter half of the seventeenth century had at his disposal the archives of Goa gives in full the text of the testament, which was dated 12th November 1583 and witnessed by the King's secretary, three other native dignitaries, one of whom was probably the Adigar Don Emmanuel who had succeeded in that office to Don Francis Barreto Senerat Banda, two Portuguese officers, John Correa de Britto and Emmanuel Coutinho, Fr. Edward de Silva Guardian of the Franciscan convent of St. Antony in Colombo, and Fr. Vieira parish Priest of Colombo.

Thus ended the second period of the history of the Portuguese in Ceylon.

In the first period, which lasted from 1517 to 1554, there was only a treaty of alliance between them and the Kings of Kotta in force of which they were allowed free trade in the kingdom on the onerous condition to help the King, when required, against his enemies. They had a commercial establishment at Colombo, a factory as it was called. They had built a small fort in which they kept a handful of soldiers, scarcely sufficient to defend their stores against a rising of the Moormen or an attack of Mayadunnè. The small garrison was not even permanent and each time that the King in force of the treaties claimed the aid of the Portuguese, the Viceroy had to send troops from Cochin or from Goa. The King of Kotta paid the expenses of these expeditions.

During the second period which lasted from 1554 to 1597, the Portuguese commercial interests in Ceylon having increased immensely, and at the same time rendered insecure by the death of Bhuwaneka Bahu who had always protected their trade; Mayadunnè being their enemy, and the Regent of the kingdom of Kotta, Weedeya Raja, a man whom they could not trust, it was deemed necessary for the protection of the important commercial interests to have a regular fort in Colombo and to keep there a stronger and permanent garrison. There was as yet no thought of possessing themselves of a part of Ceylon, on the contrary, each time that the Portuguese had conquered some district, they surrendered it to the King of Kotta, and they respected the rights of Sovereignty of the native Kings. But their influence was increasing, they interfered, more and more in the political affairs of the Island, and, by and by, established their protectorate over the kingdom of Kotta, a real Suzerainty over that of Jaffna and a nominal Suzerainty over Kandy. The three kingdoms remained independent.

During the first period the Portuguese in Ceylon were protected by the King of Kotta, in the second they protected the King of Kotta. With the death of Don Juan Dharmapala in 1597 begins the Portuguese Rule in Ceylon.

# Part III

# THE PORTUGUESE RULE

1597 — 1658

## CHAPTER 1

# THE PORTUGUESE RULE

After King Don Juan's funeral Don Jerome d'Azevedo convoked his Council to deliberate on the best manner
1597 of obtaining the pacific adhesion of the people to the new state of things, and it was decided to issue a proclamation that each district should send to Colombo two representatives to take the oath of allegiance to the King of Portugal their new Sovereign.

The proclamation was published in all the districts of the kingdom and none failed to respond. The delegates, who were the leading native chiefs came to Colombo.

The Governor Azevedo held a solemn Durbar, explained to them that having become now the subjects of the King of Portugal, they would enjoy the same rights and privileges, as those born in Portugal and that if they peacefully accepted the new order of things they would be moreover confirmed in all privileges and immunities granted to them by the Kings of Kotta.

The chiefs replied that it was a serious matter which required mature consideration. They did not reject the proposal which was made to them, but they asked for two days to think it over, and meanwhile the Governor could rely on their loyalty.

After two days they returned bringing to Azevedo the following answer: That they were born Singhalese and were brought up in Singhalese customs to which they were much attached. That it would be difficult and even dangerous to try to induce the people to abandon their old laws and customs for others unknown to them. That such radical changes if introduced suddenly always led to rebellion, and it is to be feared that the people would forget the old laws, and never learn to observe the new ones, which certainly would not be in the interest of the King. That they had no objection to recognize the King of Portugal as their Lord and Master, but in return they would ask that the King and his representatives, maintain the customs, rights and privileges, they had enjoyed till now. Then they would serve the King of Portugal as if he were born on their native soil, and swear him fidelity and allegiance, if the Governor too takes his oath in the name of the King, that their ancient customs and privileges would not be violated.

The Governor acceded to these wise and dignified demands of the chiefs, to which on his part added the following articles: That the Catholic Missionaries should be left unmolested and free to preach the Faith of Jesus Christ; that no one should be hindered to profess the Catholic Religion. That parents should not oppose to the conversion of their children, nor the children to that of their parents. That all offences against Religion would be judged by the Ecclesiastical Court. That no one should be forced to become a Catholic, but each one would be left free to embrace and profess the Catholic Faith, if God grants him this grace and enlightens his heart.

The agreement was signed, and each of the delegates took a

copy with him and returned to his respective district, and everything was later on ratified by the King.

The facility with which the Singhalese accepted the Portuguese Rule is the best proof how groundless are the assertions of certain Protestant writers regarding the alleged tyranny of the Portuguese and their cruelty towards the natives.

At that time there was only a handful of Portuguese in Ceylon, whom the Singhalese would have easily crushed, if they but tried to impose on them submission by force. Then, they had only to appeal to the King of Kandy, who was then at war with the Portuguese, the same as the Kandyans had appealed to the King of Kotta when Raja Singha imposed on them his rule.

The submission of the low countries to the Portuguese Rule was voluntary. We see that it was the Singhalese chiefs who imposed their conditions, which they did with as much wisdom as firmness, and the whole business had almost the appearance of an election.

All that shows that, during the eighty years of intimate contact with the Portuguese, the low country Singhalese, far from having learned to consider them as cruel and bloody tyrants, appreciated, on the contrary, their beneficient and civilizing influence. For the rest any one acquainted with the colonial history of European nation knows well, that none of them knew so well to identify themselves with the natives, as the Portuguese. Race and colour prejudice had no meaning for them. They treated the educated natives in the same way as they would have treated a European of the same birth and rank. The Kings of Portugal and the Governors, especially the present, Don Jerome Azevedo were glad to see Portuguese officers of noble birth marry Singhalese girls of high and influential families, and we see already at this epoch the powerful Singhalese houses of Samarakòn, Correa-Wikramasingha, Diaz and others, related in this way to the highest nobility of Lisbon.

The Portuguese Rule having thus been peacefully accepted and the kingdom of Kotta added to their extensive
1598 Eastern empire, the Governor's first care was to organize the new Colony.

As regards the army, the old feudal system introduced by the Kings of Kotta had only to be perfected. Since ancient time the Kings had in reality no standing army, but in case of war each chief had to place himself under the royal Standard with a number of soldiers proportioned to the extension of his territory and the number of its inhabitants. The chiefs gave land to people who instead of paying rent had to render military service.

These soldiers were very brave and devoted to their chiefs, for whom, often, in battle they risked their own life. They were armed with swords with very broad blades. They were very good archers and shot their arrows with marvellous exactness. Others had muskets with barrels eight feet in length and weighing 40 pounds. The bullets weighed four ounces each. These muskets needed a support, and produced an effect something like that of small falconets. The King of Kotta had 4,000 and the King of Kandy 5,000 of these singular weapons.

With this organization the King of Kotta could always count on a force of 60,000 men, but discipline and unity of action was wanting, and that to such a point that a body of 500 European soldiers could easily defeat a native force of 10,000 to 15,000 men.

The Governor Jerome d'Azevedo kept the old organization, but had the soldiers better armed and well drilled.

Three entrenched camps were established to defend the country against an invasion of the Kandyans.

The best fortified was that of Manicavere, midway between Colombo and Kandy. 350 Portuguese infantry under the command of six officers, and a body of native troops under the command of the local Dessawe or native Governor of the province were quartered there. The commander of Manicavare rank next to the Governor of Colombo and they had a Franciscan Father as military Chaplain.

The second entrenched camp was situated near the limit of the province of Uva, and had about 4,000 native troops and a few Portuguese soldiers under the command of the local Dessawe. Later on we see more frequently European Portuguese troops commanded by Singhalese officers. They too had a Franciscan as military Chaplain.

In time of war the garrisons of these entrenched camps were reinforced, and armed bodies were stationed in different parts of the country.

Colombo was surrounded by fortifications, formidable for those days. The fort commanded the harbour and was defended by 237 guns. The fortifications of Galle, Kalutara and Negombo were also improved.

The military organization however did not absorb all the Governor's attention. He promoted agriculture and industry and sought to develop the products of the country. Colombo and Galle had become harbours of great commercial importance and were visited by merchant ships, from Europe, the Red Sea, Arabia, India and Burma.

Cinnamon seems to have been in those days the chief product of export. It was not cultivated but brought out from the jungle where it grew in large quantities. The duties on its export was the principal revenue of the colony, and it brought large sums of money to the Crown.

After cinnamon, elephants brought the largest revenue to the treasury. It would seem that already in those days elephant hunting was a monopoly of the State. They were caught in kraals and exported to India, where the Rajas paid high prices for them, as they were reputed to be tamer and more intelligent than those of India and Burma.

Little attention was paid to precious stones, which yielded to government an annual revenue of only 24,000 crowns. It seems that at that epoch rubies alone were valued.

The greatest care however of the Governor Don Jerome d'Azevedo was for education. The Franciscan College
1602 at Colombo was no more sufficient for the number of Singhalese boys who went for higher studies, and the Governor approached again the Jesuits in India, who now consented to come over to Ceylon. The first Father who landed at Colombo had a

grand reception from the people. Azevedo had prepared for them a commodious house, and gave them from his own private purse a large sum of money for the erection of the College building. The Catholics of Colombo too helped generously, and the Jesuit College was started, and well provided with funds by the Portuguese Government.

Another Jesuit College was started in the same year at Jaffna by the Fathers Bonaventure d'Abreu, John-Mary and Peter Rebello, whom the Franciscan Fathers entrusted with the care of education of the Tamil boys.

The Bishop of Cochin Dom Andrew of St. Mary, himself a Franciscan, having come to Ceylon on a Pastoral Visit, seeing that with the increased number of Christians the Fathers of his Order could no more do alone all the work, asked help from the Jesuit Provincial of Malabar, and the Mission of Ceylon was now divided between the Franciscan and the Jesuit Fathers. The Jesuits took over the Missions of Caymele, Madampe and Malegame, the Seven Korles, and in the kingdom of Jaffna all the stations of the interior. They got moreover a church at Colombo and another at Jaffna.

The apostolate of the Jesuit Fathers brought quickly good results. Their principal Mission station was Beligama where they built a large stone church with three naves.

In the Seven Korles they were helped by one of the principal chiefs, Simon Correa Wikramasingha, the brother of the unfortunate

Dominic. In 1611 they had baptised 600 heathens and 300 more were preparing for baptism. In the following year Fr. Peter Euticius baptised the Raja of the Seven Korles who was a prince of the royal house of Kandy and 24 families of chiefs.

Another Mission which soon became flourishing was that of the Island of Caradiva. In the beginning the Jesuit Fathers encountered there great difficulties; it is always more difficult to convert the heathens in the neighbourhood of a great temple where the Devil is worshipped, and Caradiva possessed a famous temple which attracted pilgrimages from the north of Ceylon and from the southern part of India. They adorned there a black stone, which was considered as a powerful fetish.

To put an end to this stupid worship the Governor Azevedo made over the temple to the Jesuit Fathers to be transformed into a church dedicated to the Apostles St. Peter and St. Paul.

The heathens far from opposing the entrance of the Jesuits gathered in number for the Brahmin had proclaimed that no one would be able to throw down the fetish, and that whoever would touch it would instantly die a terrible death; and all gathered out of curiosity to witness the sight. But the fetish fell down broken in many pieces and none was the worse for it. This naturally shook the credit of the Brahmins, and conversions to the Catholic Faith were more easily obtained.

In the same year as the Jesuits, the Dominican Fathers came to Jaffna. Fr. Michael Varella and his companions were for eight months the guests of the Franciscans until their convent was finished, and four years later they built in Jaffna the beautiful church of Our Lady of the Holy Rosary. They built another convent at Colombo and later on worked in the southern part of the province of Sabaragamuwa.

The Augustinian Fathers too built in 1606 a convent at Colombo to which six parishes were afterwards attached.

## CHAPTER 2

# THE DUTCH

The Dutch appear for the first time in the history of Ceylon on
1602 the 29th May 1602.

The Dutch were an industrious people, and trade had enriched them. As we have seen, in the sixteenth century all the trade of the East was in the hands of the Portuguese. But the Portuguese fleets brought the products of Asia and Africa only as far as Lisbon where they were transhipped on Dutch merchant vessels, carried to Amsterdam, and thence sold on the markets of Europe by Dutch traders.

In nearly all the books written about Ceylon we read, that Philip II King of Portugal and Spain, having forbidden to the Dutch the entrance of the harbour of Lisbon, because they had become Protestant, they went to fetch the products of the East in their original countries.

This statement is not correct: Holland was at that time a province of the Spanish Empire and the Dutch subjects to the King of Spain. Having apostatized the Catholic Faith, they rebelled against their lawful King and proclaimed a Republic. The King of Spain dealt with them as any Sovereign would deal with a revolted province. Philip II did not forbid them to enter the harbour of Lisbon but they feared to enter it, as being rebels, their ships would have been seized.

Supposing Australia would rebel against England, would the Australian ships enter into the harbours of Southampton or Portsmouth?

It was nevertheless a great blow to Dutch trade; and enterprising as they were, the Dutch had resolved to send their vessels to the East, to fetch there the products they could no more get at Lisbon, and at that epoch of our history they had already been contending for some time with the Portuguese for the monopoly of the trade of the eastern seas.

On the 5th May 1601 three Dutch ships left Amsterdam, and their commander Joris Spilbergen had instructions from the Republican Government to land at Ceylon and to establish there relations and if possible make treaties with Kings and native chiefs.

Joris Spilbergen landed at Batticaloa on the 29th May 1602 and placed himself in communication with a local native chief, probably a Dessawe, who acted as if he were the Raja of the place, who promised him a cargo of cinnamon and pepper and detained him for two weeks under the pretext that he had sent elephants into the interior to bring these commodities.

In the meantime Joris Spilbergen learned from the Moormen that the place belonged to the King of Kandy, who was the most powerful Sovereign of Ceylon, so, on the 15th June he sent a messenger to Kandy with a letter to King Don Juan. The messenger returned accompanied by two dignitaries of the Kandyan court, Gonzalve Rodrigues and Melchior Rebecca, who brought to

Spilbergen the reply: Don Juan promised him a cargo of cinnamon, assured him of his friendship and invited him to Kandy.

Spilbergen started three days later taking the road through Bintenne. The King sent him a palanquin a day journey from the capital and on the banks of the Mahawalli Ganga he was met by the Adigar Don Emmanuel Diaz.

They gave him a grand reception at Kandy where he had several interviews with the King.

Don Juan asked him if he was a Christian. Spilbergen answered that he was, but not a Catholic as the Portuguese. Don Juan seemed rather astonished that there should be other species of Christianity than the One Church of Christ, and that those who protested against it should call themselves Christians. He then asked if in the Protestant churches there were images of Christ and of the Holy Mother of God. Spilbergen answered that the Protestant churches had only bare walls, because they worshipped God in the interior of their heart. This answer seemed rather to amuse the King.

As the monsoon was approaching, Don Juan asked Spilbergen how much he would pay him for a cargo of cinnamon. The Dutchman replied that he did not come to Ceylon for trading, but to propose to the King an alliance with the Dutch Republic against the Portuguese who were their common enemies.

King Don Juan was overjoyed at this proposal. He was afraid of the Portuguese, and did not feel himself safe on the throne in their neighbourhood. He embraced Spilbergen with so much effusion that he lifted him up from the ground. He then presented him to the Queen Donna Catharina and to his children who were dressed in European fashion. Then Spilbergen left Kandy escorted to Batticaloa by the Adigar Don Emmanuel Diaz where he embarked on the 2nd September making sail to Sumatra. On his way, he captured three small Portuguese vessels and sent them, cargo and crew, as a present to King Don Juan.

The relations which Spilbergen had established with the King of Kandy were continued by the vice-admiral Sebald de
1603 Weerd who, in April 1603, cast anchor at Batticaloa with a Dutch squadron of seven ships.

Don Juan wanted the admiral to begin at once the campaign against the Portuguese by laying siege to Galle. And he came personally to Batticaloa to arrange about the matter. The Dutch Admiral demanded that the King should pay him a visit on his ship. Don Juan, who either feared treason or regarded such a visit as beneath his dignity refused. De Weerd heated with wine replied: — „No visit, no siege of Galle." — An altercation followed in which de Weerd said something insulting against Queen Donna Catharina. Don Juan beside himself with rage, left the room shouting: — „Kill! Kill the dog." — His courtiers interpreting literally the words of the King drew their swords and threw themselves on de Weerd, whom they killed. A massacre ensued and nearly all the Dutch who had landed at Batticaloa were slain. A few only escaped by throwing themselves into the sea and swimming to their ships.

Don Juan was very disconcerted at the fatal result of the

imprudent words he had uttered in a moment of anger. Feeling certain that the Dutch would not fail to avenge the death of their admiral, he returned in all haste to Kandy, whence he wrote in Portuguese to captain Petersen Enchuyse who had taken the command of the squadron: — „Who drinks wine ends badly. God is just. If you wish to have peace, let us live in peace. If you wish for war, you shall have it." —

Enchuyse answered to this laconic letter in a rather humble style, making excuses and stating that the whole fault was on the vice-admiral's side, who had provoked the King to anger and had got what he had well deserved.

All the English writers are unanimous to condemn Enchuyse. They say that he had sacrificed the honor of his country to commercial considerations. And certainly it is easy to understand how much such a conduct is repugnant to the chivalrous feelings of the English. But the historian has to be impartial, and in order to be impartial one should know in what circumstances the Dutch captain did find himself.

Sebald de Weerd was certainly to blame. During his short stay at Batticaloa all were disgusted with his bad and arrogant manners. He drank, and by insulting the Queen he had himself provoked the adventure.

Now, besides trade, there were other interests to be considered. The government of the Dutch Republic had already formed the plan of conquering Ceylon, and it was evident that they could not do that without being helped by the King of Kandy. If, for avenging the admiral's death, the Dutch had involved themselves in a war against him, King Don Juan, a Catholic at least nominally, would certainly have made advances to the Portuguese, who, in front of a new and already dangerous enemy would have forgotten their old grievances and made an alliance with Don Juan.

Who knows, perhaps, Enchuyse had acted with prudence; it is rather difficult to express a judgment on his conduct, as we do not possess the text of his letter.

King Don Juan Wimala Dharma, did not long survive his adventure with the Dutch admiral. Soon after his return
1604 to Kandy he was seized with a mysterious disease. He was consumed by an interior fire which caused him excruciating pains, and to lessen his sufferings he had to remain constantly plunged in cold water. Finally in the last days of May 1604, he died as he had lived, neither a Christian nor a pagan. He was between 40 and 50 years of age. He had a pagan funeral, his remains being burned with great pomp.

He left four children, two daughters and two sons Mahastane and Vijayapala. None of them was of age to succeed to their father. Though educated in the Catholic Faith by three distinguished Franciscan Fathers Francis Negrão, Eleutherius of St. James and Joseph of St. Francis, it is doubtful if they were baptised.

Don Juan Wimala Dharma was an able and talented prince. His contact with Portuguese civilization had developed his mind and made him much superior to the other native princes of that epoch. He was tall and handsome, darker than the average Singhalese, he had courteous and dignified manners, an imposing exterior, of a clear penetrating mind, remarkable military talents, was both energetic and enterprising. He governed well his kingdom, and gave special care for the administration of justice.

In his young days he had tasted civilization. Severed from it by circumstances, he had always the thirst of civilization. Notwithstanding his wars with them, he liked the Portuguese and recognized their superiority. He surrounded himself by those whom he kept prisoners at Kandy and liked to converse with them. He felt himself out of his element among his rough Kandyans, and felt the need of refreshing himself in a more civilized sphere. And who can say, but had the Portuguese, after some years had passed, recognized his marriage with Donna Catharina and the rights he had thus acquired to the throne of Kandy, and either made him some advances or accepted his, and formed an alliance with him, events might have taken a different turn. A Catholic dynasty might have been established at Kandy, and Christianity and civilization introduced into the kingdom.

As regards his own subjects, Don Juan trusted more to Catholics than to pagans. His Adigar Don Emmanuel Diaz was a Catholic and the three dignitaries whom he sent to Batticaloa to meet Joris Spilbergen were also Catholics.

Don Juan himself never apostatized formally. To gain over his Buddhist subjects he sometimes took part in their idolatrous worship, but he despised Buddhism, and did not give himself the trouble of concealing the fact. The Catholic Religion had made on him a deep impression. In the beginning of his reign he acted as a Catholic, but being deprived of the succours of Religion, he grew colder and colder. His intercourse with the Dutch protestants made him a sceptic and, at the end of his life, he had no Religion at all. Nevertheless he gave full religious liberty to his Catholic subjects.

He did much to embelish the city of Kandy, and, in 1600 built a new royal palace, a part of which still exists and is now called Dalada Maligawa.

After King Don Juan's death, there was a contest for the succession between the powerful Raja of Uva, who openly aspired to the hand of the widow Queen Donna Catharina, and Senevirat, King Don Juan's younger brother who proclaimed the right of his elder nephew Mahastane, but in reality aspired himself to the throne. In consequence disputes and divisions arose between the leading chiefs, who sided some with one and some with the other candidate.

Donna Catharina who since the age of 15 years had led a retired life (she was now 27) showed in this occasion an energy little expected. She proclaimed that she was the Queen and by her own right Sovereign of Kandy, that Don Juan, as her husband had governed in her name. With a strong hand she crushed her opponents and re-established order. In fact, she was not adverse to the idea of marriage with the prince of Uva.

As the Raja of Uva and Senevirat attempted again to create trouble, she summoned both to appear before her, and when they refused to obey, she declared them traitors, deposed them from their offices and dignities and ordered their properties to be confiscated,

The two pretenders however had too strong parties to fear her threats, they nevertheless submitted and were pardoned by the Queen.

The Raja of Uva then resolved to murder his rival. But Senevirat being informed of the plot forestalled his enemy. One day, while they were going to an audience to the Queen, when they were at the entrance door of the palace, pretending courtesy each insisted that the other should take precedence and enter the first. Finally the Raja of Uva who was the elder entered the door, when Senevirat plunged a dagger into his back.

A great tumult issued, when Donna Catharina wishing to prevent a bloody fight between the two parties appeared in person and proclaimed that the Raja of Uva was a traitor and that she herself had ordered his death.

This energetic action of the young Queen stopped the bloodshed, but was at the same time her undoing. She should have put herself at the head of the party of Uva, call on them to avenge the death of their prince and so crush Senevirat. Now she cruelly offended that party, the chiefs with their retinue left Kandy and returned to their homes and Senevirat found himself thus master of the capital. He seized the throne and, in order to legitimate his usurpation, forced the unfortunate Queen who was his prisoner to become his wife.

## CHAPTER 3

# SENEVIRAT

## KING OF KANDY

We possess no authentic documents to enable us to form a clear
1605 idea of the political state of Ceylon during the first years of the reign of King Senevirat. This short period being involved in obscurity we can only make suppositions.

Some Protestant writers pretend that immediately after Don Juan's death, the Portuguese endeavoured to renew friendly relations with the court of Kandy and that Queen Donna Catharina and Senevirat refused to have anything to do with them. This is a gratuitous assertion which has no historical foundation.

On another hand the Portuguese historian Ribeiro pretends that a treaty was concluded and that the King of Kandy paid a tribute to the Portuguese till 1624. It seems evident that Ribeiro has confounded dates and places at the beginning of Senevirat's reign of the treaty which was concluded in 1612.

These two assertions must be put aside, neither can stand historical critic.

Donna Catharina's and Senevirat's sympathies for the Portuguese are well known. There still existed at that time in the kingdom of

Kandy more than one Catholic chief of influence, and those naturally were inclined towards an alliance with the Portuguese.

On the other hand the Dutch had left Ceylon in 1603 after the incident of the massacre of Sebald de Weerd and of his soldiers, and at the beginning of his reign Senevirat could not know if they would return, and, if they returned, would it be as friends or as enemies. Till now the Kandyans had not come in contact with other Europeans than with the Portuguese and the Portuguese would certainly not have left unpunished such an affront on their national honor. Senevirat therefore could not count at that time on a Dutch alliance.

Again, if the Portuguese did not dispose in Ceylon of an army much stronger than that of the King of Kandy, so that the latter could consider them as an enemy of equal strength or even inferior when the Kandyans keeping simply on the defensive obliged them to penetrate into their jungly mountains, Senevirat nevertheless knew well, that the south of Ceylon was only a part, and a very small part of the Portuguese empire in the East, and that the Governor of Colombo, the King of Malwana as he was called at Kandy, could at any moment get reinforcements from Goa, when he would become a dangerous enemy, against whom the King of Kandy could hardly try his strength.

Further, Senevirat was not as yet firmly established on his throne. True, his party had imposed him on the unfortunate Queen Donna Catharina, but this princess was not yet resigned to her forced marriage and the majority of the Kandyans looked upon him as a sort of temporary King, or rather Regent during the minority of Don Juan's eldest son Mahastane, who was already a grown up youth.

If therefore on his accession to the throne, there would be the least possibility of a reconciliation with the Portuguese, Senevirat would certainly have accepted it gladly.

But the Portuguese committed the same political blunder they had done with Don Juan who, once firmly established on the throne, desired ardently to be recognized by Portugal. The mistake this time was greater, since Senevirat had not done them the wrongs which, in the case of Don Juan, could not be easily forgotten. Nevertheless the Portuguese took towards the new King of Kandy a proud provoking attitude and, though during the first years of his reign there were no important disputes among them, there was certainly no question of a reconciliation.

The reason of this attitude of the Portuguese towards the King of Kandy could also be explained by the radical change in their policy, since a great part of Ceylon had been incorporated into their extensive eastern empire.

Till 1597, the Portuguese were satisfied with a nominal supremacy, as we would call it to-day a protectorate over the native Rulers of the Island. They made treaties with them by which the native Kings accepted to be vassals of the Portuguese Crown, a condition which gave a great advantage to these petty Sovereigns whom the Portuguese protected and defended against their enemies.

Till then, the garrisons which the Portuguese had kept in

Ceylon served only to raise their prestige, to protect their trade, and to safeguard the authority of the native Kings, their allies.

But, since they had become masters of one third of Ceylon, and since the Dutch hoped to evince them with the aid of the native Rulers, the conquest of the whole Island had become for them a necessity, the only practical way of defeating the Dutch.

Now, if King Don Juan and after him Senevirat desired an alliance with the Portuguese they understood it on the lines of the treaty of 1517 with Bhuwaneka Bahu.

Such an arrangement however was no more compatible with the new policy of the Portuguese in Ceylon. Far from desiring to establish these native Rulers more firmly on their throne, as they had done up to 1597, their present policy was rather to dethrone them as the conquest of the whole Island was now their only safeguard against the Dutch aggression.

The mistake committed by the Portuguese was not that they did not endeavour to renew the friendly relations with the King of Kandy. If it was now their intention to conquer his kingdom, and they were strong enough to do so with reinforcements from Goa, it was self evident that they should no longer tie down their hands with treaties.

Their mistake lay in the fact that this change of policy was made at a time when there arose on the horizon a new and formidable enemy.

And was it a mistake, or was it perhaps at that moment an unavoidable necessity?

In the face of the growing power of the Dutch in the East, did not the conquest of the kingdom of Kandy, who could become for them a base of operation, impose itself on the Portuguese?

If such was the case, and it was so undoubtedly, quick action was necessary. The Portuguese lost too much time. The government of Goa was always guilty of slowness where the affairs of Ceylon were concerned.

Such hostile attitude towards the King of Kandy, this long uncertainty, forced the King into the arms of the Dutch.

At this critical period, the Portuguese had but two alternatives: either to bind themselves closely to Senevirat by a treaty which would assure him the possession of his throne and the integrity of his territory, and clearly show him that he would gain more by remaining faithful to the Portuguese than allying himself with their enemies, or gathering together all the forces at their disposal as well in Ceylon as in Goa, conquer the kingdom of Kandy and annex it once for all to the Portuguese empire, depriving thus the Dutch of their base of operation.

In either case prompt action was imperative, they delayed matters, and this delay was the mistake they made, which compromised definitively the future of the Portuguese Rule in Ceylon.

In the meantime an armistice was concluded between the Portuguese and the Dutch. One of the articles of the
1609 treaty allowed the Dutch free trade in India till the

expiration of the armistice. The Dutch here acted in bad faith and resolved to abuse of this article for establishing themselves more firmly in India by entering into treaties with the native princes.

Ceylon had for them a special importance as a station on the route to Java and the government of Amsterdam resolved to renew the interrupted relation with the King of Kandy. When Peter Both, the first Dutch Governor General was leaving for Batavia, prince Maurice of Nassau, who was then at the head of the government of Holland, gave him a letter for Senevirat. Not being able to stop at Ceylon Both, on his arrival at Java, sent Marcellin Boschhouder as his plenipotentiary to the King of Kandy.

Senevirat received him in grand style and, on the 11th May 1612 a treaty was signed. In this document, the full
1612 text of which is given by Baldeus, Boschhouder gives to Senevirat the title of Emperor of Ceylon, and promises to help him in all his wars with the Portuguese, and secures for the Dutch the monopoly of the trade with the kingdom of Kandy and the right of building a fort on the Bay of Kottyar with a permanent Dutch garrison.

After the signature of the treaty Boschhouder wished to return to Batavia to present his report to the Governor General and to have the treaty ratified. But Senevirat objected to his departure, giving as a pretext that it would be an infraction of the treaty, which stipulated that a Dutchman should always sit in the Council of the King of Kandy. Boschhouder consented to remain, not however without making the King pay him for his condescension. Not satisfied with the rich present he had extorted from the King, the vain and foolish Dutchman made the King confer on him pompous titles, of which probably Senevirat did not understand much. And thus, in one day Boschhouder became prince of Mingone and Kockelekorle, President of the Supreme Council, Grand Admiral of the fleet and Grand Master of the Order of the Golden Sun.

Boschhouder took seriously his high sounding titles: Grand Admiral of the fleet without a single boat, he had some small vessels constructed at Kottyar and captured near Cape Comorin a few Portuguese trading vessels and brought a fairly good booty to Kandy.

Hardly had the Dutch constructed their fort at Kottyar, when it was surprised by a Portuguese force of 4,000 men, 3,000 Singhalese and 1,000 Europeans commanded by Don Simon Correa Wikramasingha. The Dutch garrison was put to the sword, and the fort dismantled. This happened on the 11th May 1612. It was the first encounter between the Dutch and the Portuguese in Ceylon, and it will be noticed that the Portuguese troops were under the command of a Singhalese General.

Simon Wikramasingha, having obtained the end of his expedition was returning to Colombo, when he met a Kandyan army commanded by the Mudeliyar Marasinghe advancing to the rescue of Kottyar. In the battle that followed Don Simon lost 600 men in slain, wounded and prisoners.

The prisoners were brought to Kandy, and King Senevirat ordered them all to be put to death. When they were informed of their fate, two officers Nuno Velho Travassos and Francis Macedo holding a Crucifix in their hand exhorted the men to die like

Christians. They threw themselves on their knees, asking God pardon for their sins, and all died praying and offering their lives to our Lord Jesus Christ for the conversion of the pagans of Ceylon.

The hostilities having thus commenced, Senevirat wishing to show his power to the Dutch, his new allies, ordered an army of 50,000 men to be assembled. It was to be divided into two bodies. The Ràja of Uva, at the head of the first division was to lay siege to Galle, and Boschhouder at the head of the other was to capture the fortifications of Balane, then held by the Pòrtuguese and then besiege Colombo.

This plan due, no doubt, to the vain imagination of Boschhouder was too good to be carried out. Time was required to collect 50,000 men and Jerome d'Azevedo opened the campaign. He marched on Kandy at the head of 700 Portuguese and 6,000 Singhalese troops commanded by Simon Wikramasingha who had under him the Dessawes of Matara, the seven Korles and Sabaragamuva.

Leaving Colombo on the 1st August, they reached Balane on the 19th. Azevedo remained fifteen days at Balane, adding new works to the already strong fortifications, after which, having strengthened the garrison of the place, he entered into the narrow valley leading to Kandy.

Meanwhile, Senevirat did not succeed to assemble more than 10,000 men, and feared for the fate of his capital. Such was the situation of Kandy that, once the enemy had mastered the narrow mountain passes that surround Balane, no other obstacle is to be encountered than the river Mahawella Ganga. This river near the approaches of Kandy was fordable in three places.

King Senevirat erected strong entrenchments to defend the fords. He had the bottom of the river strewn with thorns of a plant known in Ceylon as the elephant thorn. They are more than an inch in length and strong like nails, they were made in bundles and attached to a stone they were placed on the sand wherever the river was fordable. Such thorns could pierce the strongest shoes, and tore frightfully the bare feet of the native soldiers. Moreover a network of thorny rattan was arranged in the water.

It was thus that Azevedo's troops had to pass the rapid current under the fire of the enemy's batteries, and without any shelter where they could use their arms.

The men hesitated. Then the military chaplain, a Franciscan, Fr. Emmanuel of St. Joseph, having the Governor at his side, planted a wooden Cross on the shore and the whole army falling on their knees venerated the sign of their redemption. And many saw the Blessed Virgin Mary appear above the Cross. This gave them courage. Then, another Franciscan Fr. Casper of Madanella entered first into the river, calling to the Catholic soldiers to follow him. All followed cutting with their swords the thorny network, and notwithstanding the obstacles and the steady fire from the enemy's batteries, they reached the opposite bank, and without suffering great losses took the entrenchments. The Kandyans fled in panic and King Senevirat without entering his capital, sought refuge in the forests.

Kandy thus fell into the hands of the victors. The town was

sacked and Azevedo ordered to burn down the King's palace and the pagan temples.

The Governor Jerome d'Azevedo contented himself with the hard lesson he had given to King Senevirat and did not deem prudent to pursue his success. Senevirat was vanquished but new troops were daily pouring into his camp and, if he once took the offensive Azevedo's position could become critical. He gave therefore his troops three days rest and returned to Balane, where the victory was celebrated by a solemn High Mass and a procession of thanksgiving. The Governor left at Balane 250 Portuguese and a body of 1,000 native troops under the command of captain Dominic Carvalho Cão, and returned to Colombo with the remainder of his troops.

Meanwhile, new troops as said above, were pouring into King Senevirat's camp so that in a very few days he found himself again at the head of a formidable army and thirteen days after Azevedo's departure he came down from Kandy with all his available troops and laid siege to Balane. This siege did not last long, for, on the very first night Carvalho Cão made a sortie and inflicted him a crushing defeat and Senevirat fled to Kandy with the remains of his disbanded army.

Seeing now his army destroyed, his kingdom open to the enemy and his throne in danger, for the Portuguese could easily conquer now the kingdom and drive him out of it, Senevirat made overtures of peace. On his part the Governor Azevedo understood well, that now if ever would be the time to put an end to that kingdom and annex it to the Portuguese dominions, but he did not command the necessary forces and could not expect reinforcements from Goa. He therefore sent to Kandy the Franciscan Fr. Casper of Madanella as a plenipotentiary to conclude with King Senevirat a treaty of peace.

The Franciscan showed to be an able diplomatist, for he returned to Colombo with a treaty by which King Senevirat declared himself a vassal to the King of Portugal, promised to pay a yearly tribute and ceded for ever to the Portuguese all the provinces of the kingdom of Kandy that they had occupied, annulling at the same time the treaty he had concluded six months ago with the Dutch.

It is not known where Boschhouder remained all this time in hiding.

The ratification of this treaty was Azevedo's last public act in Ceylon, for, in the early part of December he was appointed Viceroy and left for Goa after having been Governor of Ceylon for twenty-one years.

Having thus secured peace Senevirat endeavoured to strengthen his power. Many of the most influential Kandyan chiefs were dissatisfied with his rule and awaited only the coming to age of Mahastane, King Don Juan's eldest son, to raise against him. At their head stood the Raja of Panua.

Senevirat had seized a compromising correspondence of this prince with the Portuguese. He sent now Boschhouder to take him prisoner. The Dutchman, after having devastated his province brought him in chains to Kandy. The King condemned him to death.

As the Raja was of royal blood he was executed with the honours due to his high rank. The scaffold was draped in white, the royal colour, a grand gilt chair was placed on it on which the Raja sat. He appeared calm, and looked on the crowd which surrounded the scaffold. But, when they began to divest him of the insignia of his dignity, he lost his countenance and began to ask if there was for him no hope of pardon; when answered that there was none he exclaimed: — „Unhappy prince, to what am I reduced!" — The gilt chair was replaced by the block and hê was beheaded.

His chief followers were condemned to have their head crushed under the feet of an elephant.

## CHAPTER 4

# THE DEATH OF DONNA CATHARINA

Prince Mahastane Don Juan's eldest son had now attained his majority. He was a handsome and talented youth and
1613 much beloved by the Kandyans, and King Senevirat feared that they would force him to hand over the Crown to the legitimate heir. One day, when the young prince on his way to a hunting party was crossing the Mahaveli Ganga, the boat capsized and he got drowned in the river.

All suspected the King to have had a hand in the death of young Mahastane and Queen Donna Catharina made him bitter reproaches. They made him a great funeral according to the pagan rite, and Boschhouder, though a Protestant, set fire to the funeral pile on which the corpse was burned.

Queen Donna Catharina could not be consoled after the death of her eldest son. She would hardly eat anything and was visibly sinking. She left Kandy and went to her country house at Welmantotte, where she got ill, and from the first day of her illness had the presentiment that her end was approaching. She granted life pensions to her servants and gave liberty to all her slaves.

Finally feeling death near, her greatest concern was for her children. She had one surviving son and two daughters by Don

Juan, and two sons, Xavier Cumara Banda and Raja Singha, by Senevirat. She had them brought to Welmantotte, for she feared to leave them in the hands of Senevirat, whom from the time of her forced marriage she had always despised. She summoned the Raja of Uva who was her relative and after having embraced her children asked him to protect them in case of need.

The King having entered her room she told him bitterly: — „You are the cause of my death." — Senevirat who loved her much, was greatly affected by these words.

After that, Donna Catharina did not speak to any one, but one day addressing the Raja of Uva she told him with great sadness: — „Oh! how unfortunate I am, a Christian, I have worshipped idols, I have offered sacrifices to the devil, and I knew well the truth. I see the devils who surround me and want to strangle me." —

Boschhouder hearing that, approached the Queen's bed and said: — „But don't forget that the devils can do nothing against a Christian who repents of his sins and deplores his past life. Calm yourself and pray God in the name of Jesus Christ our Saviour, to have pity on your soul." —

These words seemed to calm the Queen, and after a moment she said: — „Yes, I am a Christian, I will pray. Pray with me." —

Boschhouder began then to recite the Our Father and the Credo. Being a Protestant he omitted the Hail Mary. And yet, what could console more the dying Queen than that sublime appeal to the Mother of God.

When Boschhouder had finished, Donna Catharina exclaimed in

Portuguese: — „O Christo ajuda mi! Oh, Christ come to my assistance." —

A few days later feeling herself getting weaker she sent for her children and after having embraced them tenderly she said: — „O my poor children in what hands I am leaving you." — And then exclaiming: — „Oh! my God, receive my soul!" — she expired.

Thus died at the age of 35 years this Queen on whom such high hopes had been built.

As a small child, she followed her father into exile. An orphan in tender age, she received the news of the murder of her brother King Philip II.

At the age of eleven forced against her will from her peaceful retreat at Manaar, haunted by sad presentiments, she was placed on the throne of Kandy. After a short interval of peace and happiness, came the murder of Xavier Banda, to whom it seems she was attached. Then the hurried flight from Kandy, then the terrible day of Balane, the death of Lopez de Sousa, who was for her like a father, and herself a prisoner, treated by the conqueror with the most savage brutality and forced to become his wife. And she was only a girl of twelve years.

She never loved Don Juan, but having become a mother, she had resigned herself to her fate. He had been brought up like herself in a civilized atmosphere, a Christian, at least in name, in the midst of Kandyan barbarity he was for her a companion with whom she could live in community of ideas: and she was perhaps sorry when Don Juan died.

In the troubles that followed she showed a force of mind and an energy that surprised every one, but her misfortunes were far from ended.

Forced again to become the wife of Senevirat, a barbarian, a man without culture to whom she could never accustom herself. A pagan, he obliged her to take part in the ceremonies of his idolatrous worship.

All her love was for her children, and she must have suffered much to see them brought up like pagans. Her only consolation was that, thanks to Senevirat's Portuguese sympathies she could give them Catholic teachers, the most distinguished among whom was Fr. Francis Negrão. And as we will see later, two of her surviving sons, Vijayapala and Cumara Banda, returned to the Faith of their mother.

At last when dying broken hearted, full of fear and remorse, she had at her deathbed only a Protestant to speak to her about God!

What a life for a young woman, and what a pathetic figure in history was this Catholic Queen of Kandy!

Senevirat gave Donna Catharina a splendid funeral, but a pagan one. After that, gnawed by remorse, for he had loved in his own way the unfortunate Queen and was deeply moved by the bitter reproaches she made him on her deathbed, Senevirat fell dangerously ill, and it was thought he would die.

The events that followed Donna Catharina's death are not clear.

1615 It seems that Boschhouder lost much of his credit with King Senevirat, who now understood how little profit he had got from his Dutch alliance and desired to remain on good terms with the Portuguese.

Seeing his influence gone Boschhouder left Kandy in 1615 and returned to Holland, where he wanted the government of the Republic to recognize the pompous titles of prince of Mingone and Kockelekorle and Grand Master of the Order of the Golden Sun, he had extorted from the King of Kandy. The government treated him rather coldly, he then quarelled with the Directors of the Dutch East India Company. He left Holland and went to Copenhagen where he entered into the Danish service, after having promised to King Christian IV of Denmark to deliver him the Island of Ceylon.

After having concluded a treaty with the Danish government which he signed in the name of the King of Kandy as his plenipotentiary, Boschhouder left for Ceylon with two Danish ships, which were followed by five others under the command of Admiral Gule Gedde.

Boschhouder died during the voyage. Admiral Gule Gedde after a passage of 22 months cast anchor in the Bay of Kottyar. He sent a messenger to King Senevirat to announce him the death of Marcellin Boschhouder, and sent him a copy of the treaty signed by him at Copenhagen, and in which among others it had been stipulated, that the King of Kandy was to repay to the Danes the value of the seven ships and the costs of the expedition.

Senevirat indignantly replied that he had not authorised Boschhouder to sign any treaty, and that, if the Danes liked to make distant travels, they could make them at their own cost.

Admiral Gedde seeing that his expedition had failed, since

Senevirat absolutely refused to have anything to do with the Danes, seized Boschhouder's property found on board, giving only a portion of it to his widow. He gave the Dutch adventurer whose remains were on one of the ships a honorable funeral and, towards the middle of 1620, left Kottyar on his return voyage to Denmark.

Thus ended the attempt of the Danes to make themselves masters of Ceylon.

## CHAPTER 5

# THE PRETENDER NICAPETI

Don Jerome d'Azevedo having been appointed Viceroy, the Governorship of Ceylon was given to Emmanuel Homen
1616 Mascarenhas. Being an able administrator he took great care of the organization of the country and the well being of the native population.

He was succeeded by Nuno Alvarez Pereira, a younger brother of the Count of Feira, who since the beginning of his administration had to deal with a rather serious rebellion.

We have related in another chapter, how, after the conquest of Sitawacca, the infant Nicapeti, Raja Singha's grandson, was baptised at Colombo, under the name of Philip, and later on sent to Portugal to complete his studies at the University of Coïmbra where he died in 1618.

A young Singhalese of low caste, but carefully educated at Colombo, appeared in some distant villages of the coast, pretending to be Don Philip Nicapeti, secretly returned from Portugal to reconquer his grandfather's throne.

In a short time he found himself at the head of 5,000 followers, and made incursions into the Portuguese territory sacking and burning down the Christian villages.

On the 6th December he captured Mategama a village of some

importance. While the rebels were pillaging the houses, some of them approached the church. The parish priest Fr. Louis Matthew Polingotti, S. J. went to meet them, probably to protect the Christians, and they pierced him with a lance. Feeling himself mortally wounded, he dragged himself to the foot of the Cross which was raised before the church and throwing himself on his knees he invoked the Holy Name of Jesus whilst the pagans dispatched him with their lances.

Fr. John Matella, also a Jesuit, was at Mategama on a visit to Fr. Polingotti. He tried to run away, but seeing himself surrounded by the rebels, he fell on his knees and recommending his soul to God awaited death. They pierced him with lances.

Then they cut off the heads of the Fathers and fixed them on spears from both sides of the door of the church. They sacked the church and mutilated the figure of Christ on the Cross at the foot of which the Fathers had been murdered.

Fr. Polingotti was an Italian aged 38, Fr. Matella aged 32 was a Portuguese. They were buried at Mategama. Later their bodies were taken to Colombo.

1617 When the news of the murder of the Missionaries reached Colombo, the Governor sent a body of troops to avenge their death, but, crushed by the number, they took to flight, and were running in disorder through the village of Mategama, when passing near the Cross stained with the blood of Fr. Polingotti, a young officer, Don Emmanuel Correa, probably Don Simon Wikramasinghe's son, showing to the fugitives the mutilated Christ, exclaimed: — „Look at that, we must either conquer or die for Christ!“ — And he turned his horse towards the enemy. The soldiers, they were all Singhalese, followed him, and they inflicted to the rebels a crushing defeat.

Another day, during the battle, a body of Singhalese troops commanded by the Dessawe of the Seven Korles, Don Louis Gomez Pinto, whom the King of Kandy had secretly gained for the pretender whom he favoured, was on the point of passing over to the rebels already hailing the false Nicapeti as King, an officer of royal blood called Don Constantine barred them the way and exclaimed: — „Stop! If you are looking for your King, I am the man, for, as you all know, I am a descendant of your ancient Kings.“ — And placing himself at their head he led them on the rebels and inflicted them a bloody defeat. For this gallant deed the Governor appointed Don Constantine Dessawe of the Seven Korles instead of the traitor Louis Gomez Pinto.

The Governor employed against the rebels native troops commanded by Singhalese officers. It consisted chiefly of skirmishes and pillage and would have been easily ended but that King Senevirat favoured the pretender.

The self called Nicapeti was an able leader of bands of partisans. He worked on the superstitious minds of the native soldiers by all manner of tricks, which to us would seem childish, but which impressed their simple minds. So, when the Governor's troops were encamped for the night in the forests, they heard mournful voices from the top of the trees upbraiding them for serving under the Portuguese banner, when, at a distance of a few miles stood

Nicapeti, their King, their god, the right eye of the Sun. At other times they would find writings attached to the trunks of the trees, spreading the most alarming news.

Notwithstanding all this, the false Nicapeti was driven into the forests of the centre of the Island. He made his last stand near Anuradhapura, was defeated and disappeared; his followers surrendered, and that was the end of the rebellion.

King Senevirat sued for peace and the Governor made him sign a new treaty on the base of that of 1612. Senevirat once more declared himself a vassal to the King of Portugal and promised to pay a yearly tribute of four elephants and a certain quantity of arecanuts and of cinnamon.

Probably this treaty was the reason why he refused to enter into relations with the Danes. He now feared the Portuguese and had lost confidence in the support of the Dutch who, after the treaty he had concluded with Boschhouder, in which they had promised him their aid against the Portuguese, never again came to Ceylon and had abandoned him to his own resources.

Constantine de Saa de Noronha who, in 1617, had succeeded to Alvarez Pereira as Governor of Ceylon, did not deceive himself as to the value of the treaty with King Senevirat. He well knew that the King of Kandy would break it at the first occasion. He now felt himself abandoned by the Dutch who were too much occupied elsewhere to be able to attempt the conquest of Ceylon, but it was but too clear that, when the Dutch returned, Senevirat would again ally himself with them.

Now, the Portuguese were always exposed to loose their possessions in Ceylon, so long as the Dutch could make Kandy their base of operations. The Portuguese in Ceylon were certainly strong enough to resist the Dutch alone, but they could not resist the Dutch allied to the King of Kandy. Thus the conquest of Kandy forced itself necessarily upon the Portuguese and became for them a matter of vital importance.

Another danger which equally menaced the Portuguese in Ceylon was the kingdom of Jaffna. Not that they feared an alliance between the Dutch and the King of Jaffna. The King of Jaffna was not strong and powerful enough for the Dutch to take the trouble to ally themselves with him, but they could easily conquer his kingdom and make it their base of operation against the Portuguese.

Now the experience of one hundred years had thought the Portuguese how little they could rely on the treaties concluded with the native Kings, and now that they found themselves face to face with the Dutch there was no other way than to dethrone these Kings, and unite the whole Island under their immediate Rule. The two kingdoms of Kandy and Jaffna were a permanent danger, they had to be suppressed. And, once masters of the whole Island with a great native army and their European contingent, there was no fear of the Dutch being able to dislodge them from Ceylon.

And therefore, the government of Lisbon decided the conquest of the whole Island. Unhappily for the Portuguese, and more so perhaps for the Ceylonese as well Singhalese as Tamils, this decision was taken too late.

Having received such orders from Lisbon, the Governor Constantine de Saa de Noronha, decided to take profit of the armistice concluded with Holland and which he knew to be only a temporary peace, to conquer the whole Island, and so assure definitively its possession to the Crown of Portugal.

Remembering that the King of Kandy had always escaped a final defeat and that the Portuguese expeditions into that hilly country had often ended in a disaster, the Governor conceived the bold plan to conquer first the kingdom of Jaffna, establish there the Portuguese Rule, and then invade the kingdom of Kandy at the same time from the north and from the south. The events in Jaffna which we will now narrate gave the Portuguese the occasion to interfere into the affairs of the northern kingdom.

## CHAPTER 6

# THE KINGDOM OF JAFFNA

We have left Jaffna thirty years ago, at the moment when in
1587 1587 Andrew Furtado de Mendoza had installed on the throne King Sagara Raja II. The appointment was confirmed by the Viceroy Edward Menezes Count of Tarouca, and it turned out a most fortunate choice for, during the 18 years that Sagara Raja sat on the throne, the kingdom was well governed and peace never disturbed.

Sagara Raja was a wise man of a mild and sympathetic character,
1588 he loved peace and took great care that justice be well administered.

At the bottom of his heart he was a Catholic, but postponed always Baptism through fear of a rebellion of his heathen subjects.

He protected the Missions and helped generously the Franciscan Fathers whenever they wanted to build a church or to start a new school, although sometimes it happened that, when some powerful chief protested against it, he hindered them to establish a Mission in some place, where there was hope to make many conversions.

Fr. Francis of the East was at that time Superior of the Mission

1602 of Jaffna. He was the only survivor of the founders of the Mission of Ceylon, where he had come from Portugal in 1542, on the same ship with St. Francis Xavier and Fr. John of Villa Conde. The venerable old man had worked now for 60 years in the Mission of which he was one of the founders.

It happened in the year 1602, that old Fr. Francis of the East was on a visit to the Christians of the Island of Tanadiva, when walking on the sea-shore he saw two fine pieces of timber floating in the surf. He had a large Cross made of them which he planted on the place where the timber was stranded. Now it happened that the land belonged to a prince of royal blood who, not daring to remove the Cross, complained to the King who gave orders that the Cross be removed.

When a Tamil magistrate was approaching the place with a troop of armed men, to carry out the King's order, old Fr. Francis threw himself on his knees at the foot of the Cross, and embracing it exclaimed: — „Oh! sweet Jesus, grant me the grace to die a martyr at the foot of Thy Cross!" —

The magistrate drew back and turning to his soldiers said: — „Let us be off. Let the King order me something else, I will obey him, but we are not going to fight this venerable old man." — And the King approved of his conduct.

About this time the pagans had set fire to the church of Our Lady of Victories, and the roof being of cadjan the flames enveloped it in an instant. Fr. Andrew of St. Joseph, who lived in a small room, attached to the church would certainly have perished if a

Catholic youth called Augustine had not courageously dashed through the flames and saved his life. The King had hastened to the place, consoled Fr. Andrew and promised him that he would re-build him a much finer church, and did it at once.

Another Missionary mentioned at that epoch for his great zeal was Fr. Angelo of the Saviour. He erected at Manaar the church of St. John which later on in 1642 the Franciscans gave over to the Dominicans. He also built St. James' church at Parangalim and others at Aripo, Navati and Chilavali.

Towards the end of 1602 Fr. Francis of the East, broken down by age and the fatigues of 60 years of Apostolate, resigned his post of Superior of Jaffna. He requested that his successor be Fr. Peter of Betancourt who then resided at the convent of St. Antony at Bassein, and had already been a Missionary in Jaffna, and was much beloved by the King and by the people. Under the administration of this great Missionary the Apostolate in the north of Ceylon took a great extension.

One day Fr. Peter of Betancourt having to build a large church and the site at his disposal not being large enough, wanted to acquire an adjoining piece of land. But the place belonged to some Mahomedans, who had built on it a small mosque and they refused to sell. Fr. Peter went to King Sagara Raja asking his help in this affair, as, without this land, he could not build the church.

The King answered that it seemed to him that nothing could be done, for, he said, once the Mahomedans had built a mosque, they could never be turned out from the place.

— „ Oh ! said Fr. Peter, if it is only a question of turning them out, although I am not the King, I will do that ! " —

— „ And how will you manage it ? " — Asked Sagara Raja.

— „ Very simply, said Fr. Peter. I will set fire to the mosque, then you will give them another piece of land and some money to re-build there their mosque." —

The King laughed at the good joke. But, on the following night the mosque burned down to the ground. The Mahomedans who had their suspicions went to the King and accused Fr. Peter of Betancourt. Sagara Raja asked for proofs. They said they had none but, that it was well known in the town who had set fire to the mosque, and that the Father required the site for building his church.

— „ Well, said the King, you say that he has set fire to your mosque, because he wants the grounds, and you intend to re-build it on the same place. But do you know Fr. Peter ? I know him, he is a terrible man. If he needs the site for his church, were you to re-build your mosque twelve times, twelve times he will burn it down." — So saying he offered them a much better site in the Mahomedan quarter of the town.

And Fr. Peter of Betancourt got the land and re-built on a larger scale the church of Our Lady of the Victory, which, later on was called Our Lady of Miracles.

Meanwhile King Sagara Raja II had grown old, and his nephew

1614 Changali, was acquiring influence in the palace. He was known for his hatred against the Catholics. Once, on the 24th July 1614 great arrangement being mad for a procession through the streets of the town with the statue of Our Blessed Lady, Changali sent word to Fr. Peter of Betancourt, that the King forbade the procession to pass before his palace. Fr. Peter sent at once two Portuguese, Anthony Alvarez and Anthony de Fonseca to Sagara Raja who was astonished at the message and answered: — „Go to the Father, and tell him, that, not only the procession may pass this way, but, if needed, I myself will come in person to honor the Holy Mother of God." —

Towards the end of 1615 King Sagara Raja II fell dangerously ill. Knowing perfectly the Christian doctrine, and
1615 feeling himself on the point of death he sent for Fr. Peter of Betancourt to baptise him. But his nephew Changali closed the gates of the palace, and the King died.

## CHAPTER 7

# CHANGALI

Sagara Raja II left only one son, an infant of three years, who was prociaimed King under the Regency of his uncle
1616 who, like the late King his brother, was of a generous and amiable character and had always favoured the Christians.

But the ambitious Changali had already formed a party. In an attack on the palace the Regent was killed and Changali seized the power.

As he aspired to the throne his first resolve was to put the little King to death. He was however not sure if, in that case, he would not loose the support of his party, as the Jaffnese had been much attached to Sagara Raja II. He did not dare to harm the royal child and for the time being had to remain content with the title of Regent.

Whilst these events were happening in Jaffna, the Viceroy Don Jerôme d'Azevedo had ratified the choice of the first Regent and, when the commander of Manaar came to Jaffna to install him solemnly, he found the Regent dead and Changali holding the power.

Fr. Peter of Betancourt exposed to the commander the present state of things. He told him that Changali, who was backed by a strong party, could not be put out without a war and, as he was now in possession of the power, he deemed it would be more prudent to leave alone the past and to acknowledge him as Regent. The commander of Manaar did so after having made Changali responsible for the safety of the young King, and obtained from him the promise that he would never ally himself with the enemies of the Portuguese. This act of the commander was never ratified by the Viceroy, but matters were left as they were.

Changali's government was tyrannical and rebellions became frequent.

Once the rumour spread in the town, that he had put to death the infant King. The people rose to arms and surrounded the palace. Changali went out on a balcony holding the child in his arms and showed him to the people. They prostrated themselves on the ground before their little master and dispersed satisfied.

Since Changali had come into power, the Queen mother, the widow of Sagara Raja II had lived in terror for the life of her child.

Once she succeeded in escaping at night from the palace, and brought the little King to Fr. Louis of St. Diego who had succeeded Fr. Peter of Betancourt as Superior of the Mission: — „ Take him, Father, she said, guard him as if he were your own son. They refuse me the right to call myself his mother. Protect him against Changali. You shall answer for him to God." —

Fr. Louis took the child in his arms, did his best to console the unfortunate Queen and promised her to protect the young King against his enemies.

Changali grew furious when he learned that the child had escaped from his power and he summoned Fr. Louis to restore it to him. But the courageous Missionary answered that the boy had been confided to his care by his mother and to her alone he would restore him.

Then Changali sent to the Franciscan Convent two of his grandees with soldiers to take the boy by force. The little King sobbed in the arms of the Father, and when they wished to take him, he clung to the Father's habit with his hands and with his teeth. Changali's messengers were so touched with emotion that they retired with tears in their eyes, and the tyrant did not dare to make another attempt to get back the child, for fear of the Jaffnese who had a great affection for their little King, and knew him safer in Fr. Louis' hands than in those of Changali.

The Jaffnese were tired of the tyrant's Rule and rebellions became more frequent. One day there was a serious
1617 mutiny in the army. The soldiers led by their officers, marched in arms to the palace. Fr. Louis of St. Diego endeavoured in vain to stop them. Seeing that his words produced no effect on the mutineers he informed Changali of his danger, and the prince with his family fled from the palace and took refuge in the Franciscan Convent where they remained in hiding till 5,000 soldiers who had remained faithful to him were called over from another place to protect him against the rebels.

Placed in this position Changali instead of asking help from the commander of Manaar, broke his word and called to his aid the

Raja of Tanjore, who sent him troops with whose aid he suppressed the rebellion with an incredible cruelty.

Finally seeing that with the animosity of the Jaffnese who detested him he would never attain the goal of his
1618 ambition, to become King of Jaffna, and well knowing that the Portuguese would always give their support to the rightful King, though he was but a child, he entered into communication with the Dutch, who had already settled in India. He offered them several strong stations in the kingdom of Jaffna, and proposed that together with the Moors of the Malabar Coast they attack the Island of Manaar and capture it from the Portuguese. The commander of Manaar made all necessary preparations to repel the invasion, but it would seem that Changali's arrangements with the Dutch did not come to anything, for the fleet which was daily expected did not appear in the waters of Manaar, and the commander easily beat off the war junks of the Moors who rowed along the coast and pillaged the villages of the fishermen.

The Governor Constantine de Saa de Noronha, acting on the representations of the Missionaries, who wished at all cost avoid a war, which would scatter their Christians and disorganize their Missions, contented himself for this time by strongly admonishing Changali who, being Regent of a kingdom vassal to the King of Portugal had allied himself with the enemies of his Lord paramount.

But it seems that the admonition had no great effect for, a few months later a fleet of Moorish junks attacked the Island of Tanadiva. There were no troops to defend it. The Franciscan

Fathers sent for aid to the commander of Manaar, and meanwhile set themselves to organize the defence.

Fathers Anthony of St. Bernardine and Andrew of Loureiro at the head of their Christians prevented the Moors from landing, while Fr. Francis of St. Anthony having erected a battery on the shore sunk the enemy's largest vessel, and they defended the Island, till the arrival of a Portuguese squadron from Manaar put the Moors to flight.

Changali continued to treat with the Dutch, in the hope that with their aid he would become King of Jaffna, and as he knew how unpopular he was among the Jaffnese, he caused many influential chiefs, who could be an obstacle to his ambitious plan to be put to death.

Then the Governor saw clearly that more stringent measures had to be taken against Changali. It had become now
1619 an urgent necessity to deprive Changali of his power in order to prevent the Dutch establishing themselves at Jaffna and thus becoming an immediate danger for the Portuguese Rule in Ceylon.

Constantine de Saa de Noronha sent therefore a small army under the command of Philip d'Oliveira to subdue the Regent or else to dethrone him.

When Oliveira landed near Jaffna Changali, some say out of bravado, but more probably moved by fear, sent a messenger to welcome him. Oliveira answered by sending Fr. Anthony of St. Bernardine as a plenipotentiary to dictate him the conditions of peace. Changali refused, and notwithstanding all the endeavours of the Missionary to bring him to submission, persisted in his refusal.

Oliveira then marched on Jaffna and, after a desultory fight under the walls of the city captured it.

Changali with his family took to flight. They embarked on a boat to go to Point Pedro, but they were captured and brought to Jaffna.

The young King whom Fr. Louis of St. Diego had restored to the care of his mother was not found at the palace, and they already feared that Changali had put him to death, when captain Louis de Seixas discovered him hidden in a temple. The child was nearly mad with fright, he was only six years old. Oliveira did his best to quiet him down and to console him, the boy being bare-footed he got a pair of small shoes of red velvet embroidered with gold which pleased much the little King, and when he saw Fr. Louis his old foster-father he was quite happy. With the capture of the little King ended, so to say, the conquest of Jaffna.

Next morning, Philip d'Oliveira, and the little King, followed by all the officers, went to the church of Our Lady of Victories. At the door Fr. Emmanuel of Elvas presented a palm to the General. But Oliveira refused it saying: — „ Father, give it to Louis de Seixas for it is to him that we owe the victory."— „ I accept it, answered de Seixas, not as a recompense for my merits, but as a token of the goodwill of my chief." —

They entered the church, Philip d'Oliveira prostrated himself before the altar and they sang the Te Deum. Then, Oliveira raising the royal child in his arms offered him to the Holy Mother of God.

After that he was put again under the care of Fr. Louis of St. Diego, for whom the boy had a great affection.

Meanwhile the Raja of Tanjore, who pretended to be the Suzerain of the kingdom of Jaffna, had sent reinforcement to Changali; notwithstanding that they had come too late, their leader seeing how few were the Portuguese, disembarked his men with the object of re-capturing Jaffna. Oliveira who suffered from a wound he had received when capturing the town, had given up the command of his troops to his son-in-law Anthony de la Motte Galvão. All the soldiers went to confession, assisted to a solemn Mass, received Holy Communion and, on the evening went to meet the enemy. Oliveira and the Franciscan Fathers passed all the night in prayer in the church. Next morning when they were singing the Litany of the Blessed Virgin a messenger arrived and announced that Motte Galvão had gained a complete victory. 1,200 soldiers of Tanjore lay dead on the battlefield the remaining had taken to their ships and fled. The Te Deum was sung and now the conquest of the kingdom of Jaffna was an accomplished fact.

Up to the present Changali had been kept a prisoner at Jaffna. Peace being now restored, Oliveira sent him to Colombo under de Motte Galvão's escort. The Governor sent him to Goa where he was judged for high treason and for the many crimes he had committed and condemned to death.

Whilst expecting in prison his fate, he sent for the Superior of the Franciscan Fathers and told him that since his youth he had known the truth of the Catholic Faith and the depravity of heathenism. The many talks that he had with Fr. Peter of Betancourt, for whom he had a great veneration had confirmed him in his belief; but the ambition of becoming King of Jaffna which he could not attain, without the help of the heathen party, had always held him back. He was baptised, and passed his last days in sincere repentance for the many atrocities and crimes he had committed, his eyes fixed on the Crucifix, which he had asked to be put in his prison.

On the morning of his execution Don Philip Changali confessed again and received Holy Communion. On the way to the scaffold he told the Priest who accompanied him: — „Father, if I had the choice I would rather be a poor Catholic cooly than a heathen King." — When on the scaffold they wished to bind his hands, he said: — „It is not necessary. I gladly offer my life to Our Lord Jesus Christ in expiation of my sins." — He was beheaded. The Franciscans claimed his body, they dressed him, as he had asked, in the habit of their Order and buried him in their church.

Philip Changali's wife Donna Maria, who had been baptised with him, settled in Goa, where she devoted herself to works of charity.

As we have said above, the little King of Jaffna had been entrusted to the care of Fr. Louis of St. Diego who in the days of misfortune had held the place of a father to the poor royal orphan. But as they could not give him in Jaffna an education suitable for his high rank and exalted destiny, he was brought down to Colombo where his mother followed him.

He was a very intelligent boy and his piety was so great that his teachers had to moderate it. He was not yet baptised, but he so ardently asked for Baptism that when he reached the age of ten years his prayer was granted.

It was a proud day in Colombo that of the 18th June 1623 when the young King of Jaffna was baptised together with his mother the Queen Donna Clara, his sisters Isabella and Mary, his cousin Don Diego to whom Changali had caused both eyes to be pulled out, with his wife Donna Maria who was the sister of King Sagara Raja II, their children Philip, Francis, Bernardine and Agnes, and 65 other catechumens.

They were taken in procession to the church. The Governor who was the King's god-father put round his neck a rich gold chain to which a reliquary was attached. The King was named Don Constantine.

The Viceroy Francis de Gama Count of Vidiguera, wishing to supervise himself the boy's education, called him to Goa where he placed him in the College of the Three Kings.

It seems that at that time the Portuguese Government had the intention to restore him on his father's throne when he would have attained his majority, but the boy's aspirations were for monastic life, and as soon as his age allowed him to do so, he entered the Franciscan Novitiate at Goa and, under the name of Fr. Constantine of Christ distinguished himself later on by his learning and the sanctity of his life.

Thus the three old dynasties of Ceylon died out Catholic.

That of Kotta ended with King Don Juan Dharmapala and young Don Philip Nicapeti. That of Jaffna with King Constantine a Priest and a Franciscan Friar. That of Kandy with King Don Juan I who also became a Priest. Don Juan II Wimala Dharma founded a new dynasty related to the old one which lasted till 1739, when it was followed by a Tamil family, which governed or rather tyrannized the country till the British conquest in February 1815.

The kingdom of Kandy had the greatest number of Catholic Kings: We have already mentioned: Emmanuel Jayaweera I, Don Philip Jayaweera II, Xavier Banda, Philip II, Don Juan I, Donna Catharina, Don Juan II Wimala Dharma, and Senevirat's son and successor Raja Singha, as we will see later on was on the point of becoming a Catholic, when Pròtestant influence threw him back into heathenism:

Kotta had only one Catholic King, Don Juan Dharmapala and Jaffna one, the child Don Constantine if we do not count King Sagara Raja II, who asked for Baptism on his deathbed but was prevented to receive it by his nephew Changali.

History mentions moreover 19 princes of the royal family of Jaffna, 14 of that of Kandy and 11 of that of Kotta who were Catholics.

## CHAPTER 8

# FATHER ELEUTHERIUS OF ST. JAMES

We must now leave for another chapter the sequel of the event
1619 that happened at Jaffna after the kingdom had been conquered by Philip d'Oliveira, and return to Colombo, where the Governor Constantine de Saa de Noronha was pursuing his plan of the conquest of the whole Island, but at the same time organizing that part which was under his immediate Rule.

The Government of Lisbon had always at heart the education of the natives. No Colonial Government had ever done so much for education as the Portuguese in their immense dominions. If to-day we find in Ceylon no traces of their educational establishments it is because the Protestant Dutch have destroyed all the fine institutions which the Portuguese Government, with the aid of the Missionaries had founded and endowed.

If the Portuguese Rule had lasted for one century longer, Ceylon would be to-day the most civilized country of the East. The Protestant conquest arrested civilization just at the moment when it was taking the greatest expansion and re-plunged into barbarity one of the ablest people of Asia.

Now the progress of the Catholic Faith, increased yearly the number of boys who needed higher education, (the Buddhist at that time did not care much for it) and the necessity arose of a broader development of the educational system. There were at present two Colleges at Colombo, one, St. Anthony's under the direction of the Franciscan Fathers, the other under the Jesuits. In March 1619 the plan was made of starting a third College at Colombo, and opening two others, one at Galle and one at Negombo. They could not do that at once as neither the Jesuits nor the Franciscans could find a sufficient staff for these establishments and funds had to be provided for. For this reason, the idea of a third College at Colombo was abandoned and instead of it the existing Jesuit College was much increased and provided by Government with new funds, sufficient for the maintenance of one hundred boarders. Fr. Anthony Rubino a man of great learning and extraordinary virtue was appointed Rector. He died a martyr in Japan on the 21st March 1643, and the first formalities for his beatification had already been made.

In the meantime everything had to be prepared for the opening of Colleges at Galle and at Negombo.

The Jesuit Fathers were working with great zeal. In Colombo alone during that year they had baptised 150 adults and a great number of catechumens were preparing for Baptism. Their Missions in the outstations were directed from the College, the Rector being at the same time the Superior of all the Fathers of the Society of Jesus in Ceylon.

Fr. Peter Mexia, military chaplain of the fortified camp of Manicavere, exercised a great influence over the soldiers and the people of the neighbourhood. He trained them so well in the practice of true Christian life, that those who saw them used to say that it was only now that they truly understand what it was to be a Christian.

Eleven Jesuit Fathers had the care of twenty-one Mission stations, and they worked with so much zeal that in the year 1622 alone they had baptised 700 heathens. Fr. Anthony Rubino and the professors of the College were strengthening the Faith of the Catholics of Colombo with their preaching and their ministry.

We possess a letter written in 1621 by a Jesuit Father who gives us a good idea of the work of the Missionaries of the Society at that time:

—„ There are now, he writes, at the College, seven Fathers, two scholastics and two lay brothers. They have just
1621 finished their yearly spiritual retreat. During Advent they devoted themselves with more zeal for the salvation of souls, and their labours have been rewarded by a rich harvest. The devotion for processions which are made during Lent, has much increased this year, and not only the common people, but many persons of high standing take part in them, carrying lighted candles. Every Saturday the Fathers set out from the College carrying baskets of bread which they distribute to the poor in the town and to the prisoners in the jail. And many persons followed their example. Many enemies had been reconciled by the good Fr. Rector. The confessionals are besieged by a large crowd of penitents, the teaching of Catechism is well organized, and the Fathers preach every Sunday in the churches of the city.

At Kalpentyn, two Fathers are zealously at work instructing

the Christians dispersed in villages often far away from one another and administering the Sacraments in the five churches of the district. 100 adults have been baptised.

The Father in charge of the Mission of Munecerão, hopes to baptise the whole village and besides several others.

The Father recently sent to Chilaw, had already learned the language and baptised thirty heathens.

The Missionary at Caymela, loved and esteemed by all, has lately converted 39 pagans, and among them an old man aged 109 who died immediately after Baptism. The same Father visits the soldiers in their barracks, hears their confessions, and is so beloved by them, that he had no difficulty to stop the soldiers when they were so indignant against their general that they had resolved to kill him.

At Malwana, where the Governor has a palace, lives another Father, who aids him much with his wise counsels and Constantine de Saa de Noronha is very thankful for the services he renders him and is a great friend of our Society.

At Moratuwa 72 pagans have been converted by the Father who resides in this place, and people look on him as on a man sent from heaven. Though 72 years old, he spares himself no fatigue, where there is question of saving a soul or of helping the Christians.

Great progress has already been made in the residence of Galle, which has been started only in the month of March. One half of the church has already been built, thanks to the liberality of the commander of the fort and of the local Christians. And with God's help much good has been done during Lent. Besides a great number of confessions, the sermons on the Passion of Our Lord were heard with such emotion that more than once the preacher has been interrupted by the people who threw themselves on their knees weeping and sobbing. The same Father preaches three times a week, on Sunday in the principal church, on Wednesday in the chapel of the Confraternity of Mercy and on Saturday in the church of St. Dominic. Every afternoon according to the established custom, he teaches Catechism, which is followed by singing of hymns so well conducted, that many people are attracted by the beauty of the music. The Father has already opened a school in which he teaches himself. He still dwells in the house of the Confraternity of Mercy, but he has already taken possession of a village which the Governor, when visiting Galle, has given him for the support of his Mission. Four heathens had been already converted in that village." —

This letter shows that the conversions of pagan were not much easier at that time than they are now, and that the Missionaries had to work hard to baptise a few. It also clearly shows how false is the assertion of some modern Protestant writers, that the Portuguese used force and compulsion to bring the natives to the Catholic Faith.

It is a great pity that this letter and many others do not give the names of the Missionaries whose labours it narrates. But they were written to the Superiors in Europe who knew them well, and at that time, it was customary, when speaking of their merits not to mention the name but say simply: the Father who works at such a place.

Once master of the kingdom of Jaffna, Constantine de Saa de Noronha pursued his plan of isolating the kingdom of
1622 Kandy. Seeing that the Dutch and the Danes had held communications with the King of Kandy through the Bay of Kottyar which forms one of the best natural harbours of the world, he determined to get the mastery over it. Trincomalee was the chief commercial town on the shores of that Bay. He captured the town at the beginning of the year 1622, had the famous Hindu temple which overlooked the sea demolished, and with the materials thus obtained built a strong fort.

The Governor was within his rights for, though Trincomalee had not been included in the conquest of the kingdom of Jaffna by Philip d'Oliveira, it was nevertheless a dependence of that kingdom. Fearing nevertheless that King Senevirat would feel offended as Trincomalee was the only outlet for the trade of his kingdom, and not wishing to break the treaty of peace concluded with him in 1617, sent as his special envoy to the court of Kandy a very able Franciscan, Fr. Eleutherius of St. James, who fulfilled so well his peacemaker's Mission, that he and King Senevirat became great friends. The King kept him always near his person and not only entrusted him with the education of his sons, but allowed him to teach the Christian doctrine to the young princes.

Fr. Eleutherius, while playing the part of a diplomatist, never forgot however that he was a Missionary, and never omitted an occasion to speak of Religion with the King and the dignitaries of the court, and the King often pointed him out good humourously, saying: — „Look at this Portuguese, whenever he speaks to us of

Religion, he shuts so well our mouth, that we do not know what to answer to his arguments." —

Unfortunately Fr. Eleutherius was re-called from Kandy. When leaving, he proposed to the King the appointment of Fr. Francis Negrão as tutor to his sons, who were already big boys, a proposal that King Senevirat accepted with pleasure. He also left at Kandy his companion Fr. Joseph of St. Francis. At the moment of parting, the King embraced affectionately Fr. Eleutherius, and those present said, that they had never seen Senevirat so moved.

As a proof of the good relations renewed by Fr. Eleutherius of St. James between the King of Kandy and the
1623 Portuguese Government we possess a letter which Senevirat wrote to the King of Portugal on the 24th September 1623. He writes:

—„Ceylon is so far from Europe that your Majesty will excuse me for having delayed so long the fulfilment of my duty as your vassal, but it was only last winter that the news of your Majesty's accession to the throne has reached me. May God increase your power and grant you a long life and peaceful relations with your vassals. I beg your Majesty to command your officers to keep peace with me in order to allow me to govern my kingdom in a manner that would be to your Majesty's advantage and so as to enable me to grant to your officer all that is expected from me.

I have confided the education of my sons to the Franciscan Fathers in order that they might learn from them their duties to God and to your Majesty.

These good Fathers deserve your Majesty's regards, especially for the good work they do in this kingdom of Kandy, where many have shed their blood for their Faith and for their King. They do not seek gold and riches, their only aim is to gain souls to God. Men like them, who love poverty are the only ones who can exercise with success their holy ministry in this country. I want no others for my kingdom. We are pagans and ignorant but we know that virtue consists in the detachment from earthly things and from the riches of the world.

May God protect your Majesty and grant you a long life." —

Fr. Francis Negrão had already been teacher to the sons of the King, when they were but small boys. It was Queen Donna Catharina who had obtained from Senevirat to entrust the education of her children to a Franciscan Father. And many years later, her youngest son King Raja Singha, still remembered his good old tutor when, on the 1st March 1643, he wrote to King John IV of Portugal: — „To my mother's great joy, they entrusted my education to Fr. Francis Pedroso of the Franciscan Order. He taught me to read and to write and, thanks to his training, I acquired good manners and all what is required from a prince of royal blood.

Unfortunately the peace between the Portuguese and the King of Kandy was of short duration. A year later, in 1624 we see them again at war.

1624

The Governor Constantine de Saa de Noronha, foresaw that a final struggle with the Dutch for the possession of Ceylon was now unavoidable, and he prepared himself for it. He reinforced the camp at Manicavare and fortified Trincomalee, Batticaloa and Galle.

Senevirat got alarmed; he now saw his kingdom cut away from the sea, and surrounded from all sides with Portuguese territory. He hastily assembled his army and entered the Portuguese dominions, but repulsed by the Governor he retired to Kandy. The Governor marched on the capital, which, being unable to defend, the King retired with his army into the forests of the province of Uva, and Constantine de Saa de Noronha entered Kandy as a conqueror. But, not being strong enough to retain his conquest, he burned down the town and followed the King into Uva. Here he vainly endeavoured to draw Senevirat into a decisive battle, but the prudent King persisted in continuing a guerrilla war, which so exhausted the Portuguese troops that the Governor abandoned the pursuit and returned to Colombo.

## CHAPTER 9

# PHILIP D'OLIVEIRA

After the conquest of Jaffna in 1619, the Viceroy, having made the experience how little he could trust in the fidelity
1624
and loyalty of the princes of the royal house, appointed Philip d'Oliveira Regent during the minority of the young King Don Constantine. He kept this title till the day when Don Constantine, renounced to the Crown and entered the Franciscan Order. The kingdom of Jaffna was then incorporated into the Portuguese immediate dominions and Philip d'Oliveira appointed Governor of Jaffna, dependent however on the Governor of Colombo whose jurisdiction extended over the whole Island.

Philip d'Oliveira was a man of great virtue. He was devoted to the natives, who in return were very affectionate to him.

As soon as he saw his government firmly established he published a proclamation to the people of Jaffna in which he said that now that they were subjects to the King of Portugal, his Majesty's most cherished desire was to see them all Catholics, faithful and obedient to the Law of Christ, Our Lord and Our God. That none shall be induced against his will to embrace Christianity, but that the King would consider himself as well served by those who would give up the worship of their idols and become Catholics and that he himself as Representative of the King would favour them as much as was in his power.

In order to give the people a high idea of Christianity he treated with the greatest regard even the lowest Christian who came to speak with him. He himself gave them the example of a good Christian life: Every Sunday they saw him passing through the crowd in the church to kneel humbly at the confessional. He was a man of extraordinary piety, and his influence on the people was very great.

With Oliveira's support, the Franciscan and the Jesuit Fathers could now well organize their Missions. The whole
1625 kingdom of Jaffna was divided into 34 parishes, churches erected in each, and some of these churches were large and beautiful. Each parish had its school. The parishes on the coast were in the hands of the Franciscan Fathers, the Jesuits had those of the interior. The conversions were numerous: In four years, the Jesuits alone baptised 40,000 heathens. They had some Fathers who distinguished themselves by their zeal and indefatigable labours: Fr. Peter Bergnim, a Portuguese; Fathers Ignatius Bruno and Sebastian Andreotti, Italians and above all Fr. Emmanuel d'Acosta, a native of Colombo who died at the age of 35 years. He wrote the first Singhalese grammar and left after him a collection of beautiful sermons in which he explained the Christian doctrine to the pagans.

Towards the end of Oliveira's government, a great calamity fell over Jaffna: On Saturday the 20th February 1627, a
1627 terrific cyclone burst over the town. It lasted the

whole night and next day until 2 P.M. when the storm seemed to lessen. The people gathered in the church where Fr. Francis of Jesus preached a sermon on Our Lord's passion, but when after the sermon the procession was leaving the church, the storm broke out afresh with such violence that all had to run for shelter: some went home others were taking refuge in the churches. The storm lasted till Monday, overthrowing houses and uprooting trees. People were running in the streets uttering lamentable cries, and the violence of the wind was so great that they could not stand on their legs.

Soldiers were sent to their aid. They tried their best to maintain order, taking the women and the children to the church of Our Lady of Miracles, to the Governor's palace and to the house of the Confraternity of Mercy.

The sea had raised very high and the Franciscan Fathers seeing that the Governor's palace was unsafe, the waves battering against the walls, tried to persuade him to come to their Convent. The Governor replied that he could not abandon the poor people who had sought shelter under his roof. But soon it was clear that the palace was doomed and hasty arrangements were made to bring all the refugees to the Franciscan Convent. Oliveira's wife was afraid to go out into the raging storm, he told her gently: — „Come, where could we be safer than in the church, at the feet of Our Holy Mother, and under the protection of the Blessed Sacrament.“ — When all were in safety the Governor was the last to leave the tottering palace.

The church however did not seem to be a safer place. The violence of the storm made the tiles fly like dry leaves and was tearing the boards from the roof. In the midst of this frightful tumult a man came running with the news that an enormous tidal wave was advancing on the city and would swamp it. All were preparing to death. Then the Governor, asked for the banner of the Order of Christ, which had led him to so many victorious battles, and throwing it at the foot of the altar and prostrating himself on the ground: — „Oh! God, he exclaimed have pity on my people! Oh! Holy Virgin Mary, obtain from Thy Divine Son that they be saved from death. If they have sinned, may the punishment for their sins fall on me and on my children. I offer Thee my life and theirs, but save these unfortunate people." — And he remained so prostrated in prayer.

The wave rushed on with a deafening noise tearing down the houses of the town. When it came to the church it divided in two, the church remained surrounded by high walls of water rushing with great fury. All thought death imminent, but the waters slowly subsided, the wind fell, and soon they could leave the church.

For two days more the storm returned and always at the same hour, but less violent and of shorter duration.

The cyclone caused terrible ravages in the whole of the kingdom of Jaffna. Churches and villages were reduced to splinters. All the land was sown with uprooted cocoanut, panemaram and tamarind trees. Boats were found thrown a quarter of a mile inland. The wave ten feet high had penetrated one mile into the interior. No one knew the number of deaths. Many were drowned, others crushed under the ruins of their houses. A Franciscan Missionary and Fr. Peter Mexia S. J. saved themselves, by remaining all day on the top of a tree.

The town of Jaffna was in ruin. The Governor, had some houses which still remained slanting cleaned and arranged into a hospital, where he had gathered the sick and the famished. He himself looked after the men, whilst his wife and two daughters nursed the women, and his son-in-law Emmanuel Mesquita Pimentel with some soldiers took care of the children.

The Priests passed all the day in burying the dead whose bodies lay scattered in the street and among the ruins of the houses.

On the following Friday, those who survived gathered in the church of Our Lady of Victories. After a sermon preached by Fr. Sebastian of the Mother of God, which greatly moved all present, the procession left the church. The Governor carried the Cross before the officiating Priest, then came the clergy, Franciscans, Jesuits and Dominicans, and all the Christians of Jaffna.

Fr. Paul Godinho, the Rector of the Jesuit College, seeing that the Governor was so weak that he could scarcely walk, took the Cross from his hands and carried it before him.

God had granted Oliveira's prayer and had accepted the sacrifice he had made of his life for the salvation of his beloved people. He fell seriously ill, and on the 12th of March he knew that he was dying. He regulated the affairs of his government, and then prepared for death. On the 22nd March after hearing Holy Mass, which was said on an altar in an adjoining room so that he could see it from his bed, he received with great piety the Holy Viaticum and

Extreme Unction from the hands of Fr. Anthony of St. Mary, whom he then asked to read to him the Passion of Our Lord from the four Gospels, then the profession of Faith, and, when pronouncing with the Priest the last word, he peacefully expired.

He died at the age of 53 after having governed for nine years the kingdom of Jaffna, which he had found in a sad state of semi-anarchy and now left prosperous.

His body was exposed in the hall of the palace, dressed as he had desired in the Franciscan habit and the mantle of the Order of Christ. It was surrounded by the humble and the poor to whom he had always been like a father. The funeral was grand. They buried him in the church of Our Lady of the Victory, also called of Miracles under the very flagstone on which he lay prostrated during the cyclone offering to God his own life for that of the people of Jaffna.

The church was desecrated by the Protestants in 1658, it fell in ruins, and to-day, after two and a half centuries had passed, even the place remains unknown where lay the ashes of the noble Governor, who had deserved the proud surname of: the Apostle of Jaffna.

Philip d'Oliveira's successor was Ladislas de Seixas Cabreira, a man of good will but devoid of military and administrative talent.

In the meantime the war between Senevirat and the Portuguese had been again renewed. Always avoiding a decisive encounter, the King of Kandy made frequent incursions into the Portuguese territory, devastating the country and carrying on a guerrilla warfare in which the Kandyans had always excelled.

Tired at last of this desultory fighting, Constantine de Saa de
1628 Noronha marched on Kandy, took the town, and established there his headquarter.

Senevirat, wishing to make a diversion, sent the whole of his army against Jaffna. His plan was to localize the war on the territory of Jaffna, force hereby the Portuguese to go to defend their own dominions, thus evacuating the kingdom of Kandy, where he would then be able to organize a new army.

The new Governor of Jaffna Ladislas de Seixas Cabreira, committed a great mistake. Instead of endeavouring to stop the Kandyans at the very frontier till the Governor of Colombo would send reinforcement from Kandy, when taken between two fires they would be easily defeated, he caused all the garrisons in the inland to be abandoned in order to concentrate all his forces in and about the city of Jaffna. He opened thus the country to the Kandyans, who invading it in different places devastated everything on their way.

Here we meet with a difficulty: John Ribeiro, almost a contemporary says, that the Kandyan army was commanded by Attapattu Mudeliyar a fervent Catholic, a modest, very brave man, whom everyone respected, and he adds that if one wished to relate all his noble deeds a volume would be filled. And Rebeiro's testimony has certainly much weight, as it is the tribute of an enemy.

On the other hand Fr. Cesar Cordara, a reliable and truthful historian, who gives more details about this war, says that the Kandyan army, in their advance were particularly destroying the churches and pillaging Catholic villages.

These contradictory statements can easily be explained: The

Kandyans did not invade the Jaffna territory in one body. They entered it from different places, in so many detachment, all converging towards Jaffna. Attapattu Mudeliyar was certainly a good Catholic, but although commander-in-chief, he could not control other distant detachments, commanded by heathen chiefs, and prevent their excesses.

At the news of the Kandyan invasion, three Missionaries, stationed not far from the frontier, set out for Jaffna in order to escape the fury of the enemy. They were the Jesuit Fathers Bernardine Pecci, Matthew Fernandez and Jerome Froes.

They were already near Jaffna, when they received from their Superior Fr. Peter Paul Godinho, Rector of the Jaffna College, a letter exhorting all the Missionaries to remain at their stations, as in view of the reinforcements sent by Constantine de Saa de Noronha they would be in no danger.

Fr. Godinho had been informed that the Governor had sent an army in pursuit of the Kandyans, but he did not consider the length of the time it would take to such an army, encumbered with artillery and baggages, to reach its destination through a country where there were no roads. Whilst the Kandyans lightly armed as they were could advance rapidly.

The Fathers well knew the danger, but in obedience to their Superiors they returned to their Stations.

Fr. Pecci and Fr. Froes were surprised by the Kandyans on the night of the 16th October 1628. The night being very dark, they tried to save themselves by flight. Fr. Froes being young and strong managed to escape. Fr. Pecci was 49 years of age; he found his way barred by a hedge and had not the strength to get over it. He was most cruelly murdered. Fr. Pecci was of the same family as Pope Leo XIII. When he was sent to that Mission Station he had the presentiment that he would very soon shed his blood for Christ. His body was found a few days later without any signs of corruption.

After having murdered Fr. Pecci the Kandyans hastened to Nugamale, a Mission Station distant three miles from that of Fr. Pecci, and murdered Fr. Matthew Fernandez. They pierced him with lances and then cut off his head. Fr. Fernandez was a native of Cochin, he was 64 years old and had worked among the Parawers. During the five years that he had passed in the Mission of Jaffna he had baptised 5,000 pagans.

The bodies of the two Martyrs were brought to Jaffna and buried in the Jesuit church.

Two Franciscan Fathers were also murdered by the Kandyans: Fr. Andrew who was an Englishman and Fr. Amador of Rangel, Portuguese.

A number of native Christians who had been taken prisoners were brought to a temple and ordered to worship the idols. They refused and were all put to death.

As soon as the Governor Constantine de Saa de Noronha heard that the Kandyans had invaded the kingdom of Jaffna, from his headquarters at Kandy, he sent after them six companies of Portuguese and a contingent of 3,000 Singhalese troops under the command of John de Pinha and Louis Texeira de Carvalho. They advanced in two bodies, and met no resistance, as now the whole Kandyan army besieged the town of Jaffna. The Portuguese took them by surprise and the garrison making a sortie, they were caught between two fires. Attapattu Mudeliyar fought with an extraordinary courage and fell on the battlefield. The Kandyans took to flight, leaving 3,000 dead on the field. The Portuguese pursued them to the borders inflicting on them considerable loss.

Pinha and Texeira de Carvalho re-joined then the Governor in the entrenched camp of Manicavare, whence the latter went to Malwane, his summer residence near Colombo to attend to state business and to fill up the ranks of his army which had been decimated by the war.

While the Missionaries of the north of Ceylon were repairing the ruins of their Missions, those of the south continued

**1629** to work with their accustomed zeal.

The Franciscans had within the limits of the ancient kingdom of Kotta 56 churches. In 1623, they had built St. John's church at Mutuwal to which a small College and an orphanage was attached. They had two churches at Negombo, that of the Holy Ghost, and of the Mother of God. At Galle their church of the Immaculate Conception had a parish of 2,000 souls.

The Jesuit Fathers evangelized the Seven Korles, where they built churches at Chilaw and at Madampe. They had besides the parishes of Morotuwa, Velgampiti, Coylabata, Caymele, Maravila, Maripo, Manusaram, Anaulandana and Kalpentyn; in the kingdom of Jaffna: Caradiva, Batecotta, Tripule, Changani, Pandatiripu, Malagão, Chiveli, Maylati, Tambama, Maragama; five churches in the Island of Manaar, the principal that of St. Thomas; four Colleges: that of Colombo erected by the Governor Don Jerome d'Azevedo, that of Galle founded in 1614 by the commander of the fort Dominic Carvalho Cão, one at Jaffna and one at Manaar.

The Dominicans had at Colombo the church of St. Sebastian a small Convent at Galle, founded by Peter Velloso a native of that town; 12 parishes in the province of Sabaragamuva, 4 in that of Seven Korles, and at Jaffna, a Convent and the church of Our Lady of the Rosary.

The Augustinians were military chaplains in the entrenched camp of Mampane and had besides 16 parishes.

The Capuchin Fathers and the Recolects were few. They were busy with preaching in the churches in Colombo and in the out-stations.

There were in Ceylon in 1629 more than 130 churches, some of them, says Fr. Queiros were beautiful and could be compared with the best churches of Goa. Thirty years later, they were all desecrated and destroyed by the Protestants, so that no trace of them remains.

God confirmed the labours of his faithful servants by miracles which showed to the pagans the truth of the Catholic Faith and caused many conversions.

Between Galle and Weligama there is the village of Kogalle situated between the sea and a lake. There was a church dedicated to St. Joseph. A Portuguese, Anthony Sieco Moniz, a man known for his piety and great charity to the poor, lived in this village with his wife Catherine de Sousa. They had a son born blind. Doctors were consulted in vain. The child's eyes were closed and blood and matter issued from them. The parents were much afflicted and on the fortieth day after the child's birth they brought him to the church and begged the saintly old parish Priest Fr. Peter of the Holy Angels to say Mass for the infant's cure. They placed him on the steps of the Altar and both on their knees prayed fervently. Before the end of the Mass, the child opened large limpid eyes, and not a trace of his blindness remained.

A Singhalese woman who lived in the neighbouring village of Kattukurundu, had a daughter named Catharina who was born deaf and dumb, and probably an idiot, for she remained all day seated in a corner grinding her teeth. A neighbour, Madanella Fernandez, having heard of the miraculous cure of Anthony Sieco Moniz's child persuaded her to take the girl to Kogalle to St. Joseph's church. Fr. Peter said Mass for the girl, recited over her the gospel and sprinkled her with holy water, and she was completely cured.

Another church in the kingdom of Kotta, renowned for the graces which were obtained in it, was that of Our Lady at Mandavaly. Fr. Queiros mentions a great number of miracles which took place in that church.

Thus God not only raised Apostolic men to labour for the conversion of the natives of Ceylon, but also confirmed their preaching with miracles, which greatly impressed the pagans, and gave them a great idea of the Catholic Faith.

## CHAPTER 10

# THE BATTLE OF BADULLA

On his return to Malwana the Governor Constantine de Saa de Noronha fell seriously ill. Believing himself on the
1629 point of death, he received the last Sacraments with great piety and resignation. The illness lingered. The natives and above all the poor were disconsolate, for they looked upon him as a father. He had always protected them with all his power against oppression and exactions from subordinate officers. Thus, when finally he was on the way of recovery, all attributed it to the prayers of the poor.

King Senevirat was reckoning on the death of the Governor, for he feared that this great general would deprive him sooner or later of his Crown, hence his convalescence increased the King's anxieties.

He had planned to profit by the disorders which he hoped would follow the Governor's death to invade the Portuguese territory and if possible to capture Colombo.

To attain this end he endeavoured to gain to his side some influential low-country chiefs. His agent Don Ferdinand Samarakon had succeeded in corrupting Don Andrew, the Governor's private secretary, a Singhalese of high birth who had Noronha's full confidence and through whose hands passed all important papers.

He took advantage of his position to keep the King of Kandy informed of all the correspondence that passed between the Governor and the Viceroy.

Having experienced how easily the chiefs could be gained over either with money or with promises of high dignities, Don Ferdinand Samarakon continued his intrigues even after the Governor's recovery. Himself a Catholic, and a scion of one of the greatest Singhalese families, he could best sow treason among the Catholic nobility. Thus he succeeded to gain to his interest four of the most influential chiefs: Don Cosimo Colatunga, Don Balthasar, Don Alexis and Don Theodore. It was a master-stroke of Ferdinand Samarakon to gain over these four chiefs, because they were who commanded the whole native contingent of the Portuguese army in Ceylon.

Don Cosimo Colatunga was the soul of the conspiracy. What evil spirit possessed him: He was very rich, had attained the highest dignities, and was connected by marriage with the highest Portuguese families. The secret was so well kept that, at Colombo they had not the least suspicion. And the conspirators who were only awaiting a favourable opportunity to throw away their mask, were honoured and enjoyed the Governor's confidence and favour.

The new Viceroy Michel Noronha Count of Linares landed at Goa on the 21st October 1529.

The Court of Portugal was growing every year more uneasy of the growing power of Holland. Ceylon was a most important strategical position for one party as well as for the other, and the great danger for the Portuguese lay in an alliance of the Dutch with the King of Kandy. Once masters of the whole Island, the Portuguese could easily repel all attempt of a Dutch invasion. It was therefore decided at Lisbon to take profit of this moment when the Dutch were busy elsewhere, to complete the conquest of Ceylon by annexing the kingdom of Kandy to the Portuguese dominions.

Hardly therefore had he landed at Goa, the new Viceroy sent to the Governor an order to proceed without delay to the ultimate conquest of the kingdom of Kandy.

Constantine de Saa de Noronha understood better than they knew at Lisbon the difficulties of such an enterprise, above all, at that time, when the recent war had reduced the already small forces at his disposal in Ceylon. He had only 600 Portuguese soldiers most of whom he could not safely withdraw from the garrisons among which they were distributed, and his native army was inferior to that of the King of Kandy. He knew by experience how easily Kandy could be captured, he had taken it already twice. But the capture of the capital meant nothing so long as the King had his army. With the superior tactics of the Portuguese, this army could be annihilated in a decisive battle, but Senevirat knew it too, and therefore he avoided battle, entrenching himself in inaccessible places where artillery could not be used, and harassing the Portuguese by a guerrilla war, which caused them to suffer great losses and had a demoralizing effect on their troops. And then, there was always the danger of the native troops in the Portuguese army fraternizing with the Kandyans. On both sides there were Singhalese, on both sides

Catholics and Buddhists. They were not enemies, and fought only with one another, because they served two masters who had quarrelled, and they had no interest in this quarrel.

Constantine de Saa de Noronha represented to the Viceroy the impossibility of such an enterprise, he said it would be more profitable for the Portuguese to secure peace with the King of Kandy, but the Viceroy answered him haughtily, that he should rather think of the war than of commercial interests, and the old general who had done more than any Governor to establish firmly the Portuguese Rule in Ceylon, was accused of cowardice, and it was even insinuated that it was for reasons of private interests that he wished to delay the war. At last the Viceroy gave him a peremptory order to begin the campaign, but he did not send him either reinforcements nor money.

From that moment, the Governor only thought of making the
1630 necessary preparations.

The chief officers and the Missionaries, above all the Franciscan Father Anthony Peixoto, endeavoured to dissuade him, and represented him the impossibility of such an enterprise with the forces at his disposal. Noronha answered that he knew it better than themselves. That he would have gladly given his own life to avoid the disaster which he foresaw, but that, he was a soldier and as a soldier must obey to his chief.

Don Cosimo Colatunga and the Mudeliyars Don Balthasar, Don Theodore and Don Alexis renewed their correspondence with

Don Ferdinand Samarakon. The Governor's secretary Don Andrew kept the King of Kandy informed of all that was passing at Colombo. And they worked so skilfully and with such secrecy, that there was not the slightest suspicion of their treason; and they were to command all the native troops.

The Governor prudent even in a desperate position, had resolved to carry the war into the Kandyan province of Uva where he hoped for better success than from a march on Kandy.

The army left Colombo on the 25th August 1630. The four traitors commanded the native troops who numbered 20,000 men, and were secretly sowing disaffection among them. The Governor had reserved to himself the command of the Portuguese contingent, whose number he had raised to 1,500 men, by withdrawing the troops from all the garrisons, and calling under arms all the Europeans who lived in the south of Ceylon.

Two Jesuits, Fathers Simon de Leiva and Anthony Pedroso and four Franciscans, Fathers Anthony Peixoto, Joseph of St. Francis, Mark of St. Catherine and Emmanuel of the Immaculate Conception accompanied the army as military chaplains.

Meanwhile King Senevirat, to whom the secretary Don Andrew had sold the Governor's plans, having collected an army of 40,000 men, established his headquarter at Badulla the chief town of the province of Uva. At the approach of the Portuguese, not having heard from the traitors for some time, he evacuated the town, and encamped with his army in the neighbouring mountains. In this retreat he caught a chill followed by a severe fever and was obliged to betake himself to Kandy, leaving the command of his army to the three royal princes, his sons Raja Singha and Xavier Cumara Banda, and Wijayapala the son of the late King Don Juan.

The Governor entered Badulla, burned the town and encamped on a hill to give rest to his men.

The traitors at once sent a messenger to the camp of the Kandyan princes and meanwhile worked the native troops. They could not do so however without raising some suspicion, and Fr. Anthony Peixoto was the first to warn the Governor.

Next morning Don Jerome, a superior Singhalese officer, brought to him clear proofs of the treason of the four Mudeliyars. The Governor asked him what was to be done. Don Jerome answered that he should without delay summon the traitors, under the plea of holding a council of war, and have them put to death. Once they were done away, the faithful officers would easily bring back the troops to their duty.

But Constantine de Saa de Noronha knew from Fr. Anthony Peixoto and from the other military chaplains, that the spirit of mutiny among the soldiers had deeper roots than Don Jerome supposed; he therefore answered that this suggestion could have been good if they were sure that the traitors would answer the summons without suspecting that their plot had already been discovered, but it was almost certain that, at the present moment, they knew that their treason had been found out. Hence, it would only force them into immediate action and bring out a general massacre. He thought therefore more prudent to wait till next morning and meanwhile consider the course to be adopted.

A few hours later the whole Kandyan army was seen emerging from the mountains, and encamped in the plain below. The day was too far advanced to begin the battle. The Governor summoned the superior officers to his tent to hold a council of war. While so engaged, a letter was brought to him from the Kandyan princes, telling him to prepare to death, for on the morrow he would die.

By this, the Governor understood that the treason had been completed, and he dismissed the officers saying: — „ We have often fought for glory, to-morrow we shall have to fight for our lives.“ —

But he knew that all was lost. He sent a messenger to the commander of the fort in Colombo to inform him of his desperate position, and of the danger for the town. He distributed rations for three days to his soldiers and burned all his baggages. The military chaplains passed the night in hearing confessions of the officers and the men, whilst in the camp of the Kandyans drums were beaten, and great rejoicing going on.

Next morning both armies stood in battle array. Don Cosimo Colatunga was commanding the Portuguese vanguard. At the moment when the fight was to commence he gave the signal of desertion by cutting off the head of a Portuguese soldier called John Bernardes, who happened to be near him and having it put on a lance. Then they marched off to join the enemy.

The majority of the native troops hesitated to follow, but Mudeliyar Don Alexis, the commander of the rearguard, which was purposely composed of soldiers devoted to the traitors, pushed them on ahead.

Only 500 Singhalese, officers and men, all Catholics and the most part educated in the Colombo Colleges, refused to follow the traitors and rallied themselves around the general.

The fight that followed was one of the most glorious mentioned in history. 2,000 heroes, surrounded by an army of 60,000 men, fought the whole day, and when night came to interrupt the carnage the survivors still held the battlefield. Constantine de Saa de Noronha was always at the front, fighting with heroical courage, or helping the Priests to drag the wounded from the thick of the fight.

When night came, all the survivors gathered round their chief and begged him with tears to save his life and escape with his guard whilst they would cover his retreat. The Governor deeply touched answered that his duty was to stand by his men, and fight and die with them.

Then all prepared to die like Christians. They made again their confession and remained in prayer till midnight. When they went to rest, they were drenched by torrents of rain, which lasted till dawn.

Next morning at sunrise when they were ready for their last stand, they perceived with despair that the rain had drenched their ammunitions and that they could no longer use their muskets. Meanwhile the Kandyans perceiving their distress sent on them a shower of bullets and arrows, decimating from a distance the disarmed warriors.

The Priests were seen in the places where death claimed the

greatest number of victims, carrying away the wounded, administering to the dying the last Sacraments: Fathers Joseph of St. Francis, Mark of St. Catherine and Emmanuel of the Immaculate Conception fell dead pierced with arrows. Fr. Anthony Pedroso was seriously wounded, lost consciousness, and might have died amidst the combatants, had not a Kandyan soldier, a Catholic, recognized him, and carried away to a place of safety.

What followed was but a massacre. Constantine de Saa de Noronha, wounded on the shoulder by an arrow, called Fr. Simon de Leiva to once more hear his confession. Whilst on his knees, another arrow pierced his cheek. He drew it out and continued his confession. Then, at the moment when the Priest had given him absolution, the Governor was struck by a bullet and fell dead at his feet. Fr. de Leiva bent over him, when he too was killed by a bullet.

The Kandyans brought the Governor's head to Raja Singha, who had the battlefield searched for the body which he sent to his father to Kandy where the King gave it a grand funeral.

Senevirat treated the prisoners with great generosity. He told Fr. Anthony Pedroso to consider himself as his guest and to take over the duties of parish Priest of Kandy, and to take care of the welfare of the other prisoners. He honoured him and often conversed familiarly with him.

Had the Kandyan army marched now straight on Colombo, the city and with it all the Portuguese possessions in the south of

Ceylon would have fallen into their hands. But King Senevirat was still ill at Kandy, the young princes had no experience and they lost their time in pillaging and devastating the nearest Portuguese districts.

On the news of the defeat and death of the Governor reaching Colombo, Ladislas de Seixas Cabreira, the same whom we have seen at Jaffna assumed the command. This time he showed himself equal to the occasion. With the aid of his son-in-law Jerome d'Azevedo, he took energetically to improve the fortifications of the town. The walls were repaired and widened, trenches erected. All, even the women and children were helping the work.

A vessel from Malacca brought them reinforcements. It was but a small number of men, but they were heartily welcomed as the whole garrison of Colombo consisted of only 200 men. But they had brought also a large consignment of guns which were sorely needed for the defence of the fortifications. All men even the slaves were armed and the Jesuit Fathers formed a battalion of their bigger school boys, and these Singhalese lads, full of courage and determination, proved very useful.

They had no officers, so four secular Priests, Fathers Emmanuel Vinagre, Lazarus Fernandez, Diogo de Silva and Gonzalo Alvarez took the command of the most exposed bastions, so that in a short time all were ready for the defence.

The Kandyan princes, with an army of 60,000 men besieged
1631 Colombo in the early months of 1631. They were

young, full of ardour and unexperienced, and in their impatience to capture the town they did not spare their men. In a single assault they lost more than 2,000 men.

On the other hand Ladislas de Seixas Cabreira, and Jerome d'Azevedo were brave and prudent leaders. But the soul of the defence was Fr. Dominic de Negreiros, the Vicar General of the Bishop. The defenders were few and so exhausted with fatigue that they scarcely could stand on their legs. In order to give rest to the soldiers, the Missionaries, Jesuits, Franciscans, Dominicans and Augustinians as well as some secular Priests, took their place on the ramparts where they kept guard at night.

The siege had already lasted three months. The ranks of the defenders were sadly decimated and the famine was terrible. It was clear that they could not resist any longer.

Informed of the extremity to which the brave defenders of Colombo were reduced, Fr. Godinho the Superior of the Jesuit Fathers of Jaffna hastened to Cochin to bring them aid. He represented to Philip Mascarenhas that if Colombo were taken by the Kandyans the conquest of Ceylon would have recommenced. Mascarenhas gathered together all his available troops, and sailed for Ceylon.

At the sight of the Portuguese squadron, the Kandyan princes who had already lost a great number of men raised the siege and entrenched themselves near the frontier on the Kandyan territory.

The Viceroy Michael de Linares offered to Philip Mascarenhas the post of Governor of Ceylon, but he answered that, at the present critical situation, an abler man than himself was required, and recommended George d'Almeida an old general of renown, whom the Viceroy at once appointed.

New reinforcements having arrived from Goa, George d'Almeida attacked the Kandyans in their entrenched
1632 camp, and gained a great victory. He then defeated them in several encounters, so that the King of Kandy, having lost nearly all his army was reduced to sue for peace. The fortunes of war had turned.

In April 1632 Senevirat sent an embassy to Colombo. Fathers Pedroso and Peixoto who since the battle of Badulla were retained as prisoners, accompanied the ambassadors who brought two letters from the King, one to the Governor, another to the Rector of the Jesuit College, whom Senevirat asked to act as arbitrator of peace between him and the Governor.

A treaty was concluded on the terms of that of 1517. Besides the usual conditions of alliance and suzerainty, it was stipulated: that the King of Kandy would have no communication whatever with the Dutch. That he would allow the Catholic Religion to be publicly professed in his kingdom, a church to be built at Kandy large enough to hold a congregation of 200 to 300 persons and a comfortable house for the Missionaries. That he should set free all the prisoners, and return the arms, money and other valuables taken in the last war. In return the tribute which he had to pay annually to the King of Portugal was reduced from four to two elephants.

Senevirat was further obliged to send an embassy to Goa to pay homage to the Viceroy and obtain from him the ratification of the treaty.

Thus, a year and a half had not yet elapsed since the disaster of Badulla, and the Portuguese were again the masters, and more powerful than ever in Ceylon.

Old King Senevirat did not live long time after this treaty. He
**1634** died in 1634.

He was far from having the talents of his brother King Don Juan, but he was not wanting of ability. He was of a peaceful character and always endeavoured to avoid war.

He did not conceal his sympathies for the Portuguese yet he was obliged by circumstances to be always at war with them.

He had entrusted the education of his sons and of his nephew to Catholic Priests; besides the other things which formed the basis of solid education he had them taught Latin, music and equitation, and the young princes intelligent and full of life as they were, profited well by their training.

There was even a time when Senevirat allowed them to be instructed in the Christian doctrine, and the influence of their teachers Fr. Francis Negrão and Fr. Eleutherius of St. James, appeared in more than one action of their life. They never forgot their Catholic mother the unfortunate Queen Donna Catharina, and as we will see later on, two of them became Catholics, and the third was on the point of becoming a Christian, when the Protestant Dutch threw him back into heathenism.

## CHAPTER 11

# THE BATTLE OF GATEMBE

King Senevirat left his Crown to his youngest son Raja Singha, who was also the ablest. It is curious that he should
1635 have given to his favourite child the name of the greatest enemy of his race, Raja Singha Raja of Sitawacca.

The elder Cumara Singha who already in his father's life-time wore the title of Raja of Uva got the government of this province and Wijayapala the last surviving son of King Don Juan, a scholar, a man of retiring habits and the least able of the three brothers got the government of the district of Matale with the title of Raja.

Changes had also taken place at Colombo. On the 25th November 1635, the Governor George d'Almeida was replaced by Diogo de Mello de Castro, a mean avaricious man whom nobody respected.

The first years of Raja Singha's reign passed in peace. The Portuguese did not desire war, and the Kandyan princes rather desired to live in peace with their powerful neighbours. They had inherited the Portuguese sympathies of their parents, and King Raja Singha was often heard to say, that there was no nation in the world that could be compared with the Portuguese and that if they would only abstain from eating beef, they would be in no way inferior to the Singhalese.

As for religion they had none. Educated between Catholicism and heathenism, they had learned enough of the former to conceive a great contempt to idolatry and not so much to have the courage to abandon it.

King Raja Singha pretended to profess hinduism; he did not take any pain to conceal his contempt for Buddhists, especially for the Bikshun and had all the Buddhist books which fell into his hands thrown into fire. On the other hand he always showed great respect for the Catholic Religion and treated the Priests with great regard.

Cumara Singha, Donna Catharina's favourite child, whom she called always Xavier, inclined openly towards the Catholic Religion and Wijayapala the eldest of the three brothers had marked Catholic tendencies.

The peace was broken towards the end of 1637. The reason of the rupture is not very clear. We will follow the
1637 version of Ribeiro who was an officer in the Portuguese army and was in position to know the details as he came to Ceylon only two years after the events he relates.

The rupture which had to be followed by so serious consequences commenced by a petty quarrel:

A Portuguese who resided at Kandy, and had frequent intercourse with the court, when on the point of leaving the city, presented the King with a beautiful horse, a case of rose water which, at that time was a rarity much valued at Ceylon, and a box of sandalwood.

Raja Singha touched with this act of homage which was altogether disinterested, gave to the Portuguese some precious stones and one of his finest elephants. He brought the valuable beast to Colombo to embark it for India. This arose the cupidity of the Governor who seized the animal. The dejected Portuguese, having pleaded his cause in vain before the Governor, returned to Kandy to beg the King to intercede for him.

Raja Singha evinced great surprise but affected to treat the matter lightly. He said that for himself personally it was a matter of indifference that the Governor has seized the elephant, but he regretted the pain it has caused to his friend. That de Mello must be a bad and avaricious man to treat a countryman and a fellow Christian in that way. He knew, he said, the Portuguese for a long time as honorable men, and he was well aware that the Catholic Religion inculcated justice, meekness, love, disinterestedness, generosity and charity towards our neighbours. These virtues, he himself as well as all men of honour esteemed highly, and he knew by experience that all Portuguese, except the Governor, practised them. But certain men, when raised to high positions, forget all principles of morality, abandon themselves to vice and become true devils. But we must excuse them on account of their corrupt nature. He had known other Portuguese who had committed equally mean deeds, but he is happy to be able to say, that they had always been punished by the Viceroys.

After this sermon about the Governor, the King gave to the man two elephants and other presents and advised him to embark better at Chilaw, so that the Governor may not rob him again.

In the meantime, the Governor wrote to Raja Singha, excusing himself and saying that he had seized the elephant, because the King had neglected to pay the tribute which his father had bound himself to pay to the King of Portugal.

Raja Singha answered courteously that the elephant was no more his, since he had given it to the Portuguese. That he would certainly not refuse the yearly tribute promised by his father.

And he ordered that two elephants be sent without delay to Colombo as stipulated in the treaty of 1632. Thus the incident seemed to have been settled.

But Governor de Mello was, as we have said, a greedy and avaricious man. He thought that Raja Singha had given the elephant as a prize for the horse, and hoped to be able too to make a profitable bargain. He got some horses in India, good enough to tempt the King who was a great lover of horseflesh, and sent them for sale to Kandy.

Raja Singha had the horses seized on their way, and when de Mello wrote to him asking for the delivery of his property, the King answered, that the Governor may be at ease, that the horses are well fed and well cared for, and that he would give them back in good condition, when he has got the elephant of which his friend has been unjustly deprived.

The Governor got into a rage and wrote to the King that he would come himself at the head of his army to fetch his horses.

Raja Singha answered, he would be welcome, but would do well to bring the elephant with him.

We have related this matter in full to show how such trivial matter can have an influence on the fate of nations.

Diogo de Mello de Castro touched to the quick by Raja Singha's answer began to mobilize his army. Raja
1638 Singha, who wished to avoid war, wrote to the Governor asking him if it was right to shed the blood of their subject for a personal quarrel of so little importance. He desired peace, he said, and would gladly make reparation for the offence to the Governor.

He wrote at the same time to the Municipal Council of Colombo a letter in which he pointed out how small was the offence, compared with the evils caused by a war, and asked them to support his overtures of peace before the Governor.

As however de Mello would not give way, he sent for his brothers for help: Cumara Singha brought him 10,000 men and Wijayapala 6,000.

Meanwhile the Governor had assembled all the troops he could gather in the south of Ceylon: 700 Portuguese and 28,000 natives. He left Colombo on the 27th February 1638 and established his quarters at Balane at the frontier of the kingdom of Kandy.

Raja Singha tried once more to avoid bloodshed. He despatched to the Governor's camp the parish Priest of Kandy, an Augustinian Father with a Crucifix which had belonged to his mother and a letter to Diogo de Mello in which he wrote: — „Does your God, who died for you on the Cross, not forbid you to invade my country when I am at peace with your King, and have acquitted myself of the tribute you have asked in his name. Is it just to shed the blood of our subjects for a mere personal quarrel. I desire for peace, but, if you persist in wishing for war, God will be our Judge, and will punish the one who is guilty." —

The Governor did not listen to the entreaties of the parish Priest, who begged him not to expose the country to the horrors of war. In answer to the King's letter, early in the morning of the 26th March, he marched on Kandy.

Following the usual tactics, the King evacuated the town and retired to the surrounding mountains. On the 27th March the Governor entered Kandy without having encountered any resistance. He gave up the city to pillage and then intended to retire to his headquarters at Balane. But his soldiers were worn out with fatigue, he was therefore obliged to camp for the night at Gatembe about three miles from Kandy.

Next morning when they were about to continue their march they found that Raja Singha had cut their retreat and taken a position with his army between Gatembe and Gonaruwa.

A panic seized the native troops, many deserted, others passed to the enemy, and the Governor Diogo de Mello found himself with only 700 Portuguese surrounded by 16,000 Kandyans, and without any hope of escape.

Reduced to this extremity, he sent to Raja Singha's camp, his nephew Ferdinand Furtado de Mendoza and two Priests, one Franciscan the other Augustinian, to sue for peace, on the sole condition of being free to return to Colombo with his Portuguese soldiers.

Raja Singha detained Ferdinand de Mendoza, saying that he was too young to die, and advised the two Missionaries, if they valued their lives they would do better not to return to the Governor.

Whilst the Raja of Matale surrounded the Portuguese so that they could not escape, the King ordered the Raja of Uva to begin the attack. The forces being so unequal, it was rather a massacre than a fight. The Portuguese with their accustomed courage sold their lives dearly and all were killed except 100, other say 33 who were made prisoners.

The Governor was among the dead. The King caused his body to be searched for to give him a honourable burial, but it could not be found.

Raja Singha treated the prisoners with great consideration. He gave some of them to his brother the Raja of Uva, among whom young Ferdinand Furtado de Mendoza.

Among the military chaplains who had accompanied Governor de Mello on his unfortunate expedition was Fr. John Sociro S. J., who had come to India on the same ship with Fr. Bernardine Pecci. He was now 61 years of age and had been labouring in Ceylon from the time of the establishment of the Jesuit Mission. His zeal for the conversion of the heathens was great, and he was often seen walking 20 or 30 miles on foot when there was some hope of saving a soul.

The soldiers loved him dearly and considered him as a saint.

They said that the victories which they had gained over the Kandyans in 1631 were due to his prayers.

During the campaign the army was encamped in a place where there was no water. The heat was very great and the soldiers were suffering terribly from thirst, and Fr. John Sociró felt a great pity for them. Moved by the spirit of God he fell on his knees and prayed for a long time. Then, getting up, he struck a rock with his walking staff, and there gushed forth from it an abundant flow of water, so that the whole army could quench their thirst and also take ample supply for the march.

Fr. John Sociró was made a prisoner at the battle of Gatembe. The Kandyan soldiers knowing that the King's wish was that the Catholic Priests were to be treated with due respect took him before their chief, who recognizing him exclaimed: — „ You, cowards! you know this Priest to be the greatest enemy of our gods, and you did not kill him?" — The soldiers, excited by these words of their leader, seized him. The Father fell on his knees and, whilst they were piercing him with their lances, he was offering his life to God for the conversion of his executioners.

After the battle of Gatembe, and the death of the Governor, the position of Colombo and of the Portuguese possessions in the south of the Island was desperate. De Mello had taken with him all the available troops, even the garrisons of the forts. There was no hope of getting any reinforcements from India. Had Raja Singha marched on Colombo, the town and all the south of the Island would have fallen without a struggle into his hands. But he disdained to take profit of his victory, and contented himself with forbidding his subjects from having any communication with the low country Singhalese who were Portuguese subjects.

Anthony Mascarenhas was appointed Governor and landed at Colombo on the 24th May 1638.

## CHAPTER 12

# THE RETURN OF THE DUTCH

De Mello's unjust aggression which violated the treaty of 1632, exasperated Raja Singha, and made him clearly
1638 understand that peace with the Portuguese was no longer possible since the conquest of the kingdom of Kandy was now their acknowledged aim.

Raja Singha well knew, that if his father and himself had often conquered the Governor of Ceylon, when the latter had been left to his own resources, still they had always to beat a retreat when reinforcements had arrived from Goa. And it was clear to him that if the Viceroy landed a large force in Ceylon, he could easily accomplish the conquest of the kingdom of Kandy, and depose him of his throne as he had deposed the King of Jaffna.

These considerations made him finally decide to throw himself into the arms of the Dutch.

The Dutch who since twenty-five years seemed to have abandoned the idea of conquering Ceylon, had once again turned their attention towards the Island.

Commodore William Koster had visited in 1636 the eastern coast of Ceylon and after that an exchange of correspondence had taken place between Raja Singha and Charles Reniersz, the Dutch commander of Paliacotta.

After the battle of Gatembe Raja Singha placed himself in direct relations with the Dutch colonial authorities, and sent an embassy to Batavia to propose an alliance against the Portuguese.

The Dutch Governor General Anthony Van Diemen, who had already taken informations regarding the commercial potentialities of Ceylon, received the Kandyan envoys with honor and they settled that a Dutch agent was to be sent to Kandy to arrange the preliminaries of a treaty.

The Dutch agents left Batavia towards the end of the same year and were received with great pomp at Kandy.

Raja Singha gave them an audience, and with his accustomed loquacity explained them at length his grievances against the Portuguese.

The Portuguese, he said, wanted to deprive him of his kingdom, although he regularly paid them the tribute. He could not rely on any treaty with them, since all depended on a whim of the Governor, who, when he took the fancy of doing it, would invade his kingdom, burn his cities, and set fire to his own palaces. In the space of two years they had pillaged and burnt his two capitals, Kandy and Badulla. He had often defeated them, but they never get discouraged and are always ready to recommence war again. He now well knew, that so long as the Portuguese possessed one inch of territory in Ceylon, he would be always exposed to their insults, he was therefore resolved to seek the friendship of the Dutch, and propose them a treaty of alliance that would be equally advantageous to both contracting parties.

This speech of Raja Singha was certainly eloquent but he seems to have forgotten that it was not the Portuguese but the Kings of Kandy who violated the treaties, and that the Portuguese, in fact, renewed them again only to gain some time of reprieve and knowing they would not last.

If de Mello's aggression was a violation of the treaty of 1632, that treaty had already been broken before by Raja Singha, when he entered into correspondence with the Dutch commander of Paliacotta.

The Dutch agent's answer to the King was in the same pompous style. He said: that the Dutch East India Company and the States General of Holland were well aware of the treacherous conduct of the Portuguese, and that they knew that the grievances of the King were well founded and true, and that it was with the object of expelling the Portuguese from Ceylon that the Governor General had sent them to Kandy to offer his alliance to the King. That the Dutch were powerful enough to drive out the Portuguese from the Island, and that they would do that, not in their own interests, but only to restore these territories to the King of Kandy who was the lawful Sovereign of the whole Island. And that they would do that without asking any recompense for the services they would have rendered to the King.

After that they proceeded to lay down the preliminaries of the treaty:

The Dutch were to have the entire monopoly of the trade of cinnamon, spices and other products of Ceylon.

They would declare war against the Portuguese, and would give up to the King of Kandy wholly and without any afterthought all the towns and fortresses they would capture from the Portuguese, with the exception of Batticaloa and Kottyar where they would retain Dutch garrisons.

That the King of Kandy would keep an army as great as possible to co-operate with the Dutch.

That the King would repay to the Dutch the costs of all their wars against the Portuguese.

The King further engaged himself to pay to the Dutch government a fixed sum of money for each arm, leg or eye lost by their soldiers in battle, more for the right arm, leg or eye than for the left. Besides he would pay for each wound according to its gravity.

This last article was a regular market in human flesh, and it must be said in justice that this queer article was not inserted in the final treaty.

In one word the meaning of the proposed treaty was this: The Dutch would have the monopoly of the trade of central Ceylon, and they would make the conquest of the Island at the expense of the King of Kandy. The clause that they would surrender to Raja

Singha all the towns and provinces conquered from the Portuguese was only a blind as we will see hereafter.

One feels inclined to ask if Raja Singha gave himself the trouble to compare these conditions inserted in the treaty with the speech full of disinterestedness made by the agent at the audience.

The preliminaries being signed the agent returned to Batavia.

The first hostilities between the Portuguese and the Dutch
1639 began in February 1639.

The Dutch admiral Adam Westerwold, having been obliged to abandon the blockade of Goa arrived in Ceylon waters. He had sent in advance a messenger to Raja Singha to combine an attack on Batticaloa.

Westerwold brought six men of war, 840 soldiers and all the necessary engines for a siege. Raja Singha joined him with 2,000 men, and without delay they laid siege to the fort.

The garrison of Batticaloa consisted of only 40 men but they defended the fort with great determination. The enemy having cut the water supply they found themselves in great straits. 40 men against 2,840, they fought for two days on the ramparts and did not surrender until they had obtained honorable conditions. They left the fort with their arms and baggages and Westerwold had to give them a vessel to carry them to Nagapatam, the nearest Portuguese fortress on the Indian Coast.

Raja Singha and the Dutch treated cruelly the defenceless

inhabitants of Batticaloa. 50 of the principal were impaled, the others sold as slaves. The fort was razed to the ground.

Then Raja Singha and Westerwold signed a treaty, the 17th article of which stipulated that: — „ The King of Kandy will not allow any Priest, Monk or other ecclesiastical person to reside in his kingdom, and he will expell all those who are residing there at present." —

That was the first attempt of the Dutch Protestants to destroy Christianity in Ceylon.

After having spent 12 days, the King and the admiral marched on Trincomalee. The fort of that place was untenable. Its walls were crumbling down, the fortification in a most dilapidated state. It was garrisoned with only 50 soldiers and they had no ammunitions. Nevertheless they fought for two days on the ramparts, and only when 23 of them were dead, the remaining 27 capitulated.

The fort was demolished, and Westerwold set sail for Batavia. Raja Singha returned to Kandy satisfied with his successes. With an army of 2,840 men he had gained the victory over 90 Portuguese soldiers.

After the return of Westerwold to Batavia the Dutch East India Company decreed definitely the conquest of Ceylon.

**1640** On the 15th January 1640 a Dutch fleet of twelve vessels appeared before Colombo, but, not daring to attack the town which they supposed to be better defended than it was in reality, they set sail for Negombo.

As Negombo had practically no garrison, the fort being manned with a company of invalids, the Governor Mascarenhas ordered Francis de Mendoza, who was in command of Manicavare, to succour the town.

Mendoza marched immediately, and the Dutch general Lucassan informed of his approach, landed 3,500 men near the village of Caymele. Mendoza who had but a handful of men, overpowered by the number, was completely defeated and had to fall back on Colombo where he reached with a few men, nearly all wounded.

Lucassan captured Negombo and had all the company of invalids stationed in the fort put to death.

He repaired the walls and the bastions which he found dilapidated, surrounded the fort with palisades and moats and having put it into a state of defence, garrisoned it with 300 men amply provided with arms and ammunitions.

The reason why the Portuguese forts were so dilapidated was that they were not meant for European warfare. They were made against the Kandyan, whose ways in war were simple, so that common earthen works were sufficient against them, and these even were not kept in a state of repair for, as it took time to the King of Kandy to get his army together, they could be easily renewed. The present aggression of the Dutch took the Portuguese by surprise and they were unprepared.

After having fortified Negombo, the Dutch general Lucassan marched on Colombo, but the Governor Mascarenhas at once perceived that it was only a faint to turn away his attention from Galle. He therefore sent 280 men to reinforce the garrison of that town, but when they were approaching they found that it was already besieged by the Dutch commodore William de Koster.

With the customary impetuosity of the Portuguese the officer who commanded the troops, resolved to cut his way through the ranks of the besiegers to enter the place. He was defeated, but the victory was dearly purchased by the Dutch who lost 400 men.

Lorenzo Ferreira de Britto the commander of Galle bravely defended the place; he was always on the ramparts, and his young wife, a lady of truly heroic courage, never left his side, animating the soldiers by her presence and her coolness amidst the greatest dangers.

Three Missionaries distinguished themselves by their devotedness to the wounded and to the poor who were suffering great hardships. They were Fr. Louis Pinto, Superior of the Jesuits, and the Franciscan Fathers Anthony Pedroso and Francis of the Mother of God.

For eighteen days the Dutch battered the walls with their powerful artillery. The bastions crumbled one after the other. Finally a breach was made in the walls and the Dutch assaulted the fort.

Lorenzo Ferreira de Britto fought in the front rank. He had received four serious wounds, yet he stood always at the head of his men. Finally a fifth wound stretched him senseless. Some soldiers advanced to kill him when his wife covered him with her body. A

Dutch officer ran to her aid and had her husband carried out of danger.

When Koster heard of this event, in order to avoid useless bloodshed he ordered to cease fighting. He made his best to reassure the people, and took possession of the town on the 13th March 1640.

Galle was now lost for ever to the Portuguese, and the fall of this city was the beginning of the Dutch conquest.

The new Viceroy John de Silva Tellez de Menezes, Count of Aveiras, landed at Goa on the 20th September 1640. He was determined to push actively the war against the Dutch, for, as long as they possessed Negombo and Galle, they were a permanent danger for the Portuguese Rule in Ceylon.

The Governor Anthony Mascarenhas, having completed his term of office, the Viceroy, wishing to make him pleasure appointed as his successor his younger brother Philip, who was yet a young man, had not seen much service, but had already given proofs of great ability. He was very rich and very generous.

The two brothers, had a tender affection for one another, but they had been always separated by the duties of their career. Now that they were reunited, Anthony refused all appointments offered him by government, to remain near his brother and help him with his experience.

Philip Mascarenhas landed at Colombo on the 12th October. He brought a squadron of sixteen men of war and 400 European soldiers. With a contingent of Parawers, whom the Bishop of Cochin Dom Michael Rangel had armed at Tuticorin and brought to Colombo, and the reinforcements brought over from Jaffna by Anthony de Motte Galvão, the new Governor formed a small army, strong enough to attempt the recapture of Negombo.

Anthony de Motte Galvão marched against Negombo and, after a siege of twelve days, the Dutch garrison, which had suffered considerable losses and was reduced to only 200 fighting men, surrendered.

All the time that the siege lasted, the Blessed Sacrament was exposed in all the churches of Colombo, and there were always full of people. When the news of the victory reached the capital a solemn Te Deum was sung, and salves of artillery fired.

The terms of the capitulation stipulated that the Dutch were to leave the place with military honors, and that the Portuguese would supply them with a ship to go wherever they liked out of Ceylon. In spite of this condition they landed in Galle. The Portuguese however could not complain of this violation of the capitulation, for the vessel they had given them was in such a bad condition, that they could hardly have gone farther.

At the news of the siege of Negombo, Raja Singha sent 20,000 men under the command of Mudeliyar Don Balthasar, one of those who had betrayed Constantine de Saa de Noronha, to help the Dutch; but when they approached Negombo, the town had been already conquered by the Portuguese. De Motte Galvão met them with six companies of Portuguese soldiers and 2,000 well trained natives. They were completely defeated, Don Balthasar was killed, and Raja Singha who had come to Ruanwelle fled in haste to Kandy.

We know nothing about the fate of the three other traitors, Don Cosimo Colatunga, Don Theodore and Don Alexis.

After this first success, Philip Mascarenhas resolved to try to
1641 recapture Galle. But he could not besiege it properly as
he had no ships at his disposal. The operations were commanded by Anthony Amaral de Menezes who blockaded the town from the landside, preventing the Dutch from coming out of their fortified walls, and each time that they tried a sortie he inflicted them heavy losses.

Meanwhile Anthony Mascarenhas on one side and de Motte Galvão on the other expelled the Kandyan garrisons from the districts which Raja Singha had occupied, so that, before the close of 1641, the whole of their territory, excepting Galle, had been reconquered by the Portuguese.

The Dutch in Galle blockaded by Amaral de Menezes, so that they could not venture to go outside the walls of the city, were vainly looking for the help promised by Raja Singha, and their position was becoming every day more critical.

The fact was that Raja Singha, after the late success of the Portuguese, remained undecided. He asked himself if, in casting his lot with the Dutch, he had not accelerated the danger of his downfall.

Meanwhile, the position of Galle having become untenable,

commodore Koster who was in command of the town resolved to go himself to Kandy to hurry the matters.

The King received him coldly; he did not refuse the promised aid, but always delayed matters giving evasive answers to the Dutch commodore. Koster did not hide his vexation before the dignitaries of the court, and went even so far as to utter threats against the King.

At last, the King annoyed by his importunity, informed him that he has his permission to quit Kandy. Koster well understood that it was an order to leave the place, and that if he did not do so his life would be in danger. He therefore immediately departed for Batticaloa, but never reached the place. He was killed on the way, it is said, by Raja Singha's order.

## CHAPTER 13

# THE SONS OF DONNA CATHARINA

As mentioned in the preceding chapters, Queen Donna Catharina had left three sons: Wijayapala, whose father
1641 was King Don Juan II, her first husband, and two other sons by King Senevirat, namely Xavier Cumara Singha and Raja Singha King of Kandy. None of them had been baptised, but having past their childhood under the influence of a Catholic mother, and educated by Catholic teachers, the Franciscan Fathers Francis Negrão, Eleutherius of St. James and Joseph of St. Francis, they all had conceived a high idea of Christianity and a deep contempt for idolatrous worship. They had great affection for their teachers, and above all for good Fr. Negrão who, now a very old man, had retired to the Franciscan Convent at Goa.

Wijayapala, the eldest of the three brothers, had the greatest inclination towards the Catholic Faith. He was of a mild and amiable character, and passed his time amidst his books in his residence at Matale where he lived a retired life. He liked the Portuguese and found among them a society more sympathetic to his ideas and to his education than among the rough Kandyan chiefs by whom he was surrounded.

The wars of his brother Raja Singha kept him separated from more civilized society which suited him better, so that he could only enjoy the company of the Portuguese prisoners whom Raja Singha always divided with his brothers.

It is related that once a Portuguese officer paid him his ransom in false money, which fact was not discovered till too late, when the liberated prisoner had already departed and could not be caught again. One of the courtiers, indignant at the fraud remarked before the prince that this was an action unworthy of a Christian and of a Portuguese. — „Well, answered the Raja laughing, we have robbed him of his liberty, he has robbed us of his ransom, we are quits." —

Wijayapala's love of study and the frequent intercourse he had with Portuguese prisoners, inclined him more and more towards the Catholic Faith, till finally, in March 1541 he came to Colombo to ask for Baptism. The Governor Philip Mascarenhas had doubts of the sincerity of his conversion, thinking that perhaps he wanted to become a Catholic in the secret hope that the Portuguese would raise him on the throne of Kandy, to replace their enemy Raja Singha by an ally. He therefore advised him to go to Goa.

The Viceroy Count John of Aveiras spoke to him openly, saying that he could hope for nothing from the Portuguese, who had the hands too full at this moment to even think of helping him. Wijayapala replied that, far from aspiring to the throne of his brother, he had given up his own principality of Matale to become a Catholic.

He was then baptised and settled himself in Goa, where he

lived on a liberal pension granted him by the King of Portugal, and always maintained his position as a royal prince.

Cumara Singha the Raja of Uva was the second son of Donna Catharina, and after Mahastane's death he became his
1642 mother's favourite child. She always called him by the name of Xavier and endeavoured to turn his mind towards the Catholic Faith. He had been more than his brothers under his mother's influence, and his Catholic and Portuguese sympathies were well known. He was a prince of superior mind and of a mild, simple and amiable character, a better warrior and an abler man than his elder brother Wijayapala.

Some months after Wijayapala's conversion Cumara Singha had a quarrel with his brother King Raja Singha. It happened thus: After the battle of Gatembe when the prisoners and booty were being divided, Cumara Singha received as his share eighteen Portuguese prisoners among whom were young Ferdinand Furtado de Mendoza and two Franciscan Fathers, and Cumara Singha treated them with every consideration, and took a great fancy to young Mendoza whose career was suffering by his captivity which lasted already since four years.

At last, seeing how much the prisoners desired to return to their homes, he gave them their liberty and an escort to bring them safely to the Portuguese frontier.

King Raja Singha informed of what was happening at Badulla by the spies he had at his brother's court, had the prisoners seized on their way and brought back to Badulla with a letter to his brother in which he advised him to look better after his prisoners.

Cumara Singha was very much annoyed with his brother. He consoled the prisoners and assured them that, in spite of the King, he would find means to restore them to their liberty.

He felt particularly sorry for young Furtado de Mendoza, on account of his military career. He therefore advised him to escape without waiting for the other prisoners for whose flight he would find later some good opportunity.

Having secretly arranged everything, Cumara Singha gave him for companion one of the Franciscan Fathers, and an escort of four men on whom he could rely.

In taking leave Cumara Singha embraced them affectionately, then turning to the Missionary, with whom he had often spoken of religion and of his Catholic mother: — „ Father, he said, we shall meet again. In spite of the King, my brother, I will soon be of the same Faith with you." — The two departed and after eight days' march they reached the Portuguese territory.

Cumara Singha, after having received the news of Mendoza's and the Missionary's safe arrival to Colombo, made arrangements for the escape of the other prisoners. He gave rich presents to those who were poor, and a parting gift for each, and they started so as to reach Colombo by a roundabout way through the forests. But Raja Singha informed by his spies, set an ambuscade on a forest path through which they had to pass, and had them all murdered.

When the news were brought to Cumara Singha, he shut himself in his room and for three days refused to see or speak to anyone. Then he wrote to Raja Singha bitterly reproaching him for his cruelty.

Now Raja Singha who after the conversion of Wijayapala had taken possession of the small State of Matale, only waited a pretext to get rid of Cumara Singha and to take under his immediate rule the great province of Uva.

Pretending therefore to having taken offence at his brother's letter, he marched against him at the head of 20,000 men. Cumara Singha, fearing to fall into his brother's hands left Badulla and sought refuge on the Portuguese territory, where the Governor Philip Mascarenhas received him with the honors due to his rank, and the inhabitants of Colombo made their best to show him gratitude for his generosity towards the prisoners.

The Governor assembled his Council to deliberate on the best means of aiding the Raja of Uva to regain his State. All the councillors except two were of the opinion that the honor of Portugal required that they should help him. Some even proposed that Cumara Singha be placed on the throne of Kandy, as he was a wise, prudent and just prince and much beloved by his subjects. The Uvians, who were the bravest among the Singhalese would certainly raise in favour of their Raja, and with the help of a European contingent, they could overthrow Raja Singha and put Cumara Singha on the throne. The arrangement was propitious as the Dutch had only 500 soldiers in Cevlon and these were shut up in Galle, still blockaded by Amaral de Menezes.

The matter was at this stage when doubts commenced to be

entertained, if under the present critical circumstances the Governor had the power to undertake a new campaign on his own responsibility, without the consent of the Viceroy It was above all to be noted that Raja Singha seemed to hesitate, whether he should continue his alliance with the Dutch, or rather abandon them and ally himself with the Portuguese. It was true that, at that moment the Dutch were not strong in Ceylon, but reinforcements could arrive any day from Batavia, and how were they to be repulsed if a part of the Portuguese forces were engaged in the campaign against Kandy.

The more prudent advice prevailed, and it was decided to refer the matter to the Viceroy.

Cumara Singha, following the Governor's advice, went himself to Goa towards the end of December. The Viceroy received him cordially and provided him amply with means for keeping up his royal rank but left him no delusion about the support asked for. He told him clearly that all the forces he could dispose of where required to fight against the Dutch who were endeavouring to become masters of all the Portuguese settlements on the coasts of India.

Understanding that there was no hope of returning to his States Cumara Singha settled at Goa and henceforth thought about nothing else than to realize his long since cherished desire of becoming a Christian. He prepared himself seriously for it, studying the Christian doctrine and holding conversations with learned Priests.

The Baptism of Queen Donna Catharina's second son took

place about the beginning of 1645. The Archbishop of Goa, Dom Francis of the Martyrs officiated. All the clergy and high dignitaries of the State, with the Viceroy as godfather were present. Cumara Singha stood up and spoke, explaining the motives that prompted him to become a Catholic, spoke of the graces with which God had favoured him and then in a clear voice made his profession of Faith.

He was baptised and took the name of Theodose. Four Uvian chiefs were baptised with him. He lived nine years at Goa, edifying all by his great piety and died in 1654.

Donna Catharina's third son King Raja Singha, had been the favourite of his father King Senevirat, and, in consequence less under the influence of his Christian mother, and much more under that of the pagan court of his father.

Nevertheless he always showed a great respect for the Catholic Religion and did not conceal his contempt of heathenism and especially for Buddhism. Practically he had no religion whatever.

He had thrown himself into the hands of the Dutch in the hope of preserving his Crown for which the Portuguese were a constant menace. But now, when he perceived that, notwithstanding the protestations of disinterestedness, which the Dutch had so lavishingly professed to him, their intention was to conquer Ceylon for themselves, he thought that, after all the Portuguese alliance was perhaps more desirable.

In this state of mind, his thoughts turned to his early years, and to his Christian mother, to the good Franciscan Fathers who had brought him up, to his early Portuguese companions whose ways were more in accordance with his training than the society in which he lived at present, and more than once the thought came to him of becoming a Catholic like his brothers.

The Archives of Lisbon possess the original of a letter written by the Superior of the Franciscan Fathers at Goa to John IV King of Portugal:

— „Sire, he writes, I wish to mention to Your Majesty a very important matter, which had been communicated to me by Fr. Constantine of Christ, the last King of Jaffna. I have already mentioned it to the Viceroy and to the Archbishop of Goa, but, as the matter relates to the vital interests of Christianity in these countries, I deem it necessary to communicate it to Your Majesty.

Your Majesty knows that we are now at war with the King of Kandy. Now the Queen, who is a cousin to Fr. Constantine wrote to him, that her husband desires to become a Catholic, and to bring all his people to our Holy Faith, if we send him some of our Missionaries to instruct them, and if Your Majesty would renounce to Your rights of Suzerainty over his kingdom and enter into a sincere alliance with him.

As however they are people on whose sincerity one cannot much rely, I should like to have Your Majesty's instructions, to know what action I should take.“ —

Some months later, Raja Singha himself wrote to the King of Portugal the letter which we have given in chapter 8.

Raja Singha therefore was the only surviving son of Queen Donna Catharina who did not become a Christian. And he would have become one,-if the influence of his new allies the Protestant Dutch had not thrown him back into heathenism

With the progress of the Dutch, the prospects of Christianity in Ceylon were becoming darker and darker.

Wherever they became masters, they drove out the unfortunate Christian villagers from their homes and from their fields. They desecrated the churches, expelled the Missionaries and destroyed the fine schools established by the Portuguese.

The wars we have already written about, and those we will relate in the following chapters, disorganized the Missions, and dispersed the Christians. The pagan soldiers of Raja Singha and the Protestant Dutch, wrecked equally their fury on the unfortunate native Christians. They massacred whole villages, thousands were put to death, and as the Portuguese army was mostly composed of native Catholics, and many fell on the battlefields, the number of Christians in the south of Ceylon had greatly diminished; the Missions were on their decline.

The Missionaries were much concerned about the turn the events were taking. Nevertheless they did not allow themselves to become discouraged. On the contrary, they laboured bravely, with even more zeal, in order to prepare for the terrible crisis they saw impending, for they clearly understood that the Protestant conquest meant for their Christians persecution and death.

Hence we possess less letters referring to this period. The Missionaries had too much work and were too much preoccupied to write.

It was the beginning of a sad and dark period, so sad as few are found in history.

## CHAPTER 14

# THE ARMISTICE

Meanwhile important events had happened in Portugal. Dissatisfied with the union with Spain which had now
1642 lasted for sixty years, the Portuguese rose against Philip III (Philip IV in Spain). The Duke of Braganza called to the throne in 1640, under the name of John IV, established a new dynasty.

The new King concluded in 1642 an armistice with the Dutch, for ten years, during which they had to arrange the condition of a definitive peace. It was agreed that each of the two contracting parties, during this period, were to retain the places which were in their possession in India and in the colonies. But news in those days took so long time to reach India from Europe that, notwithstanding the armistice concluded in Lisbon, hostilities still continued in Ceylon.

Thirteen Dutch Men-of-war appeared before Colombo and blockaded the harbour. As the Portuguese knew that there were 3,500 soldiers on board those vessels, they expected daily their landing. The Governor therefore concentrated in the town all the available troops. They had to be always under arms, prepared for the eventuality of a sudden landing of the enemy's forces, which harassed the troops and demoralized the inhabitants of the town. This state of things lasted for 35 days after which, the Dutch departed without having dared to attack the town.

It was only in the beginning of 1643 that the news of the armistice reached India. The Dutch Governor of
1643 Batavia sent at once an officer called Peter Burel to Ceylon, to arrange with the Governor Philip Mascarenhas for the suspension of hostilities.

As said above the treaty stipulated that both parties will remain in possession of the places they occupied. Burel giving to this article his own interpretation, wanted the Governor to surrender to the Dutch the whole southern province which they coveted because of the large quantity of cinnamon which this province was producing.

Now, the Dutch actually possessed Galle, but being blockaded by the Portuguese, could not even set their foot outside the walls of the city, and the whole southern province was exclusively in the hands of the Portuguese.

Peter Burel insisted, and Philip Mascarenhas referred him to the Viceroy. The latter refused to yield to such extravagant demand and referred the matter to Lisbon.

Meanwhile the blockade of Galle continued. The Portuguese had cut off all communications from the land side; but, as the Dutch could always revictual themselves from the sea, Philip Mascarenhas was only awaiting the arrival of some vessels from

Goa, to commence a proper siege, but these vessels never came, and the partial blockade seemed to be doomed to continue indefinitely.

Of course, during the blockade there were fights and skirmishes. The Dutch tired with the life they were forced to live within the walls of the city, made sorties from time to time, but they were always repulsed with loss. Seeing that they could do nothing on the land side, one night they embarked a strong body of troops, and proceeded by sea to Welligama with the object to surprise the Portuguese camp at Curaza, where there were only 200 European troops and a small company of Singhalese mostly very young, new recruits natives of Colombo and Galle.

The battalion formed by the pupils of the Jesuit College during the last siege of Colombo had proved such a success, that it had suggested to the Governor the idea of forming a permanent battalion of Singhalese lads, and the camp of Curaza was for them a kind of military school.

On the 11th May, the day following the departure of the Dutch from Galle, all the boys were at church assisting at Holy Mass, when they heard the firing of guns. They were all much excited for they knew that, on that day, they would have their first battle. But the officer gave no command, and they assisted piously to the end of the Mass, after which they ranged themselves round their captain.

This officer, knew well that there was no haste, for the commander of the camp had sent a strong detachment under captain Peter de Sousa to stop the Dutch at a place where they would be taken at their disadvantage, and that was the firing they heard.

Wishing to test the coolness and the discipline of the boys, he told them quietly to go to their breakfast. Then he ordered the lads to march and to attack the flank of the enemy.

The battle lasted from 9 in the morning to 2 o'clock afternoon. The Dutch completely beaten fled to their vessels leaving their colours and part of the arms in the hands of the Portuguese.

All admired the pluck of the Singhalese youths. One of them Peter Queiroz, a boy of seventeen made prodigies of valour and he brought to the camp two Dutch prisoners. Whilst the commander was complimenting him, he said rather astonished: — „ Oh! captain! it was not difficult. You could have done the same. Instead of showing fight, as they should, they marched before me like lambs." —

The hostilities continued but as orders were expected daily for their cessation, both sides carried the campaign in a half hearted manner and, up to the end of the year only insignificant skirmishes took place.

Towards the end of December 1643 the Dutch having got reinforcements, declared that, by refusing to deliver to
1644 them the whole southern province and in continuing the blockade of Galle, the Portuguese had violated the armistice.

Francis Caron who commanded the Dutch reinforcements set sail for Negombo, and his ships appeared before that town on the 3rd January 1644. The Governor hastened to send to the rescue six companies of soldiers under the command of his brother Anthony Mascarenhas and of Anthony de Motte Galvão.

Caron had landed his men. The encounter took place on the 4th January. The Portuguese were crushed by the number, Caron having landed 4,200 men. Anthony Mascarenhas and de Motte Galvão perished in the fight and Negombo fell again into the hands of the Dutch.

The news of the catastrophe produced an indescribable confusion in Colombo. Nearly all the inhabitants of the town had lost a brother or a relative. The widow of Anthony de Motte Galvão abandoned herself to the most terrible despair. Groups of frightened people ran about the streets, disorder reigned supreme, and at any moment the enemy was expected to come and besiege the city.

The Governor Mascarenhas putting on his grand uniform rode then on horseback through the streets of the town. It was on the 10th of January. He spoke to the people, explained them the folly of abandoning themselves to despair in a moment of supreme danger, and succeeded in raising their courage. He then worked with energy to reorganize the means of defence.

Meanwhile the Dutch general Caron was fortifying Negombo. He repaired the bastions and the ramparts and placed on them 32 guns. This took him twelve days after which he marched on Colombo. But the town had already been placed in a state of defence. For ten whole days he tried to force the passage of the river Kelany, which was bravely defended by the Portuguese. Finally he desisted and retired to Negombo, where he left a garrison of 600 men and sailed for Batavia with the rest of his troops.

When Caron had departed, Philip Mascarenhas determined to

try to reconquer Negombo, but he was well aware of the difficulty of such an enterprise, for, though the Dutch garrison was small in number it was composed of brave and determined men, well provided with arms and ammunitions so that they could easily sustain a siege till they got reinforcements from Java.

The Governor therefore resolved to try to renew amicable relations with King Raja Singha. He sent an embassy with rich presents to Kandy, to propose an alliance on the base of a mutual guarantee of the integrity of their respective territory.

Raja Singha received cordially the Governor's envoys for he had begun seriously to distrust the Dutch who in violation of the treaty he had made with them, retained the towns of Galle and Negombo instead of delivering them to him as had been stipulated. He now perceived that their intention was to conquer Ceylon for themselves, and that, if the Portuguese were expelled from the Island, he would find himself face to face with another European power who would follow the same policy.

Now, Raja Singha in allying himself with the Dutch, was moved by the same political principles that were followed by Bhuwaneka Bahu when he so persistently spared the rebel Mayadunnè.

Raja Singha had no desire to give new masters to the south and the north of the Island. All he wanted, was that the Portuguese should spend their strength and their energy in struggling with the Dutch, instead of spending them in endeavouring to conquer his own kingdom.

He was already disgusted with the Dutch. On the other hand he feared the Portuguese: His brother Don Theodose was a favoured guest of the Viceroy at Goa. The armistice concluded with the Dutch would soon be proclaimed in Ceylon. He had not been included in it. Would not the Portuguese take profit of the truce which had to last till 1652, to endeavour to get rid of him and to place on the throne of Kandy his brother Don Theodose.

He therefore gave the Governor's envoy a kind and courteous reception, but he told him that the Dutch had not given him as yet sufficient cause to justify a rupture, and that the Portuguese should understand, that they themselves by their haughty and aggressive conduct had forced him to seek a foreign alliance. His sympathies, he said, were always with the Portuguese amidst whom he had passed his youth, and who had taught him to distinguish between good and evil. He should like to come to their aid but, in the present moment, he really did not see how he could do it. He added that the Portuguese had committed a mistake not to have ceased hostilities at the first news of the armistice. They had hoped to reconquer Galle, and now they had lost Negombo. His opinion, he said, was that the Governor should concentrate all his efforts in retaking Negombo before the armistice was proclaimed. He could not help the Governor, but he would neither help the Dutch.

With this promise he dismissed the Portuguese embassy, overwhelming them with honours and loading them with rich presents.

The Governor Philip Mascarenhas was well satisfied with the issue of the step he had taken. All that he wanted was to assure Raja Singha's neutrality in his campaign against Negombo.

He gave the command of the expedition to Ferdinand Furtado de Mendoza who had arrived from Goa with 400 men.

They laid siege to Negombo on the 19th April. But young Mendoza lacked in experience. He lost three whole months in useless skirmishes. His officers were divided in opinion. Some desired more energetic measures others being discouraged wished to abandon this useless enterprise.

A Council of war was held. Each gave his opinion, but it soon became evident that the majority was for a prompt and decisive action:

Among the officers there was an old German, one of those adventurers common at that epoch, who were selling their services to whom paid him best. He had passed his life amidst the wars in Europe and had come to seek fortune in the East.

He was listening in silence to the animated discussion, and, when all the officers had spoken, he put them a question which none of them expected:

— „ Has any one of you, he said, ever assisted to a regular siege of a town? "—

None, not even Furtado de Mendoza could answer: Yes.

— „ Well, answered the German veteran, since I was a lad I have done nothing else, believe therefore my experience: In the way you proceed, you will never conquer Negombo."—

— „ Do you doubt, they exclaimed, the courage of the Portuguese? "—

— „ Doubt it, answered the German, in all you have said now

there is more courage and determination, than prudence and knowledge of military tactics! "—

And he began to explain the tactics of the epoch in besieging of a town; how they should surround it with earth works, and bring them progressively nearer to the walls......

The officers rose from their seats and interrupted him: All that, they said is good perhaps for Germans; the Portuguese confide in their swords, and when they take a town they take it by assault.

A general attack was decided upon for the next day. The Dutch informed of it by their spies prepared for a vigorous resistance.

The assault of the 25th July was one of the bloodiest feats of war in the history of Ceylon. The fight lasted from early morning till eleven at night when the Portuguese were obliged to give up the battle. Ferdinand Furtado de Mendoza was among the slain, and of the 950 Portuguese who had marched in the morning to the assault only 398 remained. These retired in good order carrying their guns with them and entrenched themselves near the village of Vaygampitya on the road of Colombo, to check the Dutch should they march on the capital.

This day decided of the fate of Negombo, which was never to return again to the hands of the Portuguese.

On the 13th October 1644 the Dutch general John Maatzuyker arrived at Goa bringing to the Viceroy despatches from Lisbon relating to the armistice concluded in 1642. He remained some weeks at Goa arranging the details of the truce, which having been proclaimed in India, he came to Colombo in the month of December.

Everything having been already settled by the Viceroy, it remained only to proclaim the armistice in Ceylon. which was made amidst great rejoicing, for the people were tired of this war which caused them so much suffering.

Galle and Negombo remained to the Dutch, with comparatively large territories around these two cities. It was only stipulated that the Catholic villagers who had been expelled from their homes by the Protestants, would be allowed to return, but in the meanwhile many of them had died of misery and starvation.

Philip Mascarenhas had been appointed Viceroy, he left Colombo in March 1645. His successor was Emmanuel
**1545** Mascarenhas Homem.

It was about this time that Raja Singha's brother Don Theodose Cumara Raja of Uva was baptised at Goa. It made the King very uneasy, as he had not been included in the armistice, and knew the love the Kandyans had for his brother. He feared lest the Portuguese would attempt to place him on the throne, and did therefore his best to remain on good terms with the Governor and carefully avoided any pretext for a quarrel.

The only event of some importance during the truce, was the
**1546** invasion of the Dutch territory by the Kandyans.

Raja Singha had a quarrel with Adrian Van den Steel, the Dutch commander of Negombo, who had seized some tame elephants belonging to the King. Raja Singha marched on Negombo. As he could not reach the town without passing through the Portuguese territory he asked the Governor's permission, which the Governor granted, giving at the same time orders to all the officials to show great honor to the King.

Raja Singha, gained a complete victory over the Dutch. Adrian Van den Steel was killed in the battle, and his body brought to Kandy with 680 prisoners.

John Maatzuyker who, since the armistice had remained in Galle as Governor of the Dutch territory in Ceylon was much disturbed by this event. He knew that Raja Singha wavered between the two parties and was afraid lest the aggression on Negombo might not be a sign that he had finally inclined himself towards the Portuguese alliance.

He hastened therefore to send an embassy to Kandy with a humble letter in which he condemned Van den Steel's conduct, protested to his devotedness to the King, and took God for witness, that the Dutch had come to Ceylon without any afterthought of conquest, their only object being to defend the King against his enemies, the Portuguese, and that it was for him alone that they were fighting and shedding their blood.

Raja Singha, in whose interest it was to remain on good terms with both parties, as long as he did not know which would be the stronger, took profit of this occasion to foment the animosity among them. He replied to Maatzuyker's humble epistle, by setting the Dutch prisoners free, and bringing to his notice the fact, that in spite of the armistice, the Governor had allowed him free passage across the Portuguese territory. He cared little, he said, about the elephants seized by Van den Steel, and the chief object of his expedition has been to show to the Dutch how little they could rely on the loyalty and the good faith of the Portuguese.

After friendship had been thus restored, there arose a singular question of etiquette, namely as regards the title which the Dutch should give to the King of Kandy in their official correspondence. Raja Singha wanted the Dutch to call him their god, but that seemed too much even to such a godless man as Maatzuyker, and the King had to content himself with the less exalted title of Emperor of Ceylon.

Meanwhile, Maatzuyker, whose protestant bigotry seemed to have no limits, had all the Christian villagers expelled again from the Dutch territories of Galle and of Negombo. Many died of misery in the forests, and those who could reach the Portuguese dominions were charitably taken in by the authorities who provided for their pressing needs.

Whilst the Missions in the south of Ceylon were thus declining, those of the kingdom of Jaffna, where the Protestants had
1648 not yet penetrated, were still in a prosperous state.

The old apostle of Madura Fr. de Nobili S. J. was sent to Jaffna by his Superiors in 1648 where they hoped that rest and a less trying climate would restore his health impaired by many years of hard missionary labours. He was appointed Superior of the

Jaffna Mission, and notwithstanding his infirmities, he worked yet as much as he could. He was nearly blind. It was a touching sight to see the venerable man, going daily to the church, feeling his way with his staff. Then the Christians would hasten to meet him, they surrounded him with signs of sincere love, and carried him to the church.

But his strength was failing. He was ordered to Mylapore to have complete rest, where he died in 1656.

In 1650 John Maatzuyker was succeeded by Jacob Van
1650 Kittenstein.

Meanwhile Raja Singha was maturing his plans. He saw now clearly that the Portuguese power was on its decline, and that the government of Goa had abandoned Ceylon to its own resources. The fears that the Portuguese would profit by the truce to overthrow him and place on the throne of Kandy his brother Don Theodose were dispelled now that the end of the armistice was approaching, and he finally decided to cast his lot with the Dutch.

Wishing to bring him to their side, the Governor, by order of the Viceroy, sent on an embassy to Kandy, Jerome d'Azevedo and Fr. Sebastian de Fonseca Rector of the Jesuit College in Colombo, with rich presents. The King refused to receive them and notified his refusal to the Dutch commander of Galle.

The end of the armistice was approaching. The greatest activity reigned in the Dutch towns of Galle and of
1651 Negombo. During the truce, they had strongly fortified

these places, putting the ramparts into a state of defence, filling their arsenals with arms and ammunitions and their granaries with provisions of all sort.

The Portuguese on their side had remained the whole time in a state of inaction which cannot be easily explained. Had they any reason to believe that a treaty of peace would follow the truce or were they discouraged by seeing themselves abandoned to their own resources without any support from Goa and from Lisbon? This last supposition seems the most probable. The assertion of some Protestant writers, that these descendants of so many heroes had become degenerated cannot be admitted. The heroism they displayed in the last struggle gives it an emphatic denial.

Nevertheless, the fact remains that, during all the years of the armistice, whilst the greatest activity reigned in the Dutch camp, the Portuguese remained in a state of complete inaction and seemed not to think about the renewal of the struggle, which nevertheless was inevitable. They allowed matters to go so far, that the ramparts of Colombo had been planted with cocoanut trees. All available space inside the fortress was built over with houses so that the citadel had become a small town with 4,000 inhabitants of whom only 1,200 were soldiers. The 237 guns which stood on the ramparts were covered with rust and their carriages rotten, eaten by white ants. And there were no provisions even to feed the soldiers.

They had therefore a terrible awakening when in October 1652, the Dutch commander of Galle sent several officers
1652 to Colombo to notify to the Governor Emmanuel

Mascarenhas Homem that the armistice was ended and that he was going to resume hostilities.

The people and the soldiers became exasperated and all blamed the Governor, for his inactivity. They shouted in the streets that Mascarenhas Homem was a dog, and incapable of commanding even in a war with hares.

The mutiny was increasing and its centre was the infantry camp situated at a short distance from the town. Mascarenhas Homem thinking that his presence would calm the excited soldiers went himself to the camp, but he was received with cries of: Death to the traitor, long life to the Faith of Christ, long life to King John IV, death to the Governor. The tumult was indescribable and it was only owing to the energy of the military chaplain, a Capuchin Father, that the Governor could escape with his life.

Then the principal Missionaries and some notabilities of the town, seeing the threatening turn the mutiny was taking, advised the Governor to resign and leave the government to the officer next in rank, for since it was against him personally that the people and the army had a grudge, all would be again restored to order by his resignation.

The Governor replied, that he had been appointed by the King and would not leave his post without an order of his Sovereign. That it would be a dangerous thing to yield to the mutineers. That he would do his duty to the end, and if need be, fight the mutineers at the head of the troops which still remain faithful.

In vain they tried to make him understand that such would

certainly be his duty in ordinary circumstances, but not at the present moment when the enemy was at their gate, when the life of every soldier was precious, and when a civil struggle would deliver them defenceless into the hands of the Dutch. The Governor remained obdurate, the Missionaries and the Municipal Councillors decided to leave him to his fate.

Early next morning the Governor went to the Jesuit church, where he confessed and received Holy Communion. Then, followed by his staff, he went to the parish church where he addressed the people explaining them in what danger the present mutiny placed the state. He then declared that he was determined to punish the rebels with the greatest severity, and then commanded all present to swear him allegiance as the Representative of the King of Portugal.

The Blessed Sacrament was exposed and, to give the example, all the Priests present took the oath, but, when the turn came to the soldiers, some swore fidelity to the King, others to die in the defence of the Faith of Christ, but none in obedience to the Governor. It was a bad sign, but the number of those who swore in this way was so great that even the Governor, excited as he was, deemed it more prudent to overlook the fact. The ceremony was closed with a sermon preached by Fr. Peter da Costa, a secular Priest, who exposed to the congregation the danger of domestic quarrels, when the enemy was gathering his forces to expel them from the country.

When the news of the Governor's doings reached the mutineers in the camp, they swore that they would not submit, and would rather put to death the Governor and his family than obey his orders.

Then the mutineers held a meeting and decided to march on Colombo, and to depose the Governor. They elected for their chief captain Figueira de Serpa. The latter was an able and loyal officer, but seeing how exasperated were the soldiers, he deemed it prudent to accept the leadership, in the hope that he would be able to use his authority to stop the mutiny or at least prevent excesses.

Mascarenhas Homem had lost his head. He grew more and more obstinate in his determination to cling to power. He had fortified his palace, and with the few companies which remained faithful to him he prepared to fight the rebels.

The whole town was in tumult. Crowds in the streets vociferated that it was not right to shed blood for a man, who seemed to have lost his reason, for it was clear that with the few men at his disposal, he could never conquer the rebels, not even arrest their progress, the more so as the troops on which he counted were already deserting and joining the mutineers in their camp. The consequence therefore would be the loss of many lives and the pillage of the town, and worse yet, because when the news of what was going on in Colombo reach the Dutch commander in Galle, he would certainly march on the capital and take it easily.

Then the Mayor summoned the Municipal Council and, after mature deliberation, they went in a body to the Jesuit College, and asked the Rector to join them in a last endeavour to persuade the Governor to renounce to useless bloodshed. They went then to the Governor s palace, but Mascarenhas Homem did not let them speak calling them traitors and exclaiming that he would fight to the end.

Meanwhile the rebels had encamped under the walls of the city, and were asking Priests to confess them as they were determined to assault the town on the morrow.

Figueira de Serpa sent a messenger to the Franciscan Fathers entreating them to come, as their influence could do much to calm the spirits of the mutineers. They came, passed the whole night in the confessionals, with the result that next morning, the 30th of November, the hatred of the soldiers against the Governor had abated, they were calmer and more inclined to obey to their officers. Nevertheless they were determined to become masters of the town.

At sunrise, they marched in good order towards the bastions which commanded the Queen's gate. As they approached the gate was flung open, and they saw coming forth a procession with the Blessed Sacrament. They stopped at once, and, on the command of the officers threw themselves on their knees. Then the Jesuit and the Franciscan Fathers barred their way and told them that they would not let them enter the town, unless they swear before the Blessed Sacrament, that they would abstain from all excesses, and commit no offence against the Governor. All took the oath.

The Governor, seeing that the troops in the town as well as the citizens fraternized with the mutineers, sought refuge in the Convent of the Dominican Fathers whence he sent his aide-de-camp Diogo de Sousa da Cunha to proclaim in the city that he resigned his office, and at once peace and order were reestablished.

They then proceeded to the election of a provisory government composed of three members, whose first act was the imprisonment of the Governor and his family in one of the bastions of the fort. They did that in order to save his life from the fury of the excited populace who wanted to put him to death.

Fortunately, the Dutch could not recommence the war, before receiving reinforcements from Java, for had they been able to take profit of these disorders, they would have even then become masters of Ceylon.

This state of anarchy lasted in Colombo till May 1653, when the Viceroy, Count of Obidos, appointed Governor of
1653 Ceylon Francis de Mello de Castro, a very able man, who arrived at Colombo with twelve ships and 250 Portuguese soldiers.

His first care was to set at liberty the late Governor Emmanuel Mascarenhas Homem. He then proclaimed a general amnesty. The late mutineers however refused it, saying that an amnesty presupposed guilt, and far from that, they had rendered a great service to the Portuguese Crown by deposing an incapable Governor. In view of the critical position in which he was placed, the new Governor had to allow this matter to drop.

Mello de Castro's victory over the Dutch in the battle of Tebuana calmed the spirits and restored the courage of the Portuguese in Ceylon.

During the next year there were only a few unimportant skirmishes. The Dutch, too weak to attempt a decisive
1654 stroke, were awaiting reinforcements.

The battle of Kaluamodere, fought on the 10th January 1654, was the only important event, when captain Casper Figueira gained a brilliant victory on the combined forces of the Dutch and of King Raja Singha. Notwithstanding the crushing number of the enemy, the Portuguese remained masters of the field on which lay 11,000 Kandyans, and 1,600 were taken prisoners.

Francis de Mello de Castro had retired on account of his advanced age, and the Viceroy appointed Governor Anthony de Sousa Cutinho, whose first care was to put Colombo in a state of defence, and to remodel the garrison. But he could not do much for, in this moment of extreme distress the government of Goa and that of Lisbon had abandoned Ceylon to its own resources.

The greatness of Portugal was gone; their glorious deeds for nearly two centuries, the extension of their conquests which necessitated a strained life, had exhausted the nerves of the nation. The part in history which God had assigned to this most faithful nation, was to implant in the Asiatic East the Faith of Christ and civilization. They had fulfilled their vocation, their work was done, and now they had collapsed under its strain.

## CHAPTER 15

# THE SIEGE OF COLOMBO

On the 30th of September 1655 the Dutch general Gerard d'Hulst arrived at Galle from Batavia with a squadron of
1655
26 vessels. He brought 3,000 European soldiers and a contingent of Malay troops. He had orders from his government to accomplish the conquest of Ceylon.

Fr. de Queiroz says that Gerard d'Hulst was a warrior of renown, a good general, very rich and generous. Of an energetic and enterprising nature; when the Council refused to approve any plan of his as being too risky he undertook it at his own cost and responsibility, and nearly always succeeded.

After his landing at Galle, prudent general that he was, and man of great experience, he began by studying the strength of the Dutch and of the King of Kandy and the state of the Portuguese forces. Then he laid siege to Kalutara.

The garrison of this place numbered 490 men under the command of Anthony Mendez d'Aranha. They defended bravely the fort, but being unable to resist the overwhelming forces of the enemy, they capitulated. The conditions were that they leave the place with military honours to the Dutch camp at the entrance of which they would surrender their arms. Mendez d'Aranha alone would be taken prisoner to Galle, to be released in case the Portuguese retake Kalutara. General d'Hulst had demanded that all the soldiers should bind themselves, not to fight against the Dutch during the present war, but they answered, that they would rather perish under the ruins of their fortress than agree to such a condition. And the Dutch general admiring the heroism of this handful of men, did not further insist on this condition and the capitulation was signed on the 14th October 1655.

At the news of the siege of Kalutara the Governor had sent from Colombo the choicest troops under the command of Casper Figueira de Serpa, the victor of Kaluamodere. On the way they learned that the place had been capitulated. Instead of returning to Colombo, Figueira de Serpa, who in his military career had never lost a battle, marched on the Dutch who were occupying a very strong position. But he was completely defeated, and lost in the battle the greatest part of his soldiers and his best officers. This rash deed of Figueira de Serpa was unpardonable at a moment when Colombo threatened by overwhelming forces had a garrison unadequate for the struggle which was imminent.

We now come to the last act of the glorious history of the Portuguese in Ceylon, the siege of Colombo, which was one of the greatest and most heroic feats of arms mentioned in history.

After Figueira's defeat Gerald d'Hulst marched on Colombo. At the news of the approach of the enemy's army, all the villagers of the neighbourhood sought refuge in the town and the Governor Anthony de Sousa Cutinho taking pity of their distress, committed the imprudence of admitting them, trebling thus in one day the number of people he would have to feed during the siege.

The town was soon surrounded by the Dutch. The number of Malay troops which Hulst had brought from Java is not recorded. He had 4,800 European soldiers and Raja Singha sent him a contingent of 16,000 men. 26 vessels brought from Galle all equipments necessary for the siege and blockaded the harbour.

The garrison of Colombo numbered only 800 men, but arms were distributed to the citizens, and all fought with determination.

For these poor native Christians it was a holy war, not only in defence of their homes but also of their Faith, for wherever the Protestants were masters, they polluted the churches, and cruelly persecuted the Christians, and acted as if they were the enemies of God.

The operations of the siege commenced on the 21st of October. Then began a sequel of assaults, of sorties in the night and fighting on the ramparts. The Dutch who are a brave and plucky people fought with double ardour, for they knew that the capture of Colombo would be their final triumph, the definite conquest of Ceylon and their gallant chief, general Gerard d'Hulst gave them the example, being always in the front.

On the other hand, the defenders of Colombo proved themselves heroes. They had to multiply themselves to repel the assaults, being only a handful of men against such overwhelming forces. Old

Anthony Mello de Castro, the late Governor, was always on the ramparts. They say that, during the seven months that the siege lasted, he was rarely seen without his armour.

The Missionaries gave no less proofs of heroism. They too were always on the ramparts, taking care of the wounded, administering the last Sacraments to the dying, taking the place of the sentinels during the night, to give the soldiers some rest. They accompanied the soldiers in the sorties; unarmed, the Crucifix in hand, they inspired to the soldiers such courage as only true Faith can give.

They also took care of the non-combatant. They visited them in their houses, consoled the widows and the orphans, they preached, they organized processions and public prayers, in one word they did all to prevent the demoralization that often during long sieges overcomes the non-combatants.

The Missionaries who distinguished themselves especially by their courage and charity were the Franciscan Fathers Francis of the Mother of God, and Francis of St. Matthew; the Jesuits, Fr. Emmanuel Vellez, Fr. Anthony Nunez and Peter Rebello; the Capuchin Fr. Paul; the Dominican Peter Castillo Branco.

The Augustinian Fr. Anthony Nunez was the first victim of the devotedness of the Missionaries. He fell struck by a bullet when tending the wounded on the bastion of St. John. Fr. Emmanuel Vellez was severely wounded in a sortie.

One only, among the Missionaries, Fr. Damian Vieira, a Jesuit, made himself a bad name. Forgetting that he was a Priest, forgetting the sublime duties of a Priest in such moments like these, he made himself a soldier. With sword and musket in hand, he commanded bloody sorties and created great havoc among the enemy. Gifted with indomitable courage and with remarkable military talents, he was considered by the generals as one of their best captains. After the siege he was expelled from the Society of Jesus.

Meanwhile the siege continued. The Protestants were pillaging the suburban churches, and polluting the altars and all sacred things.

Having found in a neighbouring church a wooden statue of St. Thomas the Apostle they brought it to their camp, and exposing it on the ramparts of one of their batteries, the nearest to the walls of the city, so that the besieged could see it well, they submitted it to all kind of insults and abominations. Finally, on the 16th December they studded the statue with nails, and having cut off the nose and the arms they loaded it in a mortar and shouting: — „Take back your Saint" — they fired it against the town. It did not reach the ramparts and fell into the moat.

This ignoble deed exasperated the garrison. Fr. Damian Vieira with two officers, Emmanuel Seixas and Emmanuel de St. Jago Garcia and a few soldiers, made a sortie, and, under the fire of the enemy's batteries took from the moat the mutilated statue, and brought it into the town to the Jesuit College. In the evening the statue was carried in procession through the streets of the town to the Franciscan church where they held a service of expiation for the insults offered by the Protestants to the Apostle of Jesus Christ.

Then Fr. Francis of St. Matthew preached a sermon, which animated the courage of the besieged.

With the beginning of 1656 the provisions were exhausted and soon the famine became terrible. They ate dogs, rats
1656 and everything, even the most unclean that they could get. The streets were full of people dying of starvation. Then came fever, dysentery, berry-berry, the inevitable companions of famine, and more than 300 people were dying daily. The Blessed Sacrament was exposed day and night in the church of the Capuchin Fathers, which was always full of women and children. The men who could not carry arms, passed the whole day in burying the dead, but soon they found themselves incapable of carrying on this work of charity, and the corpses remained lying in hideous piles in the streets. The soldiers fought from morning to night without more food than a handful of rice.

A heathen mother, having had nothing to eat for days, and seeing the terrible sufferings of her little child, killed it, then prompted by the pangs of hunger she ate it. She was condemned to death, but some of the chief citizens represented to the Governor the unspeakable misery which had led the unfortunate woman to commit the unnatural deed and obtained her pardon.

Being reduced to such extremity, having no food for the people who were dying every day of starvation, the authorities of Colombo were finally compelled to have recourse to an extreme measure, that of expelling all the villagers who had taken refuge in the town before the siege, that they might look for their food in the country. It was the only way of saving them from death by starvation as, once outside the besieged walls, they would be easily helped by the Catholic villagers and even by the Buddhist Singhalese who were kind and charitable people. But the Dutch did not allow to pass their lines. They hung hundreds of them on trees and gibbets around their camp, and the others, driven back to the narrow space between the ramparts of the city and the enemy's batteries, were killed to the last man.

It was now the month of April, and the siege had already lasted for six months. Gerard d' Hulst wished to push now vigorously the operations of the siege to put the matters to an end.

On the 10th April, whilst he was inspecting the works of a new battery he was struck by a Portuguese bullet. Feeling that he was mortally wounded, he exclaimed: — „Oh! my God, help me." — and expired.

Thus the Dutch lost one of their ablest generals. Adrian Van der Meyden, a man of no less ability, took now the command.

The town held out a month longer, but the famine was terrible. The citizens were dying of starvation and there was not an able bodied soldier left. Then the Mayor approached the Governor with a petition from the citizens, begging him to save from a cruel and lingering death the women and children that yet survived, and to enter into negotiations with the enemy for the surrender of the city. Their sufferings were too terrible.

The Governor Anthony de Sousa knew well himself that a

longer resistance was not possible. They could not repulse the first assault, and he well understood to what the city would be exposed, if it fell unconditionally into the hands of the enemy. He therefore called to a Council in the convent of the Dominicans, the ex-Governor Francis de Mello de Castro, the officers who still survived, the Superiors of the Religious orders, the Magistrates and the Mayor with the Municipal Counsellors. The discussion did not last long, for it was evident that with the 63 officers and men who remained out of the 800 they had at the beginning of the siege, they could fight no more, and that all was ended.

Lawrence Ferreira de Britto, Jerome de Lucena Tavora and Diogo Leitão de Sousa were directed to draw up the conditions of the surrender.

Next morning, the 10th May 1656 they hoisted the white flag, and an officer of superior rank, Manuel Cabreira de Pontes, went to the enemy's camp, not to ask the victor the terms of capitulation, but to dictate them to him. And Adrian Van der Meyden, admiring their heroism, accepted the honorable terms they asked, making only a few minor modifications as a matter of form.

The first condition was that the churches and holy images were not to be profaned, and that the Priests would be left free to leave the town, carrying with them all sacred vessels and vestments.

This article duly signed by the Dutch general was violated only two days later, when St. Francis' church was polluted by the Dutch, ministers holding in it their protestant service.

The seventh article secured to the Catholics full and entire religious liberty.

We will see in the next chapters how this condition was observed.

For the rest, the garrison was to leave the town with full military honours, with arms and baggage and colours unfurled. Each gunner had to hold in his hand a lighted match, each soldier a musket and carry a bullet between his teeth. The Dutch had to supply them with ships, to carry them to Jaffna with all their belongings.

Adrian Van der Meyden not only signed these conditions, but he assured Cabreira de Pontes that the Portuguese officers and men would be treated with all regards due to their heroism, and that himself would see, that nothing necessary for them was wanting.

On the same day at 3 p. m. the officers and men of the garrison to the number of 63 left the town with full military honors passing amidst the inhabitants of the town, who were crying and lamenting. It was a sad sight, for the greater number could hardly walk. Some were cevered with wounds, others were consumed with fever or the legs swollen with berry-berry, and all exhausted by famine and privations. not one who was not an invalid.

They marched so to the enemy's camp. Adrian Van der Meyden received them with courtesy, and told them that next day he would come to Colombo to pass the garrison in review :

--- „ But the whole garrison is here before you." — Answered a captain. The general grew pale and turned to his officers to hide his emotion.

Thus ended the Portuguese Rule in Ceylon. They had remained in the Island for one and a half century. For 17 years they had contended inch by inch with the Dutch invaders, and the last act of this heroic drama was the memorable siege of Colombo, when a garrison of 800 men bid defiance for seven months to an army of more than 25,000 and did not yield till they were reduced to 63 men, and not before they had imposed on the conqueror their own conditions of surrender.

The Portuguese yet held the kingdom of Jaffna and the Island of Manaar but it was evident that they could not hold those territories against the Dutch, now masters of the south of Ceylon, and that their ultimate loss was only a question of time.

In the treaty of alliance between the Dutch and King Raja Singha of Kandy signed by both parties in 1638 it had been stipulated that: The Dutch would declare war against the Portuguese, and that they would make over to the King of Kandy, wholly and without any afterthought, all the towns and all the fortresses which they would capture, with the exception of Batticaloa and Kottyar where they would be permitted to keep their garrisons.

Now, on the strength of this treaty, King Raja Singha demanded that Colombo should be made over to him. The Dutch general gave him an evasive answer, then Raja Singha sent him the following letter:

— „ Your Excellency is free to act as you think proper till the Prince of Orange and the East India Company is informed of the matter. But you must keep in mind that he who denies God and does not keep his word will suffer the consequences. God and justice are on my side. You may put forward your frivolous arguments to whom you like, but not to me. Henceforth I shall have no faith in your word. " —

Adrian Van der Meyden replied to the King's letter on flattering terms, but Raja Singha was not satisfied. The army which he had sent to help in the siege of Colombo was still encamped in the vicinity of that town. He put himself at its head, marched against the Dutch and gained over them a complete victory, and occupied the whole of the late Portuguese territory, so that the Dutch found themselves reduced to their fortresses on the coast: Galle, Kalutara, Colombo and Negombo, and could not even venture out of the walls of these cities.

Raja Singha saw now too late that in allying himself with the Dutch, he had only given new masters to Ceylon, and far more dangerous masters, for, if he could have obtained much from the chivalrous character of the Portuguese, it was not the same with the mercantile, practical disposition of the Dutch.

Raja Singha was disgusted and so he turned again towards the old friends of his youth. He took many Portuguese into his service; gave shelter in his kingdom to those Catholics who emigrated from the southern provinces, for their protestant masters had already begun to persecute them, and allowed them to settle down at Kandy and in the villages of Ruanwelle, Galgamuva, Wawodda, Kalugalla and Wahacotta, where they built churches.

The church at Kandy situated in the Bogambra quarter was now ministered by 12 Priests driven out of their missions by the protestants, and 700 Portuguese families from Colombo established themselves at Ruanwelle.

Ribeiro, the Portuguese chronicler, speaking of Raja Singha whom he knew personally says: — „ The King of Kandy remembers us with affection, and regrets us, for he does not find in the Dutch, the courtesy, politeness and generosity and other qualities which are natural to the Portuguese. He was brought up among us, had adopted our habits and customs and, even if he had quarrels with our Governors, that, nevertheless, did not diminish his goodwill for us."—

And Robert Knox who lived for many years a prisoner at Kandy and knew well King Raja Singha writes: — „ The King and people like the Christian Religion, and respect and honor the Christians as Christians, and admit that there is a God greater than their gods. The King does not in any way persecute the Christian Religion, nor has he any aversion for it. It rather seems to me that he esteems and honors it.

The people like men who act to the dictates of their conscience, and it is on that account that they respect the Christians more than others, because they think them just and incapable of lying.

When the King appoints a Dessawe, he shows him proofs of his love and favour especially to those that are Christians, for he has more confidence in them than in people of his own religion, and believes that they will fulfil their duties more conscientiously and be more faithful." —

Such is the testimony given by two contemporary writers, who knew well King Raja Singha, of his sentiments towards the Portuguese and towards the Catholics in the first years of the Dutch Rule.

1657 The Dutch weakened by the siege of Colombo which caused them heavy losses, and by the defeat they had suffered at the hands of the King of Kandy ten days after the surrender of that town, could not think about a new campaign, and abandoned for the moment all thought of expelling the Portuguese from the north of the Island. They were engaged in preparing their defences against a new aggression of King Raja Singha and building small fortlets in the interior to protect their crops of cinnamon which was their chief commodity of trade.

The Portuguese on their side were busy in strengthening the defences of Jaffna and of the other forts they possessed in the north.

1658 About the beginning of 1658, the late Governor of Ceylon, Emmanuel Mascarenhas Homem was appointed Viceroy. He sent reinforcements to Jaffna and appointed Governor Anthony d'Amarel de Menezes.

The Dutch began to feel uneasy; they saw that even after the loss of Colombo, fresh reinforcements were forthcoming from Goa, and if the Portuguese should enter in an alliance with the King of Kandy who seemed inclined to be reconciled with them, they were still a dangerous enemy and could yet dispute with them the possession of the Island.

They therefore determined to complete the conquest with the definitive expulsion of the Portuguese from Ceylon.

An army was sent to the north, and after having captured Manaar and Kayts, they laid siege to Jaffna, the last stronghold of the Portuguese in Ceylon.

The siege was stubborn and lasted for three months, from the 16th March to the 24th June 1658. The Portuguese defended the place with the same heroism as they had done in Colombo. Famine and pestilence caused more deaths than the enemy's fire. A new horror was added to the sufferings of the besieged by the want of water, for the wells became infected by the multitude of corpses that lay unburied.

Finally, after three months of glorious defence, the white flag was hoisted. They signed honorable terms of surrender, the same as they did at Colombo. But the Dutch paid no heed to their engagements. They gave themselves up to pillage, ill-treated the garrison whom, notwithstanding the capitulation, they sent prisoners to Batavia, and brutally expelled the 50 Missionaries, Jesuits, Dominicans and Franciscans whom they found in the town.

The men had changed, and the Dutch who came to Ceylon after the capture of Colombo were no more noble warriors like Gerard d'Hulst and Adrian Van der Meyden.

We possess less details of the siege of Jaffna than of that of Colombo, but the struggle was not less heroic. When the town surrendered there remained only 140 men of the garrison, and these were so exhausted, that they no longer could carry their muskets, and, when the Dutch entered the fort, they did not find even one habitable room. The place was a heap of ruins.

Thus ended the Portuguese Rule in Ceylon.

# Part IV

# THE DUTCH RULE

1658 — 1796

## CHAPTER 1

# THE PROTESTANT RULE

The Dutch period of the history of Ceylon which lasted for one
1558 hundred and forty years is far less interesting than the precedent one. It was a gloomy, dark period, the decline of civilization and of the prosperity of the Ceylonese, which were both making such rapid progress in the first half of that century: and the horrid persecution which the Christians had to suffer at the hands of their protestant masters, gives to that period a repellent character.

Nevertheless, it seems to me, that some historians of Ceylon have been unjust, and speak too badly of the Dutch, I say of the Dutch as a nation.

It is certain that their rule in Ceylon will always compare very unfavourably with that of the Portuguese who, above all, were Christians and brought to the people of their extensive conquests, who till then lived in a state of half barbarity, the Faith of Christ and civilization. But we must make here a distinction between such conquests which are made by a nation, and those which are made by a commercial company. In the first case we see a high ideal, the love of the mother country, the desire of acquiring glory, a deep feeling of their duty towards the conquered people. In the second case there is no other object than gain.

The Portuguese sent to Ceylon the flower of their nobility, gallant knights in whom was still alive the spirit of the Crusaders, their ancestors. The Dutch sent only merchants, and with them the refuse of the population of Holland.

The Portuguese fought for the glory of God and the glory of their King. The Dutch fought for cinnamon and money.

In order to appreciate in an impartial manner the history of that period, we must always keep in mind that the conquest of Ceylon has not been made by Holland, but by the Dutch East India Company. Not by the nation, but by a company of powerful merchants, whose only aim was to draw out of the conquered country as much money as possible, and being men who had no Faith, they did it without the restraint which Religion and Christian morals impose on avarice and on the human passions.

We must not impute to the whole nation the evil done by a few.

We must not impute to the Dutch nation the destruction of Christianity in Ceylon. If the new conquerors persecuted without relaxation the unfortunate Christians of Ceylon, so much that all sentiments of humanity seemed to be extinct in their soul, they did it not because they were Dutch, but because they were protestants, and at that epoch the same persecution of the Catholic Church raged in all the countries where the followers of the new religion had got the upper hand.

What happened therefore in Ceylon, would have happened in the same way if any other protestant nation had then conquered the Island. It was not a Dutch persecution, as the historians call it unproperly, it was a protestant persecution; and Christianity has been destroyed in Ceylon not by the Dutch, but by the protestants.

The first care of the Dutch after having taken Colombo was to fortify the town. They pulled down the old Portuguese ramparts which had been constructed in view of a siege by the Kandyans and were no longer serviceable against the tactics of the times, and rebuilt them again more solidly on a more modern plan. The old fortifications were too extensive and required for their defence a rather large garrison. The area of the fort was therefore much reduced, and surrounded with a deep moat fed by the waters of the lake. A new citadel was constructed on the site of the Augustinian Convent which commanded the town.

The Dutch feared the return of the Portuguese, they had no confidence in their ally, the King of Kandy, and did not trust the people.

The Christians soon began to perceive how little they could rely on the good faith of their new protestant masters, and what treatment they were to expect from them.

On the 12th May 1656, the Dutch had signed the capitulation, the seventh article of which guaranteed to the Catholics full and entire religious liberty, and only a few days later they brutally expelled the priests, desecrated the churches, destroyed the beautiful educational establishments endowed by the Portuguese and on the 19th September 1658 proclaimed the notorious law, which forbade under the pain of death to give shelter to a Catholic priest.

Thus was the protestant rule inaugurated in Ceylon.

Some English writers affirm that the inhabitants of Ceylon were overjoyed to see themselves liberated from the tyranny of the Portuguese and sheltered under the beneficial rule of the protestant Dutch. Percival says: — „The joy of the Ceylonese of being „delivered from the yoke of their tyrannical invaders, and their „gratitude to their deliverers knew no bounds.“ —

It is the most impudent assertion ever made by a sectarian writer.

Certainly it was not the Catholics, who formed at that time a very large section of the population as well Singhalese as Tamil that rejoiced at that change.

As regards the heathens, although they were not persecuted like the Christians, they were nevertheless subjected to incessant annoyances, and they had certainly no reason to congratulate themselves for having changed the easy going Portuguese rule, for the brutal and exacting government of the Dutch East India Company.

The Dutch themselves regarded the Portuguese sympathies of the people as a danger against which precautions had to be taken, and the fear of their love for the Portuguese was the excuse they gave for their cruel persecution of the Christians. For the rest, the historical facts themselves prove the attachment of the Ceylonese to their late masters.

A few weeks after the capture of Jaffna, the Dutch having sent a part of the garrison to reinforce their troops who were besieging Nagapatam, the Jaffnese and among them a large number of pagans whom the Dutch had enrolled as soldiers prepared a revolt. The object of the conspiracy was to seize by surprise the fort of Jaffna, expel the Dutch from the town and restore it to the Portuguese. The matter was discovered, the conspirators were arrested and put to torture by order of the commander of Jaffna Jacob van der Rhee.

There still remained at Jaffna an old Jesuit, Fr. Caldeiro who being paralysed and unable to move from his bed, could not leave the place when the other Missionaries were expelled. Van der Rhee had him dragged from his bed and, under the pretext that he knew of the conspiracy in the confessional, condemned him to death. He was beheaded.

The three leaders of the conspiracy a Tamil man from Manaar, a Jaffnese called Louis and an Eurasian from Jaffna died a terrible death. First they struck them with a hatchet on the back and on the breast, they were attached to crosses and their bowels torn out, then their heart, which they put in their mouth.

Such atrocities would seem improbable if they were not related among others by a contemporary author, Philip Baldeus, an unprejudice witness, because himself a Protestant minister, who in his work printed at Amsterdam in 1672 gives even a picture on which we see Fr. Caldeiro beheaded and next to him, a man crucified to whom they are tearing out the bowels.

All others were either hanged, impaled or stretched on the wheel, and their bodies attached to trees for pasture to the birds of prey.

Deprived of their priests, driven from their churches, tracked by the protestants, so that it was only at night and in hiding that they could gather in some solitary house to pray in common, the constancy of these native Christians was really admirable. Neither afraid of threats nor seduced by temptations, they clung with fervour to their Faith and, though deprived of their spiritual guides, they nevertheless continued to hold their religious meetings at their houses in the middle of the night.

— „ Notwithstanding every persecution, writes Emmerson „ Tennent, the Roman Catholic Religion retained its influence and „ held good its position in Ceylon. It was openly professed by the „ descendants of the Portuguese who had remained in the Island after „ the conquest of the Dutch, and in private it was equally adhered to „ by large bodies of natives, both Singhalese and Tamils, whom „ neither corruption nor coercion could induce to abjure it.“ —

Thus it was how the Dutch were demolishing Christianity in Ceylon. Let us now look at their endeavours to rebuild it on Protestant lines. To avoid the danger of being accused of partiality, we make ourselves a rule to give regarding this matter up to the end of this book, only the testimony of Protestant writers.

Let us begin by Emmerson Tennent :— „ In the meantime, he „ writes, the Dutch proceeded steadily and systematically with the „ work of the *Protestant conversions*. In the peninsula of Jaffna „ they took possession of the Roman Catholic Churches. They „ established one school at least in connection with each : and „ Baldeus one of their earliest *Missionaries* relates with minuteness

„ the small amount of religious instruction, which he found it „ expedient to insist upon, preparatory to admission into membership „ with the reformed church of Holland.

„ Within five years of the arrival of the Dutch 65,000 converts „ had become *Christians*, men and women in the kingdom of „ Jaffnapatam.

„ How imperfectly even the smallest of these members, must „ have been looked after, both as regards elementary teaching and „ spiritual instruction, may be inferred from the circumstance „ deplored by Baldeus, that for the care of all these churches and „ schools, he had in 1663 but two or three clergymen of the reformed „ religion, when the Portuguese had formerly employed upwards of „ forty Roman Catholic ecclesiastics. And as if in anticipation of a „ doubt as to the sincerity of the outward profession made by these „ *converts*, he candidly states that, though Christians in name and „ qualified to discourse rationally on the commandments and other „ doctrinal points, they still retained many of the superstitions of „ paganism."—

He speaks then of the dishonesty of the teachers in these miserable schools with which they had replaced the fine Catholic educational establishments and where they educated the young generation of their converts, and forced the Catholic parents to send their children.

— „ Whilst matters were proceeding thus amongst the Hindoos „ of the north of the Island, the progress of the Dutch ministers was „ not quite so rapid and remarkable in the Buddhist districts of the „ south and it was found expedient, if not open coercion, at least,

„ some *gentle violence* to quicken their apprehensions. With this „ view, proclamation was publicly made, that no native could aspire „ to the rank of Mudeliyar, or to be permitted to farm land or hold „ office under Government, who had not first undergone the „ ceremony of baptism, become a member of the protestant church „ and subscribed to the doctrines of the helvetic confession of faith." —

What Emmerson Tennent calls a *gentle violence* was the deprivation of civil rights and for those who could not otherwise provide for the support of their families than seeking public employment, it meant either the pretence of conversion to the protestant creed or misery and starvation.

— „ The operation of this announcement was such as may be „ ready anticipated. Many of the lowland chiefs, who have been „ recently baptised by the Portuguese, and who still bore the family „ names of their Catholic sponsors abjured *the errors of Rome*. The „ landowners and those who aspired to be petty headmen and police „ viddans of their villages, were equally prompt to exhibit themselves „ possessed of the necessary qualifications for offices. And even „ Brahmans from Jaffna and Manaar, unwilling to forego their „ prospects of dignity and emoluments, which were attainable upon „ such easy conditions, made a ready profession of Christianity, „ although they forbore to lay aside their beads and other symbols „ of heathenism." —

We are grateful to Emmerson Tennent that he gives to this sad business the name of: *protestant* conversions.

## CHAPTER 2

# KANDY

King Raja Singha now bitterly repented the mistake he had made in allying himself with the Dutch. He had hoped,
1659 as they had promised him, to become master of the whole Island, and now he understood that they had duped him and made a tool of him to acquire for themselves the provinces which he coveted.

To get rid of them by force of arms was now what he had planned but, rendered prudent by experience, he knew that he could never conquer European troops in the open field, and therefore he made his best to provoke the Dutch to declare him war and invade his kingdom, when he could have easily crushed them in the forests and in the narrow mountain passes.

The Dutch traders, on their side made all they could to avoid a conflict which would endanger their cinnamon trade and diminish for a time their gains, so they answered with base adulation to Raja Singha's insults and provocations.

The Dutch Governors sent him ambassadors who, on bended knees presented him, wrapped in precious silks letters full of humility in which the Governor protested that the Dutch were his most humble vassals and faithful servants. That it was only to show their loyalty and to prove their subjection that they constructed forts along the coasts of Ceylon, only to prevent the enemies of the King from invading the country. That considering themselves as his humble servants they thought it their sacred duty to watch over their master's interests.

All the while, however, they were strengthening their defences. They filled their fortresses with war ammunitions and provisioned them so that each might easily stand a siege of one year.

Raja Singha was too intelligent a man to allow himself to be deceived by such low duplicity. He clearly saw how the matters stood and did not restrain himself from showing his contempt to his new neighbours.

Nothing however could move their patience. Raja Singha repelled with contempt the rich present which the Governor was sending him, answering that they were not good enough for a King of Kandy. He ill-treated his envoys, had one put to death and retained four others prisoners.

The first, Francis Hoes, had given refuge in his house to a Kandyan woman who had fled from the cruel treatment of her husband. He fell in love with her and the King allowed him to marry her on condition that he would settle in Kandy and enter his service. Having however after some time seized a letter in which Hoes informed the Dutch Governor of the King's doings, he had him beheaded.

The second Henry Draak died a prisoner in Kandy.

The third whose name is not known saved himself by an act of comic daring. Tired of his captivity, he determined rather to risk his life, than submit longer to his fate. Dressed in his state uniform he went to the King's palace and entering the audience hall, and standing before the empty throne he made a profound bow, as if the King were sitting on it, and, in presence of the amazed courtiers, placed on the vacant chair his letters of recall, and with another bow he made a farewell speech, left the palace and mounting his horse galloped on the road to Colombo. This adventure amused Raja Singha who gave orders not to molest him on his way, and procure him all the necessary to reach safely the Dutch territory.

The fourth John Baptista was less fortunate and had to undergo a long captivity.

The fifth envoy, whose name was Buquoy, was still a prisoner in 1697. It is not known what became of him after that.

All authors are unanimous in condemning this undignified conduct of the Dutch Governors of Ceylon and they say that neither the Portuguese nor the English would have suffered such insults. But, as already said above, it was not the Dutch Commonwealth, but a Dutch commercial company who had conquered Ceylon. The so-called Governors of Ceylon at that time were not appointed by the Dutch Government but by the Directors of the Company, they were rather a kind of commercial agents, and they had less to look about the national honor than to give dividends to the share-holders.

And at that epoch the Dutch knew very little as yet of the interior of Ceylon, and rendered prudent by the knowledge of the disasters of the Portuguese, they did not dare to risk a campaign against Kandy.

These relations with the Dutch, the manner in which they humbled themselves before him, the adulations with which they answered his impertinences entirely changed Raja Singha's character, or to express it better revived in him the barbarian.

Brought up since his infancy amongst the Portuguese, he had acquired their polished manners, and showed rather the magnanimous and chivalrous side of his character. He affected the manners of a European prince. Son of a Catholic mother, having lived on intimate terms with many Catholics, in his letters and in his discourses he would not speak of the gods but of God. Knox, who knew him personally, says of him: — „And now lastly for his religion, you cannot expect much from him. Of the religion of the country, he makes but a small profession, as perceiving that there is a greater God than those that through long custom they have and worship. The Christian Religion he doth not in the least persecute or dislike, but rather, as it seems to me, esteems and honors it." —

Being now removed from all Christian and civilizing influence he became a brute and a tyrant.

He assumed most extravagant titles. The Kandyans when they addressed him had had to style him: His divine Majesty, and call themselves: Bones of a Dog. He once endeavoured to impose on the Dutch that they call him god in their official correspondence, but resigned himself to the more humble title of: Emperor of Ceylon, King of Kandy, of Jaffna of Kotta and of Sitawacca; Grand Duke of Manaar and Matale; Duke of Uva, of Bintene and of Trincomalee; Marquis of Tumpane and Jattanuwara; Count of

Kottyar, of Batticaloa, of Matara and of Galle; Lord of Colombo, of Chilaw and of Madampé; and Sovereign of the Pearl Fisheries.

If he had yet added: Baron of Putlam, of Kurnegalle and of Ratnapura, we would have the whole geography of Ceylon.

Finally Raja Singha's tyranny reached such a degree that his own subjects rebelled against him. He was then residing
1664 in his country seat at Nilobe. In the night of the 21 December 1664, the conspirators to the number of 200, marched in arms to the King's residence and attacked it. Many dignitaries of the Court and guards were killed. The object of the conspirators was to kill the King and to place on the throne his son, a boy of 15 years whom they held in their power.

In the last moment however, when they were sure of their stroke, their courage failed them, and they put off for the next day the attack of the pavilion in which the King had sought refuge. This gave him time to escape. He was pursued by the conspirators who overtook him at a place called Golada. The King's position was now desperate, but the courage of the rebels failed them again, and they returned to Kandy where they proclaimed King the young prince.

The boy, who till then had led a very retired life, was frightened at seeing so many new faces that prostrated themselves before him, when they made him mount the throne, and disconcerted by all the pomp and military display that surrounded him. One night he fled from the palace with one old servant and sought refuge with his father.

This unexpected event broke the power of the rebels. They began to quarrel among themselves, and then Raja Singha crushed them easily.

The King's vengeance was terrible. He caused whole families of which one member had taken part in the conspiracy to be impaled or put to death in the most cruel manner, and he had the barbarity to poison his own son, the poor faithful boy who had fled to him.

1668 The position of the Catholics was very precarious.

Raja Singha allowed them full liberty in his Kingdom and even favoured them, for he considered them as more honest and more faithful than his heathen subjects, nevertheless their lot was pitiable.

Already in the last years of the Portuguese rule with the intrigues of the Dutch protestants and with the wars, they found themselves often deprived of the ministry of the priests and of their spiritual help. The old Christians bore it better, for they had been initiated into the practice of Christian life, but it was not the same with the new converts, who, in order to persevere needed to be under guidance a long time, otherwise they would relapse by and by into their own pagan ways.

The arrival of twelve Missionaries, who being expelled by the protestants from Colombo had sought refuge in Kandy, revived for a time the faith of these poor neophytes. But some of the priests had been re-called to India as they were too many for the needs of the Christian community of Kandy. Others died and could not be replaced, for the Dutch watched carefully the coast to prevent the landing of any Catholic priest.

In this way, ten years after the loss of Colombo, there remained at Kandy only three priests, and two of them, forgetting their sacred character had accepted high positions at Raja Singha's Court.

It does not seem that these two wretches had apostatized, and it is not even probable they did, for the King did not like it, and would have taken their apostacy rather badly. He gave willingly offices to Catholics. But forgetting that they were priests, and the duties of the priest, they were leading the life of laymen busy with secular affairs.

One priest only remained therefore at Kandy in 1668, Fr. Vergonse S. J. a venerable old man, but rendered almost useless by age and infirmities. He took care as much as he could of the Christians of the town, but those who lived dispersed in the Kingdom were for long years deprived of all religious aid. And Knox, a contemporary, gives us a sad picture of their religious state:

— „ If any enquires, he writes, into the religious exercise and „ worship practised among the Christians here, I am sorry I must say „ I can give but a slender account. For they have no churches „ no priests, and so no meetings together on the Lord's days, or „ Divine Worship, but each one reads and prays at his own house as „ he is disposed. They sanctify the day chiefly by refraining from „ work, and meeting together at drinking houses. They continue „ the practice of Baptism; and there being no priests, they baptize „ their children themselves with water in the Name of the Father „ and of the Son and of the Holy Ghost, and give them Christian „ names. They have their friends about them at such a time, and

„ make a small feast to their ability. And some teach their children „ to say prayers, and some not.

„ Indeed their religion at the best is but negative, that is they „ are not heathens, they do not comply with the idolatry here „ practised, and they profess themselves Christians in a general „ manner, which appears by their names, and by their beads and „ Crosses that some of them wear about their necks.

„ Nor indeed can I wholly clear them from compliance with „ the religion of the country, for *some of them,* when they are sick, do „ use the ceremonies which the heathen do in the like case, as in „ making idols of clay and setting them up in their houses, and „ offering rice to them and having Wavers to dance before them. „ But they are ashamed to be known to do this; and I have known „ some to do it, but such as are Indians born. Yet I never knew „ any of them, that do inwardly in heart and conscience incline to „ the ways of the heathen, but perfectly abhor them; nor have there „ been any I ever heard of that came to their temples upon religious „ account, but only would stand by and look on.

„ Without it were one old priest named Padre Vergonce a „ Genoez and of the Jesuit Order, who would go to the temples and „ eat with the Wavers and other ordinary people of the sacrifices „ offered to the Idols: but with this apology for himself, that he ate „ it as common meat and as God's creature, and that it was never „ the worse for their superstition that had passed over it."—

Here, Captain Knox, in his great simplicity is mistaken. The Buddhist do not offer food in sacrifice to idols. The food they bring to the Pansalas is destined for the meals of the Bikshun, and occasionally to feed the poor. And it certainly could have happened, that once or twice, good old Fr. Vergonse, tasted the food of the poor, or even sat with them to show them by this act of sympathy that he did not despise their poverty.

— „ But however this may reflect upon the Father, continues „ Knox, another thing can be related for his honour. There „ happened two priests to fall into the hands of the King, on whom „ he conferred great honours for, having laid aside their habit they „ kept about his person and were the greatest favourites at Court. „ The King one day sent for Vengonce and asked him if it would not „ be better for him to lay aside his old coat, and to do as the other „ two priests had done, and receive honour from him. He replied to „ the King, that he boasted more in that old habit and the Name of „ Jesus, than in all the honours that he would give to him. The „ King valued the Father for this saying.

„ He had a pretty library about him, and died in his bed of old „ age: Whereas the two other priests in the King's service died „ miserably, one of a cancer and the other was slain. The old priest „ had about thirty or forty books, which the King, they say, seized „ on after his death and keeps. These priests and more lived there „ but all deceased, excepting Vergonce, before my time."—

Knox relates a few anecdotes about old Father Vergonse.

Raja Singha's whim was to keep a prisoner at Kandy any European who was caught within the frontier of his Kingdom. He gave them generally some honorable employment, but they had to put away all hope of regaining their liberty, and were not allowed to go out of the town. These were the means that the King had imagined for showing himself surrounded with a European Court, and to enjoy their society which suited better to his taste and to his education than that of the rude Kandyan Chiefs, but also to profit by their culture and superior knowledge.

They brought one day to him eleven English officers and sailors from a ship that was wrecked on the coast near Putlam. The King received them with great courtesy:

— „ This civil reception upon their first coming to the city — „ says Knox — put these Persia merchantmen in hope, that the King „ would give them their liberty.

„ There was at that time an old Portuguese Father, Padre „ Vergonse by name, living in the city. With him they discoursed „ the probability of their liberty and that the favours that the King „ had shown them seemed to be good signs of it. But the Father, „ told them the plain truth, that it was not customary there to „ release white men. For saying which they railed at him calling „ him Popish dog and Jesuitical rogue, supposing he spoke as he „ wished it might be. But afterwards, to their grief, they found it to „ be true as he told them.

„ Their entertainment was excellently good, according to the „ poor condition of the country, but they thought it otherwise very „ mean and not according to the King's orders. Therefore, that the „ King might be informed how they were abused, each man took a „ limb of a hen into his hand, and marched rank and file in order „ through the streets, with it in their hand, to the court as a sign to „ the great men whereby they might see how illy they were served;

„ thinking hereby the King might come to hear of their misusage, „ and so they might have order to be better fed afterwards. But „ this proved sport to the noblemen who well knew the fare of the „ country, laughing at their ignorance, to complain where they had so „ little cause. And indeed, afterwards, they themselves laughed at „ this action of theirs, and were half ashamed, when they came to a „ better understanding of the nature of the country diet.

„ Yet notwithstanding, being not used to such a short commons „ of flesh, though they had rice in abundance, and having no money „ to buy more, they had the desire to kill some cows, that they might „ eat their bellies full of beef, but made it somewhat a point of „ conscience, whether it might be lawful or not to take them without „ leave. Upon which, they apply themselves to the old Father „ abovesaid, desiring him to solve this case of conscience, who was „ very ready to give them a dispensation and told them: That for „ as much as the Chingulays were their enemies, and had taken their „ bodies, it was very lawful for them, to satisfy their bodies with „ their goods. And the better to animate them in this design bid „ them to bring him a piece, that he might partake with them. So „ being encouraged by the old Father, they went on boldly in their „ intended business." —

These details show that old Fr. Vergonse was of a jovial and cheerful disposition.

He was the last surviving priest of the old Portuguese Missions and, after his death, the Christians of Kandy saw themselves abandoned and deprived of all spiritual help.

# CHAPTER 3

## THE LOW COUNTRIES

Meanwhile the Dutch were organizing themselves in the south of Ceylon. As mentioned above, all the towns on the
1668 coast had been fortified and placed in a state of defence, with the exception of the forts of Batticaloa and Trincomalee which had not been rebuilt because the Dutch had not sufficient forces to supply them with a garrison, and the eastern coast being less productive, they did not care to occupy it. There was no more the fear of an invasion from the sea side, since the Portuguese power in India was broken.

What the Dutch traders wanted was cinnamon, which at that time brought them enormous gains.

Up to now, cinnamon was never cultivated in Ceylon. The precious spice grew abundantly in the jungle. It was worked in this way under the old Kings of Kotta, that land was granted to villagers of the so-called Cinnamonpiller Caste, and instead of paying rent, they had to deliver to the Government stores a certain quantity of cinnamon bark.

This system was continued by the Portuguese, but since the Dutch conquest, the forests where cinnamon grew in abundance, were too much exposed to the incursions of Raja Singha who, having quarrelled with his allies, endeavoured to injure them in their chief commercial interests. The Cinnamonpillers being continually harassed by bands of Kandyan pillagers, could no longer pursue their trade of gathering cinnamon bark in the jungles, and the Dutch were obliged to keep a small army on a war footing in order to protect them, which in the long run became very expensive.

Then the Dutch, with their innate prompt determination, resolved to try to cultivate the spice, and started plantations of cinnamon under the protection of their fortresses, around the towns and the villages on the coast, and they succeeded so well, that the cultivated plants having proved to yield a much better quality of bark, the working of the cinnamon in the jungle was entirely abandoned.

Cinnamon became a Government monopoly which was so jealously guarded that the selling even of the smallest quantity to any one but to Government was regarded as a crime punishable with death.

Any plant that sprouted out by chance on a private property belonged to Government, and the Cinnamonpiller had right to enter the property, and the owner of the garden in which the unlucky plant had sprouted was not allowed to cut or uproot it, under severe penalties.

Elephants too were a monopoly of the State. They were caught alive in the forests and exported in large number to India.

The other State monopolies were arecanuts, salt and toddy.

They did not encourage the cultivation of coffee, nor of pepper which were largely cultivated in their Colonies of Java and of the Malabar Coast, in order not to lessen their price.

In a word the Dutch Government in Ceylon did not care about the well being of the people, but considered exclusively their own commercial interests.

In spite of this in a few years, they were already disappointed, and complained that Ceylon was far from bringing them the wealth they had expected, and the expenses of keeping up this new possession, obliged as they were to maintain a comparatively large army for fear of the King of Kandy, and of the raising of the oppressed people, were great.

The low country Singhalese were exasperated against their new masters and were only kept in subjection by a display of military forces:

—„ Nor was the discontent confined to the Singhalese alone, „ writes Emmerson Tennent. Disappointment was felt in Holland „ at the failure of those brilliant estimates which had been formed on „ the wealth of Ceylon. The hopes of the emigrants who had rushed „ to the Island were crushed by the reality. And the Company's „ officers and servants were loud in their complaints of the „ impossibility of subsisting on their salaries and perquisites. The „ former were absurdly small; the permission to trade, formed the „ great supplementary inducement, and as trade was improductive, „ discontent was inevitable.“—

One can easily imagine what a broad door to corruption was opened by this permission given to Government officials to trade with those who were under their rule, when the accused could sell to the Judge his stock of copra.

The great mistake that was made in Holland was that, instead of sending to Ceylon honest men and good administrators, men who had at least some feelings of patriotism, they were sending the refuses of Holland and as they were not restrained by the moral principles which Religion imposes, one can easily imagine what was their conduct, when they found themselves in a position of power.

— „ The Dutch here love drink, writes Knox, and practice their „ proper vice in this country. One who was a great man in the „ Kandyan Court would sometimes come into the King's presence, „ half disguised with drink, which the King often passed over; but „ once asked him: Why do you thus disorder yourself, that when I „ send for you about my business, you are not in a capacity to serve „ me? He boldly replied: that, as soon as his mother took away the „ milk from him, she supplied it with wine, and ever since saith he, I „ have used myself to it. With this answer the King seemed to be „ pleased.

„ And indeed, the rest of the white men, are generally of the „ same temper: in so much, that the Chingulays have a saying that „ wine is as natural to white men as milk to children." —

Corruption was general. The Governors had so small salaries, that they were not even sufficient to live on them decently, nevertheless, in two or three years that they were in office, they made considerable fortunes. And the commanders of Galle and Jaffna, provided they were on good terms with the Governor, grew rapidly rich. And all that was done by oppressing the people:

— „ Successive Governors were obliged to admit the fact of „ habitual oppression by the headmen and officials: and to record the „ conviction that the condition of the Singhalese was no better under „ the Dutch than it had been under the Portuguese, so would they „ one day turn on them as they had before shaken themselves free of „ their predecessors." —

Emmerson Tennent draws this conclusion from a report made in 1677 by Governor Henry Adrian Van Rheede, to the Directors of the Dutch East India Company but with the habit common to all protestant writers of that time to calumniate the Portuguese, he omits to make the distinction, that they were the Kandyans with their King at their head who fought against the Portuguese, whilst the low-country Singhalese, who were Portuguese subjects, fought bravely side by side with the Portuguese against Raja Singha and the Dutch invaders.

Now what the Dutch Governors feared was that the same low-country Singhalese who had been faithful to the Portuguese, and were now exasperated by the oppression of the Dutch, do not rise against them.

As regards the Catholic low-country Singhalese, this general oppression was further aggravated by a cruel religious

**1669** persecution, and their perseverance and attachment to the Catholic Faith were admirable.

They had not seen a priest now for ten years, when they were secretly informed that, on a vessel which had cast anchor in the harbour of Colombo, there was Spanish Dominican Fr. Dominic Fernandez Navaretto. He could not land for the Dutch Protestants would cast him into prison. The Christians ran to him to receive the Holy Sacraments of which they had been deprived for so many years.

Fr. Navaretto wrote: — „ There are at Colombo 3000 Catholics who have had no priest among them since the Portuguese left the Island. A great number came on board to make their confession, and they brought rosaries and candles for me to bless, and asked for holy water, and edified all of us by their piety." —

The Protestants seeing the invincible faith of the Christians, and on the other side the contempt which the heathens
1670 showed to their ministers, who were endeavouring to *convert* them by the bait of material gain, remunerative employments and the favour of Government, began to grow discouraged.

They had thought it would be for them an easy task to uproot the Faith of Christ in the Island, ignorant of the deep roots that religion had taken in the hearts of these simple people. They contended in vain against the vitality of the Catholic Church, and had at last to confess, that it was not easy to fight against God.

— „ For nearly thirty years, writes Emmerson Tennent, matters „ wore the appearance of proceeding successfully under the combined „ system of encouragement and compulsion. But about the year „ 1670 the records of the (Protestant) consistory begin to exhibit „ evidences of uneasiness on the part of the labouring clergy (the „ Protestant ministers), and contain complaints of the stubborn „ opposition of the idolators, and the hostile interference of the „ Roman Catholics and their Priests." —

Emmerson Tennent is again mistaken. It was now 14 years since the missionaries had been expelled from the south of Ceylon, and 12 years since the Protestants had driven them out of Jaffna, and since that time there had not been a single Priest in all the Dutch territories, and all these ignoble proceedings, the cruel persecution and all the means at the disposal of a tyrannical Government failed in an uneqnal struggle against the courage and the faith of a depressed flock whom they had deprived of their pastors and leaders.

Let us return to Emmerson Tennent: — „ Notwithstanding the, „ facility and the encouragement thus hold out by the civil „ Government for the extension of (protestant) Christianity, the „ history of its progress was but the history of its struggles with „ inherent difficulties and opposition, before which the energies of „ its promoters were gradually exhausted and the result of their „ labours eventually disappeared.

„ Foremost amongst these was the resistance offered by the „ genius and influence of the national idolatry of the Singhalese. In „ the southern provinces above all the contest was unequally „ sustained by the Dutch; and nothing but coercion and pecuniary „ fines served to keep up a show of pupils in their schools and enforce „ attendance on their instructions in the principles of (protestant) „ Christianity.

„ According to the reports of the (protestant) chaplain of Galle, „ in 1680, idolatry was then on the increase, so much as to render „ him doubtful of the propriety of baptizing the children of the „ natives, lest that which is holy be given to the dogs. Every thing

„ was *pro forma* and by constraint, and though the authority of „ Government lead the Singhalese to adopt the name of (protestant) „ Christianity, they were utterly ignorant of its power, and not only „ refused to send their children for instruction, but declined „ themselves to attend the preaching of the Gospel.

„ Their teachers too, with but three or four exceptions, only „ laboured from the motive of gain, without the slightest regard either „ of their own soul, or those committed to their care, and some were „ even reported to the Consistory as being professional Devil dancers.

„ At a still later period (1684) the Dutch ministers at Colombo „ apparently disheartened by the deceptive results of their labours „ and embarassed by a multitudinous assemblage of *converts in name* „ *but idolaters at heart* represented to the Governor in Council, that „ the reason why they designated the natives only as *nominal* or „ *baptized Christians* was because many made a profession, only from „ consideration of personal advantage; and that native Christianity „ throughout Ceylon was in an unsound and critical condition, „ notwithstanding the peremptory orders for the prevention of devil „ worship and other heathen superstitions, as well as against the „ practices of popery, to which some are still strongly inclined.

„ This latter allusion was not without foundation; for the „ influence of the protestant *Clergy* declined, that of the Roman „ Catholic priesthood had risen into unexpected importance. Their „ worship notwithstanding every *discouragement*, had maintained its „ hold on the natives by its gaudy ceremonial: whilst the less „ attractive teaching and sterner discipline of the Dutch could only „ be sustained by prospects of personal advantage, or enforced by

„ pecuniary fines. At Jaffna in particular, and amongst the Tamils „ of the Fisher Caste along the Western Coast, its ascendency was „ neither weakened by persecution, nor undermined by corruption."—

The author again makes the mistake, when he says, that it was the influence of the Roman Catholic priesthood and of their gaudy ceremonial that maintained the Catholic Religion in Ceylon in spite of the persecution.

At that period, as said above, there was not a single priest in the whole Island of Ceylon, the Ordinance of the 19th September 1658 having decreed the penalty of death against all Catholics who would give shelter to a priest. The ceremonial of the Church was far from being gaudy when the unfortunate Christians were dispossessed of all their churches, and tracked by the protestant authorities and could only come together in some removed solitary houses to pray in common on Sundays, risking prison if they were discovered.

The most elaborate precautions were taken to prevent Missionaries from India to land secretly in Ceylon. All persons, even the poorest coolies, who wished to go to Ceylon had to appear before the Dutch commander of Tuticorin and obtain a pass from him, and the coasts were guarded by cruisers, whose captains had special instruction to watch that no priest might land in Ceylon.

It was not therefore: — „ The influence of the Roman Catholic priesthood and their gaudy ceremonial " — but the Faith of the people that sustained them in this cruel crisis, and that particular grace which God gives to His servants in times of persecution: the grace which makes martyrs.

## CHAPTER 4

# THE FRENCH IN CEYLON

Meanwhile France also was pushing forwards her Colonial
1672 policy inaugurated by Cardinal Richelieu.

The war between King Louis XIV and Holland served as a pretext to the French to attack the Dutch in India, and to make an attempt to get for themselves a slice of the wrecked Portuguese Empire.

On the 21 March 1672 the French admiral de La Haye appeared before Batticaloa with a squadron of 14 ships. Seeing that Batticaloa was well defended, he did not stop there, but saluting the Dutch flag, which salute was returned from the fort, he set sail for Trincomalee. Having cast anchor in the Bay of Kottyar, he landed there his troops, protesting however that he did so because he knew that Trincomalee belonged to the King of Kandy and not to the Dutch.

Old King Raja Singha was overjoyed at the news of the landing of the French, and conceived the plan of an alliance with them against the Dutch. The moment was well chosen for the whole native population of the part of Ceylon owned by the Dutch, tired of their oppression, which weighted so heavily on them, was ready to rise against them in a body, once they would see themselves supported by European troops.

Three days after the landing of the French, on March 25th Raja Singha sent to Trincomalee a high dignitary of his court to welcome admiral de La Haye and enter into friendly relations with him.

De La Haye returned the compliment by sending to Kandy three officers, Dorgeret, de La Garde and Fontaine. Raja Singha received them in great style. During the audience he gave them, he placed on the neck of each a rich chain of gold and presented them with swords and muskets of the finest Kandyan workmanship. Two of the officers remained in Kandy, the third returned to Trincomalee, accompanied by an ambassador who had full power of concluding with de La Haye a treaty with the object of expelling the Dutch from Ceylon.

The ambassador was closely followed by a messenger bearer of a Chart by which Raja Singha made to France the gift of the Bay of Kottyar and of the surrounding territories, and on the 17th of May, they planted the French flag both at Kottyar and in Trincomalee taking possession of those places in the name of Louis XIV King of France and of Navarre.

Two days before they had sighted the Dutch fleet commanded by the Governor Van Goens in person. He had a squadron of 14 vessels and a troop of soldiers composed of his best men.

The Governor summoned the French to evacuate Ceylon, de La Haye refused and prepared to defend Trincomalee and Kottyar, and Raja Singha was sending his army to help the French. Thus three weeks passed.

Meanwhile, the position of the French admiral was becoming

more and more difficult. His troops were unsufficient and had been affected by the bad season. 400 soldiers and sailors were invalids, and from some skirmishes with the Dutch, the admiral had already seen how little he could rely on the badly armed and undisciplined Kandyan troops.

The Governor had got reinforcements from Colombo, and, under these circumstances the French admiral deemed it more prudent to give up the contest, at last for the time being. He weighed anchor on the 9th of July and passing before the Dutch fleet ranged in battle order, which saluted the French flag, he set sail for Tranquebar.

At Raja Singha's urgent request to remain in Ceylon de La Haye replied that he would soon return with a stronger army. In the meanwhile he was sending to Kandy, Monsieur de Laisne Nauclairs de Lanerolle who would reside at the King's Court as ambassador of the King of France Louis XIV.

Lanerolle left for Kandy. We would not have mentioned this worthless individual, had he not been destined to play an odious part in the course of this history. He was a Huguenot, a rabid protestant; his sole religion was unrelented hatred against the Catholic Faith. He left Trincomalee with a brilliant suite among whom four gentlemen of noble families: Du Plessy, de Serle, de la Roche and John de Bloom.

Lanerolle's conduct from the very beginning clearly showed that he had been ill-chosen to represent the interests of France in Ceylon. He made himself obnoxious to all by his stupid vanity.

It was the custom in Kandy that no one could pass in front of the royal palace except on foot. There was certainly nothing disparaging in it, a simple show of respect to the King. Lanerolle's retinue had to pass through that street to reach the quarters which Raja Singha had had prepared for him. When Lanerolle was asked to dismount, he refused uttering words of contempt and rode under the balcony of the King's apartment.

The wretch seems to have forgotten that the French fleet was no longer in Trincomalee and that he was entirely at the mercy of the King of Kandy. Raja Singha pretended to ignore this bravado, but was much embittered against the Frenchman.

A few days later, the King had to receive him in solemn audience. They formed a grand procession. It was evening and the whole street was illuminated with innumerable torches. Lanerolle arrived at the palace and was received by the Court dignitaries. Here again it was the custom that every foreign envoy should await the royal audience for two hours, when he was served refreshments and was entertained by the dignitaries of the Court. Lanerolle had been informed of this strange etiquette, nevertheless, after a few minutes, he expressed his surprise that the King did not appear. Then having waited for about fifteen minutes, he rose, exclaiming that it was an insult to leave him waiting so long, and left the hall. All the entreaties of the gentlemen of his suite had no effect. Some officials of the Court, wishing at all cost to avoid a scandal, took profit of this altercation to have the elephants ranged in front of the palace gate, so that he might not be able to pass through it. But Lanerolle drew his sword, saying he would pass at all hazards, They let him go, and he returned to his quarters without having seen the King.

Raja Singha felt much offended, ordered Lanerolle to be seized and flogged till he fainted, then he and his suite were loaded with chains and cast into prison.

The gentlemen of his retinue managed to explain that, far from
1675 having approved the conduct of their Chief, they had done all the could to prevent this stupid conduct of their Chief and the fact being corroborated by the testimony of the Court official, they were set free, but Lanerolle passed six months in prison in chains. There was after that no more question of their return to France, they were kept prisoners at Kandy. They were supposed to be maintained at the King's expense, but in reality they were so neglected that in order not to starve, they kept a drinking shop where they were selling arrack to the natives. They bitterly reproached to Lanerolle to have been the cause of their distress, and scandalous quarrels arose among them.

Such was the state of things when Knox came to Kandy.

—„ The rest of the Frenchmen, he writes, seeing how the "ambassadors imprudent carriage had brought them to this misery, „ refused any longer to dwell with him, and each of them, by the King's „ permission, dwells by himself in the city, being maintained at the „ Kings charge. Three of these whose names were du Plessy, son of „ a gentleman of note in France, and John Bloom, the third whose „ name I cannot tell, but was the ambassador's boy, the King „ appointed to look to his best horse kept in the palace. The horse „ some time after died as it is supposed of old age, which extremely „ troubled the King; and imagining they had been instrumental in his

„ death by their carelessness, he commanded two of them, du Plessy „ and John Bloom, to be carried away into the mountains and kept „ prisoners in chains, where they remained when I came thence. The „ rest of them follow employments: some whereof sell arrack and keep „ the greatest taverns in the city.

„ Lately, a little before I came from the Island, the King „ understanding the disagreements and differences that were kept on „ foot betwixt the ambassador and the rest of his company, disliked „ it and used these means to make them friends: he sent for them „ all, the ambassador and the rest and told them: that it was not „ seemly for persons as they were, at such a distance from their own „ country to quarrel and fall out; and that, if they had any love for „ God or the King of France or himself, that they should go to the „ ambassador's quarters and live peacefully together.

„ They went back together, not daring to disobey the King, and „ as soon as they were at home, the King sent a banquet after them „ of sweatmeats and fruits to eat together. They did eat the King's „ banquet, but it would not make the reconcilement. For, after „ they had done, each man went home, and dwelt in their own houses, „ as they did before. It was thought that this carriage would offend „ the King, and that he would at least take away their allowance. „ And it is probable before this time, the King had taken vengeance „ on them. But the ambassador's carriage is so imperious, that they „ would rather venture whatever might follow, than subject to him. „ And in this case I left them." —

The fate of these poor Frenchmen is not known. Probably they died in captivity.

Of Lanerolle alone we shall have to speak: It would seem that after Raja Singha's death he got into the good graces of his successor, and took service at the Court at Kandy, where we will soon find him, allied with the Bikshun, and making use of them to further his low intrigues.

Raja Singha died on the 6th December 1687, aged 80 years, after a reign of 53 years.

He was of middle height, strong and well built. His complexion, like that of all the members of the royal family, was darker than that of the Kandyans of higher rank. He had not much hair on his head but a very thick beard. His large restless eyes would roll about, and his huge nose was quite out of proportion with the rest of his countenance.

In his youth, when he was still under the civilising influence of the Portuguese, he used to dress according to the European fashion, or wear the picturesque dress of the Kandyans of high rank. But since the adulations of the Dutch had turned his head he commenced to dress in a costume of his own invention, with a hat covered with an incredible number of feathers which made him appear like a mountebank.

We have already described his character. Educated as a European by Catholic masters under the eyes of a Catholic mother, and notwithstanding the pernicious influence of his father and of his pagan Court, he showed at first a noble chivalrous nature and great capacities. But later on, when he got separated from all Christian and civilising influence and abandoned to himself, then spoiled by the base adulations of the Dutch traders, he fell into barbarous ways, became cruel and suspicious. Notwithstanding all that, the historian must admit that Raja Singha was a remarkable man.

They accuse him that towards the end of his reign he gave himself up to inaction, but we must not forget that, at that time he was very old, discouraged and heartbroken by the experience of his alliance with the Dutch in whom he found enemies much more dangerous than the Portuguese had ever been.

They gave him a splendid funeral: His body, dressed in royal robes was placed on the throne of the audience hall, and all the Chiefs and high dignitaries of the Kingdom came and prostrated themselves before it.

They deposed it then in a coffin made of rare wood and lined with precious silks and carried it in grand pomp, preceded by elephants, drummers and dancers and surrounded with the royal insignia, and followed by an immense crowd, to the place, where the bodies of Kings and royal princes were burned.

This place can yet be seen, near to Trincomalee street, just in front of the Protestant school they call Trinity College.

The remains of the King were placed on a high pyre, to which his son Mahastane set fire. The flames of the pyre were entertained for ten days and drums beaten around. On the tenth day they extinguished it with cocoanut milk, then gathering carefully the King's ashes and bones, they placed them in an urn of clay which was secured with the royal seal.

A great procession was formed, like the first, with innumerable elephants, drummers and dancers. On the biggest royal elephant sat a man with the face covered with a mask, so that none could see his features. He carried the urn on his head. They thus proceeded to Katugastotte. On the shore of the Mahavelly Ganga, the masked man with the urn on his head got into a richly ornamented boat. In the middle of the river where the water was deep and the current rapid, in view of the vast multitude, he broke the urn with a stroke of his sword, and threw the ashes into the river, and the pieces of the urn, then jumping himself over-board he swam to the other shore, darted into the jungle, and was seen never more. He was forbidden under penalty of death to ever return to Kandy. The boat was abandoned, to be broken by the current on the big rock with which the bottom of the river is strewed, and the elephant which had carried the royal ashes, was brought far away, and set free in the dense mountain forests. Such were the rites of the funeral of the Kings of Kandy.

The throne of Kandy was in a certain way elective. As soon as the King has drawn his last breath, the three Adigars assembled the Chiefs and the people. It was a mere form since the result of the election was always the same.

If the King had left a son, the Chiefs had to answer that he being the natural heir to the late King, he has to succeed him. If the King had died without issue they answered that they left the choice to the three Adigars. In this case, it was the Adigars who really disposed of the Crown, but, unless they had been bribed, they elected the next heir to the throne.

Raja Singha's successor was his son Mahastane aged 22.

After the funeral of the King and the election, came the installation of his successor. It was a great affair.

The most important thing was to find for the new King a name that would bring good luck for his reign. The chief astrologers were called to Kandy, first to find out the propitious day for the coronation, and as the propitious days are rare, the coronation had often to be put off for months, sometimes for a whole year. And it was in the interest of the astrologers to have it as late as possible, as during all this time, they were maintained at the King's expenses.

Next a copy of the King's horoscope, made at the time of his birth was handed to each astrologer, and with its help they had to read in the stars the most lucky name for the King which they had to engrave on tablets of pure gold.

On the morning of the lucky day, the King, forgetting for the time-being that he was supposed to be a Buddhist, went in state to the temple of Vishnu, called Maha Vishnu Devale, to offer a sacrifice to the Devil.

The procession went thence to the temple of the God Nat, Nata Devale, where the gold tablets of the astrologers were presented to him, and of all the names engraved on these tablets he would choose that which seemed to him the most lucky of all, and the first Adigar raising the tablet high above his head, and turning his face to the people proclaimed in a loud voice: Behold the name which the Gods have given to the King!

Then, the Chief of the great family Pilamẹ-Talawe, attached the tablet to the Kings forehead, and gird him with the sword, the sign of royalty.

The coronation being over the King mounted his elephant, and with all his brilliant retinue, passing through the illuminated streets, returned to his palace.

The young King Mahastane took the name of Wimala Dharma Surya by which he is known in history. Notwithstanding his youth, he was a man of superior capacity, very prudent and just. He had a horror for any kind of oppression and, during the 20 years of his reign, peace was never disturbed neither by war nor rebellion.

We will not tire the reader with a detailed statement of the constitution of the Kingdom of Kandy and of the customs of the Court. Knox and Davy have dealt with this subject at length.

We will limit ourselves to a few details necessary to understand well what follows in this history.

As already noted, the government of the Kingdom of Kandy was autocratic. All the power was concentrated in the hands of the King.

The ministry was composed of three Adigars, who were at the same time commanders of the troops and supreme Judges in the Kingdom. Only the infliction of the capital penalty was reserved to the King. As their pay was rather small, and they had to maintain a semi-royal state, it was a general complaint, that the Adigars sold justice as well as offices, the distribution of which depended on them. The King could revoke their appointment whenever he liked.

The Dessawes were Governors of provinces. They levied taxes for the King and dispensed Justice. Appeals from their judgment went to the Adigars. In time of war they commanded the contingents furnished by their provinces. They had under them the Ratemahatmeyas or Chiefs of districts, and an infinity of officials of inferior rank.

The meaning of the title of Mudeliyar is more difficult to determine. There were Civil Mudeliyars or Mudeliyars of the palace, who seem to have been some kind of Chamberlain to the King, and military Mudeliyars. The rank of the latter is not clear: Sometimes we see them commanding armies, and at other times only a small company under the Dessawe. The title was given to high personages at other times to officials of inferior rank.

There was perhaps no other Court among the ruling princes of India, that used more barbarous pomp, and gaudy apparel and where more complicated and funny etiquette was more strictly observed as at the Court of the Kings of Kandy. The throne in the audience hall was inlaid with gold and precious stones. The King appeared in a sort of armour resplendent with rubies, sapphires and emerald, and he wore besides, almost priceless jewels, and to enhance the splendour of the apparel he gave as a rule his audiences at night.

The marks of respect shown to the Sovereign, were rather those for a God than a King and in fact his subjects called him God, and the greatest dignitaries of the land, spoke to him prostrated to the ground.

In his correspondence with the Dutch, the King took the long series of titles we have given above, but when he addressed his own people, in his Proclamations and Charts the following formula was used:

— „We, the most rich protector of Religion, whose glory extends from one end of the world to the other, and whose supreme excellence surpasses that of the moon, of the stars and of the half opened bud of the jessamine flower; whose feet exhale a sweeter odour than that which comes out of the noses of all other Kings; the most noble patron and god by custom; who is like to Sakrea, who gained a brilliant victory over the Assuriahs; sitting on the precious throne of Sengadagalla, the magnificent and prosperous city which alone possesses the riches and the prosperity of all the Kingdoms, like the heavenly Kingdom of Sakrea; commands etc." —

Such was the small Kingdom of which young Mahastane, now called Wimala Dharma Surya had assumed the Crown, after the death of Raja Singha, his father.

## CHAPTER 5

# THE APOSTLE OF CEYLON

We have seen, how during the last years of his reign, King Raja
1679 Singha, old and disheartened, had left the Dutch alone. The protestants took profit of these years of peace and doubled their endeavours for the complete destruction of the Catholic Religion in Ceylon.

We have seen, how the unfortunate native Christians remained firm under the persecution: deprived of the ministration of their priests, their churches polluted and turned into protestant places of worship, into which they were dragged by force; deprived of their civil rights, they nevertheless persevered in their Faith.

Now that one generation had already passed, the state of things became more gloomy. The greatest development of the Missions had taken place in the last years before the Dutch invasion, and when the missionaries were expelled from Ceylon by the new protestant masters of the Island, a large number of Christians were neophytes, recently converted, and unable yet to guide themselves and their children on the way of true Christian life, so that these children had only a vague idea of Religion, and living in the midst of pagans took by and by their habits and relapsed into heathenism.

Among the old Christians there were only a few, who tempted by the bribe of lucrative employment had become protestants.

Others in order not to see their family starving pretended to be protestants: they went on Sundays to the protestant worship, then, coming together in some lonely house to recite their Catholic prayers. However the far greater number of the old native Christians resisted to persecution and preferred to undergo the greatest hardships, rather than to pollute their Faith even by an external show of adhesion to the heretical creed of their masters.

Nevertheless, a quarter of a century of such abnormal state of things had affected much the moral standard of the younger generation. Could it have been otherwise, when Catholic parents were forced, under severe penalties, to send their children to protestant schools, where immorality had come to the point that on the avowal of a protestant minister the Rev. J. D. Palm, there were not in the whole country, more than three or four schools where the masters were not dishonest, sorcerers or devil worshippers?

And these were the schools with which the Dutch protestants had replaced the Portuguese colleges and other flourishing educational establishments.

Thirty years after the Dutch conquest there remained hardly a trace of the civilization which was making such rapid progress under the late Catholic government among the low-country Singhalese and among the Tamils of the north and the people was relapsing into barbarity.

Under such circumstances it required all the vitality of Catholicism and all the ardent faith of these peoples, to resist the hard persecution. But now Christianity was declining. The old people had kept strong, but deprived as they were since nearly thirty years of all succour of Religion, the new generation of the new converts had relapsed in great part into heathenism, and that of the old Christians, sent by force to such schools as those we have described above, became every year more contaminated by their surroundings.

We have related how in 1669 the Christians ran in crowds on board the ship to Fr. Navaretto to hear the Holy Mass and receive Sacraments. Nine years later Fr. John of Jesus of the Augustinian Order, on his way from Macão to Goa, landed secretly in Colombo, where he remained a few days, during which he heard 800 confessions, and reconciled with the Holy Church five apostates, who for the sake of an employment under Government had become protestants.

Again, two years later, a Canon of the Cathedral of Goa, whom the Archbishop Dom Anthony Brandão had sent to visit
1680 in his name the Portuguese Missions in China, on his way back from Macão to Goa, was obliged to land in Colombo, on account of repairs that the ship on which he travelled had to undergo. He had to put on a disguise and to conceal his character as otherwise the Dutch protestants would have cast him into prison. Nevertheless, he made himself known to some Catholics, and many came secretly at night to receive Sacraments, and to be consoled by him in their extreme misery.

These three, were the only priests whom the unfortunate Christians of Colombo saw during the first 38 years of the Dutch domination.

God however, who never ceased to watch over His church of Ceylon but recently established and already so cruelly tried, hastened to its aid.

The Canon, on his return to Goa, related what he had seen and spoke with emotion of the misery of the poor persecuted Christians of Ceylon. Among those who listened to him, was a young native priest, 29 years of age. His name was Joseph Vaz, and he had already gained a great reputation in Goa for his learning and his preaching. The Viceroy Peter d'Almeida Count of Assumar had chosen him for his confessor.

This young priest was destined by God to be the Apostle of Ceylon.

Struck by the Canon's narrative, he felt his soul inflamed with the desire to sacrifice his life for the unfortunate Christians of Ceylon. Full of zeal and holy ardour he confided his plan to a few priests in Goa, but all thought the matter impossible, the coast of Ceylon being so carefully guarded by the Dutch cruisers, that the landing of a priest in the Island seemed too difficult an undertaking.

Meanwhile Fr. Joseph Vaz was appointed Superior of the Mission of Canara and in obedience to the Archbishop's order he had to go to Mangalore, then he returned to his native country and was the founder of the Oratory of Goa which rendered such great services to the church in India. And so more than five years passed before he was able to fulfil his desire, but the thought of going to Ceylon never left him for a moment.

At last, in March 1687, putting aside all human considerations,

1686 he left Goa on his dangerous voyage, on foot, begging his food on the way, stopping at every place where his ministry was required. After an eventful voyage of more than a year whose details can be found in his biography, he landed at Jaffna, about the end of April or the beginning of May 1687.

Fr. Vaz had attained his object. He had come finally to Ceylon, but he was not yet at the end of his sufferings.

He had landed at Jaffna with his servant a young boy named John, both in the garb of beggars. Knowing no one in
1687 the city, they wandered the whole day in search of a lodging, but all refused it to unknown poor strangers. At last, a charitable woman allowed them to sleep in her mandou. It was simply a roof on pillars opened from all sides to the wind and the rain. They lived several days in this kind of shed, at last Fr. Vaz exhausted by the fatigue of the voyage, by the exposure to cold and damp and affected by the unwholesome food which John was begging in the streets, fell ill with a severe attack of dysentery.

This sickness being considered as infectious, the pagans of the neighbourhood reproached the woman for having allowed to the strangers to sleep in her mandou, took Fr. Vaz on a stretcher and carried him into the forest where they abandoned him.

To complete the misery the boy John who till now had taken care of the Father, was attacked with the same illness. Thus both of them found themselves in a terrible position. Stretched on the damp ground of the forest, not being able to move, exposed in the day to the heat of the sun and in the night to the falling dew, starving, and entirely abandoned, for even if they called for help, no one could hear them, they thought that their last hour had come, and both prepared for death.

It was in that moment of supreme misery, that God came to the help of His faithful servant. A poor pagan woman, who was gathering dry wood in the forest, happened to pass by that place, and seeing them reduced to such extremity, ran at once to the village and brought them a bowl of canji. She did it daily and nursed them as well as she knew and, thanks to her charity, the two recovered, and when they gained a little strength they returned to Jaffna.

Now, in order to be able to begin his ministry Fr. Joseph Vaz had first of all to make himself known to the Christians. It was not an easy task, for in order to make himself known to them it was necessary before all to find them out, and such was the cruelty of the persecution that in order to save themselves from being tracked by the protestants they kept hidden and avoided to show any external sign of their Faith.

His first step therefore was to attract their attention. He began therefore to walk in the streets, begging his daily meals wearing ostensibly a rosary on his breast. The protestants, and after them the pagans seeing a man so poorly dressed, showing himself openly a Catholic made of him their laughing stock. They insulted him in the street, struck him and pushed him in the mud. Fr. Joseph Vaz offered his sufferings to God, but at the same time observed attentively the people at whose door he was begging, for any sign whatever if any among them was a Catholic.

He specially noted a house the owner of which treated him always with kind charity, and he suspected him to be a Catholic. On one occasion therefore, when he found himself alone with him, he began to question him about the state of the Catholics of Jaffna and asked him if he would like to see a priest, to make his confession and receive holy Communion. The poor man answered with tears that they had lost even the hope of such great happiness.

From that day Fr. Vaz stayed longer at the house of the good Tamilman, who began to suspect that there was more in his visitor than his tattered rags led him to think. He spoke of him to one of his Catholic friends, a rich man who had some influence with the Dutch officials and who guessed at once, that this strange mendicant must be a priest in disguise.

Without losing a moment, he sought out Fr. Vaz and entreated him with tears that, if he was a priest, to tell him so without fear, for the unfortunate Catholics, persecuted by the protestants, were in need of consolation and of the Sacraments, of which they had been deprived for thirty years. He felt sure, he said, that he must be a priest and in his house he had nothing to fear, as the Dutch would not dare to make search there. Fr. Vaz acknowledged the truth and laid before him the letters of the Archbishop of Goa and of the Administrator of the diocese of Cochin.

The apostleship of Fr. Vaz at Jaffna, then began in earnest. The rich Tamilman who had found him out, kept him hidden in his house, and at night the Catholics of the town met there secretly, and great was their joy when, after so many years they could once more hear Mass and approach the holy Sacraments. The young people had never seen a priest, they had been baptized and instructed by their parents.

However, it was not thought safe for Fr. Vaz to remain in Jaffna, where he was too much exposed to the vigilant eye of the Dutch protestant authorities. After deliberation it was decided that he should take his residence in a village of the neighbourhood called Sillale. The inhabitants of that place were an energetic people and so much attached to their faith, that the Dutch, fearing a mutiny, did not dare to molest them or to take from them their chapel, to be turned into a protestant temple. This village therefore became the headquarter of Fr. Joseph's Mission, and from there he went to visit Jaffna and the surrounding villages.

Although exposed to the daily danger of falling into the hands of the Dutch, Fr. Vaz displayed a great activity. Wherever he went, the Christians concealed him in their houses. His apostleship turned out very fruitful. Not only did he strengthen the Catholics in their Faith, but he also converted a number of protestants and heathens. The Catholics ceased to hide their Faith, they professed it now openly. Their houses rang again with strains of pious hymns, which they sang whilst at work.

The Dutch officers could not make out the reason of such a sudden change. How was it that the Catholics who had
1688 been crushed by their penal laws, so that they did not dare to call themselves Catholics, were now openly professing their Faith? Henry Van Rhee, the military commander of Jaffna, imputed it to the Jesuits of Manapad, who he believed, had succeeded,

notwithstanding all the measures he had taken, in secretly visiting Ceylon. He therefore charged his police to keep a watchful eye on the houses of the Christians, in order to lay hold of these supposed Jesuits. But the Christians kept a good watch over Fr. Joseph who always found means to evade all pursuits.

Fr. Andrew Freire, Provincial of the Jesuit Fathers of Malabar, wrote from Manapad to the Viceroy Dom
1689 Manuel d'Almeida: — „Fr. Joseph Vaz, a Brahmin, who was sent from Goa to take charge of the Christians at Jaffna, discharges his duties with such devotion, that all consider him a saint. He not only looks after the natives but after the Europeans too. Although the heretics search everywhere for him, they can never come upon him, for, like another Proteus, he escapes them under a variety of disguise." —

Henry Van Rhee, the military commander, had given to his police the most stringent order to ferret out the Catholic
1690 priests.

On Christmas night 1690, the Catholics of Jaffna had assembled in three different houses, where altars had been erected, and awaiting Fr. Joseph Vaz to come to say Mass for them in succession, they were reciting the Rosary together.

Fr. Vaz had not yet left his lodgings when Van Rhee's soldiers surrounded the three houses, broke down the altars, destroyed the sacred pictures and carried away as prisoners all the Catholics present, men, women, children, to the number of 300. Had the soldiers come half an hour later, Fr. Vaz could hardly have escaped,

On the next morning all the prisoners were brought before Henry Van Rhee. He dismissed the women and the children, imposed on the men a heavy fine, and retained only eight of them, who were the richest and the most influential.

One of them was a young man whom they called Don Pedro. He belonged to the Vellala caste, the highest in Ceylon. He was rich and his family held a high position among the Tamil natives of Jaffna. When yet very young, he had renounced the Catholic Faith, and become a protestant, in the hope of obtaining some high appointment from the Dutch Government. But a few years later under the influence of an old friend of his father, Emmanuel de Silva, he recognized the enormity of his crime, and horrified at his apostasy, he abjured the protestant heresy, and hence became a fervent Catholic. He did severe penance and at the arrival of Fr. Joseph Vaz, put himself under his spiritual direction, and helped him much in his apostolate.

The commander Van Rhee gave to his eight prisoners the alternative, to abjure the Catholic Faith and become protestants or to be put to death. They all answered that they were ready to die for Jesus Christ. Then thinking that the sight of torture would shake their purpose he ordered Don Pedro, the youngest among them, to be beaten with rods, until he should declare himself a protestant or die under the blows.

Don Pedro bore the torture heroically until he lost consciousness. Van Rhee, seeing his body all covered with blood, ordered him to be thrown into prison with his seven companions. There Don Pedro regained consciousness; and seeing around him his companions he exhorted them to persevere with courage in their Faith, and then peacefully expired.

After vain endeavours for bringing about the apostasy of Emmanuel de Sylva and the six others, the commander Van Rhee condemned them to hard labour for life, and to the confiscation of their property. They all belonged to the leading Tamil families of Jaffna.

They were sent to a fortress, which Van Rhee was then enlarging. Heavily chained, they were made to carry up the hill the stones that were required for the masonry. Their martyrdom did not last long, they all died of want and misery, but none of them even thought of escaping this torture by renouncing the Faith.

The martyrdom of Don Pedro and of his seven companions was the most glorious fruit of the apostolate of Fr. Joseph Vaz at Jaffna.

Fr. Joseph Vaz remained for some time longer in the vicinity of Jaffna, hiding in the jungle, but he could no more freely

**1691** minister to the Christian community, which the renewed persecution had scattered, and over which the Dutch police was keeping a stricter watch than ever. His work being thus hampered, he resolved to leave for a time the neighbourhood of Jaffna, where he had so well confirmed the Catholics in their Faith, that there was no fear of their showing weakness, and to visit other parts of the Island where the Christians were completely abandoned. With his faithful boy John, and a few Jaffnese Christians he started for Putlam. He went by land on foot through the desert of the Vanni.

The church which the Portuguese Missionaries had built at

Putlam was still standing. The Christian community of the town, about a thousand souls, had well kept to their Faith, and could freely confess it, as Putlam did not belong to the protestant Dutch. It was at that time the chief maritime town of the Kingdom of Kandy. They received Fr. Joseph with great demonstrations of joy and it was a great consolation to him to see that, deprived as they had been for so many years of the ministration of priests, they had nevertheless kept their Faith so well.

But on the other hand, the Christians of the surrounding country and particularly those of the Dutch territory were in a most miserable state: Many had become protestants, some to avoid persecution feigned apostasy and practised secretly the Catholic religion; others led such a degraded life, that they scandalized even the heathens.

Fr. Joseph Vaz remained a whole year at Putlam; he continually visited the villages, preaching, and catechising the children. He worked just in the same way as, one hundred and forty years before, St. Francis Xavier had worked among the Parawers on the fishery Coast. Fr. Joseph Vaz in all his apostolic career, kept strictly to the method and the tradition of St. Francis Xavier. He too considered preaching as the best way of correcting the customs of the people and of inspiring them with piety and faith; and giving religious instruction to children, he deemed the paramount duty of the priest. He never ceased to work, and after a year's sojourn at Putlam, the Catholic community in this town and in the surrounding villages was as flourishing as that of Jaffna.

Being now fully acquainted with the political state of Ceylon,

1692 Fr. Joseph understood, that the place from which he could most advantageously extend his apostleship over the whole Island was Kandy, the capital of a native independent kingdom, which at that time extended over nearly one half of the Island, the other half being in the hands of the Dutch. He resolved therefore to establish his headquarters at Kandy and make this town the centre of his apostleship.

But there were obstacles in the way. Without being hostile to the Catholic Religion, the Kings of Kandy were jealous of their independence and had absolutely shut their Kingdom against all foreigners. Whoever entered their territory, was treated as a prisoner and kept at Kandy without hope of being allowed ever to leave the town.

Fr. Joseph Vaz was even exposed to a greater danger. The King of Kandy despised the Dutch, he knew that they were not powerful enough to deprive him of his Kingdom, but he always feared the return of the Portuguese who might claim their former possession. Now Fr. Vaz, though an Indian by birth, was a Portuguese subject; he might therefore be easily taken for a spy and that meant death at the hand of the executioner. But none of these considerations could retain him, and in his unlimited confidence in God, he resolved to go to Kandy.

## CHAPTER 6

# APOSTOLATE IN KANDY

Fr. Joseph Vaz left Putlam in August 1692 in company with Anthony Sotto, a Portuguese merchant, who traded with the Court of the King of Kandy, and who felt confident that he could obtain permission for him to reside in the capital for some time.

After a journey of eight days, they reached Vavodda where Sotto had a house. They stopped there and Sotto sent to Kandy one of his cousins to ask the King for the necessary permission for entering his capital. Unfortunately he did not know that, during his absence, this cousin had been induced to become a protestant.

Now Sotto's cousin, instead of consigning his petition into the King's own hands, as he had promised, took it to Lanerolle, who at once repaired to the palace and denounced Sotto, as a Portuguese agent, aiming at bringing them back to Ceylon, and who even at that moment kept hidden at his house at Vavodda a spy from Goa, whom he intended to smuggle into Kandy under the garb of a Missionary.

The King at once sent soldiers to Vavodda: they arrested Fr. Vaz, Anthony Sotto and the boy John and brought them to Kandy, where they were thrown into prison, and so strictly watched that, for five days, they could not procure themselves other food than a handful of kurrakan, that their keepers gave them out of pity.

A few days later the King came to see them. Wimala Dharma Suriya II was a superior man, educated, and of broader views than was the rule with the Indian princes of his time; he was afraid of the Portuguese and dreaded their return to Ceylon, but was in no way hostile to Catholics, who enjoyed a certain liberty in his dominions.

He spoke a long time with the Father and went away quite convinced that Lanerolle's denunciation was groundless. He ordered the release of Anthony Sotto, and that Fr. Vaz should be provided with more comfortable lodgings and well cared for at the royal expense. Nevertheless he kept him in jail.

There were at this time at Kandy a certain number of Catholics. One of them, Anthony de Horta occupied a prominent position. The King had bestowed on him the title of Dessave, one of the highest in the Kingdom, but it was well known how difficult it was to approach the King on any Portuguese question, so that Horta did not dare to intercede on behalf of the prisoner, nor even ask to see him.

Things went on this way for several months, but that time was not entirely lost for Fr. Joseph Vaz, for he studied Singhalese, the language spoken in the Kingdom of Kandy and in the whole south of Ceylon, and at the same time he was teaching Latin to John, whom he intended for the priesthood.

Little by little the rigour of the prison discipline was relaxed, and they were permitted to walk freely within the jail premises. Fr. Vaz wishing to ascertain whether they kept him in prison because he was a priest, or because there yet remained in the mind of the King some lurking suspicion of his being a Portuguese spy, erected, with the help of John, a small bower of kadjan, in a corner of the prison yard, built in it an altar, put his crucifix on it, and they went there every evening to sing the Litany of the Blessed Virgin. Seeing that no one interfered with his devotions, on Christmas night 1692 the Father celebrated holy Mass and as the warders and the prisoners kept at a respectful distance, he said Mass there every morning.

A few months passed, without any change in Fr. Joseph's condition, when it happened that a Catholic, whose
1693 trade it was to embroider rich vestments for the Kandyan nobles, was admitted to the palace in order to show to the King a piece of silk cloth magnificently embroidered with gold. The King after having admired the workmanship, asked for the price of the garment, but the artisan, throwing himself at the King's feet, answered that he asked nothing else for it, but the permission to see Fr. Vaz and to make his confession to him.

The King struck by the piety of the man and his attachment to his religion, not only granted him his request, but permitted all the Catholics to visit Fr. Vaz in his prison whenever they liked.

A most active life began then for Fr. Joseph Vaz. For forty years after the death of old Fr. Vergonse S. J. no priest had been seen at Kandy; the Catholics therefore availed themselves with joy of the permission granted them by the King, and went in crowds to Fr. Vaz. They came every morning to hear the holy Mass, and the remainder of the day was spent in preaching, confessing, catechizing, baptizing children and blessing marriages.

At last, after two years' confinement Fr. Vaz was released, but on condition that he should remain at Kandy, and never
1694 go beyond the limits of the royal city; and the strictest orders were given to the soldiers of the garrison and to the boatmen on the river, to take him back to prison if he attempted to trespass. This was not a provision made specially for Fr. Vaz, it was applied to all the foreigners who were detained at Kandy.

After coming out of prison, Fr. Joseph's first care was to build a church at Kandy. The King did not object. Anthony de Horta gave him a piece of ground in the best part of the town on the shore of the lake of Bogambra. He also gave the necessary funds, the Catholics worked with delight, and in a short time Fr. Vaz had the consolation to bless his church, to which he gave the title of Our Lady of the Conversion of Pagans.

With the church and a small presbytery annexed to it, he could now seriously organize his ministry among the Christians, who after having been for so many years deprived of spiritual help, wanted it badly. Fr. Vaz gathered them every day in the church and gave them religious instruction. He preached and passed hours in the confessional. He was always surrounded with children, and patiently taught them catechism. He visited in their homes the Christians whom age and infirmity prevented from coming to him.

In this way, he not only strengthened the faith of the Christians, but converted a good number of heathens, among them some officers of the King's palace.

But many Christians lived outside the town, on the other side of the river, in the valley of Dumbura and around Ganaruwa. Notwithstanding the prohibition of the King and the strict orders given to the garrison and to the boatmen, Fr. Joseph went often to visit these scattered Christians and to bring the Viaticum to the dying. He could do so, says the tradition, because God made him then invisible to the soldiers, when he was passing through the gates, and also to the boatmen when he entered their boats.

The description which Captain Robert Knox, who after a captivity of twenty years, left Kandy thirteen years before Fr. Joseph Vaz's arrival gives de visu of the way in which the town of Kandy was fortified and watched, corroborates this tradition. He writes:

— „ The Kingdom of Cande Uda is strongly fortified by nature. „ For which way soever you enter into it, you must ascend high and „ vast mountains, and descend little or nothing. The ways are „ many but very narrow, so that but one can go abreast. The hills „ are covered with wood and great rocks, so that it is scarcely „ possible to get up anywhere, but only on the paths, in all which „ there are gates made of thorns, the one at the bottom, the other on „ the top of the hill, and two or three men always set to watch, who „ have to examine all that come and go, and see what they carry, „ that letters may not be conveyed, nor prisoners and other slaves „ run away.

„ There are constant watches set in convenient places in all „ parts of the country, and thorn gates, but in time of danger, besides „ the ordinary watches, in all towns, and in all places, and in every „ cross road, exceeding thick, *that it is not possible* for any to pass „ unobserved.

„ But specially in all roads and passages, from the city where „ the King now inhabits, are very strict watches set; which will „ suffer none to pass, not having a passport, which is the print of a „ seal in clay. It is given at the Court to them, that have license to „ go through the watches; the seals were different according to the „ profession of the party." —

In another place he says again that the watchers had to ask for so many seals, as there were persons passing through the gate.

Now, at that time, Fr. Joseph Vaz, was a person too well known at Kandy, to suppose, they did not recognize him. On the other hand, he was too poor to bribe the watchers and the boatmen, and the penalty for those who disregarded the orders of the King was torture and death.

It is therefore more than probable that, if they let Fr. Joseph pass when he went to carry the Sacrament to Christians outside the town, they did it not from condescension, for who would risk torture and death? Nor was it through neglect of duty that they took no notice of him, and let him go, but rather because God, protecting his faithful servant, closed their eyes so that they could not see him.

Fr. Vaz himself alludes to this fact in a letter which he wrote to the Archbishop of Goa:

— „ The King, he says, has not yet permitted me to cross the river, to carry spiritual help to the Christians scattered in the villages; but placing above all my duty to the King of Kings, and full of confidence in his protection, I have already crossed it eight times to carry the Sacraments to the sick and to the dying. Those who were there to watch knew that I did not contemplate flight, and the keepers of the gates as well as the boatmen took no notice of me and let me go." —

The wretched Lanerolle, in his hatred of the Faith of Christ, could not bear to see the progress of religion. He

1695 used all his influence at Court to poison the King's mind against Fr. Vaz. Seeing that all his efforts were fruitless, he resolved to arouse the Bikshun against the Catholics.

King Wimala Dharma Surya II was, as before mentioned, a prince of superior mind. He had a sincere veneration for Fr. Joseph Vaz and admired his virtue and his spirit of abnegation. On the other hand he despised the Bikshun on account of their ignorance and of their indolence.

Twice did Lanerolle seek an audience from the King, and brought with him a few of the chief Bikshun. He exposed to the King the dangers which were threatening the Kingdom unless he used energetic means to stop the advance of Catholic Religion, as it was beyond doubt, he said, that Fr. Joseph Vaz was a Portuguese agent, who organized the Christians and sought to bring over the Buddhists to the Catholic Faith in order to create around himself a powerful party; then as soon as he felt strong enough, he would raise a rebellion and call the Portuguese from Goa to help. He therefore entreated the King to save his Crown, before it was too late, and to order the church to be demolished and Fr. Vaz to be expelled from his dominions.

The King answered sternly to the Huguenot, that he had caused Fr. Vaz to be watched closely, and was fully convinced that he was not a Portuguese spy, but had ventured upon such a perilous journey and exposed himself to so many hardships and dangers, only for the sake of bringing spiritual help and consolation to the abandoned Christians of his Kingdom; it would therefore be unworthy of a King to persecute a poor stranger who had sought refuge in the chief town of his dominions.

Thus rebuked, Lanerolle lay quiet for some weeks, when he presented himself again before the King surrounded by a crowd of Bikshun. He insisted on the expulsion of Fr. Joseph Vaz from Kandy, and began to explain to the King that all the strength of political power was grounded upon the religious conformity of the people with their Sovereign. He quoted as a proof that, at the time of the Portuguese rule, three Kings of Kandy on becoming Catholics, lost their throne, because their Buddhist subjects rebelled against them. The same would certainly happen with him, after Fr. Vaz should have converted all the Kandyans to the Catholic Faith. The King therefore should never tolerate a foreign religion being preached in his Kingdom, least of all the religion of the Portuguese, the greatest enemies of the Kings of Kandy.

The King heard out patiently the long speech of the protestant, and then answered him curtly, that he hated the Portuguese who had fought against his father, but valued much their Religion, which was anyhow much better than the protestant creed.

The Bikshun then came in with their complaints: The church built by Fr. Vaz, they said, was now much more frequented than the temples of Buddha, which would be soon deserted, unless the King put a stop to the Fathers' preaching; for now, the very servants of the palace, whose duty it was to provide flowers for the worship of Buddha, refused to do so, under the plea that they had become Catholics.

Wimala Dharma replied to the Bikshun, that they should do as Fr. Joseph did: preach, instruct the people, attend to the sick, give alms to the poor, gain the love of the people. If they did so, their temples would not be deserted, and the people would flock to them, as they now did to Fr. Joseph's church.

Mortified at the manner of the King who openly favoured Fr. Vaz, Lanerolle conspired with some Buddhist chiefs, who were powerful enough to act by themselves and in spite of the King. They threatened Fr. Vaz and began to excite the mob against the Christians who, when going to the church, were belaboured with blows, assailed with stones and had their rosaries torn from their necks.

This kind of persecution increased every day, and grew serious. Fr. Vaz became very anxious. The King, it is true, was favourable to the Christians and resisted the solicitations of their enemies, but would he show the same bold face when threatened with a rising of the Buddhist mob against the Christians, for this was the aim of the protestant Lanerolle and of his heathen confederates.

Things had thus come to a critical point, when God by working a signal miracle came to the rescue of His threatened church.

The rainy season in Kandy begins usually between the middle of May and the beginning of June, but in the year in which the facts just related occurred, the time had long since passed, there was no appearance of rain, and the drought was severely felt in the whole Kingdom of Kandy.

This was a great calamity, for the food of the people in Ceylon is rice, which being an aquatic plant, can only grow during the rainy season when the fields are covered with water; irrigation even was impossible, for all the tanks and water reservoirs were dried up to the bottom. Famine therefore was the fate that threatened the whole country, famine with its ordinary retinue: pestilence and rebellion.

The King felt uneasy, for at the south of his dominions the Dutch were lurking, awaiting an opportunity to invade the Kingdom of Kandy. He consequently ordered the Bikshun to offer public sacrifices and implore the help of Buddha. Yellow and white flowers were daily deposited at the feet of the idol, and the temples resounded with the beating of drums, but rain did not come. Hindu magicians were then commanded to offer sacrifices to the devil, with no better result.

As a last resource Wimala Dharma sent for some Christians employed at the palace, and ordered them to go to Fr. Joseph Vaz: — „He preaches, said the King, that his God is the only true one, let him pray to Him to save my people who, if the drought continues, will perish.“ —

Fr. Vaz replied that, in compliance with the King's wish, he would pray to God, and if it pleased Him, as conducive to His greater glory, rain would refresh the land, for He is the Master and Creator of earthly elements, and all obey Him.

He came out of his dwelling and went towards a place at the

other end of the town. He erected an altar, put his Crucifix on it, knelt down and began to pray. A large crowd surrounded him, and whilst he prayed the sky grew overcast with heavy black clouds, and such an abundant rain poured down, that in a short time the fields were covered with water, and all the tanks constructed for irrigation were filled to the brim. Fr. Vaz was praying all the while, and the people saw with amazement that, amid such a deluge, the spot where he was kneeling, the altar and the cross had remained dry, not a drop of water had fallen on them.

This miracle produced a great impression on the people: many heathens asked to be baptized and all the apostates, and they were many, who had abjured the Faith of Christ and become protestants, did penance and were reconciled to the Church.

On the place where this miracle was wrought, stands now the Cathedral of Kandy and the Benedictine abbey of St. Anthony.

The fact of this miraculous rain is related in the Mahawanse but, with the customary inexactitude of this chronicle, or perhaps even through malice, as it happened but a short time before the compilation of the Mahawanse, it is transferred to another epoch:

— „ Under the reign of this King, it says, there was a violent „ heat and dryness in the Island, by which all plants withered, so as „ to threaten a great scarcity. This terrified all the inhabitants of „ the Island in a great decree; But the King Prakrama Bahu, having „ made great sacrifices in the name of Buddhu and other deities, „ prayed for rain. Then it came to pass that there appeared lightning „ and rainy clouds from every side of the Island, and at last it broke

„forth in a heavy rain. Upon this, the people began to praise „Buddhu and the King." —

Until now, as said above, Fr. Joseph Vaz, had not been allowed to leave Kandy, and if he visited the surrounding villages,
1696 he did it secretly and at his own peril, but after the miracle of the rain, the King gave him full liberty to go wherever he liked. He availed himself of that leave to pay a visit to Colombo.

The Christian community of this town, which was so flourishing under the Portuguese, was now a complete wreck. The fine churches had been desecrated, some fell into ruins, others were transformed into protestant temples, all the priests were banished, the beautiful Portuguese Colleges replaced by miserable primary schools, where Government under heavy penalties, obliged the Catholic parents to send their children, in order that they might lose their Faith and their love of God.

The Catholics were forced to attend the protestant service on Sundays, and they had to practise their Religion in the greatest secrecy, for even prayer in common was considered a crime, which their protestant masters visited with heavy penalties.

Such was the state of things at Colombo when Fr. Joseph Vaz came to this town. The Christians at once gathered around him. They met, at night, in out of the way houses, where Fr. Vaz said Mass, heard their confessions, administered holy Communion and exhorted them to persevere in their Faith. His inspired words gave them courage. The people brought to him the apostates who, haunted by remorse, asked to be reconciled to God. He even converted a few Dutch protestants, who abjured into his hands their heretical creed.

Under such circumstances, the presence of a Catholic priest in town could not remain long a secret. The Governor issued orders to the chief of the police, to have the most active search made for him: and had the man instantly acted on these, he would certainly have arrested Fr. Joseph Vaz, but he delayed a few days, and when he began to make search, Fr. Vaz was already at Negombo.

He then visited the province of Sabaragamuva, Batticaloa, Trincomalee, Jaffna, the first stage of his Apostolate, Mantotte, Putlam, whence after an absence of many months he returned to Kandy. He had made the whole circuit of the Island, visiting all the places where there were Catholics.

Unfortunately we have no other details of his apostolic labours during these months than those which Fr. Menezes gives us in a letter which he wrote to the Superior of the Goa Oratory on the 31 July 1699.

He writes: — „ As to the kind of life Fr. Joseph Vaz leads, is really supernatural, the people of Ceylon credit him with many miracles. Even the heathens and Mahometans relate of him things which seem most extraordinary. I was not able to verify the exact truth of these narratives, but the incident with the elephant happened in my own Mission and I ascertained the truth of the fact, which was attested to me under oath by an ocular witness:

Fr. Vaz was walking a little ahead of his companions, on the road leading from Maripo to Vellevalim; he had a small book in his hand, said the eye-witness, probably his breviary, when suddenly a wild elephant emerged from the jungle, and at the sight of the beast, all his companions took to flight. The animal advanced up to a few steps before Fr. Joseph Vaz, then paused, and taking another direction, disappeared in the jungle. Fr. Vaz seemed not to have seen him and was totally unaware of the danger to which he had been exposed.

At Pulliaculão, Fr. Vaz was preaching the Gospel to the pagans. One of them, a man advanced in age, and having no children, begged him to pray to God to give him a son. Fr. Vaz instructed and baptized him, and in due time his wife gave birth to a beautiful boy.

At Putlam, a poor woman was dying in the throes of child-birth. Fr. Vaz administered to her the last Sacraments. Then, moved by the despair of her family, he went to the chapel and began to pray. He remained kneeling before the altar, until they came to tell him that the mother had been delivered of a stillborn child. He then returned thanks to God for having heard his prayer, and rose from his knees.

At Benacuddipù, the Father urged with persistence that a woman called Anna Pulle should return to her husband; but she refused obstinàtely. God punished her, for on the same day she fell ill, a loathsome tumour grew upon her head, and she was on the point of death, when Fr. Joseph Vaz, passing again that way, called at her house. He made on her the sign of the cross, and she was instantly cured. This fact is certain, and I have heard it from Anna Pulle herself.

Now, if all these facts have come to pass in my Mission alone,

Your Reverence may judge of what may have happened in others." —

A great joy was awaiting Fr. Joseph on his return to Kandy. The Bishop of Cochin, Dom Pedro Pacheco, to whose diocese Ceylon belonged, having heard from the Provincial of the Jesuit Fathers who resided at Manapad, of the great work which Fr. Vaz was doing in the Island, where until now he had been alone, sent two Fathers from the Goa Oratory to help him in his apostolate, Fr. Joseph Menezes and Fr. Joseph Carvalho. The last named was the nephew of Fr. Vaz, the son of one of his sisters, whom we saw already sixteen years ago working together with his uncle at Mangalore.

A few months later a third Oratorian, Fr. Peter Ferrão, came to Kandy; he brought to Fr. Joseph Vaz letters from the Bishop of Cochin, by which this Prelate appointed him his Vicar General in Ceylon and granted him extensive powers.

The companions whom Dom Pedro Pacheco had sent to Fr. Vaz were all very able men, full of zeal and tried in virtue.
1697 They were all Concani Indians of the Brahmin caste. With these, and with the powers granted him by the Bishop, Fr. Vaz could now well organize the Missions. He assigned to Fr. Peter Ferrão the northern part of the Island with residence at Jaffna. Fr. Joseph Menezes was stationed at Putlam and had the charge of the Christians of Colombo, Negombo, and of all those disseminated in the Dutch territory in the South. Fr. Joseph Carvalho was appointed parish priest of Kandy. Fr. Joseph Vaz himself was to

have no fixed residence, his intention was to visit the Missions continually.

Five years had elapsed since Fr. Joseph Vaz had begun his work at Kandy and he was held in veneration not only by the Christians, but also by the pagans, who admired his virtues, particularly his great charity towards all sufferers. This charity was soon to manifest itself in a wonderful manner.

Towards the middle of 1697 small-pox began to rage at Kandy and was making great havoc. The natives, at that time, were in great dread of that disease and the panic was further heightened by the superstition, that those who are stricken by this malady become possessed by the devil.

As soon as a man showed signs of being infected, he was abandoned by his family, and left alone in some lonely hut, where he died of misery and starvation. Often the sufferer was cast into the jungle, where he was devoured by chettahs and jackals. The dead were not buried, but flung away into some ravine.

The plague was spreading with fearful rapidity. The King had left Kandy, all the wealthy people sought refuge in the country, the poor fled to the hills which surrounded the city and built for themselves huts of branches and foliage, living exposed to all kind of privations. The houses of the town were abandoned and sheltered only those stricken by the plague, who had been left to their doom. Heaps of corpses were lying in the streets, the prey of stray dogs and crows.

Fr. Joseph Vaz and his nephew Fr. Carvalho, were day and

night in attendance on the sick, Christians as well as pagans. They prepared food and carried it to them. Going from house to house, they dispensed medicines, and rendered them the most menial services. They sought out those who had been abandoned in the jungle and built over them shelters of foliage. To the Christians they administered the Sacraments; to the pagans they unfolded the consoling truths of the Faith, and converted many in the sight of death. They baptized a great number of poor dying children.

The pestilence was gaining ground and Fr. Vaz and Fr. Carvalho were unable to reach all the sick in their houses. They then selected four abandoned houses in the vicinity of the church and converted them into a hospital. With the help of abundant alms, sent to them by the Catholics of Colombo, they were able to provide for the necessities of the sick. They both said Mass before sunrise, and then carried food to the sick. They did their own cooking, for they were alone, John, Fr. Joseph's faithful companion having been sent by him to Goa with letters to the Archbishop and to the Superior of the Oratory.

Whatever time they did not spend in their hospital, they devoted to giving burial to the dead; they had an average of ten to twelve funerals a day. When possible they buried the Christians with the religious pomp they could afford in such circumstances, a thing which much impressed the pagans, but more often they had to carry the corpses on their own shoulders to their last resting place. After having consigned the Christians to their grave, they buried the pagans.

The charity and self-denial of the Catholic priests excited the admiration of the pagans. King Wimala Dharma Surya spoke of them with enthusiasm before his courtiers.

The pestilence lasted for nearly a year. After it had ceased the inhabitants of Kandy who had left the town, returned to their homes, the King took again residence in his palace. He had decided to reward Fr. Vaz royally, and was much astonished when the Catholic officials at the palace told him, that the Father would accept neither money nor any high dignity. More than once he publicly declared that, if it were not for the Fathers' charity, not a living soul would have remained at Kandy.

As soon as the pestilence had ceased, and matters had resumed their usual course, Fr. Vaz, leaving the care of the
1698 Christians of Kandy to Fr. Joseph Carvalho, set out on a visit of the Missions and of the villages.

A fact had just occurred which, having deeply impressed the heathens, had increased their readiness to hear the preaching of the Faith of Christ:

In the village of Kandegama, situated in that part of the province of Sabaragamuva which belonged to the Kingdom of Kandy, the Christians had a small chapel dedicated to St. Anthony, where they were in the habit of meeting together on Sundays to recite the Rosary and to pray to God in common.

It so happened that the Dessawe, or Kandyan Governor of the Sabaragamuva province, a pagan, decided to build a granary for the King on the site of the chapel, and sent orders to the Christians to pull it down. The Christians were in despair, and in the hope of obtaining the revocation of the decree, they delayed carrying it out. The Dessawe sent another peremptory order, but before it could be executed, he was removed from his office by order of the King.

The Christians could not but rejoice, and they said openly that it was a well merited punishment for his having attempted to destroy their chapel of St. Anthony.

The pagan felt wounded in his pride and swore that he would have his revenge. By means of intrigues at Court, and bribes distributed among the dignitaries he contrived to be reinstated. He then proceeded personally to Kandegama. Having installed himself in the chapel, where he sat deciding some cases, he had his dinner brought there and whilst he was eating, his people were bringing cartloads of stones for the building of the granaries.

The Christians greatly distressed brought out the sacred images to prevent their being desecrated by the pagans and expected their chapel to be demolished on the morrow, but in the same night the Dessawe was struck by paralysis, so that he could not even turn on his couch without the help of his servants.

He sought his cure by all the means which wealth and power placed in his hands, he called to his bed-side the most renowned physicians, but they could do nothing for him. At last, despairing of ever regaining his health, and aware of the rumours current among the people, he recognized that he had been punished, for having laid violent hands on a sanctuary consecrated to God.

He called to him the leading Catholics of the place and, in their presence, he publicly confessed his guilt. He promised that he would never again persecute them and begged them to bring back the pictures to the chapel and to pray to God for him. He gave them tapers to be lighted on the altar and money enough to feed in front of the chapel all the poor of the place for three days, because, he said, he had heard that God forgives the sins of those who are charitable to the poor.

All the Christians went to the chapel to pray, and, whilst they were reciting the Rosary, the Dessawe rose from his bed, completely cured.

To show his gratitude to God, he had a beautiful little church built at his own expense on the site of the poor chapel, but the unfortunate man himself remained a heathen. Worldly considerations and fear of the devil's displeasure held him back.

These facts made a great impression on the heathens of the vicinity and many asked to be baptized.

It was therefore with a thankful heart, that Fr. Joseph Vaz set out to visit the place where the name of God had been manifested in such a wonderful way. He made on foot the 72 miles from Kandy to Colombo, by narrow paths through mountains covered with a dense jungle, hiding and in disguise whilst on Dutch territory.

He only just passed through Colombo, his presence there not being necessary, for Fr. Menezes often visited this town from Putlam, and his labours were blessed with great success. In spite of the vigilance of the Dutch protestants, he not only ministered to the Christians, but had in a relatively short time converted over 3,000 heretics and pagans.

Fr. Vaz therefore went to Gurubevelle, a large village to the east of Colombo. The reports of the events at Kandegama had produced in the whole district a movement towards Catholicism among the Buddhist population; many had been instructed by the Christians, and now Fr. Joseph Vaz went there to baptize them. He found them all well prepared and sufficiently instructed and in the short space of thirteen days he baptized more than a thousand.

Gurubevelle was in the Dutch territory, and the Governor of Colombo, informed of what was taking place there, gave orders for Fr. Joseph's arrest.

A company of Dutch soldiers entered the village unexpectedly, and surrounded the house in which the Father had taken his abode, that there was no possibility of escape. God then came to the help of His faithful servant in a miraculous way. The soldiers searched the house, and although Fr. Joseph Vaz remained all the time among them, they did not see him. The terrified Christians saw the Father standing in the room in the midst of the infuriated soldiers, they expected him to be arrested every moment, but the soldiers could not see him. They searched all the houses and returned to Colombo to report to the Governor the failure of their expedition.

Fr. Vaz could not remain longer at Gurubevelle, he took boat
1699 up the Kelany river, and established his headquarters at
Sitawacca, a large village in the Kingdom of Kandy, on
the very limits of the Dutch territory.

His first care was to make a pilgrimage of thanksgiving for his miraculous escape, to a small sanctuary in the neighbourhood of Sitawacca, he then devoted himself entirely to his work. He had already converted a good number of pagans, when he got the crushing news that Fr. Joseph Carvalho had been exiled from Kandy, and the church demolished.

Fr. Joseph's absence from Kandy was an opportunity for his enemies to carry out the plan, which they had laid already a long time, to ruin his work.

It is uncertain whether or not Lanerolle was again concerned in the plot: his name is no more mentioned at this epoch, and probably he was dead. A powerful Kandyan Chief put himself at the head of the anti-Catholic movement. His house was not far from the church and adjoining the four houses which Fr. Vaz had used as a hospital during the pestilence, and which he had purchased to make them into a permanent hospital. The name of the Chief is unknown. Two of the greatest Lords of the Kingdom, Molligodde and Ehelapola, had their residences not far from the Mission establishment.

The Chief pretended that the vicinity of the hospital was injurious to the health of his family. He summoned Fr. Carvalho, ordered him to remove his quarters elsewhere and to demolish the houses. The Father replied, that he was not their actual owner, and could not dispose off the property. The Chief then sent his men, they threw the sick out on the street and pulled down the hospital.

After such a deed of violence, the conspirators began to dread the justice of the King. A number of the leading men of their party, supported by as many Bikshun as they could get from the two temples of Malwatte and of Asgyria, repaired to the palace with the above mentioned Chief at their head. They requested the King to take strong measures to prevent the progress of Christianity, to arrest Fr. Carvalho and above all, to forbid Fr. Joseph Vaz to set foot again in Kandy. They first urged their claim with reasons of policy, but seeing that these made no impression on the mind of the King, they threatened him openly with rebellion. The Chief who stood at their head was very powerful and the King began to fear. He yielded partly to their proposals, and consented to order Fr. Carvalho's exile from Kandy, but at the same time he sent to him one of the Catholic officials, to assure him that he would suffer no harm and that he was at liberty to take away with him whatever he possessed.

In spite of the royal assurance, the conspirators handled him very roughly, and he had much trouble to save from their hands even the requisites for Mass. He took refuge in a country-house belonging to Anthony de Horta, a few miles from Kandy on the other side of the river.

Twenty-five days after his departure, the pagans, led by the beforementioned Kandyan Chief, razed the church to the ground, he himself directing the operations. But the unhappy man was soon to suffer the punishment of his misdeeds. He was struck with a terrible illness. His legs became like those of a corpse, a loathsome ulcer appeared on his tongue, and the whole body was covered with purulent abscesses; and all the inhabitants of Kandy, Christians as well as pagans, looked upon his fate as a just punishment from God.

This was the state of affairs when the news were brought to Sitawacca, to Fr. Joseph Vaz. On hearing he wept, then throwing himself on his knees he remained a long time in prayer. It was the ruin of all his hopes, and he foresaw the saddest consequences, for it was evident that, expelled from the Kingdom of Kandy, and persecuted in the Dutch dominions, the Missionaries, having no single spot where they could enjoy a relative safety, would be ultimately compelled to abandon Ceylon.

It was with these gloomy apprehensions that Fr. Vaz left Sitawacca and set out on his way to Kandy about the middle of Lent 1699. But it was only when he came to Horta's country-house that he learned all the details of the disaster. Before that he did not know that the church had been demolished.

Fr. Vaz wished to proceed to Kandy, but the boatmen refused to carry him over the Mahavelli Ganga, as they had received strict orders not to allow any priest to cross the river. Moreover Anthony de Horta was of opinion that nothing ought to be done in a hurry. He would go himself to Kandy, find out what could prudently be done and ascertain what the King would say, if he heard that Fr. Vaz had re-entered his Kingdom. He went to the town and left both the Fathers at his country-house.

No news came from him. It seemed evident now that the King, who generally was well informed, had already heard of Fr. Joseph's return, and as yet no measures had been taken against him. The decree of banishment did not mention his name and had been enacted only against Fr. Carvalho. All that considered, the two Fathers came to the conclusion that Fr. Joseph's hesitation to return to Kandy might be misconstrued at Court, and be looked upon as a tacit confession that the two priests were really guilty of the offences imputed to them, and they decided that Fr. Joseph should no longer delay his return to Kandy.

After a night spent in prayer, Fr. Vaz started for Kandy. The boatmen made no objection to his crossing the river, and he rejoined Anthony de Horta in his town residence.

From him he learned that the King was always well disposed towards him, and that at Court there was a strong party which openly disapproved of Fr. Carvalho's exile and the demolition of the church. The time was therefore ripe for action.

Fr. Vaz assembled a number of Christians and told them to pray whilst he was deliberating with Horta on the best manner of approaching the King. Whilst they were taking counsel together, an unexpected visitor knocked at the door. It was the King's physician, a pagan, and a man of great influence. Before any word was spoken to him, he greeted Fr. Vaz and offered his services, to settle the affair with the King. Fr. Vaz had never known him before, he did not even remember ever having seen him, nevertheless he accepted his offer most thankfully.

On the same evening the man returned with a message from the King, that not only should Fr. Joseph remain, but Fr. Carvalho should also return to Kandy, and that the church should be rebuilt in the shortest time possible. Moreover, they were both at liberty to preach their religion and convert the people throughout his whole Kingdom.

The fatiguing journeys through the Missions, and the anxieties he had undergone had shattered Fr. Joseph's health. He was prostrated with a malignant fever. The King sent him his own physician, the same who had lately befriended him and desired to be informed daily of the state of his health.

Whilst still convalescent, Fr. Vaz undertook the rebuilding of the church. Anthony de Horta supplied him with a great part of the necessary funds; the Christians worked with zeal so that, in five months, the church was ready. It was sufficiently large to accommodate the Christians of Kandy and those of the surrounding villages. Fr. Vaz blessed it solemnly on the feast of the Nativity of the Bl. Virgin Mary, the 8 September 1699. He then rebuilt the presbytery and the hospital.

The Church at Kandy being rebuilt and the King having granted

1700 permission to preach the Gospel all over his Kingdom, it seemed that an era of liberty and prosperity was to begin for the Mission. But the devil in his unrelenting struggle against the Church of God, was preparing a new and severe storm. It happened in this way.

In the first year of his Apostleship, Fr. Joseph Vaz had baptized a bright Kandyan boy, the scion of one of the richest and most powerful families of the country, whose father Gobbada-Balla-Nilame, held a high position at the royal Court. He was a pious and virtuous lad, but as his conversion had taken place only a short time after Fr. Joseph Vaz had been released from jail, and the Mission was yet in a rather precarious position, he thought it more prudent to keep the boy's conversion secret, for he dreaded the resentment of his family which was influential enough to do great harm to the Mission. But the secret could not be easily kept, for the lad, being a page at the royal Court, was bound to accompany the King when he offered sacrifices to his gods in the temple, and it was not always possible to find an excuse for non-appearance, the more so, as one of the temples the Dalada-Maligawa, was part of the royal palace.

Fr. Vaz had carefully instructed the boy and bore him a great affection. Seeing now the dangerous position into which he was thrown, he advised him to withdraw from the Court and to go to live in the country.

But there the idle life he led again, far from the influence of the Father and amid pagans of dissolute life, made him lose his innocence; by and by he neglected his daily devotions and plunged into vice. At last Fr. Vaz was told that he had married a heathen girl, and was living like a heathen.

The good Father never ceased to pray to God for him, and when some one mentioned the young man in his presence, he quietly replied that he was not doomed to perish, but on the contrary he would yet become an instrument in the hand of God for the salvation of many.

One night when the young man vainly tried to sleep, the remembrance of his early youth, of Fr. Joseph Vaz, and of his pious instructions recurred to his mind. Struck with horror and with remorse at his apostacy and at the bad life he had since led, he spent the remainder of the night in prayer and, as soon the day dawned, he called a Christian from the neighbourhood to accompany him, and went to Kandy. Fr. Joseph Vaz was absent. Finding there only

Fr. Peter Saldanha whom he did not know, the young man dared not tell him who he was and only begged humbly, to be admitted among the catechumens. After a few days, Fr. Saldanha, edified by his piety, and seeing that he was perfectly instructed in the Christian Religion wished to baptize him without more delay. Then the young man prostrating himself at the father's feet told him his story; he made a general confession and resolved to expiate his crime by working generously for the glory of God. On his return home, he prepared his wife and his four children for baptism and brought over to the Faith of Christ forty more persons. Fr. Saldanha went to his place, baptized them all, and blessed their marriage.

The news of such a notable conversion excited the anti-Christian party, the more so as they were afraid that the conversion of the young Kandyan Chief would induce others to follow his example, and that he himself would use his influence to help the Fathers in their apostolate.

The party repaired again to the King, but knowing from experience that neither political considerations, nor the menace of open rebellion could move him in his sincere affection to Fr. Joseph Vaz, they sought to rouse his religious feelings or rather his superstition. They related to the King that Fr. Saldanha had baptized the young Chief and all his companions with the blood of a cow, and as such blood is necessary for baptism, it was evident that Fr. Joseph Vaz and his Missionaries were killing many cows.

Now King Wimala Dharma Surya was more or less a Buddhist, but, at that time, the Buddhists of Ceylon had all the superstitions of the Hindus, and for the Hindus there is nothing more sacred than the cow, in fact, in many countries of India, the pain of death was decreed for killing a cow. It was the greatest crime that a man could commit, equal to that of murdering three Brahmins on the shore of the sacred Ganges.

The King could not be shaken, as we have seen before, by the menace of a new Portuguese invasion of his Kingdom, nor by the threats of a rebellion of his subjects, but killing cows was a more serious matter, and in his indignation he ordered the six last converts, whom Fr. Saldanha had baptized, to be thrown into prison and their property to be confiscated.

This was the great blow to Fr. Joseph Vaz. Fearing a renewal of the persecution, he betook himself to prayer beseeching the Lord to avert this new danger from His Church.

Fortunately, as we have before mentioned, there were then two parties at the royal Court of Kandy: the one clinging to the old heathenism and therefore hostile to Fr. Joseph Vaz, the other more enlightened, or indifferent, and consequently more favourably disposed towards him.

The latter proved to the King that the Catholic Missionaries had been slandered; that they never killed cows and baptized their converts with water to which they added a little oil with balm, and they pursuaded the King so well, that he immediately ordered the six prisoners to be released and their property to be restored to them. And these men went straight from the jail to the church to thank God for their liberation.

It was the last persecution that the Christians of Kandy had to suffer during Fr. Joseph's life-time, and henceforth he was able to work in peace in the whole Kingdom.

## CHAPTER 7

# FR. JOSEPH VAZ'S DEATH

A short time before the events related in the last chapter took place, the Superior of the Goa Oratory had sent six more Missionaries to Ceylon. They were the Fathers: Peter Saldanha, Joseph of Jesus-Mary, Emmanuel de Miranda, Ignatius d'Almeida, Basil Baretto and James Gonzalves, whose name is still venerated in Ceylon for his virtues, his science and his indefatigable zeal.

There were now ten Oratorian Missionaries in Ceylon, all natives of India, and with them, Fr. Joseph Vaz could seriously organize the Mission, which was progressing rapidly.

Fr. Emmanuel de Miranda who had been sent to Colombo, the most dangerous and exposed station, had organized the Catholics of that town so well, that they no more remained in concealment and had begun to protest openly against the Dutch penal Laws.

Fr. Joseph Vaz, their Superior, directed the work of all the Missionaries, paying them frequent visits, stirring up their courage and their zeal, and he was cherished and venerated by all.

The unbounded charity of Fr. Joseph Vaz, was one of the reasons, why the King paid so much respect to him. The Father was for him an enigma, some awe-inspiring supernatural being.

The King in these countries was considered as a kind of deity. He rarely appeared before his people, even the greatest dignitaries of the land approached him only prostrated on the ground. Great was therefore their astonishment when they saw Wimala Dharma taking Fr. Joseph Vaz to his private apartments and conversing familiarly with him.

A few days after the death of Fr. Joseph Carvalho, the King was passing before the church with a large retinue. He ordered his elephant to stop and sent one of his courtiers with his condolence to Fr. Joseph Vaz, whom he desired to bring to Kandy more priests of such great virtue as his deceased nephew. He allowed Fr. Carvalho to be buried in the church, notwithstanding the law of the country, that the remains of the dead should be buried outside the town. Later on he extended this privilege to all the Oratorian Fathers. Such instances of royal favour were making a great impression on the people, and paved the way for Fr. Joseph's Apostolate.

We can see the hand of God in those good dispositions of the King of Kandy, who reigned precisely at the time when the protestant persecution was raging in the other half of the Island, which was under the rule of the Dutch. Without the protection which these heathen Kings afforded to the Missionaries, the present flourishing Catholic communities in Ceylon could not have been established.

Having now resident Missionaries in all the principal centres of Ceylon, Fr. Joseph Vaz was continually on the move. In company of one or two priests and of some devoted Christians, he was visiting the Missions, going from village to village wherever there were Christians or the hope of converting some heathens. He went sometimes far out of his way to visit a single Christian or a poor family who were dwelling among the heathens, in order to give them an opportunity of hearing Mass, making their Confession and receiving holy Communion.

In the Kingdom of Kandy travelling was difficult but when once they came to a village the Missionaries could freely exercise the sacred ministry. But on the Dutch territory they were continually exposed to danger. With the progress of the Catholic Church the persecution had increased, and the spy-system was so well organized, that the Missionaries had to remain in hiding, and could only administer the Sacraments to the Christians secretly, under cover of the night.

It had therefore been arranged that, wherever Fr. Joseph Vaz was expected, the Christians should be warned beforehand, and should gather together in some out-of-the-way house. The Father came in the evening, preached, instructed them, heard their Confessions until three o'clock in the morning, when he celebrated the holy Mass, and, before daybreak, left, in disguise, for another locality. If some circumstances or the number of Christians made it necessary to remain longer in the same place, they took the precaution of meeting every night in another house.

In this way, with the help of God, Fr. Joseph Vaz could always elude the vigilance of the protestants. I say with the help of God, for, at times, without a special and often wonderful help of Divine Providence, he could not have escaped their pursuit.

One day, at Colombo, a renegade informed the Dutch authorities in which house the Catholics were to meet for holy Mass. The Governor gave very stringent orders to capture the priest who had to celebrate it. At the very moment when Fr. Joseph Vaz was vesting, the soldiers surrounded the house and entered it. All the Catholics fled, and Fr. Joseph, encumbered with the box containing the requisites for Mass, passed among the soldiers without their noticing him.

The invaders overran the whole house, sure that the priest was somewhere in hiding and that they would capture him. But they found nothing, not even the slightest indication that there had been a meeting at that place. In one room, however, they saw a lady standing, at whose sight they were struck with stupor. She asked them what they had come for, and whom they sought. The officer and the soldiers were seized with such a terror that they all fled. When they found themselves outside the house, ashamed for having run away from a woman, they re-entered the room and found nobody there. Only on the spot where the lady had been standing, they saw a statue of the Blessed Virgin Mary. Filled with awe, they went away without touching the statue.

The news spread at once through the city that the Blessed Virgin had appeared in that house, and crowds of people repaired to the spot to contemplate the statue. The protestants were unable to conceal their disappointment, and the Governor sentenced the ill-fated renegade to be flogged publicly.

It will be easily understood what an impression such events made on the mind of the Christians, how they confirmed them in their Faith, and how great a veneration they had for Fr. Vaz. Some protestants also, notwithstanding their hatred to the Catholic Faith could not but admire Fr. Joseph's virtue, and the courage with which he faced so many perils, in order to save the souls of his brethren.

Fr. Vaz having once come secretly to Colombo, some of the leading protestant ministers went to the Governor John Simonsz insisting that he should take the necessary measures to have him at last arrested. The Governor answered that, if they had no other business of greater interest to Government, he could not speak any longer with them, as he was very busy.

Notice of the Apostleship of Fr. Joseph Vaz had reached Rome, through the Jesuit Fathers of Manapad, and Pope Clement XI was watching with interest the revival of the Church of Ceylon.

It was about that time that the Legate of the Holy See Mgr. Maillard de Tournon, landed in India. The Pope had given him special instructions to bring himself into communication with Fr. Joseph Vaz, and to support him in his apostolate.

Mgr. de Tournon wrote several times to Fr. Joseph Vaz, and sent him a Crucifix blessed by the Pope. He wished to separate Ceylon from the diocese of Cochin, and appoint him Bishop of the Island. But Fr. Vaz declined the dignity, explaining to the Legate that under the present difficult circumstances, with the unceasing persecution in one part of the Island, whilst the Missionaries had to perform their duties in disguise and in hiding, tracked like wild beasts by the protestant masters of the land, the presence of a Bishop would only increase the difficulties.

Such progress of the Catholic Faith exasperated the protestants, and they resolved to stop it at any cost. Seeing that half a century of persecution has been of no use, and that the vitality of the church of God was now on the increase they resolved to try other means for overthrowing it.

Buddhism was at that epoch in full decline, and its disappearance was only a question of time. The institution of the Bikshun, which helped to keep it up, was in a state of complete disorganization, there were only in Ceylon Bikshun of the lowest degree: Samanaras, I think, they were called.

The protestants therefore decided to give a new life to Buddhism, to throw the Singhalese, not only in the Dutch dominions but also in the Kingdom of Kandy back into heathenism, thus hoping to put a stop to the revival of Catholicism.

The Government of Colombo entered into communication with the King of Kandy, in order to re-establish in Ceylon some sort of higher hierarchy of Bikshun, importing them from Burma.

— „ At this juncture, says the protestant author Gordon „ Cumming, the Jesuit (it should be Oratorian) Missionaries, very „ naturally endeavouring, to secure a firmer footing, but the Dutch „ Government therein scenting the political influence of Portugal „ (which at that time was null) determined to counteract their action. „ They therefore gave assistance to the Buddhists, by lending them „ ships to convey a special Mission to Arrakan whence a number of „ fully qualified *priests* (Bikshun) were imported to reanimate their „ Brethren, and effectually oppose the efforts of the Roman Catholic „ Missionaries." —

Thus did the protestants reestablished the declining Buddhism in Ceylon, in the hope to prevent the spread of the Catholic Religion, and, in part, they succeeded, for had they not done so, the number of Christians in Ceylon, would be now, to say the least, double.

Not satisfied with fighting the Missionaries and procuring the revival of heathenism, they tracked the Catholic priests like wild beasts whenever they ventured to enter the Dutch territory.

Fr. Joseph Vaz was now 55 years old; he had toiled already 17 years in Ceylon, and his strength was exhausted, his constitution worn out. He continued nevertheless to work with the same energy, visiting the Christians even in the remotest parts of the Island. His bodily strength was decreasing, but his confidence in God was so great that, when the welfare of the souls committed to his care was in question, he did not hesitate to undertake the most fatiguing journeys.

One day he was going with his customary escort from Kandy to Putlam. They came to a river at the usual fording-place and found it so swollen by recent rains that it was impossible to pass it. Many travellers who had arrived before Fr. Vaz, were encamped on the shore, having built shelters of branches, for they knew they would have to stay there a few days, before the river would subside to such a level as to render its fording possible.

Fr. Vaz, on reaching the encampment, asked them why they were waiting. They answered good-humouredly that they did so, because they preferred to wait rather than be drowned. The river, they said, had risen to such a height, and the torrent was so strong, that the ford was impassable. They had repeatedly tried it, but were always carried off by the stream. These travellers were Mahometans and heathens.

Fr. Joseph Vaz came to the river. He stepped into the water, and sounding the depth with his stick, went on, as far as the middle of the stream, with the water rising only up to the knees. Then he stopped, shouting to the crowd on the shore to follow him. His escort and a few heathens entered the water. Fr. Vaz remained standing, until they had reached the other side of the river, then he too followed them.

The men who had remained in the encampment, seeing how easily they had crossed the ford, also entered into the stream, but scarcely had they taken a few steps when they were neck-deep in the flood, and had to rush back in haste.

King Wimala Dharma Surya, Fr. Joseph's protector, died in 1707, and was succeeded by his son Sreeweera Praakrama
1707 Narendra Singha, commonly called Kundesala, who, having known Fr. Vaz from his childhood, had a great veneration for him.

He was only seventeen years old. Once when, on his way to Peradeniya, he was passing in State before the church in Kandy, surrounded by a great retinue, Fr. Vaz went as far as the gate in order to present to him his homage. The King stopped, spoke most cordially with him, and would not resume his ride, until Fr. Vaz had re-entered his house.

At that period, the state of the Catholic Church in Ceylon was very different from what it was when Fr. Joseph Vaz had
1709 landed in Jaffna. The greater part of those Catholics

who had been compelled by the protestants to apostatize, or had done so for worldly interests, had been again received into the church after doing an exemplary penance. Thirty thousand pagans had been converted. The Faith had taken such deep roots in the hearts of all, and the Church was so well organized, that the Catholics felt themselves strong enough to resist openly the penal laws enacted against them by their protestant masters, and to oppose resistance to their persecution. And all that was the work of Fr. Joseph Vaz and of the nine Indian priests who laboured under him.

1710

In the last month of 1709 Fr. Joseph Vaz was suffering from a kind of low fever, which subsided for a short time and then recurred with renewed force. Though very weak, he nevertheless took advantage of the intermittence of the fever, to visit the Missions as usual. He went even as far as Kottyar and was there, in January 1710, when he was taken very dangerously ill. He had no proper lodging, and there was no physician, so, as soon as he felt somewhat better, he resolved to return to Kandy. They placed him on a cart drawn by bullocks, and after a journey of eight days, they brought him to Kandy, where, owing to good medical attendance and careful nursing, the fever left him, and he began to regain strength. But his legs remained partly paralysed. So much work, and years of fatigue and hardships had at last broken his constitution.

Nevertheless, he did not cease to work. He could no longer go on distant excursions, but he was daily seen about the streets of

Kandy, dragging himself on painfully with the help of a stick. He thus visited the sick in their houses. Every morning sitting before his door, he gathered the children and was teaching them Catechism, and when his sufferings did not allow him even to do that, he spent the whole day in prayer. He called to Kandy Fr. James Gonzalves, and entrusted him with the care of the Christians.

Fr. Joseph Vaz languished thus to the 16th January 1711 when
1711 he died assisted by Fathers James Gonzalves and Ignatius d'Almeida.

Young King Kundesala was greatly affected by Fr. Joseph's death and ordered all Catholics of his Court to attend the funeral which was grand, for many Christians had come from Colombo and other parts of Ceylon. The remains of the great Missionary were buried in front of the high altar in the church he had built on the shore of the Bogambra lake.

Sometimes afterwards, the news spread that the Oratorian Fathers had carried his body to Goa. This distressed so much the King, that Fr. Gonzalves was obliged to open the tomb in presence of a few nobles of the Court, and show them that the body was still there.

The highest praises were bestowed on Fr. Joseph Vaz after his death, we will only mention the letter of King John of Portugal dated 11th April 1726 in which he calls him: The model of Missionaries, a great servant of God, and founder of a truly apostolic Mission.

The question of his beatification was raised by Dom Francis de Vasconcellos Bishop of Cochin to whose diocese Ceylon then belonged and the preliminary of the process had been made in Goa in 1737, but the disturbances that followed in Portugal by the coming to power of the infamous Marquis of Pombal arrested its progress.

The reader will perhaps be surprised that we have devoted so many pages to Fr. Joseph Vaz. History generally concerns itself with the doings of warriors, of those who have filled the world with their fame and their glory.

The mistake of many historians is that instead of writing the history of the nation, they write the history of its wars.

Now, we ask who is a greater hero, a general, who gains a victory at the cost of the tears of thousands of widows and orphans, of much despair and desolation, or a man like Fr. Joseph Vaz, who sacrificed 24 years of his life, in poverty, alone and abandoned in the midst of dangers, often tracked like a wild beast, to bring to a people the Faith of Christ and its natural sequel, civilisation.

Fr. Joseph Vaz was one of the grandest figures in the history of Ceylon, and its place in it is the same as that of St. Francis Xavier in the history of Southern India.

The protestants had destroyed Christianity in Ceylon; they had reduced to a heap of ruins the glorious work of the Portuguese. Fr. Joseph Vaz laid the foundations of a new edifice. He is rightly considered as the founder of the present Missions, not only for having revived the Faith of what Christians were left and converted many thousands of heathens, but also because he left after him a method and a tradition, and to this method and this tradition is due the present flourishing state of the Catholic Church in Ceylon.

## CHAPTER 8

# THE CHRISTIANS

Fr. Joseph Menezes succeeded Fr. Vaz as Superior of the Mission and Vicar-General of the Bishop of Cochin. He

1712 continued to reside at Putlam, where he was better protected from the intrigues of the protestants, and had the advantage of being farther from the royal Court. Young King Kundesala, had not the energy and the high intelligence of his father. Although he had much regard for the Fathers of the Oratory, and was favourable to his Catholic subjects, there was more danger, than was the case with his father, of his being influenced by their enemies.

It was therefore deemed more prudent to have the Missions directed from Putlam, the more so since now the larger number of Catholics were on Dutch territory, and could be more easily administered from Putlam than from Kandy.

Fr. James Gonzalves remained as parish priest at Kandy, and he was on the best terms with the King, who scarcely knew Fr. Menezes.

Whilst the Catholics were thus enjoying full liberty in the dominions of the King of Kandy, the persecution on the Dutch territory was increasing. No priest could remain there to minister to the numerous Christians, and they were exposed to the greatest dangers when visiting them, and every man who gave them shelter risked the penalty of death.

— „ Notwithstanding these disadvantages, writes Harward, „ Romish Missionaries from the Portuguese Settlements of Goa con- „ tinued their exertions. They succeeded in erecting a considerable „ number of churches, and in attaching to their communion thousands „ of devoted adherents. It is but justice to this class of native „ Christians to state that, in general, they are more detached from „ the customs of the pagan inhabitants, more regular in their „ attendance on the religious services of their communion and their „ general conduct more consistent with the moral precepts of „ Christianity, than any other religious body of any magnitude in the „ Island." —

Harward calls this ugly persecution a simple disadvantage.

1613 By: — „ any other religious body" — he means the native converts of the Dutch protestant ministers. Let us see what was their moral and religious state:

— „ All the time, says Gordon Comming, heathenism continued „ rampant, the Dutch themselves declaring, that multitudes of their „ nominal adherents (to protestantism) were incorrigible Buddhists, „ who regulated every act of life by the teaching of Astrologers, always „ calling in the aid of the devil-dancers rather than the *clergy*, wearing „ heathen charms, and making offerings to the idol-temples." —

This statement is corroborated by the testimony of the Rev. Palm, a protestant parson at Colombo, who gives to his *parishioners* the following rather curious testimony:

—„ When a child is born, they still consult the Astrologer;
„ when it is sick, they hang charms round its neck; and even after
„ baptism, they discontinue the use of its Christian name, and a
„ heathen name is given it as usual on the first occasion of its eating
„ rice; and when sick or in adversity, they send for the devil-dancers
„ in preference to their (protestant) *clergy*. When they marry, it
„ must be in the propitious hour; and when they die, their graves
„ are decorated with leaves of the tree sacred to Buddha, and
„ cocoanuts and rice piled around as food for the departed. They
„ make offering to the idols of Katragam, they bestow gifts on the
„ mendicants, servants of the temples and, in short, the highest
„ benediction they can pronounce on their friends is: may you
„ become a Buddha." —

This was the kind of Christianity which the protestants were building in Ceylon on the ruins of the Catholic church. And their ministers boasted of having converted to such Katragamo-Buddhistic protestantism 428,684 natives, which, at that time, must have been about one-third of the total population of the Island.

Meanwhile by the operosity and devotion of the Indian
1715 Oratorian Fathers, the number of Catholics was steadily increasing. The protestant ministers could not bear the sight of these Christians who did not worship Katragam and Buddha, who did not call astrologers and devil-dancers and did not bless their friends in the name of the Supreme Lord Buddha.

Their only means of opposing such *Romish* superstition lay in an increase of the persecution which now lasted since fifty-seven years:

On the 11 January 1715, a new law (placaat) was enacted forbidding Catholics to assemble in public, or even in private houses for common worship and prayer, under the penalty of a heavy fine for the first and second offence, and a heavier penalty left to the discretion of the magistrate if caught the third time.

Thus the protestant converts were left free to make offerings to the Hindu gods and to worship Buddha, whilst for the crime of praying to God, or reciting the rosary in common, the Catholics were visited with heavy penalties.

On the 8th August of the same year, another placaat forbade all Catholic priests to administer the Sacrament of Baptism, to their own people as well as to the heathens.

The end of this law was that the pagans might remain in their abject heathenism, rather than become Catholics. It is useless to say that the Oratorian Fathers disregarded this law and continued, as they did before, to convert the heathens.

A question which needs to be explained is, how did it happen that, notwithstanding all these penal laws and others yet much more stringent, which were enacted in the following years, we have no record of a Catholic priest being ever caught and imprisoned by the Dutch.

Of course one of the reasons was that the Catholics and the priests themselves, rendered prudent by the persecution, took all precautions for their safety, and not to fall into the hands of the protestants. But that alone is not sufficient to explain such a remarkable fact. The chief reason was this. The cruel persecution of the Catholics had not been originated by the Dutch Government, but by the protestant ministers.

These ministers of the word of God, as they called themselves, were at that time powerful in Holland and in Batavia, and through their influence there, they obtained orders to the Governors of Colombo to enact such penal laws. On the other hand, the Governors and the higher officials were much annoyed by the tyranny which these protestant ministers and their so-called consistory exercised over them, and, with the exception of a few, who had lost all feeling of humanity and of honor, they disapproved this persecution of peaceful law abiding people, and understood the danger of alienating from Government a well organized and influential section of their subjects, at a time, when the King of Kandy, allied with any foreign power who would attempt the conquest of Ceylon, was for the Dutch a permanent danger.

And therefore in obedience to orders received, they enacted the penal laws, taking at the same time good care that they remain a dead letter.

And that explains the fact, that we have no record of any priest imprisoned by the Dutch.

Men without faith, and practically without any religion, these Dutch Governors and official, did not mind much that the Catholics were forbidden to pray, and the priests tracked by their police from house to house and from village to village. The fines exacted from these Christians went to the treasury, and often to their own pockets, because there was much corruption among them, but there they drew the line, and the protestant ministers could not obtain from them more than that. And therefore as we said at the beginning of this period of our history, the English writers are to a certain degree unjust when they speak of the Dutch persecuting the Christians of Ceylon: It was in fact not a Dutch persecution, but rather a protestant persecution.

Fr. Joseph Menezes died in 1717, and Fr. James Gonzalves succeeded him as Vicar General and Superior of the
1717 Mission. He was one of the greatest Missionaries who had worked in Ceylon. He was a very learned man, well versed in Sanscrit and Pali litterature. He translated the Gospel into Singhalese and Tamil and wrote many useful books in these two languages.

Soon after having been appointed Superior, he had the census of the Catholics in Ceylon taken: There were at this time in the Island 70,000 Catholics, 15 larger churches and over 400 chapels. In the province of Jaffna alone the Catholics numbered 15,000.

Fr. Gonzalves himself converted many heathens. He loved the Singhalese villagers and made use of simple means which went straight to their heart.

Emmerson Tennent says of the converts made at that time by the Indian Oratorian Fathers:

— „ One fact is unquestionable, that the natives became speedily „ attached to their ceremonies and mode of worship, and have „ adhered to them with remarkable tenacity.

It is remarkable that whenever protestant writers acknowledge the fidelity of which the Catholics of Ceylon gave such eloquent proofs under such hard trials, they affect to ascribe it to their love of the ceremonies of the Catholic church, as if there were not such a thing as Faith. Faith alone could inspire simple and uneducated people with such heroism as they showed under persecution.

— „ It would appear, continues the same author, that obstacles „ to the extension of Christianity (he means of Katragamo-Buddhistic „ Christianity as described by the Rev. Palm) from the influence of „ idolatry were less apprehended than the difficulties now encountered „ from the rising ascendency of the Roman Catholics, whose number „ had actually multiplied under persecution. They had churches in „ every district from Jaffna to Colombo; and in 1734 they „ extended their operations to the southern province, and with such „ success, that the protestant *clergy* of Galle, distracted by the „ impracticability of their endeavours or apostasy of the natives, gave „ way before this accumulation of hostile influence. From 1745 „ the district was left for some years altogether without the service „ of a protestant minister." —

All the hope of the protestants was now placed in the persecution, by which they expected in the long run to
1733
crush the vitality of the Catholic Church. On the 25th March 1733, a new placaat was published renewing the ordinance of the 19th September 1658, which enacted the penalty of death against any Catholic who would have given shelter to a priest.

But the Catholic had grown too strong to be discouraged by such penal laws, and in answer to that placaat Fr. James Gonzalves sent forth Missionaries to the district of Galle, where the Catholic

Apostolate had not as yet been organized, with such result that the protestant ministers who, in this district, had on their registers, 55,159 adherents, found themselves without a flock, and after twelve years of desultory struggle with the progress of the Catholic Faith, they entirely abandoned the district. Those of their converts who meant seriously to be Christians became Catholic. The others, who had always worshipped Katragam and Buddha, ceased to call themselves protestants.

The King of Kandy kept always a hostile attitude towards the Dutch, but he carefully avoided any cause of conflict, in fact he endeavoured to avoid any kind of relation with them. Twice only during his reign we see him treating on more or less friendly terms with the Governor of Colombo: in 1707, when in order to oppose the progress of the Catholic Faith with the revival of Buddhism the Governor had proposed to the King to bring over from Burma qualified Punghees to reform the Bikshun in Ceylon. This manoeuvre of the protestants proved a complete failure, they got over the Punghees, but they proved incapable of infusing a new life into the decaying Buddhism, and only succeeded partly in exciting the Buddhists against the Christians.

Then again when in 1727 the Governor of Colombo sent Texel in embassy to the King of Kandy.

This embassy gave rise to a rather amusing incident: According to the etiquette of the Court of Kandy Texel had to wait one hour at the gate of the palace and another hour in the inner courtyard. The night was very cold. Finally they drew aside the first of the seven curtains which hid the majesty of the King, then the second and the third with an interval of ten minutes between each.

Between two of these curtains, there was a kind of tent made of precious silk, and so small that only one man could stand in it. Texel was invited to enter, and they made him understand that it was a special honor, never as yet granted to an ambassador. His suite remained outside and, whilst they were shivering in the cold after an exposure of nearly three hours, they saw that Texel seemed ill at ease, and noted that he was all covered with perspiration.

The Kandyan Chiefs seeing this were telling them: See how great is our King, and how your ambassador perspires of emotion, that he will soon find himself in his presence.

They had surrounded the small tent with burning coal-pans and the unfortunate Texel remained there broiling till at last they drew aside the next curtain.

Thus during the whole reign of King Kundesala the peace with the Dutch remained undisturbed. Once only there was danger of war.

Versluys, the Dutch Governor of Colombo, hoping to realise at one stroke a large fortune, attempted to make what would be called at present a corner in rice. The rice crops in Ceylon were not sufficient for the food of the population of the Island, so that great quantities had to be imported from India. The Governor instructed his agents to buy on his account all the cargoes of rice, which were shut up in his granaries. The local provision being exhausted, the Governor began to sell, but he had raised so the prices, that the villagers unable to afford to pay them were threatened with famine especially in the Kingdom of Kandy, where agriculture being neglected, they lived mostly on imported rice, and could not afford to pay the exhorbitant prices for which the Governor was selling.

Seeing his people threatened with starvation, King Kundesala took the advise of his Council, then dismissed them without having taken any clear decision. In the evening of the same day he sent for Fr. James Gonzalves, for whom he had a great regard and told him that he could not tolerate any more the dishonesty of the Dutch who were now even starving his people, that the majority of his Chiefs were of the opinion that the time was now ripe for declaring them war and expelling them from Ceylon and that he had resolved in consequence to send an embassy to Goa, to propose to the Portuguese an alliance and invite them to reconquer with his aid their ancient possessions in the Island.

Fr. James Gonzalves, who was himself a native of Goa, knew well that the Portuguese had lost the power they once had wielded in India, dissuaded strongly the King from embarking on such an enterprise, which would only increase the misery of his subjects, and pointed out, how little hope there was, in case of his declaring war to the Dutch, of obtaining any efficacious help from Goa.

— „Should you not rather desire this war, said the King, than dissuading me from it for, if we drive the Dutch out of the Island, your Christians would be free to worship God in peace." —

— „That is true, answered Fr. Gonzalves, but my duty, at this moment, is not to look for my own interests, but to give you a wise and prudent advice." —

The King struck by the Father's wisdom gave up the idea of war. He wanted to raise Fr. Gonzalves to the rank of Adigar, but the Father declined his offer. From that time the King always treated him as if he were one of the highest dignitaries of his Court which, naturally gave to the Father a great influence over the people.

From 1736 to 1740 the Dutch possessions in Ceylon were governed by Baron Van Imhoff, who was an able administrator, but of all Dutch Governors he was the most hostile to the Catholics, and during the four years he remained in office went always hand in hand with the protestant ministers.

**1736**

In the instruction which according to the Dutch custom he drew in 1740 for the use of his successor W. M. Bruininck, he insists on the necessity of using stringent measures to crush the progress of the Catholic Faith: In order to succeed in doing that, he says, the first condition would be to have in Ceylon abler and more competent protestant ministers, to oblige them to learn Singhalese and Tamil, and it would be desirable, he adds, that they abstain from publishing high sounding statistics of the number of their converts, when in reality the results they obtain render only religion despised, and its precepts turned into ridicule.

Then speaking of the Catholic Missionaries, he says, that they do a great harm to the Dutch East India Company in opposing to its interests, much united among themselves, active and zealous, and that in his opinion the Company would never prosper in Ceylon, until they are crushed altogether.

Van Imhoff, knowing that his successor Bruininck was an

honest and upright man, disguised thus his sectarian hatred under the cover of political considerations, but one would like to know how did he come to identify the interests of the Dutch East India Company with the maintaining of heathenism, or with the spreading in Ceylon of such kind of Christianity which consisted simply in inscribing on the registers large numbers of natives who had made a faint adhesion to the protestant creed, leaving them afterwards free to continue to worship Katragam and Buddha, and deal as much as they liked with Astrologers and devil-dancers.

Such system of Christianity, according to the very words of Van Imhoff himself, rendered religion despicable and turned protestantism into ridicule. In fact, the official statistics show us that out of more than half a million of natives who had been *enrolled into Christianity* that is whose names had been inscribed on the registers held by the protestant ministers, there were no more than 200 who were practically protestants. The others, as the protestant ministers themselves called them, were: sine Christo Christiani, Christians who knew nothing about Christ, and worshipped Katragam and Buddha.

It is clear that with such sentiments that animated Governor Van Imhoff the position of the Missionaries in the Dutch dominions became even more precarious than it had been before.

As said above, Van Imhoff went hand in hand with the protestant minister, and any priest who ventured to get out of the limits of the Kingdom of Kandy, to minister to the spiritual wants of the Christians under Dutch rule, were tracked by his police, so that even such secret visits of the Missionaries as had been practically tolerated under the former Governers had now becomė more difficult and risky. Colombo was naturally the most exposed place. The Oratorian Fathers were visiting the city from Putlam, but their visits could not be frequent, and were reduced to two or three days, for the town was full of protestant spies who watched the movements of the Christians. Now the Catholics of Colombo were in great number, these secret visits were insufficient, and many died without Sacraments and it was evident that they wanted a resident priest at Colombo.

Whilst the Superior, Fr. James Gonzalves was deliberating what to do in order to remedy this sad state of things, an
1739 Oratorian Father, a Brahmin from Goa, whose real name unhappily is not known, came to him and volunteered to settle in Colombo, at the risk of being taken by the protestants and put to death, or transported to Batavia to be kept there in prison for the rest of his life. The good of souls required it, he said, and the sacrifice must be made.

He entered Colombo disguised as a fisherman from Cochin, and remained in hiding in the house of a Singhalese fish-monger in Maliban street. He was known there under the name of Anthony Cochial, that is, Anthony from Cochin.

He thus succeeded in eluding the vigilance of Van Imhoff's police for more than a year. In the day-time he was selling fish in his host's shop, dressed as a native from the Malabar Coast, at night, in some secluded suburban house, he celebrated the holy Mass and administered the Sacraments to the faithful.

But at last he was betrayed, and had barely time to escape,

1740 before the Dutch soldiers who came to arrest him had surrounded the house.

He was running along the sea-shore towards Mutuwal where he knew the Christians would find the way to hid him, when he was stopped by a group of heathen fishermen. For several days they had been offering sacrifices to the devil to check the advance of the sea which was encroaching on the shore where they used to dry their nets.

Having recognized Fr. Anthony they seized him saying: — „ The Christians say that God grants you whatever you ask Him. If you obtain from your God that the sea does not undermine the shore in this place, we will protect you against the Dutch soldiers."— Whilst they were speaking, the soldiers who were hunting the Father arrived, and the officer in command, much amused by the priest's embarassment, began to laugh and said: — „ Yes, Father, do what they request of you, and we will leave you alone, and allow you to exercise your ministry as long as you like, but do what they request." —

Then, Fr. Anthony Cochial, inspired by God, opened his Mass box: he took from it the stole, put it on, planted the crucifix in the sand and knelt down in prayer. Whilst he was praying, the waves receded and left uncovered a sand bank of more than a hundred yards, which slowly rose, so that the sea could no more cover it. The officer and the soldiers were looking on in amazement, and then retired without daring to arrest the Father.

This event produced such an impression on the fishermen of Colombo, who are a strong and turbulent body, that the Dutch

Government did not dare to touch them, and Fr. Anthony Cochial was left in peace. This happened in 1740.

A few days after these events the term of office of Van Imhoff expired. His successor, Governor Bruininck, was a man of a different stamp. He could not bear the idea of hunting and persecuting poor and harmless people, only because they were Catholics, and he took advantage of the events just narrated to grant them considerable liberty,

He sent for Fr. Anthony, received him with great courtesy, and told him, that he ratified the promise given by the officer and that henceforth he would be free to exercise his ministry in Colombo. Moreover he gave him the ground thus miraculously gained from the sea, to build a chapel on it.

Next day, all the protestant ministers of the town came in a body to the Governor to object to this act of justice done to the Catholics, the first since eighty-four years, and threatened to accuse him to the Governor-General at Batavia; but Bruininck answered them, that the word given by a Dutch officer was sacred, and could not be broken.

Fr. Anthony Cochial built a chapel on the ground given to him by the Governor. The protestants in derision called it Cochikade, the shop of the Cochin man. He worked among the Christians of Colombo more or less unmolested to his death, and was buried in his modest chapel.

At present, St. Anthony's church, one of the most frequented of Colombo, stands on the spot of the ancient chapel, and all that quarter of the town is called Cochikade.

It was thus that Catholic worship was tolerated in Colombo for the first time since 1656, and the holy Mass celebrated again in public after eighty-four years.

The persecution however continued: The protestant ministers appealed to Batavia, and the Governor of Colombo was again obliged to renew the law which enacted the penalty of death to all who gave shelter to a Catholic priest, first by the placaat of the 10th August 1743, and then for the fourth time on the 25 January 1745. But the power of the protestant ministers was declining, and these laws remained a dead letter. The men had changed and the times were changing. Protestantism in Europe had lost its bitter, intolerant character and the Dutch officials who now governed Ceylon, did not mean to be ruled by the protestant consistories of Colombo and Batavia.

Nevertheless, the position of the Missionaries remained always precarious, and their visiting the Christians full of difficulties.

Fr. James Gonzalves died at Bolawatte in 1742 and was buried in the church of that place. Fr. Martin Xavier succeeded him as Vicar General and Superior of all the Missions of Ceylon.

## CHAPTER 9

# THE AWAKING OF THE CATHOLICS

King Kundesala died in 1739 without male issue, and with him
1740 ended the Singhalese dynasty of the Kings of Kandy.

The Adigars, bribed, they say, by the Queen Widow, elected King her brother Sri Wijaya Raja, who belonged to the Tamil dynasty of the Nayaka Kings of Madura, placing thus on the throne a foreign dynasty which had neither national nor historical ties with the Kandyans, and which reigned over the Kingdom or rather tyrannised it for 75 years.

This inconsiderate election made by the Adigars augured no good for the Christians, for Madura had always been one of the strongholds of heathenism in India, and the royal family was deeply attached to the Hindu idolatry.

In fact, the party hostile to the Catholics, which had been held
1743 in check by the energy of the two last Kings, assumed now the upper hand and acquired great influence at the new King's Court. Moved by their intrigues Sri Wijaya Raja proscribed the Catholic worship in the whole of his Kingdom, had the churches in Kandy, Putlam and Chilaw demolished and the Missionaries expelled.

It was a great blow to the Catholic Church in the Kingdom of

Kandy, which had been so well organized by Fr. Joseph Vaz and by his successors so great indeed, that a century passed before it could rise again from its ruin.

Sri Wijaya Raja, surnamed Hanguranketta, died in 1747. His brother Kirti Sri Raja Singha who succeeded him, was

1747 yet more hostile to the Christians. He had all Catholics expelled from Kandy, and from the villages of Wavodda and Kalugalla where they were numerous. But soon after their expulsion famine and plague having visited the Kingdom, the Kandyans considered it as a punishment inflicted for the King's cruelty towards the Catholics, and Kirti Sri Raja Singha, frightened by the attitude of the people, allowed the Catholics to settle at Wahacotta, a distant village in the midst of the forests, allowed them to build there a chapel and gave them all the images and statues which he had taken from Fr. Joseph Vaz's church at Kandy, but he would not allow a priest to stay there.

Such was the origin of the present Catholic settlement at Wahacotta.

It was a critical time for the Catholic church in Ceylon; Expelled from the Kingdom of Kandy, tracked and hunted in the Dutch dominions, no corner remained in the Island where the Missionaries could live in peace, and it seemed that, under the circumstances, the Catholic Church could no longer exist in Ceylon.

But the Catholics on Dutch territory, hardened by the persecution, numerous and well organized, had now grown strong enough to defy their persecutors and to claim openly their rights which the protestants had been trampling under their feet for over a century.

The Catholics of Negombo and of the neighbourhood opened the campaign by presenting a petition to the Governor in which they said:

1750

— „We are tired of being persecuted and can endure no longer the present state of things.

Firmly attached to the Catholic Faith to which our fathers had been converted two centuries ago, you force us by violence and severe penalties to send our children to protestant schools, where they are taught doctrines which we condemn, so that we must bear with disgust to hear our own children, when they return from school, repeat in our presence these perverse doctrines. You force us to have our children baptized by protestant ministers. Some submit to it for fear of your penal laws, but only after the child has already been baptized by a Catholic priest. Some through fear of your unjust laws go to your protestant worship, but, at the bottom of their heart they remain Catholics. You force us to abjure our Faith, but no forced abjuration can root out from our heart this Faith to which we remain invincibly attached. Such state of things disturbs our conscience, and endangers our salvation, and we will not endure it any longer.“—

This petition was considered as a dangerous awakening of the Singhalese Catholics, and the Governor put it before his Council.

After a long deliberation, not being able to agree regarding the steps to be taken, they determined to ask the opinion of the protestant consistory, whom, according to orders received from Batavia, they were bound to consult in all religious matters.

The consistory replied that the Catholics of Negombo should be punished with the greatest severity for their audacity, that all the penal laws made till then against the Catholics should be again renewed and most strictly enforced, and a new law made, that no public office would ever be given to one who has not made a profession of protestant belief.

The Governor and council however did not view the matter in this light. They were tired of this persecution, which could have no other result than that of alienating from the Dutch government a large and influential section of the population of the Island. They were disgusted with the tyranny exercised by the protestant ministers, supported from Batavia, and to which the government of Ceylon had been forced to submit up to the present.

They therefore answered the consistory, that, in their reply they have exceeded the limits of their attributions; that they had no right to interfere with matters belonging to the civil power; that government would certainly be glad to give employments to protestants alone, if there were competent men among them, but that it had become practically impossible, since the number of protestant natives has diminished to such an extent that they could no more select among them candidates for public offices.

And in fact, protestantism was at that time in full decadence:

— „ In 1730, writes Emmerson Tennent, there had been thirteen „ ministers employed in garrison duty and the superintendence of „ native instruction, and in 1747 there were but five employed in „ Ceylon and of these, but one, who understood the language of the „ natives.

„ From this time forward, the Dutch sought and received „ assistance from the Danish *mission* at Tranquebar, who supplied „ them with types and with printers, and educated young men for the „ ministry in Ceylon, and sent repeatedly *clergy* from their own „ establishments to assist the declining labours of the Dutch." —

Having thus rebuked the consistory, the Governor's Council decided not to molest the Christians of Negombo, but ignoring their petition leave it unanswered.

The Catholics of Ceylon however were now determined to vindicate with energy their rights to religious liberty.

A short time after the incident of Negombo, the Christians of Kalutara erected a chapel and began to celebrate publicly their feasts. They had a solemn procession through the streets of the town. The principal Catholics were then arrested and condemned to be exiled to Tuticorin.

Notwithstanding that, the Christians of Kalutara continued to celebrate their feasts publicly and with pomp, other villages followed their example, and when the protestants wanted to hinder them, they took to arms in defence of their rights and in the scuffles and more serious encounters the Catholics, numerous as they were, had always the upper hand.

This state of things went on for ten years, finally the
1760 government authorities gave up the struggle and let the Catholics celebrate publicly the divine worship.

Thus the Catholics of Ceylon, by their energy and good organization, intimidated their persecutors, and fought out for themselves the right of worshipping God openly and in public.

The protestant ministers wrote continually to Batavia denouncing the Governor and procuring orders for the framing of new penal laws: The placaat of 31 July 1748 forbade the celebration of Holy Mass on Dutch territory. Another of the same date forbade all Dutch subjects to have whatever to do with a Catholic priest, and forbade the Catholics to assemble under any pretext in public or in private.

The Catholics however took no notice of these new penal laws, which they knew their persecutors had no more power to enforce, and the persecution practically ceased.

The manifesto of Negombo had shown the protestants the strength of the Catholics, and ten years later, since 1762, that is for 26 years before the English conquest, they enjoyed under the Dutch rule of a liberty not recognized by law, it is true, but practically real, which they had fought out for themselves.

In the meantime, protestantism, which since the beginning of the Dutch rule had been but a fictitious edifice, declined rapidly in Ceylon.

To say that protestantism was declining does not express correctly the situation, for really it had never existed except on the registers of the Dutch ministers, who inscribed in them about half a million natives and in the beginning when they felt themselves yet strong, they forced them to attend to their preaching which they generally did in Dutch, a language which their so-called converts did not understand. But later, when they could no longer force them to attend to their worship, they troubled themselves little if these converts were going to heathen temples to offer sacrifices to their gods. What they wanted was to have their names inscribed on their registers to show these registers at Batavia and at Amsterdam.

If at that epoch we have more documents which allow us to see what protestantism was in reality in Ceylon, it is because the ministers being now discouraged, were less reticent, and bitterly complained about their failure.

As a matter of fact, during the whole period of the Dutch domination the protestants made no serious effort to convert the pagans. Their sole aim was to destroy the Catholic Religion and root it out in Ceylon. This they did not succeed in doing, but they destroyed every vestige of civilisation, which had made such rapid progress under the Portuguese rule, and threw back the natives of Ceylon into barbarity.

— „ The causes of this failure, writes Emmerson Tennent, are „ neither few nor obscure. Irrespective of the unsubdued influence „ of idolatry and of Caste, the doctrines of (protestant) Christianity „ were too feebly developed and too superficially inculcated to make „ any lasting impression on the reluctant and apathetic minds of the „ natives of Ceylon.

„ The Dutch ministers employed in its dissemination failed to

„ qualify themselves for the task by mastering in the first instance „ the vernacular tongues of the Island. Out of a list of 97 *clergymen* „ in Ceylon between 1642 and 1725 given by Valentyn, only 8 were „ qualified to preach in the native languages, four in Tamil and four „ in Singhalese. And the consistory in vain insisted on the inefficacy „ of instruction conveyed by the cold and unsatisfactory medium of „ interpreters.

„ In addition to this, their number were too few to render „ effectual aid to the multitude of their hearers and, in 1722 when the „ returns showed nearly half a million of *nominal Christians*, there „ were but fourteen *clergymen* in all Ceylon.

„ Notwithstanding the clear perception which the Dutch appear „ to have had of the salutary influence of elementary and moral „ instruction in preparing the mind for rejecting the absurdities of „ heathenism and embracing the pure precepts of Christianity, the „ amount of education which they communicated in their schools was „ infinitesimaly small. It seldom went beyond teaching their pupils „ to read and to write in the language of their district, and even this „ was discouraged by the supreme authorities at Batavia, who in „ communicating with the (protestant) *Missionaries* in Ceylon „ expressed strongly their opinion that: — Reading and writing are „ things not so absolutely necessary for the edification of these *poor* „ *wretches*, as teaching them the fundamentals of religion, which are „ contained in a very few points: and to pretend to propagate „ Christianity by reading and writing, would be both tedious and „ chargeable to the Netherland's East India Company. —

„ Under a system so superficial and unefficient, the labour

„ actually bestowed was productive of no permanent fruits: It was „ but seed sown on stony ground, it was scorched by the sun and, „ because it had no root, it soon withered away.

„ Again the system of political bribery, adopted by the Dutch „ to encourage *conversions* among the Singhalese was eminently „ calculated to create doubts and contempt in the naturally suspicious „ minds of the natives; whilst they could not fail to conclude, that „ there must be something defective or unreal in a religion which „ required coercion and persecution to enforce its adoption.

„ Where the former system was apparently successful, it „ produced in reality but an organized hypocrisy, and when „ persecution ensued, its recoil and reaction were destructive of the „ object for the furtherance of which it had been unwisely resorted „ to. And lastly the imprudence with which outward professors „ were indiscriminately welcomed as genuine converts to Christianity „ involved the certainty of future disconfiture. The example of „ apostasy under similar circumstances, is more dangerous in „ proportion than the encouragement wrought by adhesion; and „ thus, the more widely the field was uncautiously expanded, the „ more certain became the danger, and the more frequent the „ occurrence of such untoward events.

„ Towards the close of their career, the Dutch *clergy* had the „ painful experience of this pernicious result, and their lamentations „ became more frequent over the relapses of their *converts* first in *the* „ *errors of popery* and finally into the darkness of heathenism. At „ length in apparent despondency and in painful anticipation of „ defeat, instead of altering the system, on which they had discovered,

„ that they could no longer rely, they merely contracted their „ *missionary* operations to the narrowest possible limits; cast upon „ others the labour, in which they were no longer hopeful of success; „ and at the final close of their ministrations, the *clergy* of the church „ of Holland, left behind a superstruction of *Christianity*, prodigious „ in its outward dimensions, but so internally unsound, as to be „ distrusted even by those, who had been instrumental in its erection, „ and so unsubstantial, that it has long since disappeared almost from „ the memory of the natives of Ceylon." —

This citation is borrowed from an author who cannot be accused of partiality in this matter. Emmerson Tennent was a protestant, and his hostility to the Catholic Faith appears on every page.

Let us remember all the care that the Portuguese bestowed on the education of the natives of Ceylon; the numerous schools and the grand colleges erected by the Catholic Clergy and endowed by the Portuguese Government, which raised civilisation to such a high standard that the Singhalese were considered by the Portuguese as their equals; we see them in the highest positions in the civil service and Singhalese Generals commanding European troops.

But these were *the dark ages of the errors of popery*. The enlightened protestants who had conquered Ceylon, considered that even teaching them how to write and to read, was too much for these *poor wretches*.

— „ The latest records of the Dutch consistory, continues

„ Emmerson Tennent, contain an expression of their conviction, that „ even the *converts* of Jaffna were but Laodiceans at heart, and the „ Classis of Walchern, but a few years before, expressed their fear „ from the small number of communicants in proportion of the „ crowd of Singhalese who had been baptized, that their profession was „ unsound and the *converts* themselves: *Sine Christo Christiani.*"—

And it was certainly not an exaggeration to say, that all these protestant *converts* were in reality: *Sine Christo Christiani,* as is clearly demonstrated by the statistics given by a contemporary protestant parson the Rev. Palm:

„ In 1760, he says, of 182,226 natives *enrolled as Christians* „ in Jaffna but 64 were members of the Church; of 9,820 at Manaar, „ only 5 were communicants. And in the same year at Galle and „ Matara, there were 36 members out of 89,000 who had been „ baptized." —

It would seem that, about this period the Dutch East India Company began to perceive, that it was not the best of systems, to send to their distant Colonies the refuses of the population of the mother country, as they used to do up to that time. They therefore commenced to send there honest enlightened men, such as the last four Governors of Colombo.

As a matter of fact, Ceylon at that period was far from realising the expectation of the Dutch Company. Commerce was on the decline, profits had diminished; agriculture and plantations were in a miserable condition. The Governors and officials only thought of enriching themselves: they oppressed the people, filled their own purses, whilst the treasury of the Company remained empty.

Finally the oppression of the people under Governor Schreuder reached such a point, that the Singhalese of the West Coast rebelled and took up arms against the Dutch, ravaged the plantations and massacred a great number of Dutchmen.

The King of Kandy, Kirti Sri Raja Singha, seeing the confusion that reigned at Colombo, thought the moment favourable
1761 to take away from the Dutch a few districts and perhaps even, if the rebellion took greater proportions, driving them out from Ceylon. He came in help to the rebels and invaded the maritime provinces. The Dutch defended them weakly, yet the Kandyans could not do much against their better drilled troops. It was therefore to be foreseen that so long as the Dutch would content themselves of opposing to the Kandyans who were ravaging their provinces a simply defensive warfare, the war would last a long time.

But just at that moment, when the Dutch rule in Ceylon seemed to be at its lowest ebb, Baron Van Eck, a very able man,
1763 was appointed Governor. Seeing the state of affairs he immediately understood that it would be preferable to transfer the war on the enemy's territory and if possible end it with a bold stroke.

He invaded the Kingdom of Kandy at the head of 8,000 men, marched on the capital and entered it without a stroke. The King had fled.

Now, as we have seen above, Kirti Sri Raja Sihgha was a prince of the Tamil royal family of Madura. The Kandyans disliked the foreign dynasty whom the Adigars had placed on the throne after

Kundesala's death. As soon as Baron Van Eck had become master of Kandy, the Dessawes came to him with the proposal, that they would deliver up to him the person of the King, on condition that the Dutch recognize each of them as sovereign of the province of which they were now Governors.

Baron Van Eck hesitated on the course to be adopted, in the meantime he experienced the truth of what had become proverbial among the Portuguese, that is: that it was easy to take Kandy, but very difficult to keep it.

The Dutch troops continually harassed by the Kandyans, who intercepted all their convoys of food and ammunition,
1764 suffered much from the climate.

At that time, Kandy, surrounded with forests which covered all the surrounding hills, was considered as the most unhealthy place in Ceylon. The Dutch troops were decimated with fever, and the Governor's death demoralized them completely. They evacuated the capital and beat a hasty retreat. They were pursued by the Kandyans who defeated them in a battle, took 400 prisoners whom they brought to Sitawacca where they were all beheaded. Of the 8,000 men whom Van Eck had taken on his expedition, only a small number reached Colombo.

Meanwhile the English already masters of a part of India coveted the possession of Ceylon. The hostilities between the Dutch and the King of Kandy, and the disaster of Van Eck's expedition, seemed to the English Governor of Madras, Robert Palk, a favourable opportunity to act now towards the Dutch in Ceylon in the same manner as more than a century ago the Dutch had acted towards the Portuguese.

He therefore hastened to send to Kandy an Agent, one named Pybus to compliment King Kirti Sri Raja Singha on his victory over the Dutch, and to propose him an alliance. We have few details on this first English embassy to Kandy. Either for want of tact on the part of Pybus, or for some other reason, it seems to have been a failure: — „The embassy, writes Forbes, not only failed to produce „any satisfactory results, but it is known to have left no favourable „impression of British power and policy in the mind of the „Kandyans." —

Meanwhile Governor Falk Van Eck's successor arrived at Colombo. He was a man of great ability and a good and
1765 just ruler. The first step of the English to enter into an alliance with the King of Kandy caused him anxiety. He saw at once that he must at all cost raise the prestige of the Dutch in the eyes of the natives and consequently not allow the Kandyans to peacefully enjoy their easy victory. He began therefore to make preparations for war.

The Catholics, having regained their religious liberty, by their energy and good organisation, took now every occasion for affirming their legitimate rights.

Fr. Gabriel Pacheco was at that time Superior of the Mission. He was a zealous Missionary and a scholar. We have of him a good catechism and a life of Fr. Joseph Vaz in Tamil.

It was now 19 years since the persecution had broken out at Kandy, and since that time, the Catholics, who, in spite of the King's decree of expulsion had by and by returned to their homes, had never seen a priest and had remained deprived of all religious aid. Fr. Gabriel Pacheco laid the state of affairs before the Governor, and asked him if it would not be possible that the Missionary should follow his proposed expedition to Kandy. Falk not only agreed to this demand, but invited two Oratorian Fathers to join his staff.

Falk took Kandy, but more prudent than his predecessor he did not remain there. He contented himself with dictating

1766 to the King a treaty of peace, which the King hastened to accept, for he feared that the disaffection of the Kandyan Chiefs which manifested itself more and more might cost him his Crown.

The treaty dated 17th February 1766 gave up to the Dutch the towns of Putlam and of Chilaw, the pearl fisheries and assured them the absolute monopoly of Cinnamon and other products of the Island. The King further obliged himself not to enter into an alliance with any foreign power nor to conclude any treaty without the sanction or otherwise than through the medium of the Dutch government. The treaty then concludes that in return for all these favours so graciously granted to them, the Dutch, the humble subjects of his Majesty the Emperor of Ceylon, bind themselves to pay him an annual tribute in salt, and send every year an ambassador to Kandy.

This certainly flattered the vanity of the King of Kandy, but on the other hand Governor Falk considered the treaty more profitable to the Dutch, than would have been the conquest of the Kingdom of Kandy, as the maintaining of the conquest would have costed them enormously, whilst now this Kingdom cut off from the sea, and surrounded on all sides by Dutch possessions, could no longer export their products, and the Kandyans had no other chance left, than that of selling them to the Dutch.

And certainly, this treaty would have been very profitable to the Dutch East India Company if they had the power to make it observed, a thing which was very doubtful, and meanwhile the invasion of the Kandyans and the two expeditions of Van Eck and of Falk had costed the Company ten millions florins.

After peace had been restored, Falk seriously occupied himself with organizing the Colony, fostering agriculture and doing his best to improve the condition of the people, which oppressed for more than a century, had fallen into a miserable state.

Falk was an able and well intentioned man, but unhappily he had come too late to raise the government from the state of corruption and preserve it from an imminent catastrophe.

Under the Government of such men as Van Eck and Falk, there
1767 was no longer question of persecuting the Catholics. They were too noble minded to tolerate such a thing. The Catholics moreover had become very strong, and were too well aware of their strength to submit to persecution, and the Dutch now understood how dangerous it would be to alienate such a large and

well organized section of the population of the Island, when the King of Kandy was their enemy and the English were becoming more and more powerful in India.

The Oratorian Fathers exercised freely and openly their sacred ministry on the Dutch territory. They were established at Colombo and in all the principal places.

This religious liberty which the Catholics now enjoyed,
1776 exasperated the protestant consistory and the few protestant ministers who still remained in Ceylon. Through their intrigues, they forced Governor Falk to proclaim two new placaats which were sent to him ready made from Batavia. They were dated 19th and 24th December 1776. All marriages celebrated before a Catholic priest were declared null and void, Catholics were forbidden to have their own cemeteries and had to bury their dead in protestant burial grounds, and pay to the protestant ministers exhorbitant taxes. No Catholic could hold any public office.

Imagine the anomaly: Governor Falk living on the best terms with the Oratorian Fathers, and publishing against them such decrees. He published them, because he must, but it was well understood that they would never be executed.

The greatest confusion reigned in the protestant camp. Christopher Wolf a German adventurer who had taken service with the Dutch Government, who then resided at Jaffna and himself a protestant writes in his memoirs:

— „ And what is still worse, is that the inhabitants cannot bring

„ up their slaves in the Christian Religion because in that case they „ must necessarily be declared free, for as slaves they are not allowed „ to be baptized nor to partake the Lord's Supper. I for my part „ had eight slaves about my person, all of whom I was absolutely „ resolved to have baptized, but as the Dutch minister, agreeably to „ his instructions, did not dare to undertake to do it, on pain of being „ discharged from his office, I had them baptized by a Catholic „ Missionary." —

In order to be able to boast, that in the Dutch dominions there were no Christian slaves, it was forbidden to baptize them, and the protestant ministers, fearing to lose their pay, refused baptism to the slaves who asked to become Christians. As the Catholic Missionaries did not stop at such considerations, they baptized all the slaves whom they found well disposed.

Thus the protestant consistory understood that their prohibition of baptizing the slaves in order to be able to boast that there were no protestant slaves in Ceylon, helped only the propagation of the Catholic Faith, for many protestant masters to whom it was repugnant to force their slaves to remain heathens, had them baptized by Catholic priests.

Seeing that, the protestant consistory changed their tactics. They allowed the slaves to be baptized but under the condition that those baptized by the protestant ministers would by the very fact become free; those on the contrary who would have received baptism at the hands of a Catholic priest, would remain slaves for ever, without any hope of ever regaining their freedom.

But the result was just the contrary of what they had expected. They did not consider the masters, who anxious to keep their slaves, wanted them all to become Catholics, had them instructed and baptized by the Oratorian Fathers and were eager to send them to Church in order to show in public that they were Catholics and consequently could not be liberated.

Kirti Sri Raja Singha the King of Kandy died in 1782. He was
1782 a handsome, active, intelligent prince and a man of great strength. It was his passion to tame fiery horses, and this passion was the cause of his death. He was thrown down from a restive horse, which had been given to him by Governor Falk, and a few months later died from the effects of his fall.

He was succeeded by his younger brother Rajadi Raja Singha, a lazy voluptuous man, a good poet, they say, but a rather bad ruler.

## CHAPTER 10

# THE ENGLISH

The English meanwhile were proceeding with the conquest of India, and were already strongly established in the great
1782 peninsula.

What the Dutch had been to the Portuguese one hundred and fifty years ago, the English had now become to the Dutch. They threatened their colonial empire.

The English Governors of Madras understood well the strategical value of Ceylon for any European power who would aspire to the domination over India and the adjacent seas The harbour of Trincomalee had been lately fortified, was used as a base for the Dutch fleet, and since the English had become masters of the fortress of Nagapatam, the Governor of Madras Lord Macartney had determined to attempt the conquest of Ceylon.

On the 2nd February 1782, he despatched from Nagapatam a squadron commanded by Sir Edward Hughes, with a strong company of infantry under Sir Hector Munro to Trincomalee, where they landed two days later without the slightest opposition, and in the same night, whilst the Dutch commander was engaged in writing down the conditions of a capitulation which he intended to demand next morning to Munro, a company of Marines entered the city without striking a blow. The Ostenburg redoubt made a semblance of resistance but finally surrendered.

Lord Macartney appointed an able and prudent officer in command of Trincomalee, and gave instructions to try to conciliate the people of the neighbourhood, and make them appreciate the benefit of British rule.

At the same time, remembering how much the alliance with the King of Kandy had facilitated to the Dutch the conquest of Ceylon, he resolved to send a brilliant embassy to Kandy to conclude an alliance with King Rajadi Raja Singha, and entrusted this delicate mission to Mr. Boyd.

Boyd left Trincomalee with a large retinue. All along the route they were maintained at the expense of the King of Kandy, or to be more correct at the expense of the local people, for the villagers were ordered to supply all necessary provisions, and were forbidden to accept payment from the English for the supplies. That was called in Kandy, to travel at the King's expenses, and as the villagers were very poor, it often happened that the embassy run short of provisions.

Boyd stopped at Gonoor, a few miles from Kandy where lodgings had been prepared for him. On the day fixed for the audience a Dessawe came to fetch him and Boyd was struck by his courteous and dignified manners.

In front of the palace, there was a display of troops and fifty elephants ranged in semi-circle. After having traversed several interior courts, Boyd was taken to the audience hall. The

King was seated on a raised throne in a kind of alcove. He was a handsome man, of about 37 years of age, with very dark, intelligent features. Boyd bent his knees before him, whilst his suite prostrated on the ground.

Boyd remained a few weeks in Kandy, but the negotiations did not advance, and the only result of the mission was an exchange of courtesies and mutual protestations of friendship. It seems that the King had been informed of the turn the events had taken. In fact when Boyd on his return approached Trincomalee, he was greatly surprised to see the French flag flying over the ramparts.

It happened thus: Shortly after the capture of Trincomalee, Sir Edward Hughes had to return to Madras, as his ships wanted badly repair. The Governor sent 200 soldiers to reinforce the garrison, but they returned to Madras having found the bay of Kottyar blocked by a French squadron commanded by Admiral de Suffrein. In fact, they nearly were captured.

Sir Edward Hughes, hastened to the rescue, with all his available ships, but approaching Trincomalee he saw the French flag flying on the fort and was met and defeated by a French fleet of thirty men-of-war.

The French kept Trincomalee for some months and then, handed it over to the Dutch.

After these events, the English left the Dutch for thirteen years in peaceful possession of Ceylon.

In 1789 Van der Graaf was appointed Governor of Colombo.

1789 He was an able and upright man, but he remained too short a time in office to be able to improve the situation of the Dutch in Ceylon.

The Catholic Missions were progressing in peace under Van der Graaf's government. Fr Gabriel Pacheco died in 1790,
1790 and his successors Fathers Michael d'Albuquerque and Joseph Vaz were left unhindered in the fulfilment of their duties as Superiors of the Mission. Van der Graaf was in no way hostile to the Catholic Missionaries. The well known author and Missionary in Malabar, the Carmelite Father Paulinus of St. Bartholomew, was his guest, at government house, during his stay at Colombo in 1789.

Van Anglebeck was Van der Graaf's successor and the last
1792 Dutch Governor of Ceylon.

The conquest of Ceylon had been definitively decided in London. Lord Hobart Governor of Madras organized
1795 an expedition under the command of Colonel James Stewart, who landed at Trincomalee on the 1st August 1795, and laid siege to the town. It was an uneventful siege and after three weeks the garrison surrendered.

After resting his men, Colonel Stewart marched on Jaffna. The Dutch Commander surrendered the place without fight. On the 5th November the English occupied Calpentyn.

The King of Kandy Rajadi Raja Singha, who up to the present had repulsed all the advances made to him by the English, under the pretext that he would treat with the King of England but not with the Governor of Madras, seeing now how easily the English had already conquered nearly one half of the Dutch territory in Ceylon, sent one of his Adigars on an embassy to Madras to conclude a treaty with the Governor.

A question of etiquette nearly upset the whole thing. The Kandyan ambassador demanded that the Governor Lord Hobart should prostrate himself on the ground, whilst he would hold the King's letter raised over his head, and insisted that it was an essential ceremony due to the greatness of his King, and one that could not be dispensed with.

The Governor informed the Adigar that he greatly esteemed the King, and did not wish to be wanting in respect to him in any way, but that such prostrations were not according to English custom, nor to English Court etiquette.

The Adigar was adamant, and answered that he would bring back the letter to the King, without delivering it to the Governor, rather than hand it over without prostration.

Then Lord Hobart made a proposal: If a prostration was essential, he said, since it was contrary to English custom, and required by that of the Kandyans, why should not he hold the letter raised high above his head, and the Adigar prostrate before it?

The Kandyan envoy found the argument logical, and the King's letter was handed over with due ceremony.

But it was too evident that the English did not require the Kandyan alliance. The Adigar had not yet left Madras,
1796 when, in February 1796 Colonel Stewart marched on

Negombo. As the British approached the town, they saw the white flag fluttering on the ramparts. Both the city and the fort surrendered.

We come now to the final act of the history of the Dutch in Ceylon, the surrender of Colombo. In relating this event we will follow as much as possible Captain Percival's narrative, a British officer who took part in the campaign and who relates it as an eye-witness.

After the capture of Negombo, Stewart who had been raised to the rank of a General, marched on Colombo with three regiments of British troops, three battalions of sepoys, and a company of Bengal artillery. The route he had to traverse, boarded on both sides by an impenetrable jungle, and interrupted by many rivers presented a formidable obstacle to the march of an army, which the enemy could, so to say, annihilate without even being seen. Hence naturally, each moment the English expected some ambuscade. Great therefore was their surprise, when they were permitted to pass through this difficult country without the least opposition.

A further surprise was in stock for the English. They had come to the Kelani river, which formed on that side a natural defence of Colombo. The river to whose shores the town extends today, was at this time four miles distant from the ramparts of the town. It was defended by the fort of Gran-Pass, under whose batteries it was almost impossible for an enemy's army to cross it. General Stewart halted before this obstacle, and commenced to make the preparations necessary to surmount the difficult enterprise of crossing the river under the enemy s fire, sure as he was, that such passage would be hotly contested. But two days later he learned that the Dutch had evacuated Gran-Pass fort and thrown the guns into the river.

General Stewart thought first that it was some sort of stratagem, a manoeuvre intended for drawing him into a trap. Nevertheless, having well assured himself that the enemy had actually retired, and that the coast was clear, he ordered his troops to cross the river, partly on rafts and partly in boats provided by some British men-of-war who had cast anchor at its mouth.

The English then encamped on the opposite shore in a cocoanut plantation. The position was good, for their left flank was protected by a thick jungle, their right flank and their rear by the river, when they were suddenly attacked by a corps of Malay soldiers commanded by Colnel Raymond, a Frenchman in the Dutch service. After a rather hot fight, the English gained the day. Raymond was mortally wounded and the Malays retired.

The road to Colombo being now open, General Stewart marched on that city in which the Dutch seemed to have concentrated all their forces. The town was well fortified and could sustain a long siege, but when the English approached, they saw the white flag floating on the ramparts, and the capitulation was signed on the 16th February 1796, by which the Dutch surrendered not only Colombo, but also Kalutara, Galle, Matara and all their remaining territory in the south of the Island. The English were now masters of Ceylon with the exception of the Kingdom of Kandy.

Thus ended the Dutch rule of Ceylon which had weighted so

heavily on the Singhalese and the Tamil islanders for one hundred and forty years.

After having related the campaign, in which he had taken an active part, Captain Percival continues:

—„To examine the causes which led to this unexpected „conduct, may be of use to our own nation and the commanders „of our garrisons abroad.

„Previous to the British troops appearance before Colombo, its „garrison had been in some measure weakened by the loss of the „Swiss regiment of Meuron which, for a long time had composed „part of it. This regiment upon the terms of its agreement with „the Dutch having expired a few months before General Stewart „was sent against Ceylon, had transferred its services to our „Government, and other troops had not hitherto been procured from „Holland or Batavia to replace it at Colombo. The strength of the „garrison was by these means impaired; but the want of number „was not its principal defect, as upon marching out after the „surrender, it was found to consist of two battalions of Dutch troops, „the French regiment Wuertemberg, besides native troops, forming „in all a number fully equal to the force sent against it.

„The dissensions among both the civil and military officers of „the garrison was a cause which more powerfully hastened its „surrender. Those principles which have produced so many „convulsions and atrocities in Europe, had also penetrated into this „Colony. The Governor M. Van Anglebeck was a very respectable „old officer of moderate principles and mild disposition. Many of

„ those under him were however violent republicans of the Jacobin „ party; they declared against the Governor as a man of weak mind, „ and wished to place in the Government his son whom they had „ gained over to their own principles. The violence of this party „ had gone to an alarming height; they had already begun to „ denounce their opponents, and several respectable gentlemen „ would, in all probability have fallen victims of their fury, had not „ the sudden arrival of the English at this critical moment rescued „ them from impending destruction.

„ The state of discipline in the garrison had also fallen into a „ shameful disorder. Drunkenness and mutiny were carried to the „ greatest height. The Governor had frequently declared, at the „ tables of our officers, that he was in constant danger of his life from „ their mutinous conduct. He had resolved to defend the place to „ the last, but such was the state of insubordination which prevailed, „ that he could not, by any means, induce the Dutch troops and in „ particular the officers to march against the enemy. Personal „ safety, an object scarcely ever attended by our troops, either by „ sea or land, seemed in them to overpower every sense of duty and „ honor. A few of them went to accompany the Malay troops on „ the expedition I have already mentioned; but scarcely had they „ reached the gates of the Black town, when their courage evaporated „ and they left the Malays to their fate. Not above one or two „ European officers met in that action besides the brave Colonel „ Raymond, who was ashamed of being connected with such „ poltroons, and would have brought their conduct to public censure, „ had not his life fallen a noble sacrifice to his sense of honor.

„ This state of total insubordination, the violence of the Jacobin
„ party, and the fear of an internal massacre, induced the Governor
„ to enter into a private treaty for surrender with the English, as
„ soon as they appeared before the place. He let however his
„ troops know that such measure was in agitation, but this produced
„ no effect on their disorders, and he at length signed the capitulation
„ without their knowledge and, I believe, without their consent.

„ They were found by us in a state of infamous disorder and
„ drunkenness: no discipline, no obedience, no spirit. They now
„ began to vent the most bitter reproaches against the Governor,
„ accusing him as the author of this disgrace, which their own
„ conduct had brought upon them and seemed in a tumultuous
„ crowd to display a desperate courage, when it was now too late.
„ The Malay troops alone kept an appearance of discipline. Even
„ they however were laid away by the contagious example of the
„ rest; and several of them with the Jacobin party among the Dutch
„ attacked the Governor's house and fired into it with an intent to
„ kill him, crying aloud that he had betrayed them and sold them to
„ the English. Nor was it without much difficulty that these
„ mutineers were compelled to evacuate the fort and ground their
„ arms.

„ It was grateful to the heart of a Briton to behold the steady
„ conduct and excellent discipline of our troops on this occasion,
„ when contrasted with the riotous and shameful conduct of the
„ Dutch soldiers. An officer who was an eye-witness assured me
„ that the Dutch soldiers went so far as even to strike at our men
„ with their muskets calling them insulting and opprobrious names,

„ and even spitting upon them as they passed. This behaviour „ entirely corresponded with their former cowardice, and was equally „ despised by our countrymen. I have often since conversed on the „ subjects with the Malay officers, who seemed to have embraced „ entirely the same sentiments with regard to it. They were all „ highly disgusted with the pusillanimous conduct of the Dutch, „ particularly in the affair of Gran-Pass, where they left them „ without any assistance to fight for themselves. Their contempt „ for their former masters, and their admiration of the valour of our „ troops, has served to render the Malays our most sincere friends, „ and they are now formed into a steady and well disciplined „ regiment in the British service.

„ These facts, as regards to the easy capture of Ceylon tend to „ throw the severest reflexion on the Dutch garrison there, but by „ no means serve to show that the enterprise on our part was not „ attended with the greatest danger. The opposition of even a small „ body of men must have occasioned much difficulty and loss to our „ men, however great General Stewart's military talents, and „ however brave the troops he commanded. Nature indeed seems „ to have done everything in her power to secure the approaches of „ Colombo on this side." —

Several English authors, almost contemporary to the Dutch period, or who had later on occupied an official position, which rendered them competent to form an opinion on the Dutch Government in the Island, have written some interesting remarks on that subject.

Ceylon, they say, was considered by the Dutch East India Company as a working ground from which they wanted to draw the greatest profits with the minimum of expenditure; consequently during nearly a century and a half of tenure, they did absolutely nothing for bettering the lot of the natives, and thus, they stopped and pushed on backwards the progress of civilisation which under the Portuguese domination and under the influence of the Catholic Religion was making such rapid progress. They threw back the Islanders into barbarity, so much so, that the Ceylonese even at the present moment have not yet succeeded to reach the degree of culture and of civilisation they possessed in 1656.

North, the first English Governor of Ceylon wrote in an official report to Lord Wellesley Governor General of India: — „I have no „scruple in declaring that, as it was established and administered „under the Dutch, no system could be imagined more directly „hostile to property, to the industrial improvement and felicity of „the people.“ —

— „The administration of justice, during the domination of the „Dutch, writes Philalethes, was necessarily viciated and corrupt as it „was usually entrusted to persons who were little qualified for the „office by their education, their circumstances or their character. „Neither intellectual nor moral qualities were regarded in the „selection of men for an office, which was to determine the „important questions of property, liberty and life.

„The prosperity of Ceylon was never regarded by the Dutch „any farther than as it was connected with a large supply of „cinnamon.“ —

And Lord Valentia adds: — „The Dutch left the Singhalese no „other choice than to be poor and idle, or to work for nothing." —

Emmerson Tennent, who in 1847 was Lieutenant Governor of Ceylon, and had at his disposal the Dutch Records, gives the following account of the policy of the Dutch:

— „The *fanatical* zeal of the Roman Catholic Sovereigns for „the propagation of the Faith was replaced by the *earnest* toil of the „Dutch traders to entrench their trading monopolies, and the almost „chivalrous energy with which the soldiers of Portugal resented and „resisted the attacks of the native princes, was exchanged for the „subdued humbleness with which the merchants of Holland endured „the insults and outrages perpetrated by the tyrants of Kandy upon „their envoys and officers. The maintenance of peace was so „essential to the extension of commerce, that no provocation „however gross was sufficient to rouse them to retaliation, provided „the offence was individual and local and did not interrupt the „routine of business at their factories on the coast.

„The unworthiness of such a policy was perceptible even to the „instincts of the barbarians with whom they had to deal, and Raja „Singha, by the arrogance and contempt of his demeanour and „intercourse, attested the scorn with which he endured the presence „of the faithless intruders whom he was powerless to expel.

„He disregarded all the engagements, violated the treaties, laid „waste the Dutch territory and put their subjects to the sword; yet „in spite of these atrocities, they addressed him with adulation, „whilst he replied with studied contumely, and persisted in sending

„ him embassies and presents, although he repelled their advances „ and imprisoned and even executed their ambassadors.

„ When after twenty years of captivity Knox made his escape „ from Kandy in 1679, Raja Singha held in detention or imprisonment „ upward fifty subjects of Netherlands, including five with the rank „ of ambassadors, besides a number of French and English whose „ liberation Sir Edward Winter in vain solicited by a mission from „ Madras fifteen years before.

„ During the period which followed their capture of Colombo, a „ period neither of war or absolute peace, but involving the „ expenditure of the one, without purchasing the security of the other, „ the military policy of the Dutch had been purely precautionary and „ defensive.

„ Throughout all the records that the Dutch have left us of their „ policy in Ceylon, it is painfully observed that no disinterested „ concern is manifested and no measures directed for the elevation „ and happiness of the native population, and even when care is „ shown to have been bestowed upon the spread of education and „ religion, motives are apparent, either latent or avowed, which „ detract from the grace and generosity of the act. Thus schools „ were freely established, but the avowed object was to wean the „ young Singhalese from their allegiance from the King, and the „ better to impress them with the power and ascendency of Holland. „ Churches were built, because the extension of the protestant faith „ was likely to counteract the influence of the Roman Catholics, and

„ the spread of *Christianity* to discourage the Moors and Mahomedan „ traders. In the promotion of agriculture the interests of the „ government were identified with those of the peasants, and the time „ was eagerly expected, but never arrived, when the necessity would „ cease for the importation of rice for the troops from Batavia and „ the coast of Canara. But notwithstanding these partial efforts for „ the advancement of the people, successive governors were obliged „ to admit the fact of habitual oppression by the headmen and „ officials, and to record their conviction that the condition of the „ Singhalese, was no better under the Dutch, than it had been under „ the Portuguese; so would they one day turn on them, as they had „ before shaken themselves of their predecessors." —

This last assertion, that the Singhalese had shaken themselves of the Portuguese, that Emmerson Tennent and other equally bigotted protestant writers try to insinuate maliciously, is absolutely false, and is refuted by all available historical documents. Under the Portuguese rule, the low-country Singhalese had fully enjoyed their civil rights and all their national customs and, far from having shaken the Portuguese yoke, the fought gallantly to the last moment at the side of the Portuguese against the combined armies of the Dutch and of the King of Kandy. And for many years after they had conquered Colombo, the chief concern of the Dutch Government was the fear of and offensive return of the Portuguese, of an attempt on their part to reconquer Ceylon, because they knew well, that as well the low-country Singhalese as the Tamils of Jaffna would acclaim with joy their return, and would join them with enthusiasm in expelling from the Island their protestant oppressors.

—„ In fact, continues Emmerson Tennent, from the commencement to the conclusion of the Dutch dominion in Ceylon, „ their possession of the Island was a military tenure, not a civil „ colonisation in the ordinary sense of the term. Strategically, its „ occupation was of infinite moment for the defence of their factories „ on the coast of India and for the interest of their commerce, its „ position intermediate between Java and Malabar rendered its value „ as an entrêpot. But all attempts to render it productive as a „ settlement were neutralized by the cost of its defence and „ establishments. For series of years previous to the final abandonment, the excess of expenditure over income from all sources, „ involved an annual deficiency in the revenue, and Baron Imhoff, in „ 1740, contrasting the renown of the conquest, and the magnitude „ of the anticipations with which it had been heralded, with the „ littleness of the ascertained result, compared Ceylon to one of the „ costly tulips of Holland, which bore a fabulous nominal price, „ without any intrinsic value.

„ To such lengths did mis-government prevail, that Holland was „ at last threatened with the loss of the *jewel* altogether by the „ treason of her own officers, and the rebellion of the Singhalese.

„ Vuyst, the Governor of Ceylon in 1726 aspired to become the „ Sovereign of the Island, and visited with forfeiture, torture and „ death every Chief who opposed him. For this, he was broken on „ the wheel in Batavia, and his body burned and scattered on the „ sea. Versluys who was sent to supersede him was removed for „ extortion and cruelty; and in the midst of discontent and anarchy „ which ensued, a change in the reigning dynasty at Kandy gave

„ encouragement to the lowlanders to attempt their own deliverance „ by revolt.

„ The story of the dominion of Holland in Ceylon is not „ altogether unrelieved by passages indicative of more generous „ impulses, but they were so transient and so uniformly succeeded „ by reversions to the former pusillanimous system, that the general „ character of their administration is unredeemed from the charge of „ meanness and tyranny. The presence of such Governors as „ Imhoff[1] and Falk were but episodes in the wearisome tale of „ extortion and selfishness; and when at length, towards the close of „ the last century, the British troops made their appearance before „ Colombo, after occupying the other strongholds in the Island, the „ surrender of the fortress without a struggle for its defence may be „ regarded as an evidence, that the Dutch had become as indifferent „ to its retention, as the Singhalese were rejoiced at its capture.

„ The dominion of the Netherlands in Ceylon, was nearly equal „ in duration with that of Portugal, about one hundred and forty „ years; but the politics of the two countries, have left a very „ different impress on the character and institutions of the people „ among whom they lived. The most important bequest left by „ the utilitarian genius of Holland is the code of Roman-Dutch law, „ which still prevails in the supreme court of justice; whilst the „ *fanatical* propagandism of the Portuguese has reared for itself a

1) The author seems to be a great admirer of Baron Van Imhoff, the greatest persecutor of the Catholics among all the Dutch Governors. He was certainly an able administrator but a morbid, heinous and mean character.

„ monument in the abiding and expanding influence of the Roman „ Catholic Faith. This flourishes in every province and hamlet, „ where it was implanted by the Franciscans, whilst the doctrines of „ the reformed church of Holland, never preached beyond the walls „ of the fortresses, are now extinct through the Island, with the „ exception of an expiring community at Colombo. Already the „ language of the Dutch, which they sought to extend by penal „ enactments, has ceased to be spoken even by their direct „ descendants, whilst a corrupted Portuguese is, to the present day „ the vernacular of the middle classes in every town of importance.

„ As the practical and sordid government of the Netherlands „ only recognized the interests of the native population, in so far as „ they were essential to uphold their trading monopolies, their „ memory was recalled by no agreeable associations; whilst the „ Portuguese who in spite of *their cruelties* were identified with the „ people by the bond of a common faith excited a feeling of „ admiration, by the boldness of their conflicts with the Kandyans „ and the chivalrous though ineffectual defence of their beleaguered „ fortresses.

„ The Dutch and their proceedings had almost ceased to be „ remembered by the low-land Singhalese; but the Chiefs of the „ south and west perpetuate with pride the honorifical title of Don „ accorded to them by their first European conquerors, and still „ prefix to their ancient patronymics the sonorous Christian names of „ the Portuguese.

„ When the Portuguese established themselves in Ceylon, „ commerce was not their only object: They wished to convert the

„ natives to Christianity. Persons of the highest rank became „ sponsors when Singhalese families were to be baptized, and gave „ their names to the converts. This is the origin of the numerous „ Portuguese names amongst the Singhalese.

„ The Dutch occupied themselves less with conversion, but „ employed the more speedy means of making *nominal Christians*, „ by giving certain offices to men of that religion only. But the „ instruction given to these *official converts* was too superficial to „ rout out their prejudices in favour of the idolatry of their „ ancestors." —

We have borrowed this long citation from Sir James Emmerson Tennent because, as acting Governor of Ceylon half a century only after the fall of the Dutch rule, he was more competent than any other author to form a correct judgment on the government of his predecessors. Besides, he had at his disposal the reco-ds of the Dutch Government.

It is astonishing, how, even such serious men as he undoubtedly was, are drawn by their protestant bigotry to the most illogical conclusion.

Take a few passages from the above citations: The cruelties of the Portuguese, excited the admiration and the love of the low-country Singhalese, who were the victims of these cruelties.

The establishment of Christianity in Ceylon and the high degree of civilization to which they raised the low-country Singhalese, was in the eyes of the author, but the result of the fanaticial zeal of the Portuguese; whilst the destruction of Christianity, the cruel persecution of the Catholics, the hard oppression of the people for the sake of trade monopolies were due to the earnest toil and to the utilitarian genius of Dutch traders; and finally he gives more importance to the introduction by the Dutch of a code of Roman Law, adulterated with protestant and masonic principles, than to the strong foundations of Christianity laid down by the Portuguese.

And such and other illogical contradiction due to their protestant bigotry, are found in all the English authors of the past century who wrote about the history of Ceylon.

They make their best to calumniate the Portuguese, and on the other hand they are unjust towards the Dutch. They do not take history seriously.

They do not make the distinction, which history must make between a conquest made by a nation, and one made by a commercial Company. Unless the Company be so extensive and so powerful, that it could be identified with the nation, as was the case with the British East India Company, they do not hold in their hands the honour of the nation, and the wrongs done by such Company cannot be laid to the charge of the nation.

Emmerson Tennent speaks with emphasis of: — „the sordid government of the Netherlands" — and he seems to forget that the Netherlands, or to say better the government of Holland, had nothing more to do in these affair than to confirm the Chart of the Company who was the real master of Ceylon.

And if we speak of Government, we must divide the Dutch period in three clearly distinct epochs: From 1656 to 1740, we see in Ceylon a protestant government. The consistory and the protestant ministers, all powerful with the Directors of the Company at Amsterdam and at Batavia, imposed their will on the Governors and government officials. They were the real rulers of the Island.

And at that epoch, we see the same atrocities committed by the protestants in England, Sweden, Denmark and in a part of Germany, so that whatever of these nations would become master of Ceylon, the lot of the Christians would have been the same.

From 1740 to 1760, we see a period of transition. Protestantism in Europe had lost its primitive ferocity, the morals had improved, and these twenty years in Ceylon were a period of struggle between the Governors and officials on one side, who wished to shake the tyranny which the protestant ministers exercised over them, and the consistory and the ministers on the other, who endeavoured by all means to uphold their ascendency. The last period, from 1760 to 1796, can alone be called that of the Dutch government and, whatever were its defects, it cannot be called sordid, as the precedent period had certainly been. We see justice re-established and serious endeavours made to better the government and to better the lot of the people. But they could not repair in 36 years, the ruins accumulated during a century of misrule and oppression.

The surrender of Ceylon to the English, especially that of Colombo, without even an attempt of defence, is certainly a striking feature. But which is the nation in the world who has not in its history some fact or other which turn to its dishonour?

We have heard from Captain Percival, a contemporary and an eye witness, what was the position of the town at that time.

The Revolution, on the zenith in France, had passed thence to Holland. Colombo was undermined with Jacobin lodges. These lodges had organized every thing in order to commence in Ceylon massacres like those which at that time had inundated France with the blood of her best citizens, and Governor Van Anglebeck himself had declared, that the speedy surrender of the town to the English had alone saved it from imminent bloodshed and massacres.

Remains the question if, even in such circumstances, the Governor had the right to sign the capitulation secretly, without the knowledge of his officers, who knew of the surrender of the town only when they saw the English troops entering through the gates.

It seems that when in 1794 the French revolutionary army commanded by Pichegru invaded Holland and proclaimed the republic, and the prince of Orange sought a refuge in England with his family, he made a secret treaty with the King of England, to the effect that the British would occupy Ceylon and some other Dutch colonies and keep them till the Revolution would be over in Holland and order re-established, in order to save them from being conquered by the French.

In consequence of this treaty, the Prince of Orange, who in temporary exile remained nevertheless the legitimate Sovereign of Holland would have given to Governor Van Anglebeck orders to surrender Ceylon to the British whenever their army entered the Island.

And in fact, until the peace of Amiens in 1805, the English did not consider Ceylon as their own and took into account the eventuality of having to restore the Island to the Dutch.

# Part V

# THE BRITISH RULE

1796 – 1848

## CHAPTER 1

# PILAME-TALAWE

Ceylon being now conquered by the English the question arose who should govern the Island. The Secretaries of State
1796 Pitt and Lord Melville wished to incorporate it to the Crown, but the East India Company protested; the Island had been conquered by their armies, they said, and by right belonged to them.

Until the question was settled, it was determined to establish a kind of provisory government at the head of which they placed a Madras civilian Mr. Andrews, a man of an equivocal character, inexperienced and of little judgment, who by his proceedings nearly made England lose her new conquest.

This is what Emmerson Tennent writes about his administration: — „ No arrangement could have proved more unfortunate. Mr. „ Andrews, a Madras civilian who, in response to the overtures of „ the King of Kandy in 1796 was sent to negotiate a treaty of „ alliance, was entrusted in addition to his mission as ambassador, „ with extraordinary powers of superintending the Ceylon revenues, „ a capacity in which he was empowered to revise and readjust „ the financial system of the new colony. He was a rash „ and indolent man, utterly uninformed as to the character and „ customs of the Singhalese, and seemingly unconscious, that great „ changes amongst a rude and semi-civilised people, can only be

„ affected, if suddenly, by force, if gradually by persuasion and „ kindness. Ignorant of any fiscal arrangements except those which „ prevailed in the Madras Presidency, Mr. Andrews, by a rude „ exertion of power, swept away the previously existing imposts and „ agencies for their collection in Ceylon, and substituted in all its „ severity the revenue system of the Carnatic, introducing simul- „ taneously a host of Tamil subordinates to enforce it. The service „ tenures by which the people held their otherwise untaxed lands „ were abolished, and a proportion of the estimated produce „ demanded in substitution, together with a tax upon their cocoanut „ gardens. The custom duties and other sources of income were „ farmed out to Moors, Parsis and Chetties from the coast, and the „ Mudeliars and native officials, who had formerly managed matters „ involving taxation, were superseded by Malabar Dubashes, men „ aptly described as enemies of the religion of the Singhalese, „ strangers to their habits, and animated by no impulse but extortion.

„ Unhappily, under the belief that their functions were but „ temporary, and that Ceylon would shortly be given back to the „ Dutch, Mr. Andrews and his European colleagues exerted no „ adequate influence to control the excesses of these men, and the „ atrocities and cruelties perpetrated by them were such as most „ defy belief.

„ The result may be anticipated: The Singhalese population
1797 „ was exasperated beyond endurance: Their Chiefs and „ headmen insulted by the supercession of their authority „ and outraged by the rapacity of low caste Dubashes encouraged „ the resistance of the people. The Dutch civilians inspired them

„ with the assurance of assistance from the French; and under these „ combined influences, the population in 1797 rose in violent revolt, „ and occupied entrenched positions on the line leading from the „ low-country towards the Kandyan hills.

„ The moment was in every respect critical; three military „ Governors of Colombo had died within the five months that the „ English had been in possession of the Island. A force of sepoys „ had been sent against the rebels, severe conflicts ensued, but it was „ not until considerable loss on both sides that the insurgents were „ subdued.

„ In the meantime, Colonel de Meuron was despatched by „ Lord Hobart, from Madras, and placed at the head of a Commission „ to inquire into the causes of discontent and the means of allaying it.

„ This calamity in Ceylon had the instant effect of deciding the „ policy of Mr. Pitt and of the government at home as

1798 „ to the future disposal of the Island. It was resolved to „ administer the colony direct from the Crown and, in October 1798 „ the Honorable Frederic North, afterwards Earl of Guilford, landed „ as the first British Governor. His appointment and that of all the „ civil officers were made by the King but, in the conduct of affairs, „ he was placed under the orders of the Governor General of India, „ an arrangement which endured till Ceylon was incorporated with „ the British dominions by the treaty of Amiens in 1802." —

The choice of the Honorable Frederic North at that period of crisis was rather an unfortunate one. The contemporary English writers say that he knew how to write clever reports to the Governor General and to the Secretary of State, but that there was something rather mysterious in his politics. The whole mystery was that North was neither a statesman nor an administrator and was too fond of underhand intrigues. And the worst was, that his two principal Counsellors, Boyd the Colonial Secretary, and General Mac Dowall the Commander-in-chief, were men of the same stamp.

Instead of organizing and strengthening the government in the territory recently conquered from the Dutch, North's dream was the conquest of the Kingdom of Kandy, which was rather a risky undertaking, when they were not as yet, strictly speaking, the masters of the late Dutch possessions, which they had taken only two years ago, and whose inhabitants were at that moment in a state of rebellion, and in arms against the English.

In view of his dream of the conquest of Kandy, North granted to the rebels all what they asked for, a dangerous proceeding at the beginning of a change of Government, and which created among the low-country Singhalese the idea, that their new masters were weak.

— „ Mr. North, says Emmerson Tennent, arrived in time to „ carry into effect the recommendations of Colonel de Meuron, that „ the Carnatic revenue system should be forthwith suspended and „ the Malabar Dubashes sent back to the continent, that the native „ Moodeliars should be reinstalled in their office and dignities; the „ obnoxious taxes abolished and, till a preferable arrangement could „ be introduced by degrees, the Dutch system restored for the „ moment." —

It was not easy however to introduce reforms. The Madras civil servants whom Andrews had brought to the Island were not of the best, and necessity obliged to keep on in office a number of Dutch officials, who naturally were hostile to the new British rule:

— „The Augean task of reforming such state of affairs, „continues Emmerson Tennent, was rendered infinitely more „difficult by the intrigues, inefficiency and corruption of the Madras „civil servants, the majority of whom, he was compelled to get rid „of by suspension, dismissal and forced resignation.

„Mr. North wrote to the Earl of Mornington of: — the „infamous faction of Madras civilians — and his letters contain the „details of the plunder of Government to the extent of 60,000 „pagodas by one *gentleman* who had charge of the pearl fishery and „of another under whose judicial management in the Eastern „province: — more than 4,000 inhabitants from the single district „of the Vanny, had been driven away, since our occupation of the „Island." —

And Lord Valentia adds: — Their sole object was to accumulate „money. They impoverished the woods by cutting down all „beautiful species of timber... Mr. Andrews who held the supreme „civil authority as commercial Resident and Receiver General cannot „be acquitted of having at least connived at their enormities." —

— „Another source of annoyance, says Emmerson Tennent, „was the lapse of period allowed by the capitulation of Colombo for „the duration of the Dutch tribunals, whilst there still remained suits

„ to be decided; and although the Island was thus left without any „ legal Courts, the Dutch officials who were still subjects of Holland, „ and looked forward to an early restoration of her authority, firmly „ refused to take the oath of allegiance, and accept judicial „ appointments under the British Crown. This embarassment Mr. „ North met by obtaining legal assistance from Bengal and „ organizing circuits round the Island for the administration of „ justice. The first head of the judicial establishment was Sir „ Edmund Carrington."—

Governor North however had no time to think of solidly organizing the new colony. The conquest of the Kingdom of Kandy or, as he puts it in his official reports, the establishment of a protectorate over that Kingdom, occupied all his thoughts.

It is evident that this annexation, whatever form or name one choses to give it, imposed itself on the English, and had to be carried out some day, but it was premature to think of it before the English had solidly established themselves in the part of the Island they already possessed, and had well organized it.

About the middle of 1798, King Rajadi Raja Singha died without issue. As already said above, according to Kandyan custom, it was the privilege of the three Adigars to appoint his successor. At this time however the first Adigar Pilame-Talawe, the head of one of the most powerful families in the Kingdom, held in fact the reins of government, his two colleagues being of no account.

Pilame-Talawe, who pretended to be the descendant and heir of the old dynasty of the Singhalese Kings, aspired to the throne. He could not reach at once the goal of his ambition, as there was among the Kandyan chiefs a strong party that stood against him, and that party had first to be subdued. He wanted therefore a King who would be a puppet in his hands, whom he could use so as to get rid of his enemies, then throwing on him all blame and all odium, he would turn against him, posing as a liberator, and thus place the crown on his own head.

This was a cunning and well conceived plan, and Pilame-Talawe was certainly clever enough to bring it to the desired end.

Putting therefore aside all the members of the Royal family, he gave the Crown to the nephew of one of the Queens a youth of 18 years called Kunne Swami. The lad, he thought, had no other quality than that of being handsome, but there he made a mistake, because the young King, after having acquired experience, proved to be very intelligent and soon discovered the treacherous designs of his ambitious minister.

Kunne Swami, in ascending the throne took the name of Wikrama Raja Singha. In the first years of his reign, young and unexperienced as he was he was entirely guided by the treacherous Adigar, who persuaded him that he would never be sure of his Crown until he got rid of all the members of the royal house. Under his cunning insinuation, the young King had his uncle and the second Adigar beheaded, and all the other members of the royal family thrown into prison.

One however among them managed to escape, Muthu Swami;

who was the next heir to the late King, and had hoped to succeed him. He sought refuge in Colombo, and the Governor, from one side fearing that he would be the cause of embarassment, and on the other seeing how useful he could be for the realisation of his dream of the conquest of Kandy, sent him to Jaffna, where he lived almost a prisoner, under the care of Colonel Barbut the commander of the place, generously provided by government, so that he could live there in princely state.

Governor North had recognized officially Wikrama Raja Singha as King of Kandy and was on the point of sending a brilliant embassy with his congratulations, when a communication received from Pilame-Talawe, made him change his mind.

The Adigar had already perceived that the young King was more intelligent than he had thought at first and began to emancipate himself from his tutelage and from his influence. It was the ruin of his ambitious scheme, he therefore decided to hasten their realisation with the help of the British

He invited Governor North to an interview, but as his visit to Colombo would certainly raise suspicion, he proposed him to meet at Sitawacca or at Avisavella.

During the course of the year 1799, the Governor North, and the Colonial Secretary Boyd held several interviews with
1799 the Adigar Pilame-Talawe. Both Marshall and Lord Valentia have left us detailed relations of these conferences, but as they are not very interesting we will rather reproduce the summary

given by Sir James Emmerson Tennent who as Colonial Secretary and acting Governor of Ceylon had access to the official papers:

— „ In the course of numerous interviews with the Governor, „ Pilame-Talawe avowed unreservedly his hatred to the reigning „ Tamil family, his desire to procure the death or the dethronement „ of the King, and his ambition to restore in his own person a „ national dynasty to the Kingdom. Mr. North, while he disclaimed „ participation in projects so treasonable, discerned in the design of „ the Adigar an opportunity for establishing a military protectorate „ at Kandy, with a subsidized British force, on the model of the „ mediatised provinces of India; and it must be regretted that, in the „ too eager pursuit of this object, Mr. North, not only forbore to „ denounce the treason of the minister, but lent himself to intrigues „ inconsistent with the dignity and honor of his high office.

„ In the development of the Governor's plans, the Adigar was „ encouraged to disclose his designs for the ruin of the young King, „ whom it was his intention to stimulate to acts of atrocity, such as „ would make him at once odious to his own nation and hostile to „ the English, thus provoking a war, in which the Adigar was to „ profit by the King's overthrow. Mr. North did not consider it „ unbecoming his high position, to discuss with him the terms of a „ compromise in a matter so revolting; and stipulated only for the „ personal safety and nominal rank for the King: he came to an „ agreement, by which the Kandyan Sovereign was to be reduced to „ a nonentity, and the Adigar to be virtually invested with royal „ authority. It was even contemplated that the King should be „ induced to retire altogether from the capital, to take his residence

„ at Jaffna, within the British dominions, and that Pilame-Talawe „ was to become Regent of the Kingdom, within which a British „ force was to be maintained at the cost of the Kandyan people.

„ The project was to be carried by means of an embassy, which „ was forthwith to be despatched, ostensibly to negotiate a treaty „ with the King, but it was privately arranged, that the ambassador „ was to be the General commanding-in-chief in the Island, and the „ intended subsidiary force was to be introduced under the name „ and guise of his escort.

„ It is impossible to read without pain the letters in which „ Mr. North communicated confidentially the progress of his „ political intrigue for the information and approval of the Governor „ General of India. He labours to persuade himself, that in taking „ this disingenious course, he was adopting the only line open to him „ at once to save the life of the King of Kandy and to promote the „ political interests of Great Britain:

„ I am certain, he wrote, that, if the troops are not sent, and if „ they are not put in possession of the Capital, the poor King would „ be deposed if not murdered, or that he would be driven into „ aggression against us, which I hope will excuse me in your eyes „ and in those of the world, for not being *so delicate* as I otherwise „ should about forcing his abdication or abridging his power. —

„ The reception of an armed British force in the central capital „ he regards as: — so highly essential to British interests, that he „ will not endanger the success of the negotiations by any *over* „ *strictness* in the terms on which it has to be obtained. — His „ principal object is now, he says, to collect such a military force in

## CHAPTER 2

# MAC DOWALL'S EMBASSY

General Mac Dowall left Colombo on the 10th March 1800.

1800 His *escort* was composed of ten companies of British soldiers, five companies of Malay troops, a battery of Bengal artillery with six guns, a detachment of Madras sappers and a contingent of native Sepoys. It was a rather strange escort for an ambassador (as he styled himself), going to present his credentials to a King with whom the British Government was in terms of peace and freindship.

If however the Adigar had consented that General Mac Dowall be followed by this small army, it never entered into his views, to allow this queer embassy to enter Kandy. First of all he arranged matters so that Mac Dowall took a month to get over the 72 miles between Colombo and Kandy. Meanwhile he laboured to raise the suspicions of the King and of Kandyan Chiefs so well that they absolutely refused to allow the *escort* to enter the Kandyan territory, so that Mac Dowall had to leave the greater part of his troops on the frontier. Then they led him across inpracticable roads where he had to abandon his artillery, so that, when on the 10th April he reached the Mahavelli-Ganga a few miles from Kandy, of the army he intended to introduce into the capital, there only remained with him a handful of soldiers, whereas on the opposit bank, he saw

„ to precipitate hostilities, that he had asked: *what would be* „ *considered as a sufficient aggression;* and with how many men he „ was to invade the low country to compel the British to take arms.

„ I therefore cannot but think, says Mr. North, that a very „ minute attention to diplomatical forms would be sacrificing the „ reality of justice for the sake of appearance; and, as the troops will „ only interfere for securing the government established by the „ existing power, I do not imagine that the most rigid publicist could „ find fault with what I am about to do. It is however impossible „ that I should not feel anxious and uneasy in conducting so singular „ a business.—

„ The influence of the Adigar was sufficiently powerful to „ overcome the scruples of the King, and permission was granted for „ the advance of the ambassador with his formidable escort. This „ was announced to the Marquis of Wellesley in the following terms „ by Mr. North: — The decision is made, and General Mac Dowall „ set out with his escort on Wednesday last. The Adigar, *rogorum* „ *longe turpissimus,* is to meet him at Sitawacca. Only fancy if one „ of *our* ministers, were to behave so with King George and oblige „ the abbé Sieyès to stipulate for his life! I hope that I have not „ done wrong, but I am not certain, whether I have acted like a good „ politician or like a great nincompoop." —

All English authors excepting Lord Valentia condemn North's action in this matter as unworthy of his position and detrimental to the honor of England.

In fact, these interviews were only a game of cunning between North and Boyd on one side and the Adigar on the other. North in flattering the ambition of Pilame-Talawe and offering him, if not as yet the Crown, at least the King's removal, and a kind of regency, had in fact no other intention than that of introducing into Kandy a strong British force, thus become master of the capital, which, he thought, would be a decisive step towards the conquest of the whole Kingdom. Having obtained what he desired he rejoiced in having deceived the cunning Adigar.

The Adigar, on the other hand, consented to the entrance of the British troops into Kandy, for hé saw in this movement the realisation of his most cherished hopes of provoking a war between the English and the King of Kandy. He would then raise the Kandyans against the English and the King who had admitted the foreign troops into the capital, provoke a general massacre of the English, dethrone the King, and place the crown on his own head. Such was Pilame-Talawe's plan, and he rejoiced in having deceived the British Governor of Colombo.

Both parties therefore were satisfied at the result of their intrigues, but the facts which followed proved that Pilame-Talawe was much too clever to allow himself to be cheated by North, Boyd and Mac Dowall.

## CHAPTER 2

## MAC DOWALL'S EMBASSY

General Mac Dowall left Colombo on the 10th March 1800.
1800 His *esco't* was composed of ten companies of British soldiers, five companies of Malay troops, a battery of Bengal artillery with six guns, a detachment of Madras sappers and a contingent of native Sepoys. It was a rather strange escort for an ambassador (as he styled himself), going to present his credentials to a King with whom the British Government was in terms of peace and freindship.

If however the Adigar had consented that General Mac Dowall be followed by this small army, it never entered into his views, to allow this queer embassy to enter Kandy. First of all he arranged matters so that Mac Dowall took a month to get over the 72 miles between Colombo and Kandy. Meanwhile he laboured to raise the suspicions of the King and of Kandyan Chiefs so well that they absolutely refused to allow the *escort* to enter the Kandyan territory, so that Mac Dowall had to leave the greater part of his troops on the frontier. Then they led him across inpracticable roads where he had to abandon his artillery, so that, when on the 10th April he reached the Mahavelli-Ganga a few miles from Kandy, of the army he intended to introduce into the capital, there only remained with him a handful of soldiers, whereas on the opposit bank, he saw encamped a strong division of the Kandyan army that was keeping watch on his camp, and cut all communications between it and the surrounding country. Thus General Mac Dowall who had intended to command as a master found himself almost a prisoner.

Pilame-Talawe however having thus attained his end treated him with great honor and ceremony. But he delayed the business as much as possible. First there were endless questions of etiquette to settle. Next they had to await the day which the Astrologers had declared propitious for the Royal audience.

Finally the lucky day arrived and General Mac Dowall was received by the King. James Cordiner, one of the General's suite, has left us an interesting description of the audience:

— „ In the morning, he says, the nobles of the Court waited on „ the ambassador and requested to know, what parts of the ceremony „ of introduction, he wished them to dispense with. He replied that „ he objected to carrying the letter on his head and to the too „ frequent genuflexions, stated as necessary.

„ The matter being thus adjusted, about half past four in the „ afternoon the Dessawe of Matale and the Maha-Mudeliyar waited „ on the General and told him that the King has sent them to „ announce him, that His Majesty would give His Excellency an „ audience this evening, and that he had ordered them, to take „ charge of the presents and the letter for the King.

„ It was nine o clock in the evening before they got the „ presents across the river, and at this hour the ambassador quitted „ his house to proceed towards Kandy. Having crossed the

„ Mahavelli-Ganga in boats, he and his suite got into their palanquins, „ and after travelling very slowly arrived in an hour and a half at a „ halting place half a mile from the palace and within the limits of „ the town of Kandy.

„ Upon the road we could only remark that there were a good „ many houses upon each side of it, and that there were rice fields „ where there were no houses to obstruct the view. The road was „ pretty level but bad from neglect in several parts. In four or five „ different places, high palisades run across the road, with gates in the „ centre of them; at each of these gates, we found small guards of „ about twenty five malays each, and at three of them, we observed „ two pieces of cannon, mounted upon carriages, with their muzzles „ pointed to the moon, and probably none of them exceeded the size „ of a three pounder. But as we saw them in the night, we do not „ pretend to speak decisively. It is probable that these six guns „ compose the greater part, if not the whole of the Kandyan „ ordnance.

„ After remaining about an hour at the halting place above „ mentioned, we moved on in a heavy shower of rain attended by a „ deputation of nobles to the Bo-gaha, or Buddha tree within a short „ distance of the palace. Here, the second Adigar met the „ ambassador and led him up towards the first Adigar who was „ approaching in all possible state. Having met the ambassador, he „ said, he was ordered by the King to lead him up to the first gate „ of His Majesty's palace. Having arrived there he said he would go „ and inform His Majesty, that His Excellency was at the first gate.

„ In about an hour he returned, with the King's permission for „ the ambassador to enter the palace. During the absence of the „ first Adigar, the second amused the ambassador, by pointing out to „ him the number of state elephants, that were drawn up on the „ occasion, and like the poor Kandyan troops that lined the street „ seemed as much annoyed by the deluge of rain as ourselves. The „ Kandyan nobles who were well protected from the rain by their „ talipot umbrellas, seemed to delight in proving to us, that no „ weather could stop or shorten the ceremonies of their Court.

„ We now entered the palace gate and confidently expected to „ have got out of the rain, when we found that it only lead to an „ open Court, when we were again enjoying the pleasure arising „ from a fresh ducking.

„ At length however we got under a roof, and the two Chief „ ministers, having with their own hands turned out all the intruders, „ shut the second gate behind which were fourteen drummers beating „ on European drums, and performers on other musical instruments „ who made a noise difficult to be described.

„ At this gate, the ambassador took the King's letter of the „ Appuhamis head, and holding it in both hands level with his eyes, „ instead of putting it on his head, as was the practice of the Dutch „ ambassadors, he moved on towards the door of the hall of audience, „ the two Adigars holding him by the arms.

„ Having advanced a few paces, they stopped him to ask, how „ many of the seven gentlemen who attended him, he wished to „ carry with him. On his expressing the wish that they should be „ all admitted, no objection was made. The gallery through which

„ we were now passing was lined by His Majesty's bodyguard, who „ held their firelocks nearly in the position called by military men „ *recovered arms*, and which, as it always precedes presenting or „ levelling, might have alarmed us, had they not been cased in white „ muslin, an emblem of peace, which completely concealed them.

„ Having arrived at the entrance of the hall of audience, several „ curtains were drawn, and gave us a full view of the King on his „ throne, in a recess at the further end of the apartment.

„ The drawing of the curtains was the signal for six of the „ nobles to prostrate themselves on the ground, and for the „ ambassador and the gentlemen who were with him to kneel.

„ When these six nobles prostrated themselves in this way, nine „ different times they called out: Oh! King live for ever! and „ addressed themselves to him, as if they were paying their adorations „ to a deity. The King repeated a word three different times in a „ loud rough voice, upon his pronouncing which the third time we „ all got up and advanced a few paces, when the same ceremony was „ performed a second time.

„ We then rose once more and advanced to the edge of a carpet, „ where we kneeled, and the nobles prostrated themselves a third „ time, while the ambassador still held by the first and second „ Adigars went to the throne carrying the letter. Having reached „ the foot of the throne, the first Adigar took off the muslin that „ covered the letter, and His Majesty took the letter from the „ ambassador's hand, and led it down on his left side. The „ ambassador was now led backwards, to the spot where we remained „ all the while kneeling; having reached us, he kneeled also.

„ The first Adigar now went and sat down opposite to the right „ of the throne; the second Adigar took his post opposite to the left „ of it, with his face towards the King. The Dessawe of Uva sat „ down a little advanced in front of us, having the ambassador's „ interpreters near to him. I forgot to say, that we were all obliged „ to take off our hats, when we entered the hall, excepting the „ ambassador who did not take his off, until he had delivered the „ Governor's letter.

„ After keeping the ambassador and his suite some time longer „ on their knees, the King at last condescended, to let the whole sit „ down on the carpet.

„ This and other communications between the King and the „ ambassador took place by the King addressing the second Adigar, „ who repeated the sacred message to the Dessawe of Uva. The „ Dessawe delivered it to the Singhalese interpreter (the Maha- „ Mudeliyar), who repeated it in Portuguese to a person (M. „ Joinville) who explained it in English to the ambassador, so that a „ few words took a long time to come from the throne to the „ ambassador and vice versa.

„ In addition to all these delays, the Adigar never received „ any command from the King, that he did not, after hearing it offer „ up a prayer for his length of days, and then repeated a prayer for „ the same purpose, before he delivered it to the Dessawe, who „ heard every word that the King said, just as well as the Adigar, and „ was also obliged to repeat similar ejaculations.

„ The King now asked after the health of His Excellency the „ Governor. The ambassador was obliged to ask and obtain

„ permission, to answer the King's questions before he could reply. „ The King then asked after the Governor's family, and after the „ ambassador himself and those who were with him. He asked if „ his letter and presents have been treated everywhere with proper „ respect, and if His Excellency has met with every attention due to „ his rank.

„ Here the King stopped, and the ambassador informed His „ Majesty that he had orders from His Excellency the Governor to „ ask certain questions. Permission being granted, he asked in the „ Governor's name after His Majesty's health, then informed His „ Majesty that the Governor had entrusted him with certain presents „ to His Majesty and begged permission to send them to His „ Majesty's magazines.

„ This permission being given he retired from the hall of „ audience with the same number of genuflexions as when he entered, „ taking care not to turn his back on *the greatest of terrestrial* „ *monarchs,* as the King of Kandy is styled by his subjects.

„ While the ambassador was out of Court, the presents were „ carried in and probably examined by the proper officers.

„ After remaining in the gallery some time, it was announced to „ the ambassador that he might re-enter the audience hall, which he „ did as before, only that he kneeled the third time at the place „ where he was seated, before that he did not go up to the throne, „ and that he and his suite sat down on the carpet, before being „ desired, the former permission being considered sufficient.

„ The King having asked as usual, whether he had not forgotten „ any of the commissions entrusted to him by the Governor, he

„ replied that he had not, but that he was authorized by the „ Governor to propose a treaty to His Majesty. The King desired „ that he might submit it to the consideration of the nobles. The „ King then dismissed the ambassador, by asking him if he would „ not be glad to depart, and the ambassador departed with the „ repetition of the kneelings formerly mentioned.

„ The first Adigar led then the ambassador to a room in which „ refreshments were prepared for him: these consisted in large balls „ of flour nnd honey, sweet cakes and fruit, with *acqua pura*. „ Having remained here long enough to have made a confortable „ repast, had the hour and the provisions been agreeable, the „ ambassador was attended to the halting place as before. There he „ and his suite got into the palanquins a little before five o'clock „ in the morning, and reached the ambassador's house at Ganaroowa „ a little after six o'clock. One of the party who walked back in the „ morning computed the distance to be four miles from Kandy to the „ ferry at Ganaroowa.

„ The King seemed very vain in his dress, and very uneasy on „ his throne. He kept constantly shaking his head, to display the „ precious stones in his crown, and pulled down his vest or armour to „ show the jewels with which it was studded. He seemed „ particularly fond of a large round ornament which was suspended „ from his neck.

„ The throne is a large chair raised upon a platform, three or four „ steps high; it seemed to be plated with gold, set with precious „ stones, and to be, like his attire, very rich and magnificent. The

„ canopy over the throne, sad falling of! was composed of coarse „ cotton cloth, with a cotton fringe. Two men stood by him with „ fly-flaps, which were kept in constant motion, and he had persons „ near him, whose heads were seen occasionally, with whom he „ conversed and laughed. He is a young man about twenty-one „ years of age, with an immense large head, and stupid, vacant „ countenance.

„ The pillars and walls of the hall were covered with patches of „ chintz of different pattern, each patch vying with another in „ ugliness. There were four chandeliers, and eight hanging lamps of „ European manufacture, but no light in any of them. There were „ only ten lights in the room, these were large wax candles.

„ During the whole time we were in the palace, we had „ Singhalese vocal music, and I thought the airs pleasant.

„ The nobles appeared to take the duty of prostrating themselves „ in turn, except the first Adigar who did not prostrate himself during „ the audience.

„ There was a partition between the throne and the hall of „ audience, but it had a door in the centre, through which we saw the „ King and through which he spoke to the second Adigar. The first „ Adigar retired early probably to prompt his tool of state. There „ were large mirrors on each side of the door opposite to the throne. „ The nobles sat ranged in a semi-circular form on each side of the „ ambassador and his suite, forming a crescent, the horns of which „ extended towards the throne. The Dessawe of Uva, being „ spokesman, was more advanced, and our interpreters were close to „ him. Those of them who were Singhalese, were obliged to

„ prostrate themselves before His Majesty, whenever the nobles „ did.

„ The Adigar had now fulfilled two of his promises, that the „ embassy should arrive at Kandy without insult, and that he himself „ would introduce the ambassador to the King." —

All this elaborated ceremonial had been composed by the Adigar Pilame-Talawe for the benefit of General Mac Dowall.

The Portuguese envoys to the Kings in Ceylon observed the etiquette in use at the Courts of Europe for the reception of ambassadors, and, as a rule, after the first introduction, they placed for them a gilded chair on the right side of the throne, and they conversed directly with the King.

The Dutch, styled themselves the humble vassals of the Emperor of Ceylon, and, in the beginning of their rule, their envoys who were generally officials of lower rank, prostrated themselves before the King of Kandy, and spoke to him on bended knees. But later on, they stipulated that the so-called ambassador would not have to stand an hour at the gate of the palace, nor in the inner courtyard, the prostrations and genuflexions were suppressed, and replaced by a profound inclination on entering and leaving the audience hall.

Now, the Adigar Pilame-Talawe considered a war with the English as necessary for the fulfilment of his ambitious plans, and he thought that all these humiliations heaped on the Commander-in-chief would perhaps be considered as a *sufficient aggression.* Unhappily for his plans, General Mac Dowall looked rather on the comical side of the performance and submitted good humourously to this barbaric protocole.

The best of all was, when after having kept him for seven hours, the whole night, standing in the rain, kneeling or sitting on the ground the King asked the General, if he would not be glad to depart.

General Mac Dowall after the famous audience, remained a month longer, not at Kandy, the access of the town being forbidden to him and to his suite, but in a sort of camp at Ganaroowa, a village distant four or five miles from Kandy on the other side of the river where he was kept in a sort of half captivity, so strictly watched that he could have no communication except with the Adigar and a few grandees of the Court devoted to the cause of Pilame-Talawe.

They then commenced negotiations for the treaty of alliance.

Mac Dowall, as we have already seen, was a man of very limited capacities. He did not see the difference of the position he had dreamed about with North and Boyd, when there was question of his entering Kandy at the head of an army, and command as a master, and his present actual position, as almost a captive at the mercy of the King of Kandy. He obstinately wished to carry out the Governor's instructions to the letter, insisting on the condition, that the King for the honor and security of his person and of his dynasty, should admit a garrison of 800 British troops into Kandy, the cost of its maintenance being equally shared between the King and the British Government.

It seems even that he went so far as to propose to the King, for the greater security of his throne and of his person, to place all power in the hands of Pilame-Talawe, and to take himself refuge on British territory.

These propositions were naturally rejected with indignation, and the King gave graciously the general *permission* to depart, that is ordered him out of his Kingdom. He left Gonaroowa on the 2nd May and returned to Colombo: — „ unsuccessful and disappointed " — writes Emmerson Tennent.

— „ It is difficult to imagine, says Forbes, what delusion could „ have laid any one, to expect that a suspicious, jealous and haughty „ despot, who styled himself in his counter proposals: King of „ Lanka, as great amongst men as Iswara amongst gods, would „ delegate all power to his minister, and transfer his own person from „ possible danger to certain restraint.

„ As might have been predicted, the mission was a total failure, „ and the same consequences resulted from this as from former „ embassies, viz: that they ministered to the vanity of the Kandyan „ monarch and exalted him in the eyes of his ignorant subjects, who „ contrasted the studied splendour of the royal pageantry, with the „ degrading ceremonies enforced upon the British representative. "—

Mac Dowall's mission produced also another result: The Adigar Pilame-Talawe understood that he could no longer rely on the English for his scheme of seizing the throne of Kandy, and the King on his side commenced to see clearly through the intrigues of the Adigar.

After the failure of Mac Dowall's embassy, Governor North endeavoured on several occasions to renew relations with

1802 the King of Kandy. Unable to do so directly he decided to use as secret agent a Dessawe named Leuka and some Bikshun of Colombo, who, it was said, enjoyed the King's favour and were known as mortal enemies of Pilame-Talawe.

Dessawe Leuka however answered to the Governor that the King was ready to conclude a treaty, but only on the terms of the last treaty concluded with the Dutch, and the Bikshun declined all participation in the matter; however they kept the King informed of the Governor's proposals with the result that in February 1802 a Kandyan embassy arrived at Colombo.

The ambassador was the second Adigar, but as the King of Kandy considered one of his rank too high a personage for dealing with the Governor, he had to appear at Colombo simply as a Dessawe.

They treated him nevertheless with much ceremony. When he was to appear before the Governor for handing over to him the credentials, the Governor sent him his state carriage. When they invited him to enter it he refused exclaiming: — „Is that the way you treat me. To me who am the ambassador of the greatest King in the world, you give a lower seat, than to the driver who is a simple cooly!" — After much persuasion and explanations on the part of the Governor's aide-de-camp, he entered the carriage, but when they wished to shut the door, he pushed it violently back: — „I go, he said, to your Governor as a free man, the envoy of a

King, and not like a vile prisoner, whom you can shut in at your will into this gilded casket." — And he paraded through the streets of Colombo with both doors of the carriage wide open.

The choice of the King was not a happy one. The second Adigar was Pilame-Talawe's nephew, and it was seen since the very beginning, that he had more at heart the interests of his uncle than those of the King.

From the very first interview he started the subject of deposing King Wikrama Raja Singha and placing on the throne his uncle. The Governor gave him an evasive reply, clear enough however to make him understand that he would do better not to touch this subject any more. He next passed to the matter of the treaty, and laid down as an absolute condition that England should deliver to the King of Kandy three small Islands near the coast of Ceylon, that the Kandyans should have the right to trade all over the British territory, and that the Governor should send another embassy to Kandy.

The Governor refused and the negotiations for the treaty were broken off. The Kandyan envoy tried once more to treat with the Colonial Secretary Boyd the question of placing his uncle Pilame-Talawe on the throne of Kandy, but having failed he left Colombo.

This was the last attempt made by Pilame-Talawe to gain over North to his ambitious projects. He saw now clearly that he must not count on the help of the English.

On the other hand, his position was now far less strong than it had been in 1799. He had lost the confidence of the King, and the number of influential Chiefs that were opposed to him had increased. He saw therefore that, in order to succeed he must act quickly.

He had always cherished the idea that a war with the English would be the best occasion to dethrone King Wikrama Raja Singha and usurp his crown. Now it was the only means left to him to attain the end so much desired. He therefore decided to bring about the war. All that was needed was the famous *sufficient aggression*, and, as on the other hand North always full of the idea of conquering the Kingdom of Kandy and annexing it to the British possessions, having failed of making himself master of it by intrigue, he now dreamed of conquering it with arms, a pretext was not difficult to be found:

In April 1802 some traders of Putlam, who were British subjects, had purchased on the market at Kandy a large quantity of arecanuts, and were on their way home robbed by a minor Kandyan Chief who seized their merchandise and their beasts, the whole to the value of about one thousand pounds.

Governor North demanded a reparation from the Kandyan Government, and rumours were current that the whole affair, had been arranged by order of the Adigar Pilame-Talawe with the object of provoking war, but the fact could not be proved. The King of Kandy admitted the justice of the demand and promised to indemnify the traders, but delayed in keeping the promise, and meanwhile the Adigar was preparing for war, and had issued to all men capable of wearing arms the order to be ready to join the army on the first summons.

Nine months passed, and the reparation asked for by the Governor had not yet been made. To all his complaints they were answering with putting forwards impossible counter-demands.

At last, in January 1803 the Governor declared war against the King of Kandy.

Some almost contemporary English authors regard this declaration of war as an unjust aggression on the part of the Governor, and declare that the reason was not sufficient, but in order to be able to form a calm judgment one should know the exact wording of the correspondence passed between the two governments regarding this affair.

Certainly, Governor North desired war. Ever since the failure of the strategem of Mac Dowall's embassy war had entered into his plans of the annexation of the Kingdom of Kandy. But, on the other hand, we must not forget that, before he declared it, he had waited patiently for nine months, during which he did not cease to treat with the Kandyan Government.

Therefore, in order to be able to judge with correctness whether this war was really unjust, or whether on the contrary it was but an inevitable evil, one must know exactly what demands were made by the Governor, and what were the King's answers.

The Adigar on his side, had decided to have war, and if the affair of the traders had not been considered a sufficient cause, he would have arranged another to provoke the conflict.

— „ The ambitious spirit of the first Adigar, writes Cordiner, „ a generally well informed contemporary, longed for war, hoping „ that in the struggle which it would occasion he might accomplish „ the nefarious schemes which he had so long meditated. Relying on

„ the strength of fastness and the security of retreat as well as on the „ depths of his political sagacities, he waited with deliberate patience „ the issue of the contest, in the prospect of which he saw the „ balance preponderate in favour of his own agrandissement. „ When war was begun, he thought he should easily find an „ opportunity of despatching the King; and he trusted to secure „ his own power by offering an advantageous treaty to the English. „ This project he nearly avowed to Mr. Boyd in 1800.

„ The fugitive princes of Kandy maintained before the war that „ such was his design; and some relations of the King who dwelled „ at Trichinopoly, were so much persuaded that the Adigar intended „ to assassinate the Sovereign, that they had long solicited the „ intercession of the Nabob of Arcot with the British Government, to „ promote at all events the escape of their Kinsman from his „ dominions. The Nabob received their presents, but never forwarded „ their application.“ —

## CHAPTER 3

# THE WAR

War being declared, General Mac Dowall at the head of a small army left Colombo on the 31 December. He marched
1803 triumphantly through the city, and encamped outside the walls on the Kandy road.

The Governor still hoped that this military show and the menace of war would intimidate the King of Kandy and induce him to sign the terms of the treaty proposed to him by Mac Dowall in 1800, that he would accept the British protectorate and a British garrison at Kandy. North had no idea of the difficulties of a war with the Kandyans, of which the Portuguese and after them the Dutch had made the sad experience.

Whilst General Mac Dowall was making a triumphal start towards Kandy — „ Colombo, writes Cordiner, was almost quite „ drained of troops. The strength of the garrison consisted of only „ two companies of His Majesty's 65th regiment under Lieutenant „ Colonel Maddison stationed in the fort, and about three hundred „ Sepoys of the Ceylon infantry cantoned in the vicinity." —

At the same time another division commanded by Colonel Barbut left Trincomalee on the 4th February, and on the 20th, after having had only some insignificant skirmishes, both divisions joined forces at the ford of Kattugastotte, about one hour march from Kandy. The two united divisions numbered 3,000 men.

The same evening, General Mac Dowall sent his vanguard commanded by Major Evans to reconnoitre the fortifications of Kandy whilst his troops crossed the Mahavelli-Ganga on rafts.

Evans did not meet a living soul on his way, and approaching Kandy he found the city deserted: only some stray dogs prowled in the streets. Having sent his report to the General he encamped in the midst of the deserted city, keeping himself on guard in prevision of a sudden attack of the Kandyans.

The night however passed without surprise and on the next morning of the 21 February General Mac Dowall occupied Kandy. All the inhabitants had left the city and the King had gone, taking with him his treasures, after having set fire to his palace, which they found half consumed.

Mac Dowall triumphant at his easy victory thought that by the capture of the capital the war was ended. The English had as yet no time to acquire experience of Ceylon, and they did not guess, what the Portuguese knew so well, that the natural position of Kandy being such, the town could not be defended against an invading army, and therefore the tactics of the Kandyans had always been to let the enemy enter it, when they were caught like in a trap, and then, assuming the offensive block them in the town surrounded with mountains, which at that epoch were covered with an impenetrable jungle. Thus General Mac Dowall allowed himself to be trapped. He had however at his disposal an army of 3,000 men, which was considered by the Kandyans as a force not to be trifled with.

General Mac Dowall thinking as we said above that the capture of Kandy has ended the war and delivered into his hands the whole Kingdom committed a great mistake.

On the day after the occupation of Kandy, on the 22 February he published a proclamation in the deserted city, declaring King Sri Wikrama Raja Singha deposed and proclaiming King of Kandy prince Muthu Swami.

We have seen that Muthu Swami had sought refuge on the British territory and was kept in princely state but in semi-captivity in Jaffna. He had the cleverness to make the Governor believe that he was very popular at Kandy, and that a great number of Chiefs and the majority of the people were on his side, when in fact he was despised by all, and would never be recognized as King on account of a public and ignominious punishment inflicted on him by the late King Rajadi for some misdeed.

Having been thus proclaimed King by Mac Dowall, Muthu Swami made his entry into Kandy on the 4th day of March, and the General was much surprised that not one of the Chiefs came to pay him homage, and he resolved to use force in order to procure some subjects to the nominee of the Governor: — „Almost every day, „says Cordiner, parties made excursions into different parts of the „country, but the inhabitants fled in all directions; fear prevented „them from coming forward to declare their friendly sentiments to „the new King. An attempt to subdue them produced no „advantage.“ —

Muthu Swami's first act was to claim as his property all the booty which the English had made in the pillage of what remained of the royal palace, and Mac Dowall had everything returned to him.

A few days later General Mac Dowall signed a treaty with his improvised King, who, says Cordiner: — „ Now occupied the royal „ palace, without any other subjects than his servants, and without „ any other support than that of the British army corps." —

The treaty naturally satisfied all North's wishes: It acknowledged the British protectorate over the Kingdom, admitted a permanent strong English garrison at Kandy, gave over to the English a large portion of the Kandyan territory and several strategical positions which commanded the road between Colombo and Kandy. Marshall gives this document in full.

Unfortunately the treaty was concluded with a prince whom Mac Dowall alone regarded as King, and for whom it was not only necessary to conquer the throne to which he had no right whatever, but also afterwards to maintain him on it.

Meanwhile, the effects of the climate were more and more felt in the ranks of the British army. Fever and dysentery were decimating the soldiers and the hospital was filling daily.

This was what the Adigar Pilame-Talawe was waiting for. The invading army was too strong for him to risk a battle. He therefore allowed Mac Dowall to amuse himself with making a King of Muthu Swami, and awaited the hot season, when he knew, the British troops would be decimated by sickness, and all communications with Colombo interrupted for some time.

When this season was drawing near, Pilame-Talawe commenced to make advances to Mac Dowall which resulted in a secret correspondence between them, with the object of seizing the person of King Sri Wikrama Raja Singha who was now staying at Hanguranketty, one of his country seats.

The Adigar urged the General to capture the King, and, writes Major Forbs: — „The British commander still duped by the Adigar „despatched two strong parties under Colonel Bailie and Colonel „Logan, on a meteor chase to seize the King,“ — And so persuaded they were of the facility of the enterprise, that they omitted to send scouts to reconnoitre the country, nor even seem to have had a vanguard.

The two detachments found the route well fortified. Everywhere in the mountains the Kandyans in ambush received the troops with well directed musketry fire and inflicted them heavy losses. Finally the two Colonels arrived at Hanguranketty, only to find that the King had shifted his headquarters farther. The English set fire to the royal palace, in which they found nothing to carry away and returned to Kandy, after having suffered considerable losses.

Meanwhile the position of the British troops in Kandy became more and more precarious. Strong bodies of Kandyan partisans occupied the mountain forests which surrounded the town, and every soldier who ventured out of the encampment was shot. The King, others say the Adigar, had promised a reward of ten Rupees for each English head they brought to him, and five Rupees for each head of a Malay or Singhalese soldier. The convoys of food and every correspondence with Colombo was intercepted.

Such was the state of things when on the 26th March, the Maha-Mudeliyar who had accompanied Mac Dowall to Kandy received a letter from the Adigar, in which he wrote that he was rather surprised that the Governor continued this useless war, when he could easily arrange matters with him, and at the same time cunningly insinuated that his conditions would be the same as those he had proposed in 1799, that is to say, the deposition of the King, and his own elevation to the throne of Kandy.

The matter seemed easier now that Mac Dowall had already solemnly proclaimed the deposition of Sri Wikrama Raja Singha. It was necessary at all cost to get out of the position in which he had been entrapped. The General therefore answered the Adigar, that he agreed to treat with him on that basis, on condition that the deposed King would be delivered to him, that the province of the Vanni would be erected into an independent principality for Muthu Swami and that of the seven Korles handed over to the English.

Two days later, the second Adigar arrived at Kandy. He emphatically refused to give up the Vanni to Muthu Swami and the seven Korles to the English, a treaty however was signed by him and by Mac Dowall on the following conditions: The King Wikrama Raja Singha was declared deposed. The Adigar Pilame-Talawe was to be invested with royal power with the title of Great Prince. Muthu Swami was to retain the title of King, but was to be kept in Jaffna on a pension of 30,000 dollars. An armistice was concluded which was to be followed by a definite peace, on the day when King Wikrama Raja Singha would be delivered a prisoner in Colombo.

The second Adigar left Kandy on the 30th March midst salves of artillery.

Without waiting for the ratification by the Governor and by Pilame-Talawe of this treaty which in itself was null and void as concluded with a traitor whilst King Wikrama Raja Singha was still in possession of the whole of his Kingdom except the capital, General Mac Dowall evacuted Kandy with his army, and returned to Colombo, leaving only a garrison of 300 British and 700 Malay soldiers under the command of Colonel Barbut.

With what feverish haste the proceedings were carried on, is shown by the following dates: Pilame-Talawe made his first advances on March 26. On the 28 his plenipotentiary arrived at Kandy. On the 30th March the treaty was signed, and on the 1st April, Mac Dowall left Kandy with the greater part of his army.

Two weeks later Pilame-Talawe asked for an interview with the Governor to ratify the treaty. He named Dambadenia, on the confines of the Kandyan territory as the place of meeting. And North, who, Pridham says: — „ thought that the Adigar was sincere, „ and that he had at length determined to act in good faith" — hastened to the place and on the 3rd May the treaty was ratified.

Colonel Barbut, who commanded the garrison at Kandy, arrived suddenly at Dambadenia with an escort of 300 Malays. It was quite natural that the Colonel would come to confer with the Governor, but everyone was astonished at so strong an escort. Pilame-Talawe seemed uneasy, he seemed to be under the influence of a great agitation: his hands trembled as he spoke. It was not till much later that it became known that the treacherous Adigar had arranged everything to capture the Governor and carry him, a prisoner, into the mountains of the Kandyan territory. Colonel Barbut suspected something of the kind and his timely arrival with his escort frustrated the Adigar's plans.

Nevertheless the conference continued, and Pilame-Talawe requested that General Mac Dowall should return to Kandy, to help him to put the treaty into execution and North consented. The conference being over, the Governor returned to Colombo, and Colonel Barbut to Kandy, where he died on the 21st May. His death was a great loss, for he was a brave, able and experienced officer.

General Mac Dowall arrived at Kandy on the 23rd May, two days after Barbut's death. He did not find the Adigar who had promised to meet him there. To a letter of the General, Pilame-Talawe answered that he could not hold with him communication of any kind without the previous permission of King Wikrama Raja Singha. The General remained three weeks in Kandy, and on June 11th, without having seen the Adigar, he left for Colombo.

After Barbut's death and the departure of General Mac Dowall the command of the garrison of Kandy passed by right to Major Davie.

Two days after the General's departure, Davie received a letter from Pilame-Talawe, in which the Adigar bitterly complained that his endeavours to serve the English had brought upon him the displeasure of the King, and earnestly requested from him to send an expedition to capture the King who had again established his headquarters to Hanguranketty.

This letter of the Adigar was a cruel mockery, for he well knew to what miserable state the garrison commanded by Davie had been reduced:

The rainy season had begun, and swollen rivers rendered all communications with the British territory impossible. Mac Dowall having contented himself with the occupation of the town alone so that the surrounding country remained in the hands of the King, there was no possibility of getting provisions, and all detachments, who left the town in search of food in the neighbouring villages, were massacred by bands of armed Kandyans.

The unfortunate garrison had to live on insufficient rations of rice. The native and Malay soldiers deserted in large numbers and passed to the Kandyan army.

The effects of the climate, and the want of proper food brought on a bad type of fever, so that of the 300 English soldiers left by the General 140 were in hospital, and about six men died daily. The mortality among the native troops was still greater. They were cantoned in huts and, as no one thought of burying the dead, the dogs devoured their corpses in the streets.

It was in such a condition that General Mac Dowall abandoned the unfortunate garrison of Kandy when he left for Colombo.

Meanwhile the Kandyan army was approaching the town. The

King having concentrated considerable forces had surrounded the town erecting batteries on the hills.

The unfortunate Muthu Swami trembled in his palace and began to understand that he would have to pay dearly for having acted as a phantom King during the last four months.

On the 23rd June, as in derision of his now desperate position, Pilame-Talawe wrote again to Major Davie expressing him his astonishment at not having as yet captured the King, and urging him to do so without more delay.

Meanwhile Wikrama Raja Singha marched in person on Kandy. On the 24th June he captured a redout which Davie had erected in the morning and then ordered an assault on the royal palace where Davie had entrenched himself. Wikrama Raja Singha watched the proceedings from a hill which overlooked the town.

Major Davie had at that time only 20 English soldiers who were fit for fighting, a handful of officers and a small body of Malays. They fought like heroes. Lieutenant Blackeney was killed, Lieutenant Plenderbeath dangerously wounded. The small garrison in the palace suffered considerable losses for the Kandyans were firing from the hills that commanded the building.

Finally, after nine hours heroic resistance, a British officer in command of the Malays represented to Major Davie, that a longer resistance would only result in a butchery, and they hoisted the white flag.

A Kandyan Chief bearing too a white flag approached the palace and Major Davie went out to him. The Kandyan told him in the name of the King: that the English having invaded his territory, they would pay dearly if they did not evacuate it at once.

— „How can we remove the sick who are in the hospital, said the Major, we have no means of transport." —

— „Leave them where they are, replied the Kandyan Chief the King will see that they are well cared for." —

— „Will their lives be spared?" — Asked Davie.

— „Fear nothing, said the Kandyan, no harm will be done to them, if you depart immediately with all your valid men. If however you delay a moment, you are dead men, and they too." — Then he added ironically: — „Who knows, perhaps the King will keep some Englishmen in cages to show them to the people." —

Finally Major Davie obtained the permission to go with the Malay Captain Noureddin to Pilame-Talawe to arrange the terms of the capitulation.

These terms were as follows: Kandy was to be delivered immediately to the King with all the baggages and munitions. The soldiers who were not sick, would leave the city with their arms and regain the British territory by the road of Trincomalee; Muthu Swami would be allowed to go with them. The sick were to remain in the hospital under the Adigar's protection, well supplied with food and medicine, till it would become possible to take them to Colombo or to Trincomalee.

Thus, in the desperate position in which he was placed, Major Davie had managed to obtain honorable conditions. He returned to his men with a safe-conduct signed by the Adigar the name of the King.

At five in the afternoon, all the valid men of the garrison marched out of Kandy. They were 14 officers, 20 British and 250 Malay soldiers and 140 Indian sepoys, Muthu Swami with his family and servants.

They took the road of Trincomalee and reached the Mahavelly Ganga at a place called Wallapoloa, where the river was always fordable, but found it so swollen by the rains of the last days that it was not possible to ford it. There were neither boats or rafts, and the night was falling.

Major Davie ordered his men to camp till next morning. An old servant approached him and said: — „Have you forgotten the words of the King: Delay your departure and you are dead. Do not stop here for the night. Let us pass the river as we can, on bamboo rafts or even swimming, but do not stop." — The Major turned round quickly and said: — You have delivered me your lecture, now take mine." — And he gave the old man a stroke with his horse-whip.

It rained in torrents. The small body of men gathered on the top of a hill under an old fig tree which gave them some shelter, and there they passed an awful night. The tree still stands, the lone witness of a tragedy, and the Kandyans call it Davie's tree.

At dawn, next morning, they saw on the opposite bank of the river a group of Kandyan villagers and called to them to bring boats, but they took a hostile attitude. Then they set about to construct rafts, but the rain of the preceding night had enormously swollen the river and the rafts were dashed by the current on the rocks that rose in the bed of the river. Some soldiers tried to swim over the flooded river in order to tie a rope to a tree on the opposite bank, so that the others could swim holding to it, but they could not struggle against the current. At last one succeeded, and tied the rope. But he was killed by the villagers who cut the rope away.

The King and Pilame-Talawe, knew well that the river was not fordable, and that was the reason why they had consented to such easy terms.

In the morning a few Kandyan Chiefs, arrived on the spot with a body of soldiers and asked to speak to Major Davie. They told him that the King was very much excited against the Adigar for having allowed the English to leave Kandy instead of keeping them prisoners, but later on he seemed appeased and said that if Major Davie delivers to him Muthu Swami and five of his relatives, he would procure him boats to cross the river and give order that no one molest them during their retreat through the Kandyan territory. Davie refused.

Two hours later other chiefs arrived at the encampment, and speaking amicably told Major Davie that the King was a near relation to Muthu Swami, and certainly would do him no harm, but, not having seen him for a long time, he wished to take leave of him before his departure.

Major Davie had no faith in this sudden tenderness of the King towards his unhappy rival. His first thought however was to save his soldiers and he already had begun to waver in his resolution to protect to the end the unfortunate prince. He answered however, that he could not deliver him to the King without an express order of the Governor.

The Chiefs withdrew a short distance but soon returned, declaring to the Major that if he did not deliver to them Muthu Swami, they would take him by force, and then the King would prevent his troop from crossing the river.

The position became more and more critical. They had tried in vain to launch a raft on the river. The current took it away and broke it on the rocks. They had to cross the river to get out of the King's reach and saw the impossibility of doing so without boats.

Davie held council with his officers, and they decided, that in face of such a desperate position all resistance was impossible, and that they had no other choice than to yield to the imperious demand of the King.

The Major himself carried the sad tidings to Muthu Swami, he told him that he was powerless to protect him, and endeavoured to console him by saying that the King had promised to treat him kindly. But Muthu Swami knowing well the fate that awaited him exclaimed: — „Can it be possible that the glory of the arms of England has fallen so low, as to have to give way before the menaces of these miserable Kandyans." —

Major Davie, greatly moved handed him over to the Chiefs, together with his family and servants: Muthu Swami all the time kept a proud and dignified attitude. They took him to Kandy, where Pilame-Talawe, and the second Adigar Millawe had already received orders, to take him immediately to Ondewatte where the King had his headquarters.

When he was brought before him the King told to a powerful

Chief called Eheylapola to ask Muthu Swami, if he was not ashamed, he, a royal prince, to have been in league with the English? Muthu Swami turned to the King and replied: — „I am in your power.“ — Then the King asked him if he had had any correspondence with any of the Chiefs. Muthu Swami replied that all that he could say was, that the First Adigar Pilame-Talawe was in constant correspondence with the English.

The King refused to believe it, or pretended not to believe, then he ordered Muthu Swami and five members of his family to be beheaded, and the servants to have their noses and ears cut off.

Muthu Swami having been executed, the King summoned Pilame-Talawe and commanded him to send troops to Wallapoloa to secure and put to death Major Davie and all the English who were with him. The Adigar objected that it would be a violation of the capitulation and besides an unjust and cruel action.

The King answered in anger: — „So, you side again with the English!“ — The Adigar left the King and passing through the antechamber, where a few Chiefs were assembled he told them of the King's order. They all protested, but Pilame-Talawe said: — „It is the King's order; what can we do!“ — Yet he tried to bring the King to reason through one of his favourites, but hardly had the man opened his mouth, when the King rose in anger exclaiming: — „What, have they not yet carried out my orders!“ —

Meanwhile the Kandyans seemed to be seriously busy in preparing the means to bring over Davie's troops to the other side of the river, yet night fell and the boats had not been brought to the place.

Next morning, Sunday 26 June, large detachments of Kandyan troops were seen massing on the Kandy road. Major Davie grew uneasy, when he saw a man advancing towards his encampment, carrying a musket wrapped in white muslin, a sign of peace. The messenger said he came from the Adigar Pilame-Talawe, who desired to have a personal interview with Major Davie, in order to arrange with him personally about the passage of his men through the river, and their safe retreat through the Kandyan territory. The man said that the Adigar was waiting on the road to Kandy and begged the Major to bring two officers with him.

Major Davie took with him Captain Rumley and Captain Noureddin of the Malay regiment and followed the messenger. They did not find the Adigar on the road but only three Chiefs who told that the King wanted the Major to come to the palace.

Captain Noureddin endeavoured to persuade the Major not to go farther, as all these manoeuvres seemed to imply treason. Davie however knew well, that to disobey the King's orders meant death to his troop and moreover he hoped to obtain from the King means to cross the river.

When they were approaching the town they were surrounded by a strong body of Kandyan troops, and understood that they were prisoners.

Meanwhile, some Malay officers, in the service of the King of Kandy, had penetrated the English encampment and fomented desertion among the Malay and Indian troops, and many deserted.

Then a messenger came to the encampment and told the British officers that the river was fordable at Katugastotte, about the distance of a mile, and that Major Davie and Captains Rumley and Noureddin were awaiting them there. They set out to march for the place, but soon found themselves surrounded by Kandyan, Malay and Kaffir troops who were pushing them forwards.

Finally, half way between Wallapoloa and Katugastotte, they saw both sides of the road lined by Kandyan troops, they were surrounded and summoned to lay down their arms.

A Kandyan Chief then summoned the Malay soldiers and asked them, if it were not better for them to abandon the British and to pass over to the service of the King of Kandy. Many replied that, having sworn allegiance to the King of England, they would remain faithful to death. They were immediately tied up and placed under the guard of the Kaffirs. The Chief then asked the other soldiers if they preferred death or the service of the King of Kandy. Frightened by the fate of their companions, they consented to be enrolled in the Kandyan army and were marched under escort to the town.

Then began the last act of this terrible drama: The English officers and men were taken two by two and brought behind a hill where they could not be seen by their companions. They were handed to Kaffir soldiers who gave each a stroke with the sword on the neck, then broke their head with the butt of their muskets and rolled down the dead bodies into a ravine. Thirty Englishmen were executed in this way.

Corporal Barnsley was the only man who escaped the massacre:

With the muscles of his neck cut, and a blow of the butt-end of a musket on his head, he hid himself under a heap of corpses and, at night, dragging himself to the river and, seeing that the water had fallen, he swam across. Some Kandyan villagers moved with pity gave him clothes and some food, and he managed to reach a fort 16 miles on the Trincomalee road where the English had small garrison. Marshall gives us a stirring narration of the flight of Barnsley.

Whilst this bloody execution was taking place on the Katugastotte road, the Kandyans, by the King's order slaughtered the 120 British officers and men and the 30 native soldiers who were lying sick in the hospital.

There also only one escaped: He was a German named Thomas Thoen. Stunned by a stroke in the head, he fainted, and the Kandyans thinking him dead, threw him out of the window with the other corpses.

The shock revived him and he dragged himself to a ditch, where he remained hidden till next morning, when he was discovered and hanged on a tree. The rope broke and he fell on the ground in a faint.

Discovered again he was hanged a second time, and again the rope broke, and he sought refuge in an abandoned hut and lived for six days on herbs and roots. Recaptured again, they did not dare to put him a fourth time to death as they believed him to be a sorcerer. The King ordered to give him a house and all the necessaries for life. He escaped two years later and managed to reach the British outposts.

In the evening of the day of the massacre, the Adigar Pilame-Talawe ordered salves of artillery to be fired, and there were great rejoicings.

By and by, the people who had left Kandy at the approach of the English returned to their deserted homes.

Major Davie and Captains Rumley and Noureddin were conducted to Hangeranketty where the King was encamped.

Rumley died soon of dysentery. Major Davie was confined in a village in the district of Dumbura, where he was fairly well treated. He died in captivity some say in 1805, others in 1810. The Government of Colombo made overtures for his release, but the King asked for his ransom a harbour on the coast. They say that in his captivity Davie could hardly be distinguished from the native villagers; he had adopted their manners and their dress.

Captain Noureddin was the son of a petty Malay sultan. When he was brought before the King, he was ordered by the Adigar to prostrate. He and his brother answered that they were sons and grandsons of Kings and would prostrate before no Monarch. The King seemed to be pleased with this bold answer, and addressing them courteously invited them to enter his service, offering them the command of all his Malay troops. They answered that, having sworn fidelity to the King of England, they would not break their oath. The King angered by their refusal condemned them both to death. They were beheaded and their bodies thrown into the jungle to be devoured by the wild beasts.

This massacre of the garrison of Kandy is certainly one of the most exciting episodes of the history of Ceylon. But one is deeply struck by the fact, that, when the Portuguese found themselves in an equally desperate position, at Balane in 1589, or at Badulla in 1630, we see them passing the whole night in prayer, preparing to die as Christians. Here, among the minutest details given by contemporary writers, we can find no trace that these protestant soldiers, in the face of a certain death, had ever raised their souls to God, their Creator.

The English authors are unanimous in condemning Major Davie's conduct. But it seems to us that their judgment is unjust. It is easy to understand Cordiner or Bisset (Philalethes) sitting on the verandah in an easy chair with whisky and soda at their elbow discussing the unfortunate soldier, and telling one another the acts of heroism they would have performed if they were at his place. But more astonishing is the judgment of a serious writer like Pridham, and of military men like Major Forbes and the recent author who wrote under the name of: An Officer of the Ceylon Rifles.

— „ In our judgment of the conduct of Major Davie, at this „ unhappy conjuncture, writes Pridham, it is almost needless to „ remark, that the feelings of passion and resentment which „ naturally arise at the violation of British faith, and the first duty of „ the soldier, must, however difficult it may be, banished from the „ mind. That performed as we have endeavoured to perform it; „ every obstacle in the way being fairly considered; and last of all a „ portraiture of ourselves in the situation of the unfortunate „ commander having been mentally drawn, it may be possible to

„ arrive to a comparatively dispassionate conclusion as to the real „ exigencies of the case.

„ The result of such an investigation, will be found to be more „ fatal to the character of Major Davie, than the most hasty and „ impassionate decision.

„ He could in the first place have no right to expect that the „ surrender to a certain death of the unfortunate prince, who had „ been tempted to assume a nominal sovereignty, should free him „ from the difficulties of his situation; on the contrary, it elevated the „ spirit of the King and stimulated him to attempt that act of „ atrocious cruelty which harmonized so well with his cowardly „ character.

„ He must, however, have been devoided of all energy and mental „ resources, or a moment reflexion would have suggested, that there „ were other routes, much less dangerous and impracticable than the „ one that he selected. The Kandyans were two days in consumating „ their perfidy. Had he, during the storm of the first night, when „ the Kandyans from inability to withstand the exposure to the „ inclemency of the elements had, *in all probability*, retired to their „ houses, discumbered himself from the surplus of his baggage, and by „ his example and that of his officers inspired the troops with the „ courage and resolve which seldom fails to the British soldier in the „ moment of danger; had he, I say, marched to the Kattugastotte „ ferry, the passage of which would be far from insuperable to „ a lightly equipped force, with the simple aid of a warp, and with „ several clear hours before him threaded the defiles of Balane, the „ safety of his force would have been to all human certainty insured.

„ Had he even taken a more circuitous route by the ferry of „ Ganaroowa to Colombo, there is no ground for believing, that he „ could have failed in his enterprise.

„ It was not until two days had elapsed, and the dejection „ arising from hunger, exposure to the pitiless elements and the „ apparent certain destruction in store for them had done its work, „ that coward fear had taken possession of the troops.

„ Why had it so soon seized upon their Commander? Major „ Davie had already had a fair specimen of Kandyan faith and „ sincerety by the attack on Kandy in defiance of a solemn treaty.[1] „ The slightest attention to the offers of the Kandyans, was not then „ for a moment justifiable.

„ But what if the passage of the river at the very ferry, at which „ he took up his post was practicable? Forbes intimates as much; and „ certainly the ease with which Captain Johnston's small force „ subsequently crossed would warrant the belief. Had he crossed the „ river, a rapid march through the Atgalle pass would have placed „ him in security at fort Mac Dowall in a few hours. A march from „ twelve to fifteen miles by any one of the three routes would have „ placed him in comparative safety.

„ Our duty thus discharged, we may cordially concord with „ Forbes where he remarks: — We may mitigate our severe opinion „ of the indefensible act of this unfortunate man, who by lingering „ out his existence in a miserable captivity, expiated his errors of „ judgment, and we may imagine how much the sickness and

1) The treaty here mentioned as we have seen above, was made between the Governor, and a traitor minister and stipulated the deposition of the King, and could not therefore bind the King who attacked Kandy.

„ suffering, which he constantly witnessed, may have affected his „ mind. We were equally the dupes, and only by good fortune „ escaped becoming the victims of Kandyan treachery." —

Let us now examine the position, not in the light of events that followed but such as appeared on the memorable days of the 24th, 25th and 26th of June 1803.

The surrender of Muthu Swami to the King of Kandy was certainly a tragical episode that none can read without emotion.

Davie was in a desperate position. He was caught in a trap without possible issue. The Chiefs sent by the King asked for the surrender, but at the same time they gave clearly to understand that in case of refusal, the King would take him by force and annihilate the more or less disarmed British troop, to which the terms of the capitulation had assured a retreat to the British territory. They should have fought, they say in defence of the Governor's proteges. Yes, they had muskets without munitions, they had swords, but before they could have reached the Kandyan lines at swords length they would have been annihilated by the enemy's musketry and artillery fire.

Moreover the Major well knew, that the attack on Kandy led by the King in person meant a serious renewal of hostilities. The British possessions were in a sore want of troops and the 423 regulars he had with him would weight in the balance in such a war like that.

The King promised to provide him with means of crossing the

river, if he abandoned to his fate Muthu Swami, and once on the other bank, his men were safe. He could not save Muthu Swami, that was too evident.

Now, what was his duty, not as a private man, but as a responsible commander: Had he to resist, and sacrifice the life of his men, whose death in the case was certain, for the honour of having endeavoured to protect one, whom he could not save from his fate, or save the life of his soldiers, of whom at that moment England was in a sorry need?

We leave to military men to decide this question, he had no other alternative: deliver Muthu Swami, or cause at the same time the death of the unfortunate prince and of all the men under his command. For it must be kept in mind that, at that moment, the King did not yet mean to slaughter the English, on the contrary, he promised to provide them with boats to cross the river. He wanted Muthu Swami.

Another crime reproached to Major Davie is to have remained two whole days encamped at Wallapoloa: If the river was swollen and the ford impracticable, he should have taken profit of the moment when, *to all probability* on account of the rain, the Kandyan soldiers had gone to the homes, burn their unnecessary baggages, swim over the river, and by his example inspire to his men the manly courage and resolve which seldom fails the British soldiers in the moment of danger. Johnston forded the river at the very same place. Thus is the accusation resumed by Pridham.

The: — „*to all probability*" — is really admirable. Does it not seem rather improbable that the Kandyan soldiers, in front of an enemy, even weak and retreating, were allowed to go to their homes because it rained.

Why did he not burn the unnecessary baggage. According to the terms of the capitulation the English were but allowed to take their swords and their empty muskets, not even some ammunitions nor a provision of food for two days. What was then this unnecessary baggage ?

He should have had inspired the troops with that courage and resolve which seldom fails the British soldier. Out of the 423 men he commanded 30 only were English, all the others were Malay and Indian sepoys, demoralized, seized with an unspeakable fear, and looking only for some means of deserting.

Johnston crossed the river in the very same place. Yes, fifteen months later. I was once looking how some boys were fording the river at Wallapolao. The water rose to their breast. When I returned to the same place after two days of heavy rain, the water rose over the banks, and the current was so rapid, that whoever would have tried to swim over would certainly be dashed against the rocks.

But why Davie's obstination to cross the river at that place? Why did not ford it at Kattugastotte or at Ganaroowa ?

If the river could not be crossed at Wallapolao, it was equally impracticable at the two other fords. Secondly, according to the terms of the capitulation they had to retreat by the Trincomalee road and the strict observance of these terms could alone save his men.

Violate them would mean to show hostility to the victors at whose mercy they were.

In order to reach Ganaroowa Davie would had to cut his way through the Kandyan army what he certainly could not do with his handful of demoralized men.

One way only remained open to him, it was to follow the shore of the river and so reach Ganaroowa. But he knew that there too the river was flooded, and he was watched, and if he tried to move in that direction the Kandyans by the road of Gatembe would reach the place in half the time and cut his retreat.

Why did he accept, they say, the interview with the Adigar, when he should have forseen the treason?

Why should he have foreseen the treason of those with whom he had signed a honorable capitulation and who approached him with a message of peace, the more so, that at that moment they seemed to be seriously busy in preparing all that he needed for the crossing of the river.

Why did he not fight, they say. Fight with whom? With those who came to him bearing the white flag, and fight with swords against artillery, and when, as says the same Pridham, a coward fear had already taken possession of his troops?

But, writes: An officer of the Ceylon Rifles: — „ Major Davie, „ instead of boldly cutting through his contemptible enemies, which „ he might have done... surrendered his arms which he never should „ have done under any circumstances." —

But were the 20 or 30,000 Kandyans well armed and provided with artillery, such a contemptible enemy for a handful 400 soldiers who could use only swords and the butts of their muskets. How could he cut boldly through them, when his men were panic stricken and already deserted in number?

Davie should have never surrendered his arms. But when the troops surrendered their arms, he was already a prisoner on his way to Hanguranketty.

Finally they make a crime to Davie that during his captivity he took the habits and dress of the Kandyans. But where, I say, could he have got a laced uniform, epaulets and a periwig?

All these writers are unjust in their judgment of Major Davie's conduct. Instead of overwhelming the unfortunate soldiers, should they not rather blame the General who seeing the garrison of Kandy reduced to a desperate state abandoned it and returned hastily to Colombo and safety, and the Governor whose incapacity and love of intrigues, was the cause of the disaster.

The news of the massacre of the English in Kandy produced a general consternation at Colombo, and they hastened to evacuate some fortlets they held on the Kandyan territory.

Governor North asked urgently the Governor General of India for reinforcements of at least 3,000 men, but did not get them.

The Kandyans invaded the British territory. They entered it in different places to oblige the Governor to divide his forces, which, they knew were inadequate.

Wherever they passed the Kandyans caused the native population who fraternized with them to rebel against the English, whose position became very critical, as with sorely unsufficient forces they had not only to repel the Kandyans, but also to defend themselves against their own subjects.

On the 21 August, a considerable body of Kandyans approached within 15 miles of Colombo and captured the fort of Hanwella, and next day the news spread that they were marching on Colombo, which produced in that town an indescribable panic. On August 23 they devastated the districts of Galle, Matara and Hambantotte. On the 25th they appeared before Mulatiwu. On the 27th they laid siege to Chilaw. On September 3 they approached Kottyar and Battecaloa. The low-country Singhalese on the eastern and southern coasts were in open revolt against the English.

The Kandyans were passed masters in partisan warfare in the mountains and forests of their native country, but could not cope with European troops in the plains, where notwithstanding their number they were always repulsed by a mere handful of British troops.

Cordiner gives us a detailed account of this war, but it presents little interest; a succession of insignificant skirmishes, in which the British officers evinced their usual pluck and determination, but at times committed cruel reprisals on the revolted natives.

— „ A desultory warfare of retribution between the Kandyans „ and the English, writes Marshall, continued about February and „ March 1805. The war was conducted by both parties, Christians

„ and Heathen with savage barbarity. Numerous villages were „ burned, and large tracts of country reduced to desolation. The „ English no doubt palliated their barbarities, by the loss they had „ incurred during the invasion of 1803; but who can justify retaliation, „ when the innocent are the victims?

„ In our own territory, the disaffection of the inhabitants was „ punished by martial law with fearful severity. At Cogel (Kogalle) „ on the southern coast, the inhabitants of which village had „ interrupted the communication between Galle and Matara, fifty „ boats were burned, and all the houses of the village destroyed. „ One rioter was hanged and five others were condemned to receive „ each one thousand lashes, a favourite sentence with court-martial „ at that period and for a long time after." —

Although his armed bands were repulsed everywhere the King of Kandy, elated with pride, conceived the ambitious design of driving the English out of Ceylon and to make a brilliant stroke by capturing Colombo. Wikrama Raja Singha was perfectly aware of all that was going on in the town. He knew the discouragement that reigned there, and the weakness of the garrison, but he had probably no idea of what European fortifications meant, for he placed all his hope in a few small guns he was taking with him.

He marched first on Hanwella which in the meantime had been retaken by the English. The garrison of the fort consisted in a small number of invalids, so on the news of the Kings approach the Governor sent there a body of 100 soldiers under Captain William Pollock who had to assume the command of the place.

On the morning of the 6th September a large but undisciplined Kandyan army attacked the fort of Hanwella, they had erected batteries, and with their small guns were directing on the thick walls of the fortress a constant fire of grape shot, which had naturally no other effect than making the plaster fall.

Captain Pollock had meanwhile sent Lieutenant Mercer with a small body of men to turn the enemy by traversing the forest by a path he knew and attack them from the flank, and he himself endeavoured to draw the Kandyans as near as possible to the walls. When they were not more than 200 paces, Pollock judging that Mercer had already reached his position made a sortie.

During the fight 26 Malay soldiers and 150 Indian artillery men, of those who had belonged to Davies unfortunate body, and who had been enrolled by force into the Kandyan army, deserted and joined the English. Whilst the Kandyans were occupied with Pollock, Mercer attacked the King's quarter. The King thus surprised fled, the rout was complete. Pollock took the royal standard and all his infantry. Then, leaving the invalids at Hanwella, he pursued the Kandyans into their own territory, seized their army stores and Ruanwelle, and having freed the British territory from the invaders, returned to Colombo, with three times the number of soldiers he had taken with him, and a number of guns.

This splendid valour of Captain Pollock decided the fate of the campaign. King Wikrama Singha returned to Kandy where he appeased his rage by having many of the Chiefs of his army beheaded. When their wives claimed their dead bodies, the King refused to allow them to be buried, and two of the ladies in thelr despair committed suicide. The Kandyan Chiefs did not hide their indignation, the people murmured loudly, and seeing the general disaffection the King did not dare to continue the war for a while. He wanted all his troops to prevent a rebellion.

Governor North, on his side, discouraged by the results of his policy began to make advances to the King of Kandy:

1804

— „ The private correspondence of Mr. North, at this period „ with the Governor General, writes Emmerson Tennent, evinces the „ intensity of his anxiety for peace. Messages were sent secretly to „ the King through the chief Bikshu of Kandy, to entreat him to ask „ for pardon, as all the Governor required was not treasure and „ territories, but satisfaction for the horrid crime he had perpetrated.

„ But the only reply was a refusal on the ground that the „ butchery had been committed without his orders by the Adigar, „ from whom he had since withdrawn his confidence.

„ Cordiner states, that those advances for peace were made by „ the Kandyans, but the letters quoted above show that they „ emanated from the Governor." —

One remains simply amazed at the simplicity of North, who, seeing that his policy of intrigues had ended in a disaster, reduced to extremity by this war and sure of not being able to get any reinforcements, entreats the King of Kandy, who, far from being conquered had driven the English from his territory and invaded and devastated theirs, and was even at that moment at the head of an army of at least 30,000 men, to humbly beg him pardon, offering him generously his clemency.

North's advances having been repulsed by the King the war continued, always on British territory, which the Kandyans did not cease to invade. Driven away on one side, they reappeared on another, favoured by the natives who were in a latent state of rebellion.

Whilst the Kandyans were ravaging the British territory, General Wemyss, who had succeeded Mac Dowall, determined to cause a diversion in the King's dominions. On the 4th September 1804, he sent from Battecaloa Captain Johnston, an Irishman, at the head of 300 men. He had to effect a junction at the frontier with another company which had to be sent from Colombo and invade the Kingdom of Kandy.

Soon after Johnston's departure the project was abandoned but the dashing Captain had marched so rapidly, that the messenger sent after him did not reach him, having probably lost his way.

When reaching the frontier, Johnston did not find the other company at the appointed place, he supposed they had gone in advance. It did not struck him that perhaps they were yet on the rear. He marched on, and encountering no resistance he found himself at the gates of Kandy.

The Kandyans, not knowing the strength of the enemy, had, as was their custom, abandoned the town, and Johnston occupied it.

Getting no news of the other corps, the Captain understood the gravity of the position in which he had imprudently thrown himself, the more so that he saw himself strictly watched by a body of Kandyans dressed in British uniform, which they had taken from Davie s men and strong detatchments of the King's army were concentrating round the town.

His men whom the fear of the fate of Davie's companions had cause to lose all discipline, had discovered in the royal palace a large supply of brandy; excited with drink they fell into a disorderly panic. They gathered together on the palace square shouting like madmen : — „ We are going to be butchered. General Wemyss had delivered us up to the Kandyans. The Governor has sold us. There is no means of retreat. Let us stand where we are and fight to death." —

Johnston ran amidst the tumult, and for a moment losing his head, he too began to shout : — „ I am innocent. I knew nothing of this affair. If the Governor and the General has sold you, he has sold me also ! " — Then, suddenly, remembering his duty he said : — „ Despair will not save us. As long as we have arms, we are not lost. To remain here means destruction. We must at once beat a retreat. Spare your ammunitions, you have not too much of it, and on it depends our safety. Remember the butchery of Davie's soldiers, whose bones you have seen unburied, and which we shall see again this evening. To avoid a like fate, you ought to be firm and brave and observe the strictest discipline. Obey strictly my orders, and I will lead you all into safety." —

These manly words revived the courage of the soldiers, who set about actively making preparations for the retreat.

Captain Johnston put down in writing his plan of retreat, and after having read it to his soldiers placed the paper in his breast pocket showing them where they would find it in case of his being killed, to serve them as a guide. They then began their march.

They reached the ford at Wallapolao. Fortunately the river was low, and they crossed it under the enemy's fire. Then began an awful march through the Kandyan territory, of which Marshall gives us the details.

Harassed day and night by the Kandyans, starving, they marched on, Johnston always at the most dangerous post, reviving their courage, inspiring energy. Finally they reached Trincomalee, barefooted and in tatters, dying of fatigue and hunger. So exhausted they were that, on reaching the fort, they nearly all fell in a swoon.

Johnston's heroical retreat was as great a disaster, as the slaughter of the troops of Davie, for almost all the men who had escaped the bullets of the Kandyans, died in hospital. The Kandyan Chiefs said, that Johnston must have been in league with the devil as otherwise he could not have escaped all their ambushes. He was court-martialled for having gone to Kandy when his orders were to go to the frontier and acquitted.

In February 1805 the Kandyans again invaded the British territory but reinforcements had been received from India
1805 and they were vigourously repulsed. Nevertheless the King made preparations to march on Colombo, when the news reached suddenly, that the Adigar Pilame-Talawe had gone in haste to Kandy. All communications were interrupted, and for three weeks nothing was known of what was going on in the neighbouring Kingdom.

Finally the mystery cleared itself. The King had a severe attack of small-pox, they thought he would die. And Pilame-Talawe thinking the time had arrived to carry out his ambitious plans, had seized the power.

The Honourable Frederic North, created Earl of Guilford, left Ceylon about the middle of 1805, after having been Governor for seven years.

The results of his strange policy were: the British territory devastated, the native population exasperated and in a permanent state of rebellion; England's prestige compromised in the eyes of the Kandyans and in those of her own subjects.

Pridham gives a long enumeration of the faults committed by North and by the officials under him, but they are too uninteresting to be quoted.

In sending to Ceylon Andrews and North they committed in England the mistake, that had often been repeated by other powers, to entrust the Government of a newly conquered colony to civilians.

The disasters of the last few years opened the eyes in England and the four Governors who followed were military men.

North's immediate successor General Sir Thomas Maitland, ceased all hostilities with the Kandyans, disinterested himself of the affairs of this Kingdom and occupied himself entirely with the organisation of the territory conquered from the Dutch and whose possession had been assured to England by the treaty of Amiens.

## CHAPTER 4

# SIR THOMAS MAITLAND

We have few details of the progress of the Missions in the first
1805 years of the British rule. The Oratorian Fathers who were evangelizing the Island were simple and humble men, who carried on with wisdom and energy the Apostolic work inaugurated by Fr. Joseph Vaz, but left us few records of their zealous and truly apostolic labours.

Andrews and North were indifferent to religious matters, did not molest them and left them free to enjoy the liberty which the Catholics by their energy and organization had conquered from the Dutch thirty years before their downfall.

At the time of the British conquest, Fr. Joseph Vaz was the Superior of the Oratorians and Vicar General of the Bishop of Cochin to whose diocese Ceylon still belonged. He was probably of the family of the great Fr. Vaz. He died in the following year and was succeeded by Fr. Dominic Monteiro, who governed the Mission from 1797 to 1807. After him came Fr. Nicholas Rodriguez.

Under the rule of these wise Superiors, not only the number of Catholics increased, but Religion took deep roots in the hearts of the people. They became fervent Christians.

— „ The Roman Catholic Religion under the British adminis- „ tration, writes Emmerson Tennent, has maintained the same

„ ascendency and exhibited the same energy, which it had previously „ manifested throughout the patronage of the Portuguese and the „ proscriptions of the Dutch.

„ The number of nominal Christians, who still adhered in secret „ to the rites and tenets of Buddhism is infinitely smaller amongst „ the Roman Catholics, than amongst the professors of any other „ *church* in Ceylon, an incident which has been ascribed to the „ overruling influence of the confessional and the unintermitted „ control which it exerts over the feelings as well as the actions of its „ votaries; and Harward, himself a protestant minister, has borne his „ willing testimony to the sincerity and demeanour of the Roman „ Catholic converts, whom he describes as: — more detached from „ the customs of paganism, more regular in their attendance on the „ religious services of Christianity, and in their general conduct, „ more consistent with the moral precepts of the gospel, than any „ other religious body of any magnitude in Ceylon." —

Since Sir Thomas Maitland had set about the work of organizing
1806 the British possessions of Ceylon, he found himself in front of an embarassing difficulty:

The Dutch law of the 24th December 1776 had declared all the Catholic marriages null and void and considered as valid only the unions contracted before a protestant minister or according to heathen rites.

Catholics of course took no heed of this infamous law, and none of them would consent to contract such sacrilegious marriages.

The English Government till then had accepted the Dutch

legislation so that practically all old Dutch penal laws remained still in vigour. All marriages of Catholics contracted in the last 30 years were null before the law, and it created a great confusion each time that a question of inheritance came before the British Courts.

To obviate to this difficulty, and many others of the same kind Sir Thomas Maitland promulgated on the 27th May 1806, the following Law:

— „ Regulation No. 4 of 1806. A Regulation for taking off the restraint which were imposed upon the Roman Catholics of this Island by the late Dutch Government. Passed by the Governor in Council on the 27th May 1806.

It being his Majesty's most Gracious intention, that all persons who inhabit the British settlements on this Island, shall be permitted liberty of conscience and the free exercise of religious worship, provided they can be contented with a quiet and peaceable enjoyment of the same, without giving offence to Government. And it appearing that the Roman Catholics, who are a numerous and peaceable body of his Majesty's subjects are, by several laws passed under the late Dutch Government, rigorously excluded from many important privileges and capacities, and that although these laws had not been acted upon in all cases by His Majesty's Government, yet that they are still unrepealed and a cause of anxiety to those who profess the Catholic religion. The Governor in Council enacts as follows:

1. — The Roman Catholics shall be allowed free and unmolested possession and exercise of their Religion in every part of the British Settlements on the Island of Ceylon.

2. — They shall be admitted to all civil privileges and capacities.

3. — All marriages between Catholics, which had taken place within the said settlements since the 26 August 1795 according to the rites of the Roman Catholic Church, shall be deemed valid in law, although the form appointed by the late Dutch Government had not been observed.

4. — This Regulation shall take effect on the fourth day of June next, that day being His Majesty's birthday.

5. — Every part of any Law, Proclamation or Order which contradicts this regulation is hereby repealed." —

Thus, the religious liberty for which the Catholics had so bravely fought between 1750 and 1760, and which they had practically enjoyed since that time was finally recognized by the law.

Whilst the Catholic Missions were thus making a steady progress the fictitious edifice of protestantism erected by the Dutch ministers was crumbling down. It is very difficult to give an adequate idea of the position of protestantism in the first decade of the British rule, as we have only protestant documents to rely upon, and their testimony in this matter is not reliable. The protestant ministers greatly exaggerated the number of their so called converts, and used statistics simply as a mean to throw dust into the eyes of those who helped them with their money.

Nevertheless the documents that we have show sufficiently the state of their affairs.

Of the number of 429,684 protestant natives on the registers of the Dutch ministers in 1722, there remained on the arrival of the English according to the figures given by the protestant minister Cordiner, 342,200. It is however clear that these figures are greatly exaggerated for as we have seen, Palm, another protestant minister, who seems more or less honest in his computations, had given for the year 1760 the number of 280,057 native protestants in the Island of whom, he says, 105 only were communicants, and it was precisely between 1760 and 1796, that the number of these so-called native protestants diminished so rapidly, that the ministers finding themselves without flock, abandoned whole districts.

It is easy to explain the large number of protestant natives whom the Dutch had on their registers.

Having deprived of civil rights all natives who would not allow their names to be inscribed on these registers, and demanding from their so-called *converts* but a semblance of baptism and the attendance on Sundays to the protestant service, without caring if, on other days, they went to the temple of Buddha or offered sacrifices to idols, these natives considered their *conversion*, simply as a kind of registration which conferred on them the rights of citizenship and gave access to petty government employments, thus giving them the means of earning money without much work. To allow to be sprinkled with water, to be put to the inconvenience to sit out once a week a tedious sermon in a language of which they understood but little if in so doing they qualified themselves for renting land from the Crown, becoming clerks in government offices or village policemen, without having for that to give up their heathen customs and worship, seemed for them an easy sacrifice.

And that explains, how, out of a quarter of a million of natives registered as protestants in 1760, one hundred and five only were communicants.

Lord Valentia relates how during a tour in the interior, Governor North met a native who had to take the oath, as witness in Court:

— „ What is your religion ?" asked the Governor.

— „ I am a Christian." — answered the Singhalese.

— „ A Christian, but of what sect ?" —

— „ I am a Dutch Christian." —

— „ Oh ! a Dutch Christian said the Governor, then you worship Buddha." —

— „ Certainly, sir, he is my supreme Lord." —

And Lord Valentia adds, that: — „ Mr. North, in a tour round the Coast, found that in many parts, paganism was regaining its lost ground." —

The expression is not correct. Paganism could not regain ground, where it had never lost it, for all these native *converts* of the Dutch, were simply heathens, whose names had been written on protestant Registers. They were, as the protestant ministers themselves called them: *Sine Christo Christiani.* Christians who knew nothing about Christ.

When the British had replaced the Dutch, they already applied to the Colonies the principle of the atheistical, godless state, and openly proclaimed to the pagans their indifference in matters of religion, with the result, writes Digby, that the class of natives who were called protestant Christians: — „melted away like hail stones „in an Indian summer.“ —

Emmerson Tennent who is more explicit says: — „The natives „soon came to regard the withdrawal of compulsion to religious „conformity, only as an evidence of religious indifference on the „part of their new rulers, and they became still more convinced of „the justice of this conclusion on discovering that they were no „longer *paid* for apostacy, and that a monopoly of offices and public „employments was not as therefore to be jealously preserved for „the outward professors of (protestant) Christianity. Almost with „greater rapidity than their number had originally increased, they „now commenced to decline.“ —

In 1802 there were said to be only 34,000 protestants in the Island including Europeans and Burgers. The fine old Catholic churches which the Dutch had polluted and turned over into protestant worship places had fallen into ruins.

— „In 1806, says Emmerson Tennent, Buchanan who then „visited Ceylon describes *the protestant religion extinct*, the fine old „churches in ruin, the *clergy* who had once ministered in them „forgotten, and but one Hindoo Catechist in charge of the province „(of Jaffna).

„Vast numbers had joined the Roman Catholic communion, to „which they had long been secretly attached, and the whole district „had been handed over to the priests from the College (Oratory) „of Goa.“ —

Thus, ten years after the occupation of Ceylon by the English,

1808 protestantism was extinct in the Island. The natives had perceived that they had nothing to gain by calling themselves protestants and they abandoned in a body this dry and unpalatable form of religion for which they always had a profound contempt.

A great number became Catholics, the others declared themselves openly heathens, as practically they had always been, and protestantism was reduced to the English officials and military men and to a few Dutch families who had remained in the towns after the British conquest.

When this state of things became known in England the old bigoted spinsters, who were feeding with their money the protestant ministers in the colonies, raised such a clamour, that Government was forced to interfere:

— „ The Secretary of State, Lord Castlereagh, writes Emmerson „ Tennent, so early as 1808 addressed a despatch to Sir Thomas „ Maitland, to acquaint him with the fact, that the measures of his „ government had been freely censured for their tendency to „ discourage the progress of Christianity, and to induce the natives „ to relapse into paganism.

„ The local government thus animated by the encouragement „ of the Secretary of State addressed itself *anxiously* to the work of „ *re-establishing Christianity.*" —

Sir Thomas Maitland was in perplexity. Able General that he was, he certainly knew how to re-establish discipline in a regiment, but *re-establish Christianity* in an Island was more than he could do, and he had no protestant ministers at his disposal. On the other hand he was a soldier and a disciplinarian and knew he must obey to his Superior's orders.

He was a man of resources and managed to get himself out of the difficulty: He selected the most intelligent from among the non-commissioned officers of his troops, corporals and others, gave them the title of *Proponents,* and sent them to the districts with orders to *make* Christians.

Each *Proponent* had an escort of three drummers. When they came to a village, they stopped on the road and set about beating the drums. When the villagers assembled around them, curious to see what was the matter, the *Proponent,* sprinkled them with water, and wrote their names in his pocket-book and when they asked the meaning of this ducking, he answered that it was necessary in order that their children might inherit their rice fields and cocoanut gardens.

The native villagers called this singular ceremony: *admission to rank,* and gave to those who had been thus admitted to rank the name of *Government* or *Buddhist-Christians.*

Thus, in a short time, Sir Thomas Maitland *made* 57,000 *Christians* and *re-established* (*protestant*) *Christianity* in Ceylon. But, says Emmerson Tennent the result of his apostolate: — „ was „ however far from satisfactory." —

Then, Sir Thomas Maitland, who had now become as zealous as he had been indifferent before, called protestant ministers from England and from India to help him to *make Christians* and, to assure better success, he wished to have them of all the different sects into which the unhappy Church of England has miserably split: Wesleyans, Presbyterians, Anglicans, Baptists and others:

— „ But, continues Emmerson Tennent, after a patient trial, the „ result was pronounced to be a failure: they succeeded in establishing „ schools, which were but sparingly attended. The Singhalese (pro- „ testant) Christians in the south were represented, after four years' „ ministration among them to be worse than the heathen, thousands „ of them were actual worshippers of Buddhu, and their general „ estimation of (protestant) Christianity so low, that it was known „ by the Singhalese as: *The Religion of the East India Company.* „ As for the Tamils of the north, after a few years of hopeless „ exertions the (protestant) *Missionary* sent to them was withdrawn. „ And so universal was their relapse into idolatry that, within a few „ years, the only Christians who were to be found in the peninsula „ were the members of the Church of Rome." —

General Wilson who succeeded Sir Thomas Maitland remained one year in office, and on the 11th March 1812, Sir
1812 Robert Brownrigg Bart. was appointed Governor of Ceylon.

Peace with Kandy had not been disturbed since 1805. No treaty of peace had been concluded, but both parties were tired of the war which had been carried on under North's Government, and hostilities remained suspended.

Maitland, Wilson and Brownrigg were busy with organising the

Colony, and they were so absorbed in this labour that they seemed to be wholly disinterested of the affairs of the Kingdom.

Nevertheless, the events that were taking place at Kandy were not without a certain local importance:

— „During this interval, writes Emmerson Tennent, the career „of the Kandyan King presents a picture of tyrannous atrocity „unsurpassed, if it be even parallelled, in its savage excesses, by any „recorded example of human depravity. Distracted between the „sense of possessing royal power and the consciousness of inability „to wield it, he was at once tyrannous and timid, suspicious and „revengeful. Insurrections were excited by his cruelties, and the „Chiefs who remained loyal became odious for possessing the „influence to suppress them. The forced labour of the people was „expended on works of caprice and inutility, and the courtiers who „ventured to remonstrate were dismissed and exiled to their „estates.“ —

Tennent's statement, however, must be taken with a certain reserve, he sometimes exaggerates and likes to write in a rather declamatory style. Marshall who is calmer and less poetical in his appreciations, and who had the advantage over Emmerson Tennent of being a contemporary and of having known the King personally, says that he had a very pleasing exterior, was an intelligent man, dignified and affable in his manners. Then he adds:

— „Not having a minister in whom he could place any „confidence he lived under the constant fear of conspiracies. Until

„ he was made a prisoner, he said, he had never retired to rest „ without the dread of assassination. Fear produces oppression, and „ oppression excites fear. He trusted none of his courtiers, and it is „ doubtful if any one of the Chiefs deserved his confidence. He „ punished traitors, as traitors are generally punished, namely with „ merciless severity; and, being a passionate man, it is alleged he was „ liable to condemn accused, without adequate investigation.

„ It may be observed that, horrible as his punishments were, „ they were much in the ordinary course of things under oriental „ despotism, where subjects were beheaded, impaled or mutilated, at „ their ruler's caprice, as easily as the subjects of one European „ country are transported in another imprisoned or flogged.

„ Some of the King's most severe measures, is alleged, were „ ordered to be carried into effect when he was in a state of ebriety. „ And from the great quantity of Hoffmann's cherry brandy bottles „ found in the palace, it may be inferred that he was fond of that „ liqueur.

„ He was unpopular among the Chiefs, but not among the „ middle and lower classes of his subjects, whose rights and privileges „ he frequently defended, against the injustice and oppression of the „ aristocracy or nobles. By protecting the poorer classes against „ their tyranny and exertions, he created formidable opponents, „ enemies whose ambition, resentment and influence, he could not „ effectually restrain, and whose vengeance led to his deposition." —

The King's most powerful enemy was the first Adigar Pilame-Talawe, who after seventeen years of intrigues, treason and fruitless efforts, had not yet given up the ambition of possessing himself of the throne of Kandy.

A rebellion having broken out in a district where Pilame-Talawe had considerable landed property, he reduced the rebels by his mere presence. This event showed the King the influence his minister had among the Kandyans. Having always distrusted him, the King now began to fear him, for he was not so blind, as not to see his ambition and intrigues. The Adigar on his side, seeing the unpopularity of the King increase daily among the Chiefs and Nobles, became arrogant.

One day, when the King did not show him the regard he was accustomed to, he told him that he ought to remember, that it was he who had placed him on the throne, and reproached him with no longer paying heed to his advices and counsels. The King replied that he would not allow himself to be guided by the Chiefs, but it was he who would give them their orders. This was the beginning of breach between King and minister.

Some time later, the Adigar was summoned to the palace. Before the whole assembly of the Chiefs, the King accused him of ill-using the power which his position of prime minister gave him. He then bitterly complained, that it was Pilame-Talawe who had led him on to all the acts of cruelty which had stained his reign and that he certainly deserved punishment. Then calming down, he said that in order not to add an act of cruelty to those he already had on his conscience, he would pardon the Adigar's crimes.

A few days later, the Adigar was again summoned to the palace, and the King accusing him of new offences real or imaginary, despoiled him of all his dignities and ordered him to go and reside in one of his estates at a great distance from the capital.

Pilame-Talawe however was not a man to resign himself easily to retire into private life. He was now afraid of the King, not knowing what his anger might bring to him. He resolved therefore not to delay any more the striking of the great blow, and to make a supreme effort to gain the crown for himself.

He bribed the Malay guard who was posted in the interior of the palace. His plan was to raise a rebellion in two provinces in which his family had a great influence, the Malays would then kill the King, whilst he marched on the Capital at the head of the rebels who would proclaim him King.

But the assassins failed, the rebellion broke out sooner than was expected. Pilame-Talawe, his son and his nephew were arrested and brought in chains to Kandy.

The King condemned them to death. The ex-Adigar, his nephew and six Chiefs who had taken their side were beheaded.

The Adigar's son whose name too was Pilame-Talawe was brought to Kandy some days later, and the King pardoned him.

Thus ended the famous Pilame-Talawe who during 14 years had been so to say the central figure in the history of Ceylon. All his life he had sought a throne and ended by finding the scaffold.

## CHAPTER 5

# THE CONQUEST OF KANDY

Pilame-Talawe's successor was his nephew Ehelapola the Dessawe of Sabaragamuva. The King raised him to the
1814 dignity of first Adigar unwillingly, for he distrusted him, and suspected him of not having been stranger in Pilame-Talawe's conspiration, but he did not deem it prudent to discontent the Chiefs who clamoured for his nomination.

Chief of one of the most powerful families in the Kingdom, raised to the highest dignity which gave him a great power, Ehelapola made himself the heir of his uncle's ambitious plans. He too aspired to the throne, but he was far from possessing the strength of character and the cunning wisdom of his uncle, nor had he the patience to wait his opportunity.

Scarcely had he taken possession of his office of prime-minister he began to make advances to Sir Robert Brownrigg who gave him an evasive reply.

Having learned that the King had discovered his treason he took refuge in the province of Sabaragamuva which he had governed as Dessawe, and whose people were devoted to him, rose them against the King and placed himself at the head of the rebels.

The King sent against him an army commanded by the second

Adigar Molligode, Ehelapola was defeated and fled to Kalutara, and went thence to Colombo, in the month of May 1814.

Molligode returned to Kandy with a great number of prisoners of whom 47 were executed by order of the King. 70 other Kandyan nobles whom the King suspected of sympathy to Ehelapola, were arrested and put to death.

The Governor gave shelter to Ehelapola at Colombo, but in order to avoid a conflict with the King, refused to give him audience.

Sir Robert Brownrigg saw clearly that now the moment had come to undertake the conquest of Kandy, when nearly all the influential Chiefs sided against the King. But he was a wise and prudent general, and did not wish to commence the campaign, before he was sure of success. He expected reinforcements from India.

Meanwhile, the King had declared that Ehelapola had forfeited his titles and dignities and elevated Molligode, his conqueror, to the rank of first Adigar.

Wikrama Singa took terrible revenge on all those whom he suspected of sympathies with Ehelapola. A Dessawe named Pusilla who was found out to have been in correspondence with him had his eyes torn out, and after having been frightfully tortured, was put to death.

Since the times of Raja Singha, the custom had been established that the wives and children of the principal chiefs had to reside in Kandy, where they were kept as hostages of the fidelity of the chief.

The King had Ehelapola's wife, step-sister and children seized, and condemned them to death. Capital punishment of women was an unheard of thing in the Kingdom, and their execution took place amidst unspeakable acts of atrocity.

The King ordered all the Chiefs present in Kandy to assemble in a place in front of his palace between the Nata and Maha Vishnu temples. The condemned ladies and children were brought before the King. To the reproaches he made her, Ehelapola's wife answered that, if her husband was guilty, she, and her children were innocent, nevertheless if her death and theirs would appease the King's anger against her husband and his followers, she was ready to make the sacrifice.

Seeing that nothing would appease the tyrant, the unfortunate lady told the eldest of her sons to go and place himself in the hands of the executioner.

The poor child, a fine lad of eleven, clung crying to his mother's dress.

The younger who was only nine years old took him by the hand and said: — „ Do not fear, let us go. I will show you how to die.“ — Then advancing to the executioner he fell on his knees and bowed his curly head, which was cut off with one stroke.

Whilst the body was still palpitating, the head of the noble boy was thrown into a mortar, and they forced the unfortunate mother to pound it with a pestle.

The same was done with the eldest boy and with a girl of seven.

The poor mother was almost senseless, they had to support her whilst they forced her to pound the heads of her children. She seemed to see nothing and to understand nothing.

The youngest child was scarcely a year old; she held it clasped to her heart. They snatched it from her, and after having beheaded the infant, they also threw its head into the mortar, and forced the mother to pound it.

At the first blow, milk came out of its mouth and mixed with the blood. At this sight the unfortunate mother regained her senses. She uttered a fearful cry and fell in a dead swoon.

The crowd which assisted to this awful scene, broke out in loud sobs, and an old Chief Palihapane Dessawe, fell down senseless. The King deprived him of his office for this act of weakness.

After this execution, which perhaps has not his equal in history the mother and her step-sister were drowned in the lake of Bogambra.

A mournful silence reigned all the day over the town of Kandy. All houses remained shut. No fire was lit, and no one even thought of cooking food.

With this atrocious act of cruelty, the King had sealed his doom. It resounded mournfully from an end of the Kingdom to the other, the people were exasperated.

The forced labour which the King imposed on the villagers, for the digging of the lake of Kandy sowed disaffection everywhere, and all seemed to be ripe for rebellion.

Sir Robert Brownrigg thought now the moment propitious for attempting the conquest of the Kingdom of Kandy.

He had an interview with Ehelapola. In appearing before the Governor, the unfortunate Chief burst into tears. Sir Robert sought to console him, and treated him with delicate courtesy. They had several meetings and arranged the plan of the invasion of the Kingdom of Kandy.

The reinforcements had arrived from India; all was ready for war, it only remained to find a pretext for declaring it.

They had not to wait long for the pretext.

Kandyan villagers having robbed some Singhalese merchants who were British subjects, and fearing to be punished seized them and took them to Kandy, under the pretext that they were British spies, and it would be difficult to prove that they were not.

The King had no difficulty in believing it, for he was not ignorant of the fact that the Governor was using Ehelapola to make advances to the Adigar Molligode and to induce the Kandyans to rebellion. He knew that war was decided and it seemed to him no extraordinary thing that the Governor might send spies to gather informations.

He ordered the men to be mutilated. They cut off their noses, their ears and their hands. Seven of them died in Kandy. The three others dragged themselves as far as Colombo, where they arrived in the most pitiable condition.

The Governor considered this act of cruelty committed on British subjects, as a sufficient pretext to declare war.

Having already completed his preparations, he began to concentrate his army on the Kandyan frontier. The principal division under the command of Major Hook left Colombo on the 9th December 1814. Ehelapola and his followers joined it.

On the 15th January 1815, the Governor proclaimed, from his headquarters at Ruanwelle the declaration of war.

1815 Captain Marshall, one of the officers who took part in this campaign, gives us the text of this proclamation:

—„ To secure the permanent tranquillity of these settlements, „ and in vindication of the honor of the British name; for the „ deliverance of the Kandyan people from their oppressors; in fine, „ for the subversion of that Malabar dominion, which, during three „ generations had tyrannized over the country, His Excellency has „ resolved to employ the powerful resources placed at his disposal „ etc.“ —

Next day the British army entered the Kandyan territory. The opposition encountered in its march was insignificant, and reduced itself to a few skirmishes between the vanguards.

Major Hook tried to capture Molligode, the Adigar and commander-in-chief of the Kandyan army, who had his quarters in the neighbourhood. He attacked him once suddenly, and captured his palanquin but the Adigar himself escaped into the jungle.

A few days later, it was announced to Major Hook that two messengers from Molligode had come to the English camp and wanted to speak with him. At the beginning of the conversation the major perceived that one of the messengers treated the other with marks of great respect. This arose his suspicions and he began at once to address him as Adigar.

Molligode seeing himself recognized, did not try further to hide his identity. He openly declared to Hook that he had decided to abandon the cause of the King and to ally himself with the English.

It was arranged that Molligode would pretend for a time to be faithful to the King and remain at the head of his army, to paralyse its action, and if an encounter became inevitable, he would not give out bullets to his men, but make them fire on the English only with blank cartridges.

Captain Marshall relates that: — „During the march of the „troops from Hettymoole to Gannitenne, the Kandyans fired more „than usual upon us from the jungle. The writer was walking with „Major Hook at the head of the column, when we saw two „Kandyans come out of the jungle about twenty-five or thirty „yards before us. They both fired, and one ball struck the ground „close to Major Hook's foot. He observed at the moment: „— There has been a bullet in that musket. — It was afterwards „ascertained, that the party in question was not under the command „of Molligode.“ —

I do not know how this arrangement with the commander-in-chief of the enemy's army turned traitor, to give blank cartridges to his soldiers would be considered from the military point of view. It looks very much like slaughtering practically disarmed men. And the indignation of the Chief of the expedition at the enemy firing with bullets had rather a comical flavour.

On the 8th February, the Adigar Molligode consummated his treason. He made his submission to the English and entered their camp with drums beating and flags flying; he surrendered to Major Hook the colours of his troops and a number of war elephants. Several other Chiefs followed his example.

The same evening Molligode had an interview with Ehelapola. In entering his old adversary's tent Molligode exclaimed: — „I am a ruined man."— „And what am I?"— Answered Ehelapola. And both Chiefs burst into tears.

The English marched then on Kandy. The details of this unopposed march are uninteresting.

Wherever they had to pass, the people were running away and hiding in the jungle so that they encountered on their march only deserted villages and abandoned homesteads.

One episode only deserves to be related as an example of the pluck and presence of mind of a Kandyan lad:

Not far from the route which the English army had taken, lived a Kandyan Chief named Baddula Mudeliar a warm partisan of the King, probably an enemy of Molligode and Ehelapola. Major Hook sent a detachment to devastate his lands, burn his residence and, if possible, bring him a prisoner.

On the approach of the British, Baddula Mudeliyar fortified his house, and determined to defend himself to the end.

He sent the women to a place of security in the forests and wished his two sons to go with them; but the brave boys, still in tender years, protested saying that they would fight at their father's side. The elder, Maradhanu, a lad of 15 years, declared that he would rather die than go away with the women, and the father allowed them to remain.

Baddula's residence, thus fortified was only accessible on one side, which was the weak point for the defence, an easy incline from the top of the hill to the valley, covered with rocks which gave easy shelter to the enemy.

It was from that side that the English attacked the house. Hidden behind the rocks, they poured a shower of bullets on the besieged who, being short of ammunitions, answered by a prudent and measured fire. Each time that a helmet or an uniform appeared from behind the rocks a bullet greeted it.

The fight had already lasted for two hours, when the commanding officer had recourse to a stratagem. Forty helmets appeared above the rocks, the English held them on the end of their muskets. The Kandyans fired at them, and before they had time to reload, the English ran over the space that separated them from the house and were under the verandah. Then followed a hand to hand fight. Baddula Mudeliar fell dangerously wounded, but as he was dressed like the others, the English did not notice him and his men brought him unconscious to the upper floor.

Meanwhile the English had conquered the ground floor, and the Kandyans had barricaded themselves in the upper floor.

The officer in command did not dare to attempt the assault of the narrow staircase, for it would cost many lives, he therefore deemed it more prudent to parley.

He shouted in a loud voice to the besieged that he would let them go all free if they delivered him Baddula Mudeliyar.

A profound silence reigned round the wounded chief, who had not yet regained his consciousness, when, an old servant hastily dressing himself in his lord's robes and insigna answered the British officer:

— „I am ready to give myself up, on condition that my people will not be molested." —

— „I will not hear conditions from a rebel, answered the officer, let Baddula be given up, and the rest can go where they like." —

Then the servant in his disguise descended the stairs and surrendered to the English. But the officer would not allow himself to be caught so easily. Neither he, nor any of his men had ever seen the chief. He wanted him to be identified, and ordered to bring Baddula's son.

— „But, objected the disguised servant, they have not promised to give you up my son." —

— „It's all right, answered the officer, no harm will come to the boy, I want only to speak with him." —

Then the servant called in a loud voice: — „Maradhanu, my son, come down." —

The lad in a moment took in the situation, and answered — „I am coming, father." —

He descended the stairs, and throwing himself at the servant's feet, cried out: — „Father! Father! They have put you in chains!" —

— „All right, said the officer, let the boy go." —

The English put fire to the house and went away taking their prisoner.

Then the Kandyan who had barricaded themselves on the first floor saved themselves from the flames, taking their unconscious Chief. When they placed him on the ground before the burning house, they remembered two little boys, whom they had shut up in a room, where they were safe from the bullets of the enemy.

The boy Maradhanu threw himself into the flames to save his little brothers but the servants pulled him out and putting a ladder to the window entered the room, and found two little charred corpses.

Baddula Mudeliyar and his son remained for some time in hiding in the forests, then they took shelter in a pansala, which was not a place of much security, as the Bikshun during this war acted as spies for both sides.

We do not know the fate of the good servant. As to the boy Maradhanu who had so bravely commenced his career, his story is disappointing. Grown to a man he settled at Colombo, where he became a sort of cricketer. They called him: the sporting Mudeliyar. He led an idle, undignified life.

Whilst the English were marching on Kandy, the King discouraged by the defection of Molligode and of the other Chiefs, had fallen into a state of complete apathy, and took no steps to resist the invaders.

On the 11th February, leaving behind his treasures and two of his four wives, he fled from Kandy hiding himself in the mountains that border the District of Dumbera. He had with him only a few servants who had not as yet abandoned him.

On the 14th February General Brownrigg entered Kandy without encountering the slightest opposition. The town was deserted, as was the custom of the Kandyans at the approach of the enemy. All houses were empty not a living soul to be met. Only a few stray dogs were barking in the streets.

The General established in the town his headquarters, and was joined on the next day by Major Hook's division.

Sir Robert Brownrigg, was a man of action and intended to profit by his success, and passed experience had shown him how dangerous it was to lose time in Kandy.

Being informed that the King was in hiding not far from the town and supposing by the direction in which he had fled that his object was to reach the province of Uva, where he had followers on whom he could rely, Sir Robert sent two detachments in pursuit. The first was composed of English soldiers under the command of Captain d'Oyley, the other of Kandyans followers of Ehelapola and Molligode. They took two different routes towards a place where they supposed they would cut the King's retreat.

Flying from mountain to mountain under the beating rain, the unfortunate Wikrama Singha arrived at last in the neighbourhood of Medda-Maha-Nuwera where he took refuge in the house of a petty official.

Ehelapola's men who followed his tracks, surrounded the house, broke open the door which had been barricaded and entering found themselves face to face with the King.

At the first moment Wikrama Singha who till then, had only seen his subjects prostrated at his feet, lost countenance, but he soon regained his usual dignity. The Kandyans overwhelmed him with insults. They took his precious ornaments, tore off his clothes, and having tied his hands behind his back, took him to a near village, all the while striking him and spitting on him.

Fortunately Captain d'Oyley and his detachment had already arrived in the village. Indignant at the treatment inflicted on the unfortunate King, the Captain snatched him from the hands of the Kandyans, took him to his quarters, where he treated him with respect and all possible consideration. This happened on the 18th February.

Next day, whilst at table with his officers, Sir Robert Brownrigg received the news of the King's capture. He rose from the table much moved for he knew that now the conquest of the Kingdom of Kandy was an accomplished fact.

The royal prisoner was not brought into Kandy, he was despatched straight to Colombo under a strong escort.

Meanwhile, Sir Robert Brownrigg, through Ehelapola and Molligode, the latter having resumed his office of Adigar, summoned to Kandy all the chiefs, to make their submission and swear allegiance to the King of England.

On the 2nd day of March a durbar was held in the audience hall of the palace, and the Governor read the following proclamation:

— „ Led by the invitation of the Chiefs, and welcomed by the „ acclamation of the people, the forces of His Britannic Majesty have „ entered the Kandyan territory and penetrated to the Capital. The

„ ruler of the interior provinces, has fallen into their hands, and „ the government remains at the disposal of His Majesty's „ representative." —

After an enumeration of all the late King's crimes, the proclamation continues:

— „ Contemplating these atrocities, the impossibility of establishing with such a man any civilized relations either of peace or of „ war, ceases to be a subject of regret; since His Majesty's arms, „ hitherto employed in the generous purpose of relieving the „ oppressed, would be tarnished and disgraced, in being instrumental „ in the restoration of a dominion exercised in a perpetual outrage to „ everything which is sacred in the constitution or functions of a „ legitimate government etc." —

After that somewhat pretentious proclamation, a convention between the British Government and the Kandyan Chiefs was read: It commenced by declaring the deposition of King Sri Wikrama Raja Singha; his descendants and relations, no matter to what degree deprived in perpetuity, of their rights to the throne, and the Kingdom of Kandy incorporated with the British dominions. Some guarantees were given to the Chiefs, and certain rights acknowledged to the people. The Buddhist religion was declared inviolable, and the temples, pansalas and Bikshun protected by Government.

The convention was signed by the Chiefs, amidst salves of artillery the British Flag hoisted on the Royal palace, and King George III proclaimed Sovereign of the whole Island of Ceylon.

Every one notices, in this assembly the gloomy and dejected

figure of Ehelapola, who had leagued himself with the English in the hope that they would raise him to the throne of Kandy, and now saw that his treason had only delivered his native land to the stranger.

He obstinately refused all the dignities offered him by Government, and retired to his estates, where he occupied himself actively in organizing a general rebellion of the Kandyans against their new masters.

As for the feeling of the people, Pridham says: — „That portion „of the population who had returned to the town of Kandy, evinced „no concern in the business which was going on in the palace, and „did not leave their ordinary advocations. Apparently, they „regarded the transfer of Government from an oriental to a „European dynasty with perfect indifference." —

On the 6th March, the royal prisoner arrived in Colombo under Major Hook's charge. There he acted the part of a resigned philosopher. Having inspected the rich furniture of the house that had been prepared for him, he said: — „Since I am no longer permitted to be a King, I am grateful to be treated with so much regard." — Then turning to the British officers who accompanied him he said: — „Had my people not been such cowards, and my ministers traitors, I would have shown you that I am not a woman. Twice, during my reign you had taken Kandy, and each time, you have been only too glad to be able to escape." —

Once an allusion having been made to his cruelties he answered: — „I have ruled my Kingdom according to Hindu law. Not having a single man whom I could trust, I lived in constant fear of plots and conspiracies. Till the day I saw myself your prisoner, I never retired for the night without fear of being murdered, and in such a position, I might have committed more than one act of injustice. Your Kings in Europe have the great advantage, to have a council. That prevents them from issuing orders, in the first moment of anger, and seeing them carried out, before they have had time to reflect." —

He advised the Governor to distrust Ehelapola and Molligode: — „They have betrayed me, he said, and will betray you on the first occasion." —

King Wikrama Singha was detained in Colombo till the 24th January 1816, when he was sent to Madras. He was brought thence to the fortress of Vellore where he died in 1830.

After the British rule had been thus established at Kandy Fr. Louis de Sousa, the Superior of the Oratorians, intended to send there two Missionaries to visit the Catholics who lived at Kandy, Galgamuva, Wahacotta and in some other villages and who had been now deprived of religious ministration since 1746.

During these 70 years, once only had they been visited by priest, when the Dutch Governor Falk had invited the Oratorian Fathers to join his staff during his expedition to Kandy.

Fr. de Sousa had therefore made all preparations, when the Governor forbade him positively to send any Catholic priest to Kandy under the pretext, that it would be dangerous for them to go there. What danger did he fear, no one could guess, but as Sir Robert Brownrigg had never shown hostility to the Catholics, his prohibition was put on the account of an exaggerated prudence.

## CHAPTER 6

# THE REBELLION OF THE KANDYANS

Two and a half years had scarcely elapsed since the establishment of the British rule and already the greatest discontent reigned among the Kandyans:

1817

— „ For many reasons, says Percival, the Kandyans of all grades „ disliked the English. Differing in race, religion, customs, habits „ and mode of thinking, the British rule could not but be, for a long „ time, highly unpalatable to them.

„ The Kandyans used to inquire, when the English intended to „ return to the maritime provinces: — You have now, said one, „ deposed the King, nothing more is required, you may leave us. — „ The people showed no dislike to us individually, but as a nation „ they abhorred us.

„ The British Government assumed the despotism of the fallen „ monarch, the people having no legal power to control the decrees „ of the Governor, more than they had to modify the orders of the „ King. One despotism had given place to another; in practice, the „ common people found that the alleged moderation of the English „ Government differed very little from the exactions of their former „ ruler." —

Another contemporary, Major Davie adds: — „ There was no

sympathy between us and them, not one circumstance to draw or bring us together; and innumerable ones of a repulsive nature.

„ The Chiefs though less controlled than under the Kings and exercising more power in their districts than they before ventured to exercise, were far from satisfied. Before, no one but the King was above them; now they were inferior to any civilian in our service to every officer in our army. Though officially treated with respect, it was only officially. A common soldier passed a proud Kandyan Chief with as little attention as he would a fellow of the lowest caste. Thus they considered themselves degraded and shorn of their splendour.

„ The people in general had similar feelings on this score, at least the respectable and more considerable portion of the population, viz. the Goevanse part. Ignorant of their distinctions, high caste and low caste were treated alike by most Englishmen, who came in contact with them, and undesignedly and unwillingly we often offended and provoked them when we least intended it.

„ Accustomed to the presence of a King in their capital, to the splendour of his Court, and to the complicated arrangements connected with it, they could not relish the sudden and total abolition of the whole system. The King of Great Britain was to them only a name; they had no notion of a King ruling over them at a distance of thousands of miles. They had no notion of delegated authority. They wanted a King whom they could see, and before whom they could prostrate and obtain summary justice.

„ These are a few only of the leading circumstances, which

„ tended to render the natives averse from us and our government, „ and anxious to attempt to overthrow it." —

In such circumstances, it was not difficult to Ehelapola, chief of one of the most powerful families in the Kingdom, and to his confederates to organize the rebellion, and they did it with so much secrecy that at the very moment when everything was ready for a general rising, and they awaited only the signal, the Governor without the least suspicion, was going to Trincomalee through the Kandyan territory; and so far was he from suspecting a rising that Lady Brownrigg was going with him.

On his way back he had an interview with Ehelapola who came to meet him with great pomp, many elephants and an escort of 3,000 men. Ehelapola's plan was to seize the Governor, bring him a prisoner to Kandy and proclaim himself King. And he could have done it, for the Governor with his small escort and unsuspecting treason was at that moment at his mercy. But the courage failed him, and the interview came to an end with an exchange of many compliments. Sir Robert Brownrigg returned to Colombo, ignoring the danger from which he had so narrowly escaped.

In October 1817 the rebellion broke out. To act better on the people's imagination they set out a certain Durraswami as pretender to the throne. He made his appearance in the Uva province, where he was patronized by Kappitipola Dessawe.

The insurrection spread rapidly. In less than six months it had extended over several provinces of the Kingdom of
1818 Kandy, and in the other provinces all was ready for the

rising. And government feared that the rebellion would extend even to the low countries. Durraswami approached Kandy, he reached Dumbera, where he was acclaimed by the people and the Chiefs paid him homage, and rendered him royal honours.

— „ Before six months had expired, writes Davie, the rebellion „ was truly alarming, both from the rapidity and extent of its „ progress, and the number of Chiefs who had joined it. In March „ 1818 all the country was in arms against us, with the exception of „ the lower part of Suffragam, the Three and Four Corles Oudeneura „ and Jattineura; and, with the exception of the first Adigar, every „ Chief of consequence had either joined the rebel standard, or was „ under arrest and confined by us, for favouring or being suspected to „ favour the rebel cause. Ehelapola himself and the second Adigar „ Kappawatte were of the latter number.

„ During the three following months, our affairs assumed a still „ more melancholy aspect. Our little army was exhausted and „ reduced by fatigue, privation and disease. The rebellion was still „ unchecked. All our efforts had been apparently fruitless: not a „ leader of any consequence had been taken and not a district „ subdued and tranquillized.

„ This was a melancholy time to those who were on the scene „ of action, and many began to despond and augur from bad to worse „ and to prophesy (what indeed was far from improbable) that the „ few districts, not yet against us, would join the enemy; that the „ communications between Colombo and our headquarters in Kandy „ would be cut off; and that we would be very soon obliged, to „ evacuate the country, and fight our way out of it." —

But the Governor's energy mastered the situation, he alone remained firm in the middle of the general despondency and discouragement. With the small force at his disposal, he not only held out his ground but successfully crushed the rebellion:

— „This gloomy prospect, continues Major Davie, was of „short continuance: the aspect of our affairs brightened with the „same rapidity that they had become overcast. Kappitipola was „defeated in several attempts which he made about this time, with „all the forces of the country he could command, often amounting „to several thousand men. Dissensions sprung up among the „leaders of the rebellion. Kappitipola and the pretender were „seized and imprisoned by another rebel Chief, and another „pretender to the throne, set up in opposition to the first.

„Now our efforts were as eminently successful, as they had „been the contrary before. Hardly a day passed but some rebel „Chief was taken; district after district submitted, till, in October, „Kappitipola was seized, and Buddha's Tooth, which had been „clandestinely removed from Kandy, recovered, and the whole „country tranquillized.

„It would be difficult to give the English reader an accurate „idea of the manner in which, during the rebellion, hostilities were „carried on on either side. It was a partisan warfare which, from its „very nature and circumstances, was severe and irregular; parti- „cularly when at its height, and after lenient measures had been „tried in vain.

„When a district rose in rebellion one or more military posts

„ were established in it, and martial law was proclaimed. The „ dwellings of the resisting inhabitants were burned; their fruit trees „ were often cut down; and the country was scoured in every „ direction by small detachments who were authorised to put to „ death all who made opposition, or were found with arms in their „ hands.

„ The natives on their part never met us boldly or fairly in the „ field; they had recourse to stratagems of every kind, and took „ every possible advantage of the difficult nature of their country, „ and of their minute knowledge of their ground. They would „ waylay our parties and fire on them from inaccessible heights, or „ from the ambush of an impenetrable jungle; they would line the „ paths through which we had to march with snares of different „ kinds such as spring guns and spring bows, deep pits lightly „ covered over, and armed with thorns, spikes etc. and in every „ instance that an opportunity offered, they showed no mercy and „ gave no quarter. Such a system of warfare as this of which I have „ partially sketched the outline, had better not to be given in detail.

„ There were certain redeeming circumstances occasionally „ exhibited on which one might dwell with pleasure; traits of „ heroism amongst our men, and of undoubted courage that have „ never been exceeded and traits of parental attachment amongst „ the natives and of cool resignation to their fate, that have seldom „ been surpassed.

„ For the same reasons that I have not entered into details of „ the warfare, I shall notice only in the most summary manner, the

„ sufferings and miseries inflicted and endured, on both sides, whilst „ the conflict lasted.

„ We suffered most from the harassing nature of the service; „ from fatigue and privation; and from the effect of these and of „ night marches and an unwholesome climate producing disease.

„ The sufferings of the natives were of a more severe kind and „ complicated nature. In addition to the horrors of the war in its „ most appalling shape, they had to encounter those of disease, want „ and famine without chance of relief.

„ Our loss from disease alone amounted nearly to one-fifth of „ all forces employed. The loss of the natives killed in the field or „ executed, or that died of disease or famine can hardly be calculated; „ it was probably ten times greater than ours and may have „ amounted perhaps to ten thousand." —

As usually happens in such rebellions, the poor villagers suffered most. The first factitious enthusiasm raised by the Chiefs, having cooled down, they saw nothing before them but the most terrible misery:

— „ The hostility of the people in most of the disaffected „ districts, writes Pridham, at length abated. A predatory warfare „ had been in existence for nearly one year, during which period the „ principal part, indeed, almost the whole of the population had „ lived in the woods and on the top of the mountains. Their „ grounds had been uncultivated for two seasons. Many of their „ cattle were killed; their small stores of grain were expended, „ having been in many places destroyed and plundered by the British

83

„ troops. The monsoon rains were approaching: They had there-„ fore no other prospect before them by holding out before the „ English, but accumulated hardship and famine." —

In fact, these poor people knew well that, if they did not return to the cultivation of their fields before the rainy season was over, they would all perish of misery and starvation.

At the beginning of the rebellion, the Bikshun had carried away Buddha's Tooth from Kandy and had taken it into the insurgents camp.

The reader will remember that, in olden times, the Tooth was considered as a Fetish, which gave to its possessor the Sovereignty over the whole Island of Ceylon. Although the new Tooth fabricated in 1568 by King Wikrama Bahu never enjoyed the reputation of the old one destroyed at Goa by the Portuguese, yet the Bikshun and the Chiefs somehow managed to revive the old legend, and to persuade the ignorant and superstitious villagers, that having succeeded in taking away the fetish from the English, the victory would certainly be theirs.

This superstition cunningly propagated, had at a certain moment given life to the rebellion, but it was also its undoing, for the English having regained possession of the fetish, the people discouraged by this cruel war and all the misery they had to suffer, turned the argument against the Chiefs: The English now have the Tooth, they said, their victory is therefore assured, no use to fight them any longer.

And thus the rebellion, which at a certain moment had been nearly successful, was crushed.

Sir Robert Brownrigg acted generously towards the conquered people. He did not wish to increase their sufferings which already had been great, he only punished the Chiefs: Kappitipola and Madugalla were condemned to death and executed. Ehelapola and Pilame-Talawe, the son of the famous Adigar, were exiled to Mauritius. Ehelapola died in exile in 1829 at the age of 59 years. Pilame-Talawe obtained in 1832 the permission of returning to Ceylon, where he died a short time after.

The Kandyan Chiefs lost their privileges; the Governor abolished the convention of the 2nd March 1815, and thus the Kingdom of Kandy lost is remnant of autonomy and became a mere province of the British Colony of Ceylon.

## CHAPTER 7

### 1819 — 1848

The rebellion being now suppressed and the country entirely pacified, Fr. Joachim Monroy, the Superior of the

1819 Oratorians, applied to the Governor for the removal of the prohibition made in 1815, and permission to re-establish the ancient Catholic Missions in the Kingdom of Kandy.

At the same time, Fr. Monroy pointed out, that the reason given by Government has ceased to exist, and that there could now be no question of any danger to the Missionaries nor embarassment to Government.

As a matter of fact, Government could no longer bring forward the reasons given in 1815, the more so that the protestant ministers were allowed to go wherever they liked, and *make Christians* in their customary way.

The Governor delayed the matter as long as he could and it was not before four months had elapsed that Fr. Monroy got the answer, which forbade him to re-establish the Mission and allowed only one priest to go to visit the Christians of three localities, and that with such restrictions that it rendered the visit practically useless.

The answer dated 6th April 1819 ran as follows:

— „ Minute. By His Excellency the Governor. His Excellency the Governor, having considered the application of the Superior of the Roman Catholic Mission in Ceylon for leave to afford spiritual aid to the persons of that religious profession, actually established in the Kandyan provinces, deems it expedient to accede to the same, under the following restrictions, necessary from the political state of that country:

That only one priest shall be allowed to proceed at a time, and for a period to be limited; that he shall travel as a private person, but with few attendants and without parade.

That his visit shall be restrained to the two villages of Wahacotta and Galgomera in which they are still remaining Christians of that persuasion, with permission to reside a few days in the town of Kandy to inspect thë proceedings of the Roman Catholics of the low-country residing there, but for no other purpose.

That neither in Kandy nor in the villages shall any public procession take place." —

And they had made Fr. Joachim Monroy wait four months for this mockery of an answer.

At that time there was at Colombo an enterprising protestant minister, called the Reverend George Bisset. He was an able man and had written a remarkable book on Ceylon, under the name of Philalethes.

As we know, the protestant ministers did not require the Governor's permission to go wherever they pleased. The Reverend George Bisset seeing that the government delayed the answer to Fr. Monroy's petition, resolved to become an apostle and to rob the Catholic Missionaries of their Christians of Wahacotta.

He ordered a tailor at Colombo to make him a cassock on the model of those used by the Oratorian Fathers, went to Wahacotta and presented himself to the people, as the long expected priest sent to them by Fr. Monroy.

Great was the joy of those poor simple Christians, many of whom had never seen a priest, and in this way the cunning Reverend took possession of the church and of the presbytery.

However but few days had elapsed, when the Christians began to have doubts: The priest whom they had received with such enthusiasm, never said the holy Mass; put off to another day all those who came for confession. He preached every day, but never mentioned in his sermons the Blessed Virgin Mary. At last he distributed bibles to all the villagers. That was certainly not the way in which, as they knew from tradition, the Catholic priest acted. The principal men of the village met in the house of the Sacristan to consider the position.

In order to guard the Christians against the protestant bibles which the heretics were distributing to them, the Missionaries had pointed out to them some passages by which they could distinguish between the protestant and the genuine Catholic version. The chief villagers therefore met in the Sacristan's house, and compared the bibles given them by the sham priest with a copy of the Singhalese translations of the Gospels by Fr. James Gonzalves, which they read at church every Sunday, and no doubt could remain that the bibles which had been distributed amongst them were protestant ones. They all rose in uproar, and with strong cudgels in their hand, ran to the presbytery.

The Reverend George Bisset jumped out of the window and, embarrassed with his cassock, under a shower of bibles and stones thrown at him by the women and children, took refuge in the jungle, where he remained in hiding till night, when he got his bullock-cart, and returned to Colombo.

Such was the tragic and undignified end of Reverend George Bisset's apostolic experiment.

Davie makes an allusion to this heroical expedition when he says: — „Their village in Matale had already been visited by two „ *clergymen* of the church of England, one of whom, and the earliest „ visitor the Rev. George Bisset presented their little congregation „ with a copy of the new Testament in Singhalese, the first they have „ ever seen." —

This last statement is absolutely false: A century ago, Fr. James Gonzalves had translated the new Testament into Singhalese, and the book was in the hands of every Catholic. Emmerson Tennent speaking of the same Christians of Wahacotta says positively: — „They had one copy of the new Testament in Singhalese „ translated by a Roman Catholic priest." And most probably they had more than one.

Having at last received the Governor's answer, Fr. Joachim Monroy sent to Wahacotta a young Indian Oratorian Fr. Vincent de Rosario Diaz who, seventeen years later, was chosen by the Pope, to be the first Bishop of Ceylon.

On the 1st February 1820 Governor Brownrigg was succeeded

1820 by General Sir Edward Barnes, a man of great ability and entirely devoted to the interests of the British Empire.

It is related, that when he was leaving England for Ceylon, the Secretary of State for the Colonies recommended him to endeavour to establish solidly the British power and to take efficacious means for preventing a new rebellion of the Kandyans. Barnes answered that to do so he required a small number of soldiers and a large number of engineers.

In fact, hardly had he landed in Ceylon, that he began to make roads: large roads from one town to another, with secondary roads between.

He opened thus the interior of the Kingdom of Kandy and deprived it of its inaccessible character which was the principal strength of the Kandyans. Since regular troops and artillery could easily reach every point, the Kandyans could no more resist the British.

The roads made by Sir Edward Barnes, did more than Brownrigg's armies to consolidate the British conquest.

What he did, was a remarkable engineering feat, for he had to carry these roads all along the flanks of steep mountains, cutting rocks, throwing bridges across torrents, scaling mountains more than 6,000 feet high. The eleven years of Barnes' government in Ceylon were devoted to complete this grand work.

Some English writers express their astonishment, why the Portuguese and the Dutch, in all their wars with the Kandyans never thought of constructing roads?

The answer is plain: They did not, for the very same reason for which the English began to make them only after a quarter of a century of their rule in the Island: They were not masters of the Kingdom of Kandy.

It is easy to construct strategic roads in a conquered country, comparatively subdued and quiet, but it cannot be done, when a country is independent, hostile and possesses a strong army to repel the invaders.

If again the Portuguese and Dutch did not make roads in that part of Ceylon which was under their rule, the reason is that they had not the principal means which the English possessed later, as the low-country people were not like the Kandyans subjected to forced labour.

The low-country Singhalese paid the rent for their lands in military service, whilst the Kandyan villagers were subjected to hard and almost unlimited forced labours which they owed to their Ruler.

Sir Edward Barnes used freely of this forced labour for the construction of his roaas, so freely indeed, that according the statement of his own engineers, his great work: — „cost the life of „as many natives, as had perished in Brownrigg's wars.“ — Now how many lives had costed the conquest of Kandy in 1815, is not known; not many, probably as there was scarcely any fighting; but we have seen Major Davie's statement that in the rebellion of 1817 and 1818, the dead roll of the natives was about ten thousand.

The Portuguese were less lavish of the lives of their subjects, and the Dutch preferred the water-ways, the rivers which brought them to the very heart of the cinnamon producing country, and in the neighbourhood of the towns they had constructed navigable canals of which some still exist.

Shortly before Barnes' arrival to Ceylon, a new pretender to the throne of Kandy made his appearance in the Bintenne district. He was a young Tamil named Kumara Swami, but his few partisans styled him: Wimala-Dharma-Narendra-Singha-Maharajah. It is probable that in reality he was a member of the royal family. He had come from India. His reign did not last a week. He tried in vain to raise the people. They were tired and discouraged with the horrors of the late rebellion, and would not allow themselves to be drawn into a new revolt.

On the 12th January 1821, Kumara Swami was taken prisoner and carried to Badulla in chains. He was a very handsome young man, with noble and prepossessing manners and, during his captivity he bore himself with much dignity.

**1821**

When asked how he dared to take the name of King and allow others to call him so: — „ But it is my birth right." — He answered. When accused before the Judge of having had the presumption to give to a Chief the title of Adigar, he said: — „ I am a King, and if my reign did not last but an hour, a day or a week, I had the right to appoint my ministers." —

He was condemned to death but Sir Edward Barnes commuted the sentence to one of transportation to Mauritius, where Ehelapola and Pilame-Talawe were already detained.

Still another pretender appeared in 1823 in the north of the

1823 Island, and managed to get a small group of followers, but they were dispersed after a small skirmish near Anuradhapura, and their rising was of no consequence.

The Kandyan territory remained still forbidden to the Catholic
1829 Missionaries. The Superior of the Oratorian had great difficulty to obtain from Government the permission to a priest to go there for a short time and visit the Christians. It was not until the Catholic Emancipation Act was passed in England in 1829, that the Oratorian Fathers were allowed to settle in Kandy and build there a small church. Since eighty-six years the Catholics there had no church and no priest.

In October 1831 General Sir Edward Barnes was appointed
1831 commander-in-chief in India. He was the last military Governor of Ceylon. His successor was Sir Robert Wilmot Horton.

The disaffection of the Kandyans against the British Government still lasted. Its cause, according to contemporary writers was the arrogance with which the English treated the Ceylonese. The lowest official considered himself superior to the greatest Kandyan Chief and treated him in consequence.

The latent discontent burst out at last in 1834. It took the
1834 form of a conspiration of the Kandyan Chiefs who imagined themselves that they would be able to drive the English out of Ceylon with the help of the French and of the King of Siam.

The plot was discovered and, in the night of the 19th July twenty conspirators were arrested. After long indagations, six, the most guilty were committed to trial. They were: Molligode the younger brother of the Adigar, Dunuville Dessawe, Raddegodde Leukam all three from among the most influential Kandyan Chiefs, a native officer of the British army, and two Bikshun from the Malwatte Vihare at Kandy.

The case lasted till the 21 January 1835. The Jury was composed of six Englishmen and seven Singhalese. Although the guilt of the accused had been clearly proved, the seven Singhalese Jurymen who were the majority gave a verdict of: not guilty.

The Government was much annoyed by this fact which proved that the discontent and disaffection was also latent in the low-countries, and notwithstanding the verdict of the Jury the Governor deprived the three Chiefs of their offices and honors.

1835 In the meantime, the Catholic Religion had progressed so far in Ceylon, that Pope Gregory XVI, ordered the Island to be separated from the diocese of Cochin to which it had belonged for nearly three centuries, and erected into an independent Vicariate Apostolic.

The Superior of the Oratorians Fr. Francis Xavier was appointed Bishop, but when the Pontifical Brief reached Ceylon, he was already dead.

The Pope appointed in his place Fr. Vincent Rosario Diaz with the title of Vicar Apostolic of Ceylon and Bishop of Tamacene. His consecration took place at Colombo, on the 9th November 1835. He governed the Mission till 1843.

He was succeeded by Fr. Gaetan Antonio Pereira, who was appointed in the same year by the Pope, Bishop of Usula
1843 and Vicar Apostolic of Ceylon. Like his predecessor he was an Oratorian of the Brahmin caste and a native of Goa.

The Oratory of Goa being on the decline Bishop Gaetan Antonio Pereira could not get a sufficient number of priests for Ceylon and he saw the necessity of calling to his help European Missionaries. The first who answered to his call, was an Italian Oratorian Fr. Horace Beltachini who later on became the first Vicar Apostolic of Jaffna.

The Oratorian Fathers in Ceylon had committed the mistake of not admitting into their number young Ceylonese. Under the influence of the Caste system, they admitted only into their Congregations natives of Goa of the Brahmin and Chardos castes.

Separated as they now were from Goa, they could no more recruit themselves, and were dying out in Ceylon, and there was a great need of priests, for according to the Ecclesiastical census made in 1850, the Catholics of Ceylon numbered 116,654, of whom 83,561 were Singhalese, 31,952 Tamils and 1,141 Europeans and Burghers.

Bishop Gaetan Antonio being now old, asked the Holy See for a Coadjutor with the right of succession, and as the Goan Oratorians were now dying out and as new Missionaries could only be got from Europe he wished his Coadjutor to be an European, and Pope Pius IX appointed in 1857, Fr. Bravi a Benedictine of the Sylvestrin Congregation. Bishop Gaetan Antonio Pereira died in the same year and was succeeded by Bishop Bravi.

The last surviving Oratorian was Fr. Matthew Gaetan who died in 1874.

The Indian Oratorian Fathers had worked in Ceylon for nearly two centuries since 1687 when Fr. Joseph Vaz had landed at Jaffna.

They raised the Catholic Church from the ruin into which the Dutch protestants had reduced it. In the midst of cruel persecution they revived the Catholic spirit, converted many heathens, and gave over to their successors the Missions in a flourishing state, in fact second only to the great Catholic centres of Goa and the Malabar Coast.

The year 1848, which was a year of revolutions in Europe
**1848** witnessed too the last rebellion of the Kandyans.

New taxes had been imposed on boutiques, on firearms and on dogs, and they exasperated the people. It was certainly a rather queer idea to tax the dogs in an uncivilized country but no one even dreamed what would come out of it. A short time afterwards a capitation tax was introduced, the villagers rose all against it: — „ We are taxed like the dogs, they said, the English treat us like dogs." — The Bikshun were fomenting the rebellion. They discovered a pretender to the throne of Kandy, a descendant, they said of Donna Catharina and of Senevirat. He was proclaimed King at Dambool on the 28 July 1848, and marched on Kandy at the head of 4,000 men. He took Matale and Kurnegalle. But his success was of short duration. He had to retreat before the English troops.

In the first days of August he was defeated. Many prisoners were taken among whom was the pretender's brother who had taken the title of Raja of the seven Korles.

The self made Raja, a Bikshu, and eighteen leaders were condemned to death and shot, thirty-two condemned to prison and twenty-nine to be publicly flogged.

Towards the end of September the pretender himself was captured in a hiding place near Matale. Condemned to death, he was pardoned by the Governor; flogged publicly on the esplanade in Kandy, he was condemned to deportation.

This was the last rebellion of the Kandyans.

We finish here our narrative. The facts of the last period from 1848 up to the present time, a period of peace and of ever increasing prosperity in the Island, are well known, and it would be premature to write its history. Time must pass before it could be done in a serious and unprejudiced manner.

# APPENDIX

## THE SOURCES OF THE HISTORY OF CEYLON

# THE SOURCES OF THE HISTORY OF CEYLON

Few countries in the East possess such abundant historical sources as Ceylon, though they all belong to the modern epoch.

Of the early history of Ceylon we know absolutely nothing. Notwithstanding the importance which Turnour and Tennent give to such lucubrations as the Mahavanse, the Rajavali and the Raja-Ratnacary, these unpalatable compilations made by order of King Kundesala about the middle of the eighteenth century, have no historical value whatever. I would not perhaps call them with Davie: — „A tedious and unprofitable historical romance." — Tedious and unprofitable they certainly are, we must admit however that they contain some more or less correctly reported historical facts and some scraps of local tradition, but no serious writer can consider them as historical sources. They must simply be put aside.

The history of Ceylon, a history based on authentical documents begins with the year 1505.

The sources for the history of the Portuguese period are very rich and abundant. They consist of well preserved archivial documents, and in writings of serious and reliable authors, whose veracity cannot be attacked,

The Dutch period is poor in records and yet poorer in works of private authors. The reason is that it was strictly forbidden to all officers in the service of the Dutch East India Company to publish anything about Ceylon: — „The watchful jealousy of the Dutch, „writes Percival, both excluded the researches of strangers, and „prevented their own people from publishing any observations, „which they might have made during its stay in the Island." —

The English literature is rich in works about Ceylon, but they are all stained with protestant bigotry, with a clear tendency to calumniate all that is Catholic, to calumniate the Portuguese, because they were Catholics, and that to such an extent, that no honest man can read them without disgust. And, what unavoidably must happen when one falsifies history for a preconceived purpose, they contradict themselves.

Let us give some examples:

Emmerson Tennent Lieutenant Governor of Ceylon begins his history, as follows:

— „There is no page in the history of European colonisation, „more gloomy and repulsive than that which recounts the proceed- „ings of the Portuguese in Ceylon." —

In the historical sketch that follows, this assertion is of course contradicted.

Pridham, after having praised rather enthusiastically the Catholics of Ceylon and the devotion, disinterestedness and charity of their priests, the deep faith of the people, spits out the following bomb: — „In the case of Ceylon, it is very questionable whether „the tenets of Buddhism disvested of their idolatrious parasites,

„ would not serve as a brighter beacon, to light the path of morality, „ than the insensate and infinitely more debased tenets of Rome.“ —

Gordon Cumming, who certainly does not deserve to be placed among more serious authors, but whom I mention because she wrote at the dictation of a well known protestant minister whose guest she was, comes out with the following disgusting, rabid statement:

— „ In Ceylon, we were told of one Roman Catholic Chapel in „ which during the absence of the priest, the Congregation had „ introduced three images of Buddha and several others; and we „ ourselves saw a small Roman Catholic Chapel with the image of „ Buddha on one side, and that of the Blessed Virgin on the other „ apparently receiving equal homage. I fancy however that that „ also must have been without the leave of the priest.“ —

She takes great care however not to mention, where these singular Chapels were situated.

And such calumnies, not so infamous perhaps as this last, are found in all the English protestant authors who wrote about Ceylon, so far that, as I have said above, no respectable man reads these books without a feeling of disgust.

The Dutch writers are as a rule more honest in that matter.

But let us go back to the sources of the History of Ceylon.

Most of the archivial documents for the Portuguese period are to be found at Lisbon: The State Records, the Torre do Tombo, the Royal Library; the manuscripts of the Geographical Society and of the Society of Sciences; those of the Library of Evora contain an inexhaustible treasure of documents for the history of Ceylon.

Some documents are preserved in Brazil among the manuscript of the Library of the Historical and Geographical Society of Rio Janeiro.

Among the many Portuguese printed books, the most important is the chronicle of Barros and Couto: Da Asia, dos feitos che os Portugueses fieram na conquista e descubrimiento das terras e mares do Oriente. Lisboa 1778. 24 Volumes. Both authors held the office of keepers of the State records at Goa and at Lisbon, and had at their disposal the original documents.

Faria y Sousa (Manuel de). Asia Portoguesa, Lisboã 1675. 3 Vols.

Ribeiro João. Fatalitade historica do Ilha do Ceylão. He gives the facts which he had witnessed himself, and a historical sketch of the events which preceded his arrival to Colombo.

Saa y Menezes. Rebellion de Ceylão. Lisboã 1681. Gives a description of his father's campaign against Senevirat King of Kandy and of the battle of Badulla in 1630.

Queiros (Fernão) S. J. Conquista temporal e espiritual de Ceylão. A voluminous work written in 1687. Has not been printed. The original manuscript is kept at Rio-Janeiro in the library of the Historical and Geographical Society of Brazil; and an authenticated copy (the only one existing) in the library of the Papal Seminary at Kandy.

Castanheda (F Lopez de). Historia do discobrimento e conquista da India pelos Portugueses. Lisboã 1733. 7 Vols.

Felner (R. J. de Lima). Decade 13 da historia da India, composta por Antonio Bocarro Chronista d'aque Estado, republicado de ordem de Classe de sciencias morães, politicas e bellas lettras da Academia Real das sciencias de Lisboã. Lisboã 1876.

Many interesting details for the history of Ceylon are to be found in the works published by the Religious Orders that had Missions in the Island. The most important of these works are:

Soledade (Fernando da). Historia seraphica chronologica do Ordem da S. Francisco na provincia de Portugal.

Civezza (Marcelino da). Storia universale delle Missioni Francescane. Roma. 1857 — 1895. 11 Vols.

Bartoli (Daniello). Dell' Historia della Compagnia di Gesu. L'Asia Genova 1756.

Orlandini, Sacchini and Cordara. Historia Societatis Jesu.

Maracci (Jean). Relation de ce qui s'est passé dans les Indes Orientales, en ses provinces de Goa, de Malabar etc. Par les Perès de la Compagnie de Jesus. Paris 1651.

Camarra (Manoel de). Missoẽs dos Jesuitas. No Oriente nos seculos (XVI e XVII).

Monumenta historica Societatis Jesu. Madrid. Many volumes have already been printed and continue to be printed.

Catharina (P. Lucas de Sta.). Quarta parte da Historia de S. Domingos, particular do regno e conquistas de Portugal. Lisboã 1767.

Sousa (Fr. Louis). Historia de S. Domingos do reino e conquistas de Portugal. Lisboã. 3 Vols.

This and the preceding work give so little about Ceylon that they can be overlooked.

Sousa (P. Francisco de). Oriente conquistado. Lisboã 1710. 2 Vols.

All these authors are Catholics. Now with the Dutch conquest begins the series of protestant writers.

The most important among them is: Baldaeus (Philippus) niewsgerige beshrijvingen van Malabar Chromandel en Ceylon. Amsterdam 1672. The work is not only interesting as regards the Dutch conquest of the Island, but also for the last period of the Portuguese rule, which he treats more honestly than the others.

Valentyn (Francis). Oud en niew Ost Indien. Amsterdam 1724. 8 Vols. The second volume is about Ceylon.

Knox (Robert). An historical relation of the Island of Ceylon. London 1681. Gives many interesting details about the ways and customs of the Kandyans.

Spilbergen (Joris). T'historical journael van weghen due shepen gheva ren mgt. Zeetland: anno 1601 den 5 Mey tot t'Eiland Ceylon. 1605.

Wolf (Johan Christoph). Reise nach Zeilan. Berlin 1782.

Rego Sebastião (Catholic). Vida do Veneravel Padre Joseph Vaz. Margão 1867.

Then comes the series of the English writers very interesting for the minute details of the English conquest.

They narrate facts which the authors themselves had witnessed, and in which often they had played a part. They gather from eyewitnesses the facts which have preceded their arrival to Ceylon; they mention episodes of ancient times, and, as none of these authors intended to write history, but only give to the readers a bunch of interesting historical events, each work contains some new and partly unknown addition to the History of the Island.

These authors of the first decades of the nineteenth century are generally speaking reliable and truthful, except when they speak about Catholicism and about the Catholic Portuguese, when their sectarian spirit shows but too often the points of its horns.

We will mention them in a more or less chronological order.

Campe. Ambassade de M. Hugues Boyd à Kandy 1782.

Percival (Robert). An account of the Island of Ceylon. London 1803.

Cordiner (James). A description of Ceylon. London 1807. 2 Vols.

Johnston (Major). Narrative of the operations of a detachment in the expedition to Kandy in the year 1804. London 1810. Dublin 1854.

Marshall (Henry). Ceylon. London 1846.

Philalèthes (Bisset). History of Ceylon. London 1817. 2 Vols. The second volume is a re-edition of Knox.

Davie (John). An account of the interior of Ceylon. London 1821.

The authors who wrote about the middle of the nineteenth century are few, and their writings bristle with protestant bigotry, and morbid hatred for Catholic Religion. They are often disgusting and purposely falsify history in their sectarian spirit. They contain nevertheless precious details for Ceylon's history:

Forbes (Major). Eleven years in Ceylon. London 1840. 2 Vols.

Pridham (Charles). An historical, political, statistical account of Ceylon. London 1849. 2 Vols.

Emmerson Tennent (Sir James). Christianity in Ceylon. London 1850, and Ceylon, an account of the Island. London 1860. 2 Vols. These two works are absolutely worthless and unreliable in all that regard the Portuguese period. They are, on the contrary, important for the history of the Dutch and English periods as the author who was Colonial Secretary, and acting Governor of Ceylon, had at his disposal the Colonial records of Colombo, which he has used for writing his book, though in a rather lazy and superficial way.

# CONTENTS

# HISTORY OF CEYLON

## CONTENTS

## Second Period

## THE PORTUGUESE PROTECTORATE

## 1554 — 1597



## Third Period

## THE PORTUGUESE RULE

## 1597 — 1658

## Fourth Period

## THE DUTCH RULE

## 1658 — 1796

## Fifth Period

## THE BRITISH RULE

### 1796 — 1848



## APPENDIX



PRINTED AND PUBLISHED BY J. M. SUARES, CODIALBAIL PRESS, MANGALORE, S. C.

# HISTORY OF CEYLON

| Page | Line | Errata | Corrige |
|---|---|---|---|
| 56 | 14 | Peninsula | pansala |
| 58 | 12 | a dozen of | a dozen |
| 68 | 2 | 1546 | 1545 |
| 133 | 8 | re-trenched | entrenched |
| 197 | 20 | have | had |
| 211 | 22 | *after:* passing through that town | *add* took lodgings in his father's house |
| 221 | 19 | him | them |
| 289 | 1 | whose | which |
| 309 | 4 | slanding | standing |
| 327 | 19 | have recommenced | have to be recommenced |
| 422 | 26 | Spanish | a Spanish |
| 508 | 4 | hid | hide |
| 525 | 6 | the | a |
| 589 | 7 | Forbs | Forbes |
| 611 | 13 | soldiers | soldier |
| 614 | 17 | infantry | artillery |
| 626 | 9 | therefore | before |
| 647 | 26 | notices | noticed |